LONGSTREET HIGHROAD GUIDE
TO THE
NEW YORK
ADIRONDACKS

BY PHIL BROWN

LONGSTREET
ATLANTA, GEORGIA

Published by
LONGSTREET PRESS, INC.
a subsidiary of Cox Newspapers,
a subsidiary of Cox Enterprises, Inc.
2140 Newmarket Parkway
Suite 122
Marietta, Georgia 30067

Great efforts have been made to make the information in this book as accurate as possible.
However, over time trails are rerouted and signs and landmarks may change. If you find a
change has occurred to a trail in the book, please let us know so we can correct future editions.
A word of caution: Outdoor recreation by its nature is potentially hazardous. All participants in
such activities must assume all responsibility for their own actions and safety. The scope of this
book does not cover all potential hazards and risks involved in outdoor recreation activities.

Printed by RR Donnelley & Sons, Harrisonburg, VA

1st printing 1999

Library of Congress Catalog Number 98-89176

ISBN: 1-56352-505-4

Book editing, design, and cartography
by Lenz Design & Communications, Inc., Decatur, Georgia

Cover illustration by Harry Fenn, *Picturesque America,* 1872

Cover design by Richard J. Lenz, Decatur, Georgia

Illustrations by Danny Woodard, Loganville, Georgia

Next morn, we swept with oars the Saranac,
With skies of benediction, to Round Lake,
Where all the sacred mountains drew around us,
Tahawus, Seaward, MacIntyre, Baldhead,
And other titans without muse or name.
Pleased with these grand companions, we glide on,
Instead of flowers, crowned with a wreath of hills.

—Ralph Waldo Emerson, *The Adirondacs: A Journal Dedicated to My Fellow Travellers in August, 1858*

Contents

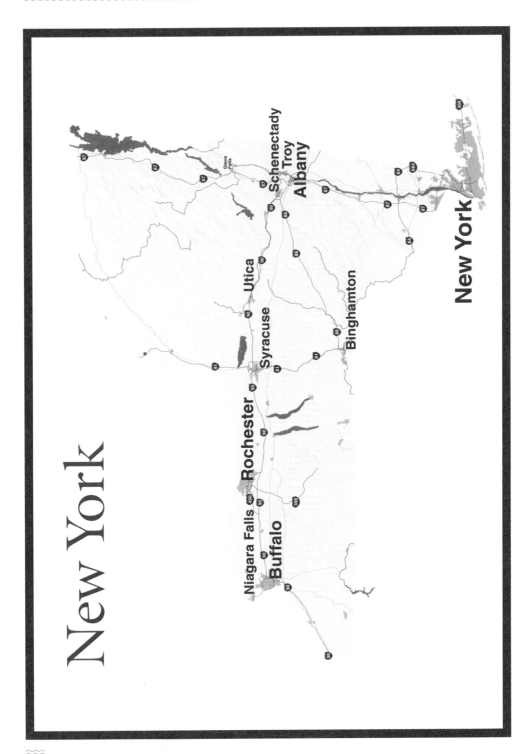

How Your Highroad Guide is Organized

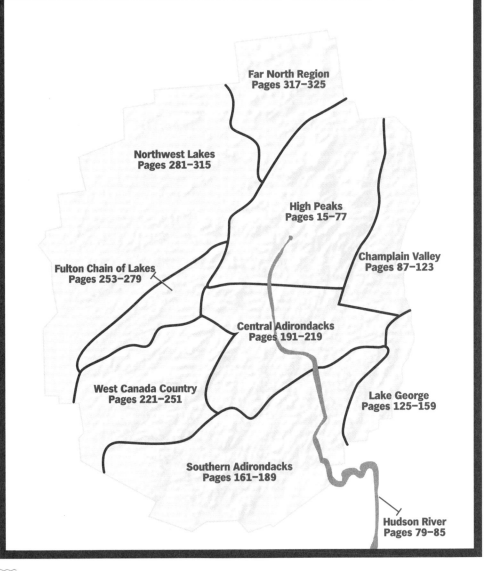

Far North Region
Pages 317–325

Northwest Lakes
Pages 281–315

High Peaks
Pages 15–77

Champlain Valley
Pages 87–123

Fulton Chain of Lakes
Pages 253–279

Central Adirondacks
Pages 191–219

West Canada Country
Pages 221–251

Lake George
Pages 125–159

Southern Adirondacks
Pages 161–189

Hudson River
Pages 79–85

How to Use Your Longstreet Highroad Guide

The *Longstreet Highroad Guide to the New York Adirondacks* includes a wealth of detailed information about the best of what the Adirondacks have to offer, including hiking, camping, fishing, canoeing, cross-country skiing, mountain biking, and horseback riding. The *Longstreet Highroad Guide* also presents information on the natural history of the mountains, plus interesting facts about Adirondack flora and fauna, giving the reader a starting point to learn more about what makes the mountains so special.

This book is divided into 10 major sections using regions in the Adirondack Park, plus one additional section that provides an introduction to the natural history of the mountains.

The maps in the book are keyed by figure numbers and referenced in the text. These maps are intended to help orient both the casual and expert mountains enthusiast. Below is a legend to explain symbols used on the maps. Remember, hiking trails frequently change as they fall into disuse or new trails are created. Serious hikers may want to purchase additional maps from the US Geological Service before they set out on a long hike. Sources are listed on the maps, in the text, and in the appendix.

A word of caution: The mountains can be dangerous. Weather can change suddenly, rocks can be slippery, and wild animals can act in unexpected ways. Use common sense when in the mountains so all your memories will be happy ones.

Legend		
Amphitheater	Wheelchair Accessible	Misc. Special Areas
Parking	First Aid Station	Town or City
Telephone	Picnic Shelter	Physiographic Region/ Misc. Boundary
Information	Horse Trail	
Picnicking	Horse Stable	Appalachian Trail
Dumping Station	Shower	Regular Trail
Swimming	Biking	State Boundary
Fishing	Comfort/Rest Station	70 Interstate
Interpretive Trail	Cross-Country Ski Trail	522 U.S. Route
Camping	Snowmobile Trail	643 State Highway
Bathroom	Park Boundary	SR2010 State Route
		T470 Township Road

Preface

Y ou don't go to the Adirondacks expecting to find a moose unless you're Al Hicks. Or tagging along with Al Hicks. Finding a moose in the Adirondacks is like finding a needle in a haystack: The moose may be a big needle, but the haystack covers 6 million acres.

That's why Al cheats. He's got this grill-shaped antenna that picks up signals from radio collars on moose he has managed to capture in the past as a state wildlife biologist. We are searching for a cow moose he shot two years ago with a tranquilizing dart. She's a skittish moose, and he hasn't seen her since.

Al holds the antenna aloft and listens. He looks as absorbed in his mysterious work as a water dowser except that this magic wand points skyward instead of earthward.

"We're close," he says. "Very close."

We are standing on a knoll just off NY 30 north of Speculator. The moose may be close, but Al isn't sure in which direction. So we drive down the road a piece and listen again. Still not sure. We drive farther down the highway. Al climbs atop a road cut and listens. Finally, he concludes she's in the woods just south of the Jessup River. Maybe 500 yards from the highway.

We plunge into the woods, pushing aside the hobblebush, weaving among the balsam and spruce, stepping over fallen trees. Every once in awhile, Al stops and listens. Each time the signal gets stronger. We come to a small rise, and Al's voice drops to a whisper.

"She's very, very close."

We soon come across a cloven hoof print in dark mud. It resembles a deer's print, but it's much larger, much deeper. You can fit your hand into one of the clefts. We tread on silently. We see more of the prints. We are very close.

Then Al stops to listen. He turns up the dial on the transmitter. All I can hear is static. The moose is gone. She has circled around us. She outsmarted us.

On the way back, I think that perhaps it's a good thing that our technology proved to be no match for the moose's instinct. It means that in the Adirondacks, at least, the wild has not been conquered, not completely.

And so I cannot guarantee that this book will find you a moose.

But I do hope it makes the search more enjoyable.

—Phil Brown

Acknowledgments

Although mine is the only name on the title page, I could not have written this book without the help of many other people. The names of some of those people are listed below. I apologize to anyone I leave out inadvertently.

I want to thank Marge McDonald, the project director of the Highroad series for Longstreet Press, for hiring me. I want to thank Richard Lenz and Pam Holliday of Lenz Design and Communications, who edited my copy, for all their encouragement and helpful suggestions.

I owe a big debt to R.W. Groneman, editor of *The Conservationist*, New York State's environmental magazine. Keep putting out a great publication. Go Reds!

Countless people at the State Department of Environmental Conservation helped me in countless ways. I'd like to single out Rick Fenton of the Bureau of Public Lands for answering numerous questions and directing me to others for the answers he didn't have. Thanks to Jim Papero, Tom Kapelewski, and Charles VanDrei for looking over parts of the manuscript. Several wildlife scientists took the time to explain things or send materials to me, among them Peter Nye, chief of the Endangered Species Unit; Al Hicks, the moose man; Al Breisch, reptile specialist; Lou Berchielli, bear specialist; and Mike Matthews, deer specialist. Rich Preall related to me the fascinating story of Adirondack brook trout. Thanks to Ron Cadieux for talking about trees. Thanks to all the forest rangers I spoke with. Finally, thanks to the media spokespersons at DEC, including Gary Sheffer, and at the Adirondack Park Agency.

Yngvar Isachsen of the New York State Geological Survey fielded many of my phone calls about rocks. I also relied heavily on his writings about the geology of the Adirondacks. I had the great fortune to live near the Adirondack Research Library, run by the Association for the Protection of the Adirondacks. It's a wonderful resource. Thanks to Dave Gibson, the association's executive director, and the staff: Ken Rimany, Pat Prindle, Edith Pilcher, and Bill White.

The Adirondack Mountain Club (ADK) publishes a shelf of books containing a wealth of information about the Adirondacks. Some of those I consulted often can be found in Appendix A. Nearly all of the trail distances used in my descriptions of hikes come from ADK's series of hiking guidebooks.

I want to thank Robert Ringlee, a former president of ADK, for sharing with me his illuminating compilation of trailhead statistics.

Thanks to John M.C. Peterson of High Peaks Audubon for talking to me about hawk migrations and bird-watching in the Champlain Valley.

Thanks to John Sheehan of the Adirondack Council for the cache of the council's acid rain brochures, hot off the presses. I had to drive 20 miles to get them, but it was a beautiful night.

A special thanks to Boy Scout Troop 709 of Caughdenoy, New York, for feeding me after I arrived at the Wanakena campsite after dark, beat from an all-day hike through the Five Ponds Wilderness.

I want to thank friends who, in one way or another, helped me get the job done. Mike Larabee and his wife, Caitlin, visited Thirteenth Lake and Taylor Pond in my stead. Gary Hahn and Tim O'Keeffe accompanied me on hikes. Tim, sorry about the snow on Vanderwhacker. Thank you, Paul Grondahl, for telling me to go for it. Thank you, Mike Virtanen, for believing in me since second grade. Thanks to all my colleagues at the Albany *Times Union*, especially those on the copy desk. There's too much radar out there!

Finally, thank you, Barbara—and Nathan, Rebecca, and Martha—for putting up with my long absences, both physical and spiritual.

—Phil Brown

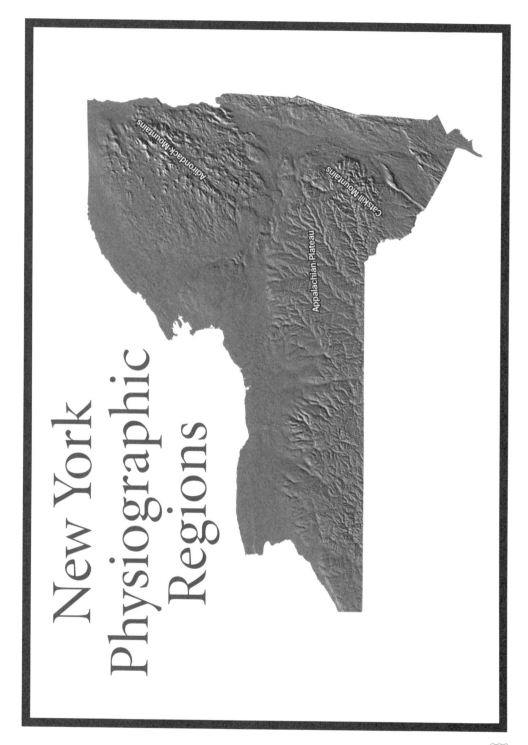

New York Physiographic Regions

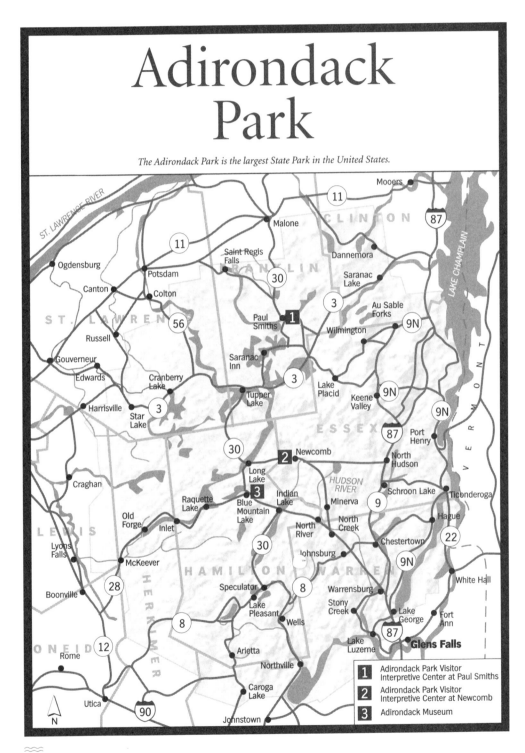

Adirondack Park

The Adirondack Park is the largest State Park in the United States.

The Natural History of the Adirondacks

T he Adirondack Park has been called the largest park in the lower 48 states. Bigger than Yosemite National Park. Bigger than Yellowstone. Bigger than Rhode Island. This is all true, since the Adirondack Park contains nearly 6 million acres. Some people may feel disappointed, however, to learn that the state owns less than half of it.

Don't be disappointed. The Adirondack experience is not just about wilderness. It's about the people and their history, the tales of the old guides, the banter in roadside diners, the cords of firewood stacked on lawns, the mom-and-pop campgrounds, and the Olympic flags fluttering above the main drag in Lake Placid.

Besides, there's plenty of wilderness here. That is clear to anyone who drives through the Adirondacks. On most highways, trailhead signs beckon motorists to park and take a walk in the woods. In the drive between the hamlets of Indian Lake and Blue

[*Above:* Avalanche Lake in the Adirondack Mountains]

Geologic Time Scale

Era	System & Period	Series & Epoch	Some Distinctive Features	Years Before Present
CENOZOIC	**Quaternary**	Recent	Modern man.	11,000
		Pleistocene	Early man; northern glaciation.	1/2 to 2 million
	Tertiary	Pliocene	Large carnivores.	13 ± 1 million
		Miocene	First abundant grazing mammals.	25 ± 1 million
		Oligocene	Large running mammals.	36 ± 2 million
		Eocene	Many modern types of mammals.	58 ± 2 million
		Paleocene	First placental mammals.	63 ± 2 million
MESOZOIC	**Cretaceous**		First flowering plants; climax of dinosaurs and ammonites, followed by Cretaceous-Tertiary extinction.	135 ± 5 million
	Jurassic		First birds, first mammals; dinosaurs and ammonites abundant.	181 ± 5 million
	Triassic		First dinosaurs. Abundant cycads and conifers.	230 ± 10 million
PALEOZOIC	**Permian**		Extinction of most kinds of marine animals, including trilobites. Southern glaciation.	280 ± 10 million
	Carboniferous	Pennsylvanian	Great coal forests, conifers. First reptiles.	310 ± 10 million
		Mississippian	Sharks and amphibians abundant. Large and numerous scale trees and seed ferns.	345 ± 10 million
	Devonian		First amphibians; ammonites; Fishes abundant.	405 ± 10 million
	Silurian		First terrestrial plants and animals.	425 ± 10 million
	Ordovician		First fishes; invertebrates dominant.	500 ± 10 million
	Cambrian		First abundant record of marine life; trilobites dominant.	600 ± 50 million
	Precambrian		Fossils extremely rare, consisting of primitive aquatic plants. Evidence of glaciation. Oldest date algae, over 2,600 million years; oldest dated meteorites 4,500 million years.	

Mountain Lake, one passes six trails in 12 miles. Visitors need not climb a mountain to see unbroken vistas of forest: they can see that from NY 28N near Newcomb or NY 30 near Indian Lake or NY 73 near Lake Placid or NY 192 near Gabriels.

You get the picture: This is a wild place. It's got bear and deer, eagles and falcons, trout and salmon. It's even got a few rattlesnakes.

But it has people, too, and that confuses outsiders who think of a park as people-less. So before moving on, let's clarify some terms:

The Adirondack Park encompasses about 5,927,000 acres of private and public land. The park's boundary is known as the Blue Line, a reference to an actual line on a map of the original park. The Blue Line encircles all of Essex and Hamilton counties and parts of 10 other counties. The Adirondack Forest Preserve comprises all the state land within these 12 counties and thus includes land outside the Blue Line. Within the Blue Line—the focus of this book—the preserve totals 2.6 million acres.

And that's bigger than Yosemite National Park. Bigger than Yellowstone. Bigger than Rhode Island.

Geologic History

The first thing to keep in mind about the Adirondacks is that they are babes in the woods, young mountains fashioned from old rocks. The Adirondack bedrock belongs to the Grenville Province, a wide belt of rocks more than a billion years old that undergirds much of eastern Canada. The province stretches all the way to Mexico, but outside Canada most of it lies deeply buried beneath younger strata. The ancient rock pokes through the surface in the Adirondacks and along a narrow corridor that crosses into Ontario at the Thousand Islands. Few other outcrops of the province exist in the United States. This means that no rocks found in the East are older than those in the Adirondacks. Still, these are far from the world's oldest rocks: some in Greenland date to 3.5 billion years ago.

The mountains did not arise until 10 million years ago. In geological time, this is so recent that some scientists believe the mountains are continuing to grow. The Appalachians, in contrast, formed about 250 million years ago and have been eroding away ever since. The common belief that the Adirondacks belong to the Appalachians probably derives from their proximity, but a close look at a good relief map of the eastern United States reveals the differences between these mountains. The Appalachians run for hundreds of miles in a path roughly parallel to the coast. The Adirondacks, unlike this linear range, appear as an isolated dome about 120 miles wide, with rivers pouring off in all directions. As the topography suggests, the Adirondacks and Appalachians formed not only at different times, but also in different ways.

The story of the Adirondacks begins in the Precambrian age, when a shallow sea covered the region that today is New York state. This sea lay off the coast of a rugged continent barren of plants and animals, for evolution had yet to advance much beyond algae and aquatic microbes. Over millions of years, sand and mud from the continent washed into the sea, building up layers of sediment that sank ever deeper under their own weight. Offshore volcanoes added lava and ash to the sedimentary pile. Eventually, the sediments attained such thickness that the bottom layers, under great pressure, turned into rock such as sandstone, limestone, and shale.

About 1.1 billion years ago, a continent to the east collided with proto-North America, crumpling and uplifting the rocks along the coast into a mountain range 5 to 6 miles high—as high as the Himalayas—in an event known as the Grenville orogeny. The rocks at the mountains' root, lying 15 miles deep, were subjected to immense pressure and heat, and they recrystallized into metamorphic rock: Sandstone became quartz, limestone became marble, and shale became gneiss. These intermingled with igneous rock forged from magma deep in the earth's crust. The igneous rocks also underwent metamorphosis, creating granitic gneiss, olivine metagabbro, and metanorthosite, the moonlike rock that hikers trod on today when they scramble up Mount Marcy, the state's highest summit.

As soon as the Grenville mountains arose, rain and wind went to work cutting them down to size. Slowly, grain by grain, the peaks wore away, but as they did, the roots of the mountain below, floating on denser rock, bobbed upward much as an iceberg rises as the top melts. After about 500 million years, the metanorthosite and other metamorphosed rocks that once lay 15 miles deep finally reached daylight. By this time, the once-great mountains had been whittled down to a peneplain, a nearly level landscape. It would be another 500 million years or so before the Grenville rocks in the Adirondack region would be uplifted into mountains.

Meanwhile, the two continents that collided during the Grenville orogeny had separated, allowing the sea to flood the region again. After millions of years, the sediments that accumulated in these shallow waters, known as the Potsdam Sea, turned into sandstone, limestone, dolostone, and shale, all of which were deposited on top of the Grenville rocks. These sedimentary rocks have long since eroded in most of the Adirondacks—once again exposing the older, more durable rocks—but they can be found around the margins of the region, such as in the Saint Lawrence and Champlain valleys. Ausable Chasm, in the northeast corner of the Adirondack Park, is a spectacular exhibit of Potsdam Sandstone. Sedimentary rocks also survive in grabens, valleys where huge blocks of crust have fallen below the surface, protecting the rocks from erosion. Lake George, the largest lake wholly within the Adirondack Park, lies in a graben.

All the rocks formed by the Potsdam Sea date to the Cambrian to mid-Ordovician periods, or from 540 million to 450 million years ago. No rocks younger than these are found in the Adirondacks. Thus, there are two gaps in the region's geological record. The first occurs right after the Grenville Orogeny, since no new rocks show up in the record until the formation of the Potsdam Sea—an interval of about 500 million years. Occasionally, a road cut on the fringe of the Adirondack dome illustrates this gap, revealing layers of sandstone lying atop granitic gneiss. The time between the Potsdam Sea and today represents another gap of nearly 500 million years. If sedimentation created rocks in the region after the mid-Ordovician Period, as seems likely, erosion has erased any trace of them.

The eastern United States has been in three more continental wrecks since the Potsdam Sea receded, but since the Adirondack region lay inland, away from the action, it did not experience another upheaval such as the one associated with the Grenville orogeny. The region may have been flooded for a time after the first of these later collisions, but the basic geological landscape remained unchanged: a peneplain of sedimentary rock superimposed on older basement rock. And that's how things stood for eons, until about 10 million years ago, when the Adirondacks began to rise.

Geologists cannot explain why the Adirondacks came into being, but the most common theory is that a thermal plume, or hot spot, heated rocks near the earth's mantle, causing them to expand and exert upward pressure until the old Grenville rocks broke through the surface and grew into mountains. A flaw in the theory is that other domical uplifts caused by thermal plumes cover an area much wider than the Adirondacks. It's as if the heat from the hot spot, instead of fanning outward as it rose, zeroed in like a laser beam on the Adirondack region. State geologist Yngvar Isachsen, one of the theory's main proponents, admits the Adirondacks seem to be anomalous, but he can think of no source of energy other than deep heat to explain the uplift.

Only two summits top 5,000 feet: Mount Marcy, at 5,344 feet, and Algonquin Peak, at 5,114 feet. Another 41 summits surpass 4,000 feet. All of these high peaks are located in the vicinity of Lake Placid and Keene Valley, in the northeastern quadrant of the Adirondack Park. The mountains are higher in this part of the park for two reasons: they lie near the center of the uplift and most are made of anorthosite, a durable rock that resists erosion. Mountains elsewhere in the park are usually made of gneiss.

Comparisons of old and new geological surveys suggest that the mountains continue to grow 1 to 3 millimeters a year, far outpacing the rate of erosion. If this were to continue for a million years, the mountains would grow more than a kilometer. But it's uncertain whether the growth is a temporary spurt or a long-term trend. Also, some geologists question whether the mountains are rising at all, for it may be that the old survey measurements were imprecise. In 1995, geologists resurveyed peaks using the Global Positioning System. Several decades hence, geologists may be able to use this data to determine if the Adirondacks are indeed still growing.

Glaciers in the Adirondacks

About 2 million years ago, at the start of the Quaternary Period, the earth entered an ice age that saw the advance and retreat of at least three continental glaciers in the Northern Hemisphere. Most likely, all the glaciers reached the Adirondacks, but if so, the last glacier erased any signs of its predecessors. This glacier, which covered virtually the entire state about 20,000 years ago, changed the Adirondack landscape by sharpening the topographical relief and transforming the region from a land of rivers to a land of rivers, lakes, and ponds.

Geologists believe that the glacier buried even Mount Marcy. Although this remains unproven, glacial erratics, boulders carried by the ice, sit as high as 4,600 feet on Marcy. The glacier sculpted the region's alpine bedrock in several ways. It gouged out weak or broken rock in fault valleys, shearing the walls so valleys that had been V-shaped became U-shaped. As the glacier rode over low mountains and hills, it smoothed the northern slopes on the way up and steepened the southern slopes, by plucking away rock, on the way down. When the main ice retreated, local glaciers lingered near summits, carving out cirques—large rock amphitheaters visible on Whiteface, Giant, and other mountains.

The glacier carried tons of boulders, rocks, and soil. As the ice melted, this debris was often deposited in valleys, damming rivers to form lakes, including Lake George, Long Lake, and Indian Lake. The glacier also created innumerable kettle ponds during its retreat. These form when an isolated block of ice gets buried in debris: after the block melts, it leaves a depression that fills with water. Kettle ponds often evolve into bogs. The glacier also left numerous eskers. Essentially, these are inverted riverbeds—narrow, sinuous ridges formed from the deposits of rivers that once flowed within or atop the glacier. For the ordinary hiker, the most obvious signs of the glacier are the large boulders that turn up in unexpected places as if dropped out of nowhere. These glacial erratics are scattered throughout the Adirondacks.

The weight of the mile-thick glacier so depressed the landscape that when the ice finally melted, the Atlantic Ocean flowed into the Saint Lawrence and Champlain valleys, and for awhile, whales, walruses, and seals dwelt on the margin of the Adirondacks. As the land rebounded, the sea retreated and Lake Champlain took its place. Geologists estimate that the land in the Champlain Valley has rebounded 500 feet since the glacier departed about 10,000 years ago.

Flora

After the glacier melted, plants began to colonize the denuded landscape. Grasses and tundra flora, such as alpine bilberry (*Vaccinium uliginosum*) and dwarf birch (*Betula glandulosa*), arrived first, but as the climate warmed, they retreated to the cold and windy summits. Today, the tundra community survives only on 85 acres scattered over a dozen or so of the High Peaks. Visitors are struck by the Spartan beauty of these islands in time.

Coniferous taiga forests, similar to those in modern Canada and Siberia, succeeded the tundra flora. As the climate continued to warm, the taiga, too, retreated up the slopes. Today, two boreal species of trees, balsam fir (*Abies balsamea*) and red spruce (*Picea rubens*), dominate the forest above 2,500 feet. Near timberline, in the *krummholz*—German for "crooked wood"—the trees become dwarfed and misshapen. The High Peaks Region contains 100,000 contiguous acres of boreal forest, which the ecologist George Davis has classified as a high-elevation boreal biome.

EASTERN WHITE PINE
(*Pinus strobus*)

The taiga also survives in the cool, moist lowlands in the northwestern Adirondacks. Davis has classified these 350,000 acres as a low-elevation boreal biome. Conifers will also be found in moist lowlands and along lakes and streams throughout the Adirondacks, but these pockets are too small to count as a biome—a broad unit of ecological classification.

The rest of the Adirondack Park, about 5.5 million acres, lies within a temperate deciduous forest biome. Here, northern hardwoods dominate. The most common climax species are sugar maple (*Acer saccharum*), yellow birch (*Betula alleghaniensis*), and American beech (*Fagus grandifolia*). Northern red oak (*Quercus rubra borealis*) and white oak (*Quercus alba*) exist in the more temperate climes on the southern and eastern margins of the park.

Even in this biome, conifers are never out of the picture: they grow alongside the hardwoods everywhere, often in great numbers. Also, local conditions may favor conifers. Tamarack (*Larix laricina*) and black spruce (*Picea mariana*) are found in bogs; balsam fir and red spruce in swamps and at high elevations; and white pine (*Pinus strobus*) and red pine (*Pinus resinosa*) in places where the soil is dry and sandy.

Human History

Native Americans hunted and fished the Adirondacks and traveled its waterways, but they did not settle in the interior. When Europeans arrived, they found a pristine forest undisturbed by man. The early records, later corroborated by the analysis of pollen in bogs, suggest that red spruce was the primary softwood and yellow birch the primary hardwood. In the centuries to come, the forest would be changed dramatically.

For the most part, the early white settlers kept to the foothills and valleys on the margins of the Adirondack region. They cleared land for farms and cut trees for local sawmills. Because of the inhospitable climate and poor soils, however, agriculture never flourished in the Adirondacks except in the Champlain Valley. That's where most farms in the Adirondacks are located today.

In the early 1800s, lumbermen transported logs to mills by floating them down rivers, so they cut only buoyant softwoods, mainly red spruce and white pine, and stayed close to river corridors. Tanneries sought only hemlock (*Tsuga canadensis*), as they used the tannin in the bark to turn hides into leather. Often, the hemlock logs would be left to rot in the woods after the bark was stripped off.

In the 1860s, the timber companies began transporting logs out of the forest by railroad, enabling them to range farther from the river corridors and to harvest hardwoods as well as softwoods. These companies selected the best of the mature trees, but iron forges and pulpwood mills cut down trees of all sizes and types to make charcoal for the iron smelters and pulp for the paper mills. This led to ugly clear-cuts.

By the late 1800s, people had become alarmed at the destruction of the forests. As early as 1857, the journalist Samuel H. Hammond wrote, "Had I my way, I would mark out a circle of a hundred miles in diameter and throw around it the protecting aegis of the constitution. I would make it a forest forever." Verplanck Colvin, the famed Adirondack surveyor, argued for the creation of an Adirondack park in a report to the state Board of Regents in 1870.

In 1885, the state legislature established as a forest preserve 681,000 acres in the Adirondacks and 33,894 acres in the Catskill Mountains. In 1892, the legislature created the Adirondack Park. In 1894, the electorate ratified a new state constitution containing a clause that strengthened protection of the preserve: "The lands of the State, now owned or hereafter acquired, constituting the forest preserve as now fixed by law, shall be kept as wild forest lands." Essentially, this means the state land cannot be developed or logged without a constitutional amendment.

Nevertheless, the forest preserve remains vulnerable to the ravages of nature. In the late 1800s and early 1900s, wildfires fueled by the slash left by loggers destroyed hundreds of thousands of acres of private and public land. The fires of 1903 and 1908 alone ruined 800,000 acres of forest. Fire towers built in their aftermath, although no longer staffed, still stand atop many summits.

In the Great Blowdown of 1950, hurricane-force winds severely damaged about 425,000 acres of forest. Another windstorm ripped through much of the northwestern Adirondacks in 1995, toppling trees and clogging trails. In 1998, a catastrophic ice storm broke or bent countless trees in the northern Adirondacks. Acid rain also has taken a toll on trees, especially on red spruce at high elevations.

Hikers probably will see the effects of the 1995 and 1998 storms for years to come: The fallen trees will make bushwhacking impossible in places. Another consequence of the assaults on the forest, both natural and human, has been the proliferation of pioneer species such as paper birch (*Betula papyrifea*) and quaking aspen (*Populus tremuloides*). These sun-loving trees sprout in clearings, but after one generation, they usually are replaced by more shade-tolerant species.

Despite the ravages of the past, several old-growth stands survive in the Adirondacks. The largest, in the Five Ponds Wilderness, covers about 40,000 acres. Giant white pine, red spruce, and yellow birch more than 230 years old can be seen there. Smaller old-growth stands are scattered throughout the park. Many are easily accessible. All of them hint at the grandeur of the forest that once was and that may be again.

Although timber companies still own and log large tracts in the Adirondacks, tourism has surpassed lumbering in economic importance. The region's first big draw was Lake George, in the southeastern corner of today's park. Thomas Jefferson, who visited the lake in 1791, described it as "the most beautiful water I ever saw." By 1817, entrepreneurs had built a steamboat to take tourists around the lake.

BEAVER
(Castor canadensis)
Beavers live in lakes and streams near trees that will be used for dams.

In the early 1800s, few people other than an occasional hunter or fisherman visited the remoter interior. After midcentury, though, more and more writers began waxing romantic about the wilderness and extolling the tonic virtues of mountain air. Among them was Ralph Waldo Emerson, who camped at Follensby Pond near the Raquette River in 1858 with a band of fellow intellectuals. Out of this trip came his poem "The Adirondacs: A Journal Dedicated to My Fellow Travellers in August, 1858."

But the tourist boom did not arrive for another decade, following the publication of *Adventures in the Wilderness; Or Camp-Life in the Adirondacks* by the Rev. W.H.H. Murray. After the book came out in 1869, the author became known as "Adirondack Murray" and his followers as "Murray's Fools." Many of the veteran sportsmen complained that the throngs of newcomers spoiled the wilderness. The old guide Alvah Dunning sniffed, "They pay me well enough, but I'd rather they stayed out of my woods."

The 1800s saw the era of the great Adirondack guides, among them Dunning, John Cheney, Mitchell Sabattis, and Orson "Old Mountain" Phelps. Rightly or wrongly, Phelps enjoyed the most celebrity, thanks to his philosophical musings, quaint expressions, and eccentricities. He once described the bliss of standing atop his beloved Marcy—or "Mercy," in his parlance—as "heaven up-h'isted-ness."

Fauna

Nineteenth-century accounts of the Adirondacks describe it as a land teeming with fish and game. Dunning and his father often shot three or four moose (*Alces alces*) in a single day. Another guide, Elijah Simonds, claimed he killed 2,000 white-tailed deer (*Odocoileus virginianus*), 150 black bear (*Ursus americanus*), 12 timber wolf (*Canis lupus*), and 7 panther (*Felis concolor*) during his career. Reports of prodigious catches of brook trout—in one case, more than 40 pounds in a day—were so common that historians refuse to dismiss them as mere fish stories.

Before the century ended, the hunters had shot the last of the moose, wolf, and

Forest Preserve Rules

Hikers should be aware of the following regulations for the Adirondack Forest Preserve:

1. If you carry it in, carry it out. Do not litter the woods or bury garbage.

2. Unless staying in a lean-to or designated tent site, you must camp at least 150 feet from the trail or any water source.

3. It is illegal to camp above 4,000 feet from May 1 to December 14.

4. Bury human waste under soil and leaf litter at least 150 feet from the trail or any water source.

5. Wash dishes at least 150 feet from water sources. Do not let soap get in water sources.

6. Avoid making campfires, but if you must build a fire, use only down and dead wood.

7. It is illegal to pick plants or damage trees.

8. Groups of 10 or more people need a permit to camp on state land.

panther; the Canada lynx (*Lynx canadensis*) had vanished; and the beaver (*Castor canadensis*) had almost vanished. Since 1980, the moose has migrated back to the Adirondacks from New England. As of 1998, it was estimated that 75 to 100 moose were in the Adirondacks, and wildlife biologists expect the population to grow. The state has even seen fit to put up moose-crossing signs on a highway north of Speculator. The beaver, too, has returned in such force that beaver dams and beaver meadows are familiar sights on hiking trails.

In the 1980s, the state released a number of lynx in the High Peaks, but the animals did not stay put. Some were hit by cars; one was shot in Vermont. There has been talk of restoring the wolf and panther, but neither project has gained popular support. One study concluded that the region no longer has a roadless wilderness large enough to contain the panther.

The brook trout—one of the enduring symbols of the Adirondacks—also has suffered since the nineteenth century. Acid rain has rendered many ponds incapable of supporting trout, but the greater threat has come from competing fish, such as yellow perch, that have been introduced into waters that once held only or mostly trout. Occasionally, the state poisons a lake to kill off the unwanted species and then restocks it with trout. The state stocks dozens of Adirondack lakes each year with brookies. Most of them belong to a strain adapted to life in hatcheries. Heritage trout, descendants of aboriginal fish, still dwell in a small number of lakes.

Despite environmental setbacks, the Adirondack Park remains a wild land, wilder today than at the start of the twentieth century. A 1988 state report estimated that the park harbors 133,000 snowshoe hare, 73,000 gray fox, 65,000 deer, 50,000 beaver, 22,000 muskrat, 7,600 raccoon, 7,500 red fox, 4,000 eastern coyote, 3,600 bear, 3,500 fisher, 3,000 river otter, 2,300 mink, and more than 1,000 pine marten. The populations of all were listed as stable or on the rise.

The same report estimated that there were 106,000 ruffed grouse, 12,300 Canada geese, 600 common loon, 100 osprey, and 68,000 waterfowl of various species. The bald eagle (*Haliaeetus leucocephalus*) and peregrine falcon (*Falco peregrinus*), both absent from the Adirondacks for years, have returned to the skies as a result of successful restorations. Both now breed within the park. Most Adirondack fauna can be found in just about any part in the park. One exception is the eastern timber rattlesnake (*Crotalus horridus*), which dwells only in the vicinity of Lake George and Lake Champlain. Also, northern species of birds, such as the boreal chickadee (*Parus hudsonicus*) and gray jay (*Perisoreus canadensis*), exist in greater concentrations in the two boreal biomes than elsewhere in the park.

The Adirondack Park

The Adirondack Park also contains a large number of *Homo sapiens*: 130,000 people live here year-round and millions visit each year. Dozens of hamlets and villages are scattered throughout the Adirondacks. Some are little more than crossroads with a general store. The more developed villages—such as Lake Placid, Lake George, and Old Forge—resemble other tourist meccas, with their pizza parlors, gift stores, gas stations, restaurants, and motels.

Private landowners hold title to about 3.4 million acres in the Adirondack Park, or about 56 percent of the total land. The Adirondack Park Agency, which regulates development, has placed the bulk of the private land, roughly 2.7 million acres, in its two strictest land-use classifications, and as a result this land remains largely forested. Only about 2 percent of the private land is classified as hamlet, the least-restrictive category.

The State Department of Environmental Conservation manages the 2.6 million acres of forest preserve within the park, but the amount of public land is in flux. In 1998, for example, the state agreed to buy 29,000 acres of timberland and protect another 114,000 acres through conservation. DEC operates 40 campgrounds, two ski areas, and several day-use areas in the park. These intensive-use areas make up less than 1 percent of the preserve. The rest of the preserve is open to the public for free, but the allowable recreation varies somewhat with land-use classification. The land is classified as wilderness, wild forest, primitive area, or canoe area.

Wilderness. The state tries to keep wilderness areas as natural as possible. Bicycles, snowmobiles, motorboats, and automobiles are prohibited. Some tracts do not even have trails. Anglers are forbidden to use baitfish in many waters, a policy aimed at preventing exotic fish from taking over trout ponds. The park has 16 wilderness areas, totaling about 1 million acres. Five wilderness areas exceed 100,000 acres.

Wild Forest. The wild forest areas are more accessible than wilderness. Often, they are bisected by local roads. In some cases, vehicles are allowed to penetrate deep into the woods via old jeep trails. Mountain bicycles and snowmobiles usually are permitted. The park has 24 wild forest areas, totaling about 1.4 million acres. Some are quite small and isolated, but the larger wild forests are as big as wilderness areas.

Primitive Areas. Primitive areas are managed as wilderness, but they are placed in a separate class because of something that detracts from their wild character, such as a road, a building, an inholding, or simply their small size. Often, they adjoin wilderness or wild forest and are indistinguishable from the larger land units. The park has 27 primitive areas, totaling about 55,000 acres. Only a few are well known, including the Hudson Gorge, Hurricane Mountain, Lake Lila, and Valcour Island primitive areas.

Canoe Areas. The Saint Regis Canoe Area, totaling 18,600 acres, is the only designated canoe area in the park. It is managed as a wilderness.

That's 2.6 million acres. Get out and enjoy it.

Adirondack Park Visitor Interpretive Centers and Adirondack Museum

Anyone who does much hiking in the Adirondacks soon becomes acquainted with a number of scenes in the woodland gallery: blue gentian blooming in a beaver meadow, a yellow birch wrapping its roots around a glacial boulder, ghostly white stalks of Indian pipe poking through leaf litter, brown rock lichen peeling off a cliff face like bad paint. Eventually, hikers desire to know more about the natural world around them. How did that boulder get atop this mountain? Why is this plant all white? Are these brown flakes really alive? Those who possess such curiosity will want to spend some time at one of the Adirondack Park Visitor Interpretive Centers run by the state in Newcomb and Paul Smiths. Either center provides an excellent introduction to the natural history of the Adirondacks through indoor exhibits and interpretive hiking trails. The centers also sponsor lectures and workshops throughout the year.

The trails wind through forest, bog, and marsh, affording hikers the chance to see a variety of birds and animals. The trails vary in length from about 0.6 mile to 1.2 miles but can be combined for longer hikes over easy terrain. In winter, visitors can ski or snowshoe at the centers. Children will delight in the butterfly house at Paul Smiths or the butterfly garden at Newcomb. Both centers have a "touch table" with a collection of natural objects that youngsters may pick up and examine, such as pine cones, rocks, and animal skulls. The centers also sponsor sundry children's activities and workshops.

For those interested in the cultural history of the Adirondacks, a visit to the Adirondack Museum in Blue Mountain Lake is a must. The museum, overlooking the lake, has about 20 buildings exhibiting all things Adirondack, from trout flies to artworks, from mining tools to antique guideboats, from a rich man's railroad car to a poor hermit's hut. Taken as a whole, the exhibits paint a comprehensive portrait of the people who lived, worked, and played in the Adirondacks.

The museum and the visitor centers complement each other, so those who take the time to do both tours will be rewarded with a deeper appreciation of the region's human and natural landscapes. Plus, visitors can cap off their trip to any of these places with a climb up a nearby mountain: Blue Mountain in Blue Mountain Lake (*see* page 209), Goodnow Mountain in Newcomb (*see* page 211), or Saint Regis Mountain in Paul Smiths (*see* page 301). All three summits have exceptional views.

ADIRONDACK PARK VISITOR INTERPRETIVE CENTER AT NEWCOMB

Directions: [Fig. 4(2)] From the village of Long Lake, drive northeast on NY 28N about 14 miles to the entrance on the left. The center is located west of the hamlet of Newcomb.

Activities: Hiking, Nordic skiing, snowshoeing, lectures and workshops on natural history.

Facilities: Indoor exhibits, hiking trails, butterfly garden.

Dates: Open year-round.

Fees: None.

Closest town: Newcomb.

For more information: Adirondack Park Visitor Interpretive Center, Box 101, Newcomb, NY 12852. Phone (518) 582-2000.

ADIRONDACK PARK VISITOR INTERPRETIVE CENTER AT PAUL SMITHS

Directions: [Fig. 4(1)] From the intersection of NY 30 and NY 86 in Paul Smiths, drive north 0.9 mile on NY 30 to the entrance on the left.

Activities: Hiking, Nordic skiing, snowshoeing, lectures and natural history workshops.

Facilities: Indoor exhibits, hiking trails, butterfly house.

Dates: Open year-round.

Fees: None.

Closest town: Saranac Lake village is about 12 miles south.

For more information: Adirondack Park Visitor Interpretive Center, PO Box 3000, Paul Smiths, NY 12970. Phone (518) 327-3000.

ADIRONDACK MUSEUM

Directions: [Fig. 3(3)] From the junction of NY 28 and NY 30 in Blue Mountain Lake, drive north on NY 30 about 1 mile to the museum on the left.

Activities: Lectures, workshops, field trips, youth activities.

Facilities: More than 20 indoor and outdoor exhibit areas, museum shop, cafeteria, picnic pavilion, conference building.

Dates: Open from Memorial Day weekend to mid-October.

Fees: There is a charge for admission.

Closest town: Blue Mountain Lake.

For more information: The Adirondack Museum, Blue Mountain Lake, NY 12812. Phone (518) 352-7311.

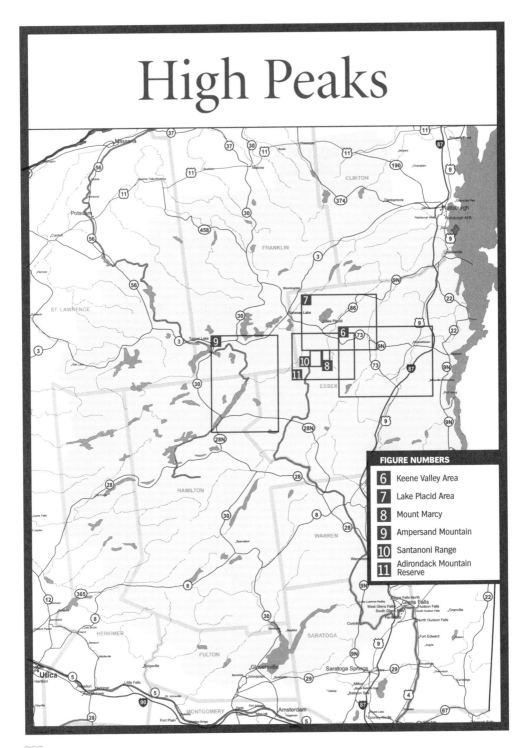

High Peaks

FIGURE NUMBERS

6	Keene Valley Area
7	Lake Placid Area
8	Mount Marcy
9	Ampersand Mountain
10	Santanoni Range
11	Adirondack Mountain Reserve

The High Peaks

When people think of the Adirondacks, they often think of the High Peaks and Lake Placid. This is unfortunate, for not all of the beauty of the Adirondacks lies within a 20-mile radius of the Olympic village. But it is understandable. After all, the Adirondacks are mountains, and the High Peaks are the biggest of the lot. Not that you have to climb Mount Marcy to enjoy the High Peaks Region. You could climb a small mountain instead, or walk to a pond, or canoe to an island, or fish the legendary West Ausable.

As defined in this chapter, the High Peaks Region encompasses the territory bounded roughly by the Northway to the east; NY 28N and the Blue Ridge Road to the south; Long Lake and the Raquette River to the west; and NY 3, Essex County 18, and the West Ausable and Ausable rivers to the north. The village of Saranac Lake, which is bisected by NY 3, and its surrounding lakes will be covered in the Northwest

[*Above:* Mount Marcy, which reaches 5,344 feet, is New York's highest mountain]

Lakes chapter. The Saranac River, which skirts the High Peaks Region, will be covered in the Far North chapter. The High Peaks Region includes six wilderness areas totaling about 365,000 acres—more than a third of park's wilderness acreage—as well as chunks of land classified as either wild forest or as primitive.

The Marcy Massif, a huge block of metamorphosed anorthosite—covering 540 square miles, with roots extending 6 miles below the surface—undergirds most of the region. This durable rock is similar to rocks brought back from the moon, except that the lunar rocks did not undergo metamorphosis. Because metamorphosed anorthosite forms at great depths, it seldom reaches the Earth's surface, but the geologists Howard and Elizabeth Jaffe indicate in *Geology of the Adirondack High Peaks Region* that some type of anorthosite constitutes the summits of 44 of the 46 High Peaks. The summits of Giant and Armstrong mountains, the two exceptions, are syenite gneiss, a rock similar to granite.

Anorthosite takes its characteristic bluish-gray cast from tiny crystals of ilmenite, a shiny black mineral trapped inside the rock, but anorthosite's hue can vary. Geologists differentiate Marcy anorthosite from the darker Whiteface anorthosite. Also, anorthosite turns whitish as it weathers. Like other Adirondack rocks, it often contains bits of red garnet. Anorthosite can be seen in many road cuts in the region.

Gneisses and other metamorphic rock make up most of the bedrock outside the massif. Because metamorphic rock is hard, it resists erosion, but in some places less-resistant igneous rock, such as camptonite and diabase, intruded the main rock. These intrusions, known as dikes and sills, occurred at various times, some as recently as 100 million years ago. After the mountains rose, the igneous rock often eroded to create stream beds and waterfalls. Rocky Falls, Roaring Brook Falls, Indians Falls, and Bushnell Falls are among the falls in the High Peaks Region that formed in this way.

Metamorphic rock will erode more quickly if it has been shattered along faults or in fracture zones, a phenomenon that accounts for some of the region's most spectacular scenery, such as the Ausable Lakes, Indian Pass, Avalanche Pass, and High Falls Gorge. The erosion took place over millions of years, but the glaciers helped by excavating the broken rock. A glance at a map reveals that all four of the geological features named above run northeasterly—the same direction as most of the region's major faults.

As in the rest of the Adirondacks, the glaciers altered the landscape in the High Peaks Region by sculpting the summits, widening valleys, and damming rivers to make lakes. When the ice melted, the water filled Lake Placid valley to such a height that traces of ancient beaches remain on the slopes of the Sentinel Range. Although geology books usually assert that the glaciers topped all the mountains, the Jaffes say the matter is in doubt. Boulders carried by the ice sit as high as 4,600 feet on Mount Marcy, but the Jaffes point out that geologists have not found striations, the grooves created by glaciers, at the highest elevations.

Hikers can find ample evidence of the glaciers' work in the High Peaks. Whenever they come across a huge boulder that seems to have dropped out of nowhere, chances are it's a glacial erratic, discarded by melting ice. Striking examples of cirques, bowl-shaped amphitheaters carved by ice, can be seen on Whiteface and the west side of Giant. An esker ridge, the deposits of a glacial stream, runs parallel to the Raquette River south of Coreys.

COMMON RAVEN
(*Corvus cryptoleucus*)
The raven's wedge-shaped tail causes it to sometimes be mistaken for a crow.

After the glaciers retreated about 10,000 years ago, the first plants to colonize the barren landscape were tundra flora: lichens, mosses, ferns, sedges, tiny flowers. Over time, as the climate warmed, the trees moved in, first the boreal species, such as spruce and fir, and later birch, maple, and beech. But the trees never could get a foothold on the highest summits, those above 4,500 feet or so, and there the tundra plants cling to life to this day. The botanist E.H. Ketchledge has called them "a living heritage and museum of post-glacial times." Their realm is Lilliputian: a mere 85 acres scattered over approximately a dozen peaks.

Much of the region above timberline is exposed rock where nothing can survive but lichen and moss, both adept at retaining moisture. Several bog plants, such as leatherleaf (*Chamaedaphne calyculata*), Labrador tea (*Ledum groenlandicum*), and black crowberry (*Empetnum nigrum*), also grow on the alpine summits, for nutrients are as scarce on the summits as in bogs. In fact, most plants in the alpine zone can be found at lower elevations, but they exist in miniature on the summits, often hugging the ground, in order to minimize exposure to the wind. One exception is the alpine azalea (*Loiseleuria procumbens*): its delicate pink blooms can be seen nowhere else in the Adirondacks.

Just below the alpine zone, boreal forest dominates the upper slopes from about 2,500 feet to timberline, a region too harsh for most deciduous trees. Balsam fir (*Albies balsamea*) and red spruce (*Picea rubens*) coexist up to about 4,200 feet, where the red spruce starts to disappear. Close to timberline, the trees that remain—which can include black spruce—become gnarled and shrunken, as if cowering from the cold winds. This is called the *krummholz*, from a German word meaning "crooked wood." Spruce-fir forest can be found in isolated patches on mountains throughout the Adirondacks, but it is so common in the central High Peaks as to constitute a separate biome, a large biogeographical community. This high-elevation boreal biome, as defined by wilderness researcher George Davis, stretches from the Dix Range northwest to the Sawtooth Mountains, taking in most of the High Peaks.

In the short growing season of the upper slopes, evergreens have an advantage over deciduous trees in that they need not expend energy regrowing their leaves each year. Paper birch (*Betula papyrifea*), however, hangs on well in the boreal zone, perhaps because chlorophyll in the inner bark supplements the photosynthesis that takes place in the leaves. Mosses, liverworts, ferns, and a few hardy flowers—such as wood sorrel (*Oxalis dilleni*), bunchberry (*Cornus canadensis*), and bluebead lily (*Clintonia borealis*)—account for much of the ground cover that is able to grow in the thin, organic soils.

Below 2,500 feet, forests more typical of the Adirondacks predominate: northern hardwood forest and mixed woods. In a mixed wood, usually found on the lowest slopes, conifers such as balsam fir and red spruce mingle with yellow birch (*Betula alleghaniensis*), red maple (*Acer rubrum*), and other hardwoods. As elevation increases, the typical Adirondack hardwoods—sugar maple (*Acer saccharum*), American beech (*Fagus grandifolia*), and yellow birch—become more common. But conifers seldom disappear entirely: white pines (*Quercus alba*) will grow in dry places and Eastern hemlocks (*Tsuga canadenis*) or red spruce in moist places. Spruce-fir swamps will be found in poorly drained lowlands.

Little old-growth forest remains in the region. Despite the steepness of the mountains, loggers managed to the cut timber at quite high elevations. Botanist Ketchledge has seen evidence of a logging road on Wright Peak at 3,700 feet. Forest fires, fueled by slash on timberlands, burned thousands of acres on Marcy, Giant, Cascade, Dix, Big Slide, and other peaks in the early 1900s. Also, the 50-mph winds of the Great Blowdown leveled and destroyed countless trees in the Western High Peaks in 1950, leaving the area impassable for several years. The beautiful stands of paper birch scattered throughout the High Peaks Region owe their existence to these and other disturbances of the forest, as this pioneer species takes over clearings vacated by other trees.

Nevertheless, old-growth stands did survive here and there. Among those in the Forest Preserve are stands at Marcy Swamp, Phelps Brook, Roaring Brook Falls, Ampersand Mountain, and Tamarac Mountain. There is another stand at the Adirondack Mountain Reserve, which has trails that are open to the public. Of course, the krummholz found on the highest mountains also qualifies as old growth, but it hardly conforms to the popular notion that old means big.

The usual menagerie of Adirondack mammals inhabits the forests, including black bear (*Ursus americanus*) and white-tailed deer (*Odocoileus virginianus*). The High Peaks, though, ranks among the worst deer habitat in the state. Not only are the winters harsh, but there are few places where deer can find adequate shelter and nourishment while waiting for spring. In fact, hunting statistics reveal that the deer take throughout the Adirondacks is low compared with other parts of the state. In Keene, a town in the heart of the High Peaks Region, hunters killed 75 deer in one recent year, whereas they killed 321 in Bethlehem, a suburb of Albany, and 833 in

Bath, a town in southwestern New York. Bears are fairly numerous, but hunting statistics suggest that they are much more plentiful in the central Adirondacks. Though seldom seen, bears sometimes show up at campsites in search of food.

Some of the larger birds that reside in the High Peaks Region are the common loon (*Gavia immer*), great blue heron (*Ardea herodias*), American bittern (*Botaurus lentiginosus*), great horned owl (*Bubo virginianus*), and spruce grouse (*Canachites canadensis*). Hikers on the bald summits sometimes see peregrine falcons (*Falco peregrinus*) and common ravens (*Corvus corax*), which nest on cliffs, soaring over the valleys. Even bald eagles (*Haliaeetus leucocephalus*), which nest a little to the north, fly overhead every once in a while. But it is the smaller birds—such as the golden-crowned kinglet (*Regulus satrapa*) or hairy woodpecker (*Picoides villosus*)—that are more likely to be spotted by hikers in the woods. All told, about 150 species of birds breed in the region.

Judging by place names, one might get the idea that Native Americans visited the High Peaks Region as often as Adirondack Mountain Club hikers. There is an Indian Pass, an Indian Falls, an Indian Carry, and an Indian Head. Then there are the many aboriginal names, some of dubious authenticity: Tahawus, Nun-de-ga-o, Oseetah, She-gwi-en-dank-we. According to lore, the Iroquois referred to the Adirondacks as *Couchsachraga*, which has been translated as "dismal wilderness." Finally, there is the apocryphal story that Boundary Peak, located between Algonquin Peak and Iroquois Peak, marked the ancient boundary between the territories of the two rival tribes.

In truth, Indians did pass through and no doubt hunted and fished the region, but they would have had little reason to frequent a place so remote and inhospitable as the High Peaks, especially if game were more abundant elsewhere. Artifacts have been dug up, but anthropologists do not believe that Indians made permanent settlements in the region.

Two centuries after Europeans arrived in the New World, the High Peaks interior remained a "dismal wilderness." Lewis and Clark crossed the Rockies and gazed upon the Pacific Ocean 34 years before the geologist Ebenezer Emmons and his party

MAYAPPLE
(*Podophyllum peltatum*)
Growing to 20 inches tall, the mayapple produces a lemon-yellow fruit that is poisonous when immature. Mature fruit are used in jellies.

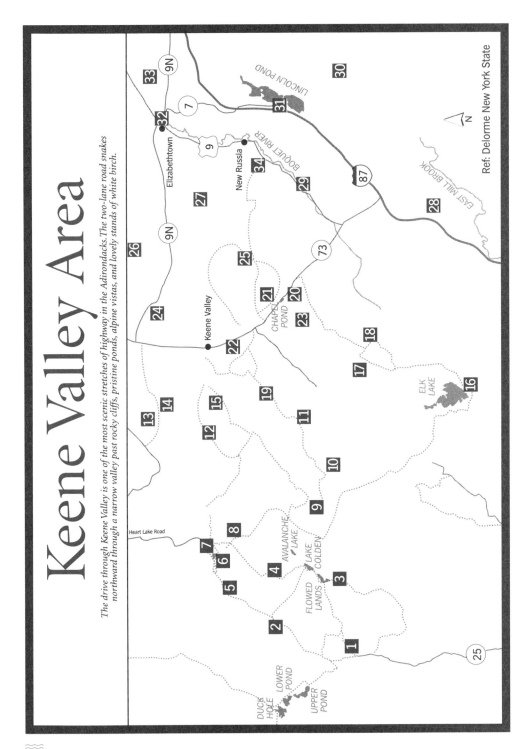

Keene Valley Area

The drive through Keene Valley is one of the most scenic stretches of highway in the Adirondacks. The two-lane road snakes northward through a narrow valley past rocky cliffs, pristine ponds, alpine vistas, and lovely stands of white birch.

1 Two-day Loop from Upper Works
2 Indian Pass
3 Hanging Spear Falls
4 Algonquin Peak/Avalanche Pass
5 Rocky Falls
6 Heart Lake Trail
7 Adirondack Loj/Mount Jo
8 Marcy Dam
9 Mount Marcy
10 Mount Haystack
11 Gothics Mountain

12 Big Slide Mountain
13 Cascade Mountain
14 Porter Mountain
15 Johns Brook Lodge
16 Hike from Elk Lake
17 Nippletop Mountain
18 Dix Mountain
19 Hike via the Great Range
20 Round Mountain
21 Giants Washbowl and Nubble
22 Snow Mountain

23 Noonmark Mountain
24 Baxter Mountain
25 Giant Mountain
26 Hurricane Mountain
27 Owl Mountain Lookout
28 Sharp Bridge Campground/ East Mill Flow
29 Split Rock Falls
30 Belfry Mountain
31 Lincoln Pond Campground
32 Adirondack History Center
33 Pauline L Murdock Wildlife Sanctuary
34 Rocky Peak Ridge
·········· Trail

made the first ascent up Mount Marcy in 1839. And British explorers discovered Lake Victoria three years before Old Mountain Phelps blazed the first trail to Marcy's summit in 1861.

Eventually the tourists did discover the High Peaks—and they continue to do so. The state Department of Environmental Conservation estimates that the number of visitors to the High Peaks Wilderness alone rose from 67,000 in 1985 to 131,000 in 1995. Thousands more hike the less-traveled paths in the region's other wilderness areas each year.

Anyone climbing the High Peaks should be prepared for cold weather, even in summer. The temperature at the summit can be 20 degrees Fahrenheit lower than at the start of the trail, and if the wind is blowing, as it often does, it will seem even colder. Moreover, the Adirondacks have a reputation for fickle weather: sunny skies can darken quickly and unleash a downpour.

For more information: State Department of Environmental Conservation, P.O. Box 296, Route 86, Ray Brook, NY 12977. Phone (518) 897-1200.

Drive Through Keene Valley

Visitors approaching Lake Placid from the southeast will take delight in driving along NY 73 through Keene Valley, one of the most scenic stretches of highway in the Adirondacks. From Northway Exit 30, the two-lane road snakes northward through a narrow valley past rocky cliffs, pristine ponds, alpine vistas, and lovely stands of white birch (*Betula papyrifea*). Many of the road cuts along the way are anorthosite.

Those who approach the region by another route might want to take a trip down NY 73 just for the scenery. The sights below are described in order as encountered when driving north from the Northway.

CHAPEL POND

[Fig. 6] This 0.5-mile-long pond bordered by white birch trees and steep cliffs makes a nice picnic stop. Rainbow trout (*Oncorhynchus mykiss*) and brook trout (*Salvelinus fontinalis*) inhabit the waters, which drain into the Ausable River's East Branch, and ravens (*Corvus corax*) nest on the cliffs. The 700-foot precipices attract a good number of rock climbers. A road cut on the other side of NY 73 just north of the pond contains a 165-foot band of granite, flecked with garnet, that intruded into the anorthosite. There is a small sandy beach on the south end of the pond. A canoe can be put in on the north end. A little north of Chapel Pond, on the other side of NY 73, Roaring Brook Falls can be seen cascading off Giant Mountain.

Directions: From the junction of NY 73 and US 9, drive about 4.3 miles north on NY 73 to a parking area on the left.

Activities: Picnicking, canoeing, fishing, rock climbing.

Facilities: None.

Fees: None.

Closest town: Keene hamlet is about 5 miles north.

CASCADE LAKES

[Fig. 7] There is another pretty picnic spot between Upper and Lower Cascade lakes. White birch trees ring the twin lakes, which lie in a fault zone gouged out by glaciers. The lakes take their name from a waterfall that tumbles down a cleft in Cascade Mountain, spilling onto a pile of talus between them. In spring, the cascade leaves mineral specimens, such as blue calcite and red garnet, amid the talus. Visitors should beware of climbing the cleft because the rock is steep and often loose. Note that it is illegal to collect minerals in the Adirondack Park.

Both lakes are stocked with brook trout. The round whitefish (*Prosopium cylindraceum*), an endangered species in New York, also survives in both; if caught, these fish must be returned to the water. Anglers are not allowed to use bait fish. Small boats and canoes can be launched into either lake. Camping along the lakes is prohibited.

Stagecoach Rock lies across NY 73 just north of Upper Cascade. The large boulder features an etching of a stagecoach, a tribute to an era when the stagecoach was the main means of public transit in the mountains.

Directions: From Keene hamlet, drive west on NY 73 about 6 miles to a parking area on the left. From Lake Placid, the lakes are about 5.3 miles past Adirondak Loj Road on NY 73.

Activities: Picnicking, canoeing, fishing.

Facilities: Picnic tables, launch for car-top boats.

Fees: None.

Closest town: Keene is 6 miles away.

HIGH PEAKS VISTA

[Fig. 7(10)] There is a spectacular vista of the High Peaks at the junction of NY 73 and Adirondak Loj Road. One looks across a large meadow—once the bottom of a glacial lake—to Algonquin Peak rising between Indian Pass on the right and Avalanche Pass on the left. In summer, it's not unusual to see an artist painting the scene or someone snapping a picture. Just before Lake Placid, there is

SNOWSHOE HARE
(*Lepus americanus*)
A shy boreal species that is more active at night. Dark brown in summer, white in winter.

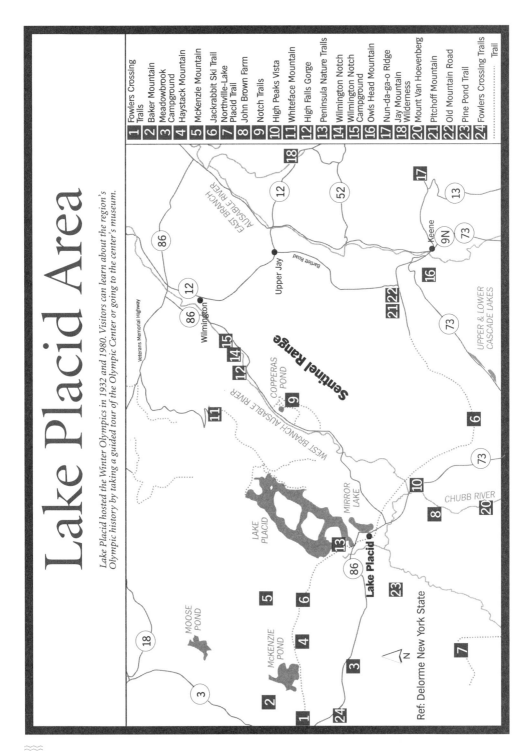

Lake Placid Area

Lake Placid hosted the Winter Olympics in 1932 and 1980. Visitors can learn about the region's Olympic history by taking a guided tour of the Olympic Center or going to the center's museum.

1	Fowlers Crossing Trails
2	Baker Mountain
3	Meadowbrook Campground
4	Haystack Mountain
5	McKenzie Mountain
6	Jackrabbit Ski Trail
7	Northville–Lake Placid Trail
8	John Brown Farm
9	Notch Trails
10	High Peaks Vista
11	Whiteface Mountain
12	High Falls Gorge
13	Peninsula Nature Trails
14	Wilmington Notch
15	Wilmington Notch Campground
16	Owls Head Mountain
17	Nun-da-ga-o Ridge
18	Jay Mountain Wilderness
20	Mount Van Hoevenberg
21	Pitchoff Mountain
22	Old Mountain Road
23	Pine Pond Trail
24	Fowlers Crossing Trails Trail

Ref: Delorme New York State

another panorama, this one of Whiteface Mountain and the Sentinel Range. They can be seen on the right as one passes the county fairgrounds.

Directions: From the south, Adirondak Loj Road is on the left about 3 miles past the Mount Hoevenberg Olympic Sports Complex. From Lake Placid, the road is on the right about 4 miles south on NY 73.

Lake Placid Village

[Fig. 7] Lake Placid got its start as a resort community in the 1850s when some of the year-round residents started taking in sportsmen as lodgers. In 1871, Thomas Brewster built the hamlet's first genuine hotel, the Lake Placid Inn, on Mirror Lake. It was a success and was soon imitated. By 1904, the tourist trade had grown so much that the Lake Placid Club decided to risk staying open for the winter. The rest is history: Lake Placid evolved into a winter sports capital that hosted the Winter Olympics in 1932 and 1980.

The Olympic Regional Development Authority operates several Olympic sites open to the public. In Lake Placid, visitors can learn about the region's Olympic history by taking a guided tour of the Olympic Center, a year-round training center for figure skating, hockey, speed skating, and curling. The center also opens its indoor and outdoor rinks to visitors for public skating and rents speed, hockey, and figure skates. Travelers can also visit the Lake Placid Winter Olympic Museum, which includes history from the 1932 and 1980 Olympic games. At the Olympic Jumping Complex, a facility for ski jumping and freestyle aerials, visitors can watch athletes training year-round for these sports. During the summer, the ski jumping ramp is lined with porcelain tiles and jumpers land on a hill lined with plastic matting to simulate snow.

For more information: Lake Placid/Essex County Visitors Bureau, Olympic Center, Lake Placid, NY 12946. Phone (518) 523-2445 or (800) 275-2243. Olympic Regional Development Authority, 218 Main Street, Lake Placid, NY 12946. Phone (518) 523-9275.

For those looking for further outdoor exercise while in town, here are some suggestions:

PENINSULA NATURE TRAILS

[Fig. 7(13)] The state maintains three interconnected trails, totaling about 2.5 miles, on Brewster Peninsula on the southwestern shore of Lake Placid. The trails go along the lake, past wetlands, and through various woods, with views of Whiteface Mountain across the lake. Signs along the way identify trees, flowers, mosses, ferns, and fungi. Among the wildflowers that grow here are large-flowered trillium, lily of the valley, and wood-sorrel (*Oxalis dillenii*). Mountain bikers, joggers, and cross-country skiers also use these trails. Pick up a map and trail guide at the Lake Placid/Essex County Visitors

Points of View

Climb a mountain, enjoy the view. Sounds simple enough. But short of climbing them all, how do you know which mountains have the best views? In most cases, you probably couldn't go wrong with taking Bob and George Marshall as your guides. Not only did these two climb all the High Peaks in the 1920s, but they also ranked all the views. They thought Mount Haystack number one. James Burnside also ranked them in his 1996 book *Exploring the 46 Adirondack High Peaks.* Gothics tops his list. Six peaks make the top 10 of both lists: Haystack, Nippletop, Algonquin, Marcy, Santanoni, and Dix. They agree that Nye Mountain—one of the hardest peaks to climb—offers the worst view. The biggest difference between them is the rating of Rocky Peak Ridge: it is 33rd on the Marshalls' list, 8th on Burnside's. When the Marshalls hiked Rocky Peak, however, the surrounding landscape still bore the scars of forest fire. Since then, the woods have grown back, and the view today is indeed gorgeous.

Marshalls	Burnside
1. Mount Haystack	1. Gothics Mountain
2. Santanoni Peak	2. Dix Mountain
3. Nippletop	3. Mount Marcy
4. Iroquois Peak	4. Nippletop
5. Algonquin Peak	5. Algonquin Peak
6. Basin Mountain	6. Mount Haystack
7. Mount Redfield	7. Giant Mountain
8. Mount Marcy	8. Rocky Peak
9. Dix Mountain	9. Santanoni Peak
10. Panther Peak	10. Saddleback Mountain

Bureau at the Olympic Center in the village.

Directions: From NY 86, just west of Lake Placid, turn north onto the road between Howard Johnson's Motor Inn and Howard Johnson's Restaurant. Turn left at fork and park in area next to barricade about 0.5 mile down the road. Walk down the gravel road on the other side of barricade to the trail network.

Trail: 3 interconnected trails totaling about 2.5 miles. Various loops are possible.

Degree of difficulty: Easy.

Surface and blaze: Gravel road, footpath. Blue blazes for Lakeshore Trail, red blazes for Boundary Trail, yellow blazes for Ridge Trail.

MIRROR LAKE

[Fig. 7] Downtown Lake Placid lies not on the lake of the same name but on Mirror Lake. There is a park and beach at the southern tip of Mirror Lake. A 2.8-mile brick promenade circles the water. Motorboats are not allowed on the lake, but small boats and canoes can be launched at the north end. The state stocks Mirror Lake with lake trout and rainbow trout.

Directions: From Main Street, turn east at the post office onto Parkside Drive.

Activities: Swimming, walking, canoeing, fishing.

Facilities: Beach, picnic tables, playground, tennis courts, basketball courts, brick walkway.

Fees: None.

🪨 LAKE PLACID: THE LAKE

[Fig. 7] Lake Placid, on the outskirts of the village, has a peculiar shape that has been likened to a ladder. The two arms of the lake—the sides of the ladder—rest in fault valleys that, as most faults in the region, run in a northeastern direction. Two other fault valleys cross them almost perpendicularly to form the rungs. Moose Island, the biggest of three islands in the lake, lies between the rungs a few miles from the village.

With 2,800 acres of water, Lake Placid is popular with motorboatists, but canoeists will enjoy paddling around its shores. The state owns most of Moose Island and maintains two lean-tos there. The state also owns the northeast shore, where there is a public dock at Whiteface Landing—a 4-mile paddle from the village. A 3.5-mile trail goes from the dock to the summit of Whiteface Mountain. There is another lean-to up the trail about 1.1 mile from the dock. Whiteface Landing also can be reached on foot by a trail that starts near NY 86. Canoeists can camp on Moose Island and hike to Whiteface the next day.

The state stocks Lake Placid with rainbow trout. Lake trout, brook trout, northern pike, and smallmouth bass also live in the lake. In the spring of 1986, an angler caught a lake trout weighing 34 pounds 8 ounces—a state record at the time.

There is a state boat ramp with a hard surface launch in the village.

Directions: From Main Street, turn north on Mirror Lake Drive to reach boat ramp.

Activities: Boating, canoeing, fishing, camping, hiking.

Facilities: State boat ramp in village, lean-tos on Moose Island and on trail to Whiteface Mountain, hiking trails.

Fees: None.

Whiteface Mountain

[Fig. 7(11)] Whiteface is not like most High Peaks: there's a road to the top. The state built the Veterans Memorial Highway in 1931 to honor New Yorkers who died in World War I. Because the land lay within the Forest Preserve, the public had to approve a constitutional amendment to authorize the project. Hikers still climb to the summit, but most people drive.

However you get there, the view from the state's fifth-highest summit makes the trip worthwhile. Whiteface's isolation from the central High Peaks—it lies 17 miles north of Marcy—offers visitors a magnificent panorama of the mountains to the south. On a clear day, it's possible to see the St. Lawrence Valley to the north.

This mountain illustrates better than most the power of ice to sculpt rock. After the main glacier retreated about 10,000 years ago, smaller glaciers remained in the valleys near Whiteface's summit. The glaciers pried away rock by alternately thawing and freezing, eventually forming rock amphitheaters known as cirques. The glaciers almost merged, leaving only jagged ridges between the cirques. Four of these rock ridges, or aretes, radiate from the top of Whiteface.

Whiteface takes its name from streaks of rock bared by landslides long ago. The name has been around since the early 1800s, making Whiteface one of the first of the High Peaks to have been given a name that's still in use.

As one of the sites of the 1980 Olymics, Whiteface is known for alpine skiing. In summer, the ski slopes are open to mountain bikers and the chairlift becomes a tourist ride.

VETERANS MEMORIAL HIGHWAY

[Fig. 7] The 8.5-mile drive from the tollbooth to the summit takes one through two hairpin turns, with great views of Lake Placid at the first turn and of the Wilmington Notch, a glacial gorge, at the second. There are several places to pull over along the way to enjoy the view or have a picnic. Take note of the loose cobbles of sandstone carried south by the glaciers. The road ends well short of the real summit. To get to the top, visitors can take a trail that follows one of the aretes or take an elevator. There is a gift shop and restaurant at the road's end. Some people walk or ski up the highway. Bicycles are not allowed.

Directions: From NY 86 in Wilmington, east of Lake Placid, turn northeast onto County 431, which is the Veterans Memorial Highway. The tollbooth is about 2.5 miles from the turn.

Activities: Hiking, picnicking.

Facilities: Picnic tables, restaurant, gift shop, coin-operated telescopes.

Dates: Open mid-May through mid-Oct.

Fees: There is a charge for the driver and passengers. No charge for hikers.

Closest town: Wilmington is about 2.5 miles from the tollbooth.

For more information: Olympic Regional Development Authority, Olympic Center, Lake Placid, NY 12946. Phone (518) 523-1655 or (800) 462-6236.

HIKING WHITEFACE MOUNTAIN

Two trails lead to Whiteface, one from the south and one from the north. Hikers also can walk up the Veterans Memorial Highway for free, but they cannot park near the tollbooth.

The south trail is longer than the north trail, but it has the advantage of passing by Whiteface Landing on the shore of Lake Placid, where sweaty hikers can jump in the lake off a state-owned dock (but watch out for rocks). This trail also passes by a lean-to, a good place to stop for lunch. The first 3 miles follow an old logging road through a mixed wood to Whiteface Landing, which is reached by a short detour to the left. The main trail turns right and crosses Whiteface Brook three times before reaching the lean-to at 3.6 miles. After passing the lean-to, the trail soon steepens, passes through the krummholz, and emerges onto bare rock above the timberline, where arctic plants live.

Directions: From the junction of NY 86 and NY 73 in Lake Placid, take NY 86 east about 3 miles to a dirt road on the left. Follow the road, bearing left at 0.5 miles, to a parking area. The south trail begins farther down the road.

Trail: 6 miles, one way.

Elevation: 1,635 feet at trailhead to 4,867 feet at summit.

Degree of difficulty: Difficult.

Surface and blaze: Old road, natural forest floor, bare rock. Red blazes to timberline, yellow blazes rest of way.

MOUNTAIN BIKING AT WHITEFACE

In summer, mountain bikers can take the chairlifts to the 3,600-foot summit of Little Whiteface and ride down. The advanced trail drops 2,100 feet in elevation. It's also possible to get off halfway to the top for shorter trails of varying difficulty. Nonbikers can just ride the chairlifts for the views. An observation deck and picnic tables are on the summit. Bikes can be rented at the base lodge.

Directions: From the junction of NY 86 and NY 73 in Lake Placid, drive east about 8 miles on NY 86 to the Whiteface Mountain Ski Center on the left.

Activities: Mountain biking, chairlift riding, picnicking.

Facilities: Lodge, observation deck, picnic tables.

Dates: Late June to mid-October, 9 a.m. to 4 p.m.

Fees: There is a fee for using bike trails or just riding chairlift.

Closest town: Wilmington is about 5 miles east.

CHIMNEY SWIFT
(Chaetura pelagica)
Nesting in hollow trees, unless chimneys are available, this small bird spends much of its day in flight, flapping its wings rapidly then holding them stiffly to sail through the air.

For more information: Olympic Regional Development Authority, Olympic Center, Lake Placid, NY 12946. Phone (518) 523-1655 or (800) 462-6236.

Mount Van Hoevenberg

[Fig. 7(20)] Once called South Mountain, this 2,860-foot peak southeast of Lake Placid was renamed in honor of Henry Van Hoevenberg, founder of the original Adirondack Lodge, shortly before Lake Placid hosted the Winter Olympics in 1932. In the 1980 Olympics, the bobsled, luge, cross-country skiing, and biathlon competitions all took place here. Year-round, visitors can pay to ride the bobsled with a professional driver. During the winter, solo rides on the Luge Rocket, a modified competitive luge, are available to the public for a fee. One day per week during the winter, visitors can pay to take a solo ride in a traditional luge. The cross-country trails are open to skiers in the winter and mountain bikers in summer. Two hiking trails lead to the summit.

SKIING AND BIKING AT MOUNT VAN HOEVENBERG

Skiers can choose from a myriad of loops along 30 miles of trails designed for Olympic competition. All of the trails begin and end at a central stadium. They also connect with the Mt. Van Ski Trail, giving access to the High Peaks Wilderness, and trails maintained by the Cascade Cross-Country Center. Skis and bikes can be rented at the center. Trail maps are available. Note that bicycles are prohibited in the neighboring High Peaks Wilderness.

Directions: From Lake Placid, drive about 7 miles south on NY 73 to the entrance to the Mount Van Hoevenberg Olympic Sports Complex on the right. If coming from the south, the turn is about 7 miles north of Keene.

Activities: Cross-country skiing, mountain biking.

Facilities: About 30 miles of trails. Warming hut.

Dates: Mid-June to early Sept. for biking. Mid-Nov. to Mar. for skiing.

Fees: There is a charge for skiing or biking.

Closest town: Lake Placid is about 7 miles northwest.

For more information: Olympic Regional Development Authority, Olympic Center, Lake Placid, NY 12946. Phone (518) 523-1655 or (800) 462-6236.

HIKING MOUNT VAN HOEVENBERG

Hikers can climb to the summit from South Meadows Road or the Olympic Sports Complex parking lot. The trail from the complex, following bobsled runs, is about 0.5-mile shorter, but there is a parking fee. The trail from South Meadows starts out flat for about 1 mile as it passes through a deciduous forest on the bed of a glacial lake and then ascends the mountain's south scarp. Three ledges on the way up offer great views of the nearby High Peaks. The geologists Howard and Elizabeth

Jaffe describe Mount Van Hoevenberg as a homocline, a mountain with rock layers that tilt in one direction, like a lopsided layer cake, creating an escarpment on one side and a more gentle rise on the other. Big Slide, one of the many peaks visible from the summit, is another example of a homocline.

Directions: From Lake Placid, drive 4 miles southeast on NY 73, turn south on Adirondak Loj Road, go about 3.8 miles to South Meadows Road, turn left, and go another 0.3 mile to the trailhead.

Trail: 2.2 miles from road to summit.

Elevation: 2,120 feet at trailhead to 2,860 feet at summit.

Degree of difficulty: Moderate.

Surface and blaze: Natural forest floor, rocky ledges. Blue blazes.

High Peaks Wilderness

The High Peaks Wilderness, encompassing about 226,000 acres, is the largest of the 16 wilderness areas in the park. Thirty-two of the 46 High Peaks lie within its boundaries, including Mount Marcy and Algonquin Peak, the only two that exceed 5,000 feet. Most of these peaks are concentrated in the eastern part of the wilderness. The western region, though not without its mountains, is as much a land of water—streams, lakes, and wetlands—as of rocky summits. Since most hikers come to climb the peaks, they tend to congregate in the eastern region. Those after solitude should look to the west (or other parts of the park).

When Bob and George Marshall set out in the 1920s to scale all the peaks over 4,000 feet, most of the summits lacked trails and several had never been climbed before. Today, the wilderness is much more accessible. The state Department of Environmental Conservation, with the help of private organizations, maintains 300 miles of trails in the High Peaks, and even trail-less summits often can be reached by unofficial "herd paths." Among the facilities found in the interior are 70 log lean-tos,

Black Bear

About 4,000 black bear (*Ursus americanus*) live in the Adirondacks. They move around a lot in search of food, mostly berries, nuts, roots, and insects, but hikers rarely see them. If you do see a bear, here's the advice of Lou Berchielli, the state's bruin specialist: "Stop and enjoy it. Once the bear realizes you're there, it should leave." If it doesn't leave, you should walk away slowly. If you run, the bear might pursue, more out of curiosity than anything else. In about two decades on the job, Berchielli knows of only one instance in which a bear attacked a hiker in the Adirondacks: A mother bear bit a teenager in the buttocks after he tried to steal her cubs. Sometimes, bears show up at campsites at night looking for food. Usually, blowing on a whistle or simply yelling will scare them off. When camping in the Adirondacks, keep your food in a bear bag suspended 15 feet off the ground on a rope stretched between trees. It's also a good idea to put in the bag clothing and other items that smell of food.

NORTHERN CARDINAL
(*Cardinalis cardinalis*)

300 primitive campsites, and 100 privies. Such amenities have made it easier to follow in the footsteps of the Marshalls, and thousands have duplicated their feat.

All told, about 150,000 people visit the High Peaks every year. Most are day-trippers hiking to such popular destinations as Marcy Dam, Avalanche Lake, Lake Colden, Cascade Mountain, Algonquin Peak, and, of course, Mount Marcy. On the busiest days—essentially, any weekend during the warm months—it can be difficult to find a parking spot at certain trailheads. The High Peaks also sees a good number of overnight backpackers. On some evenings, so many campfires and lanterns light up the woods around Lake Colden that forest rangers have nicknamed the place Day-Glo City.

Though the High Peaks can get crowded at times, the region has not lost its natural splendor. From certain mountaintops, hikers looking out over the unbroken forest might well imagine themselves transported back to a primeval time—a time before Gore-Tex boots and aluminum walking sticks. Beauty also dwells away from the summits, in the mountain passes, in beaver meadows, and at secluded waterfalls. And sometimes, even in the Eastern High Peaks, hikers will be able to soak up the surroundings in solitude, especially on the less popular trails and summits.

The High Peaks Wilderness contains 117 lakes and ponds, many of them small and nameless, and about 220 miles of cold-water streams, including the headwaters of the Hudson River. Acid rain has left some ponds barren of fish, among them Lake Colden and Avalanche Lake, both once renowned as trout fisheries. Brook trout (*Salvelinus fontinalis*) can still be caught in many ponds, but without stocking, the population would fall off. The endangered round whitefish (*Prosopium cylindraceum*) exists in four of the waters.

For more information: State Department of Environmental Conservation, P.O. Box 296, Route 86, Ray Brook, NY 12977. Phone (518) 897-1200. The DEC publishes a leaflet titled *Trails in the High Peaks Region.*

For the discussion that follows about campgrounds, trails, and destinations, the High Peaks Wilderness has been divided into two sections, eastern and western.

Eastern High Peaks

This region, lying east of Tahawus, boasts 25 High Peaks, including nine of the ten highest. Sixteen of the twenty-five have maintained trails to the summit. Most people come for the challenge of climbing the mountains, especially Marcy, but hikers can find plenty of beautiful scenery without setting foot on a summit.

CAMPING IN THE EASTERN HIGH PEAKS

Backpackers cannot count on finding a vacant lean-to or campsite on busy days and so should be prepared to set up tents at makeshift sites off the trails. No state campground abuts the Eastern High Peaks, but the Adirondack Mountain Club (ADK) maintains lodges and other facilities at two spots on the edge of the wilderness: at Heart Lake and along Johns Brook. Because they are used by so many visitors, they deserve special mention.

ADIRONDAK LOJ

[Fig. 6(7)] Each year, tens of thousands of hikers begin their journeys into the wilderness at Heart Lake, where the ADK runs Adirondak Loj and a High Peaks Information Center. Hikers can buy supplies and snacks, fill up their water bottles, take showers, check the weather forecast, or attend a naturalist's lecture. The club maintains a large parking lot on the premises, open to all for a fee.

For those who want to stay the night, the Loj offers meals and various sleeping quarters: a bunkroom, family rooms, and private rooms. The Loj also has a campground with 34 tent sites; two cabins, one sleeping four people, the other up to 16; and 16 lean-tos. The facilities are open to members and nonmembers alike.

The Van Hoevenberg Trail, leading to the interior of the High Peaks, begins at the ADK parking lot and crosses onto state land. It is the most popular trail in the Adirondacks: in one recent year, about 37,000 people registered at the trailhead, more than twice as many as at the next most popular trailhead. Other popular trails originating here lead to Mount Jo and Indian Pass.

Directions: From Lake Placid, drive 4 miles southeast on NY 73, turn south on Adirondak Loj Road, and go about 4.8 miles to the ticket booth. From the south on NY 73, Adirondak Loj Road is about 3 miles past the Mount Van Hoevenberg Olympic Sports Complex.

Activities: Hiking, camping, swimming, canoeing, fishing, cross-country skiing, snowshoeing.

Facilities: Lodge, campground, lean-tos, beach, interpretive trails, nature museum. The campground has no RV hookups.

Dates: Most of the facilities are open year-round.

Fees: There is a charge for parking or spending the night.

For more information: Adirondack Mountain Club, Box 867, Lake Placid, NY 12946. Phone (518) 523-3441.

JOHNS BROOK LODGE

[Fig. 6(15)] The Adirondack Mountain Club keeps a rustic lodge in the wilderness reachable by a 3.5-mile hike from Keene Valley. Overnight guests use it as a base for exploring the High Peaks, but it makes an excellent day hike for families with children. Upon arrival, they can relax on the deck and try to pick out the peaks of the Great Range. The lodge accommodates up to 28 people in its four bunkrooms. Overnight guests can buy meals at the lodge, including trail lunches. The ADK also rents three lean-tos and two year-round cabins near the lodge.

Directions: From NY 73 in the hamlet of Keene Valley, turn west onto a road marked by a sign that says "Trail to the High Peaks" and drive 1.6 miles to a parking lot known as the Garden. If the lot is full, as often happens, hikers should leave their cars in town and walk to the trailhead, since it is illegal to park on the road to the lot. From the Garden, take the yellow-blazed Phelps Trail to the lodge, a fairly easy hike.

Activities: Camping, hiking.

Facilities: Lodge, lean-tos, cabins, small store, water spigot.

Dates: Cabins are available year-round. From mid-June through Labor Day, the lodge is open daily; in spring and fall, it is open midweek through the weekend.

Fees: There is a charge for staying at the lodge, lean-tos, or cabins.

Closest town: Keene Valley is about 5 miles east.

For more information: Adirondack Mountain Club, Box 867, Lake Placid, NY 12946. Phone (518) 523-3441.

HIKING THE EASTERN HIGH PEAKS

The trails in this region intersect so often as to offer a seemingly infinite variety of possible hikes. The suggestions that follow run the gamut from easy to strenuous. The easy and moderate hikes precede the High Peaks climbs. Directions to the two most popular trailheads, Adirondak Loj and the Garden, will be the same as given above for the Adirondack Mountain Club lodges.

HEART LAKE TRAIL

[Fig. 6(6)] The Heart Lake Trail is a 1-mile nature trail circling Heart Lake, a 32-acre kettle pond created as the glaciers retreated about 10,000 years ago. At interpretive stops, hikers can refer to a leaflet that discusses the trees, wildflowers, birds, and animals that can be seen along the way. This is a good hike for children. The Adirondack Mountain Club, which owns Heart Lake and the surrounding land, maintains two other interpretive trails nearby.

Directions: Same as for Adirondak Loj. Start hike at Nature Museum.

Trail: 1-mile loop around lake.

Degree of difficulty: Easy.

Surface: Natural forest floor.

MARCY DAM

[Fig. 6(8)] The damming of Marcy Brook has created a lovely trout pond ringed by mountains, with views of Mount Colden, Avalanche Mountain, and Wright Peak. The place gets crowded with campers and hikers en route to and from other destinations, but it's a pleasant hike and easy for young children. Starting at Adirondak Loj, the trail winds through stands of pine, northern hardwoods, and spruce, often following Marcy Brook. Cross-country skiers often ski to the dam along this trail or the old truck road from South Meadows Road.

Directions: Same as for Adirondak Loj. From the parking lot, take the Van Hoevenberg Trail as far as Marcy Dam. (The trail continues to Mount Marcy.)

Trail: 2.3 miles from ADK lot to Marcy Dam.

Elevation: 2,178 feet at trailhead to 2,365 feet at Marcy Dam.

Degree of difficulty: Easy.

Surface and blaze: Natural forest floor. Blue blazes.

AVALANCHE PASS AND LAKE COLDEN

[Fig. 6(4)] This is a rugged hike with a rich reward: the sight of Mount Colden's bare walls rising straight up from the dark waters of Avalanche Lake. Part of the trail skirts the base of Avalanche Mountain, going up and down ladders and over wooden catwalks. Look for the Trap Dike, a 70-foot-wide cleft in Colden's cliffs where gabbro rock eroded more quickly than the surrounding anorthosite. When Robert Clarke and Alexander Ralph made the first ascent of Colden in 1850, they went up the dike and then a nearby slide. The route is still popular with rock climbers. Before reaching Avalanche Lake, look for a small waterfall in the pass that marks the divide between the watersheds for Lake Champlain and the St. Lawrence River. Avalanche Lake is a favorite destination of experienced cross-country skiers.

Directions: Same as for Adirondak Loj. Start on Van Hoevenberg Trail. Just past Marcy Dam, bear right and follow yellow blazes to Avalanche Lake.

Trail: 5.3 miles from parking lot to Lake Colden.

Elevation: 2,178 feet at trailhead to about 3,000 feet at Avalanche Pass.

Degree of difficulty: Moderate.

Surface and blaze: Natural forest floor; ladders and catwalks. Blue blazes to just beyond Marcy Dam, yellow blazes rest of way.

ROCKY FALLS

[Fig. 6(5)] A fairly easy hike through hardwoods and hemlocks leads to a series of small waterfalls along Indian Pass Brook and a pool big enough to swim in. There is a lean-to here. The waterfalls formed when softer rock (diabase) in the stream bed eroded faster than the anorthosite. One could take the trail all the

GRAY JAY
(Perisoreus canadensis)
Found in coniferous forests, this bold jay may be seen around forest camps, exploring campers' tents for food.

way to Indian Pass, but the shortest way to the pass starts at the Upper Works (*see* Indian Pass, page 36).

Directions: Same as for Adirondak Loj. The trail begins on the west side of Adirondak Loj Road just before the parking lot.

Trail: 2.1 miles from road to Rocky Falls.

Degree of difficulty: Easy to moderate.

Surface and blaze: Natural forest floor. Red blazes.

INDIAN PASS

[Fig. 6(2)] Writers in the 1800s gushed about Indian Pass and its 1,000-foot cliffs as comparable to Niagara Falls in awesome beauty. The place remains as rugged and wild as ever: Boulders clog the pass and peregrine falcons dwell high overhead on the ledges of Wallface Mountain. Summit Rock, 0.5 mile south of the actual height of the pass, affords the best view. It's possible to continue another 6 miles to Adirondak Loj.

Directions: Park at Upper Works. From Northway Exit 29 in North Hudson, drive west on Blue Ridge Road about 20 miles and turn right onto the Tahawus Road. From the west: the Tahawus Road starts about 1.5 miles east of the junction of NY 28N and Blue Ridge Road. About 6 miles down Tahawus Road, bear left at the fork down a road marked by a sign that says "Marcy and the High Peaks." Park in the lot 3.5 miles from this fork.

Trail: 4.4 miles to Summit Rock, 10.4 to Adirondak Loj.

Elevation: 1,770 feet at Upper Works to 2,820 feet at Summit Rock.

Degree of difficulty: Moderate to difficult.

Surface and blaze: Natural forest floor, rocky stretches. Yellow blazes for 1.5 miles, red blazes rest of the way.

FLOWED LANDS AND HANGING SPEAR FALLS

[Fig. 6(3)] The nineteenth-century writer Charles Fenno Hoffman applied the Seneca name *She-gwi-en-*

WOODCHUCK
(Marmota monax)
Also known as the groundhog, the woodchuck hibernates in its burrow until late winter, and usually does not emerge on February 2, as popularly believed, to look for its shadow.

dank-we, meaning "hanging spear," to this cascade along the Opalescent River even though the Senecas never frequented the Adirondacks. At certain times, a jutting rock that divides the flowing waters is said to look like a spear hanging in midair.

This loop follows Calamity Brook to Calamity Pond, continues to the Flowed Lands, a popular camping area just west of Lake Colden, and returns by a trail that passes the falls. Calamity Pond got its name after David Henderson, a partner in the McIntyre Iron Works, accidentally shot himself to death there in 1845. His children paid for a large stone memorial that was drawn by oxen through the wilderness to the shore. The return trail emerges onto the road about 0.5 mile south of the parking lot.

Directions: Same as for Indian Pass (*see* page 36). Park at Upper Works. Start on Indian Pass Trail. After 0.4 mile, turn right onto the Calamity Brook Trail. After reaching the Flowed Lands, return along the red-blazed trail that follows the Opalescent River (the last 4 miles have yellow blazes).

Trail: 13.7-mile loop.

Elevation: 1,770 feet at Upper Works to 2,760 feet at Flowed Lands.

Degree of difficulty: Moderate to difficult.

Surface and blaze: Forest floor, road. Red blazes for first 1.8 miles, blue blazes to Flowed Lands; first red, then yellow blazes on return to road.

TWO-DAY LOOP

[Fig. 6(1)] It's possible to see some of the most spectacular scenery in the High Peaks on a two-day trek that requires no overnight gear. From the Upper Works, take the Indian Pass Trail (*see* page 36) all the way to Adirondak Loj, about 10.4 miles. Spend the night at the lodge, eating dinner and breakfast there. The lodge also will prepare the second day's trail lunch. Return to Upper Works by way of Avalanche Pass, Lake Colden, the Flowed Lands, and Calamity Brook Trail, about 11.8 miles (*see* pages 35, 36). Be sure to make reservations.

Directions: Same as for Indian Pass. Park at Upper Works.

Trail: 22.2-mile loop.

Elevation: 1,770 feet at Upper Works to 2,834 feet at Indian Pass. 2,179 feet at Adirondak Loj to 3,000 feet at Avalanche Pass.

Degree of difficulty: Strenuous.

Surface and blaze: First day: Natural forest floor, rocky sections. Yellow blazes for 1.5 miles, red blazes rest of the way. Second day: Natural forest floor, rocky sections, ladders and catwalks. Blue blazes to just beyond Marcy Dam, yellow blazes to far side of Lake Colden, red blazes past Flowed Lands, blue blazes along Calamity Brook to trail junction, red blazes rest of way to Upper Works.

MOUNT JO

[Fig. 6(7)] Henry Van Hoevenberg, who built the original Adirondack Lodge, named this summit in 1877 after his fiancée, Josephine Schofield, who died before they could be married. Rising beside the north shore of Heart Lake, Mount Jo offers great views of Marcy, Algonquin, and other peaks. Soon after the climb begins, a fork presents a choice of two routes to the summit: the way left is a bit longer but not as steep. Take your pick and return by the other. Mount Jo is owned by the Adirondack Mountain Club.

Directions: Same as for Adirondak Loj. Start at Indian Pass Trail on Adirondak Loj Road, just before parking lot. A short distance from the trailhead, turn right for Mount Jo.

Trail: 2.2-mile loop.

Elevation: About 2,180 feet at trailhead to 2,876 feet at summit.

Degree of difficulty: Moderate.

Surface: Natural forest floor.

OWLS HEAD MOUNTAIN

[Fig. 7(16)] This is ideal for a youngster's first climb. Not only is the hike a short one, but it also affords several views from ledges on the way up. And blueberries grow on the summit. Porter, Cascade, and Hurricane mountains are among the peaks visible from the top. Most of the trail traverses private land, but the state owns the summit.

Directions: From the hamlet of Keene, drive north on NY 73 for 3.2 miles and look for an Owls Head Acres sign on the left. Pull in and follow the gravel road 0.2 miles to a junction. The start of the trail is marked by a small green sign around the bend. When parking, take care not to block the road.

Trail: 0.6 miles.

Elevation: 1,160 feet at trailhead to 2,120 feet at summit.

Degree of difficulty: Moderate.

Surface: Natural forest floor.

SNOW MOUNTAIN

[Fig. 6(22)] Of three approaches, the best follows Deer Brook from NY 73. At 0.8 miles up the trail, just before a small bridge, turn left for a short detour to Deer Brook Falls. The surrounding mountains, including Noonmark and Big Slide, can be seen on the way up as well as on the summit.

Directions: From the High Peaks sign in the hamlet of Keene Valley, drive south 1.9 miles on NY 73 and park on the right—about 0.1 mile before a bridge over the west branch of the Ausable River.

Trail: 1.7 miles to summit.

Elevation: 1,200 feet at trailhead to 2,360 feet at summit.

Degree of difficulty: Moderate.

Surface and blaze: Natural forest floor. Green blazes.

CASCADE MOUNTAIN

[Fig. 6(13)] The easiest of the High Peaks to climb, Cascade nonetheless offers great views of numerous mountains from its bald summit. This makes it extremely popular: close to 20,000 people registered at the trailhead in one year recently. Many people climb Cascade and nearby Porter Mountain together. The view from the latter is not nearly as good. Those who want a shorter hike can turn back after reaching an open expanse of rock about 1.8 miles from the trail-head.

Directions: From Keene hamlet, drive north 6.8 miles on NY 73 to trailhead parking on the left. From Lake Placid, the trailhead is 4.5 miles past Adirondak Loj Road. The lots are often full.

Trail: 2.4 miles to summit.

Elevation: 2,158 feet at trailhead to 4,098 feet at summit.

Degree of difficulty: Strenuous.

Surface and blaze: Natural forest floor, bare rock. Red blazes.

BIG SLIDE MOUNTAIN

[Fig. 6(12)] From the Great Range, Big Slide is instantly recognizable as a giant slab of rock sticking out among the wooded slopes of Johns Brook Valley—a distinctive feature created by an enormous landslide in 1830. The mountain probably got its name from this slide. Rock climbers have managed to find several routes up the steep slab, one dubbed Slide Rules. For hikers, a rugged but scenic trail to Big Slide starts in the Garden and goes over three smaller summits called the Brothers. Lookouts along the way afford vistas of the Great Range, Giant, and many other peaks.

GOLDEN CLUB
(Orontium aquaticum)
With waxy leaves that repel water, the golden club is also called neverwet.

On the return, take the Slide Brook Trail to the Phelps Trail. There is a spectacular view of Gothics on the way down. At the Phelps Trail, turn left to go back to the Garden. A right turn leads to Johns Brook Lodge after 0.25 mile (*see* Johns Brook Lodge, page 33).

Directions: Same as for Johns Brook Lodge. From the Garden, take the Brothers Trail to the Slide Brook Trail, just below the summit of Big Slide. Turn right for the summit.

Trail: 9.4-mile loop.

Elevation: 1,520 feet at Garden to 4,240 feet at summit.

Degree of difficulty: Strenuous.

Surface and blaze: Natural forest floor, bare rock. Red blazes on Brothers and Slide Brook trails, yellow blazes on Phelps Trail.

ALGONQUIN PEAK

[Fig. 6(4)] Reached after a steep climb, the Adirondacks' second-highest peak rewards the hiker with not only one of the most magnificent panoramas in the High Peaks, but also splendid specimens of alpine flora, such as diapensia (*Diapensia lapponica*), mountain sandwort, (*Minuartia groenlandica*), and Lapland rosebay

(*Rhododendron lapponicum*). With its many patches of grasses, flowers, and moss, the summit resembles an enchanting rock garden.

The mountain was once known as Mount McIntyre, after the founder of the McIntyre Iron Works, but Verplanck Colvin dubbed it Algonquin about 1880. Colvin, the famed surveyor of the Adirondacks, placed the disk at the summit himself in 1873. A mile southwest of Algonquin sits Iroquois Peak, and between them is Boundary Peak. The story goes—it is apocryphal—that Boundary marked the line between the territories of the two rival tribes.

Many people climb Algonquin together with nearby Wright Peak and/or Iroquois. Both peaks also feature alpine communities. There is a plaque on Wright commemorating four airmen who died when an Air Force bomber crashed into the summit in 1962. Parts of the wreckage can still be seen.

Directions: Same as for Adirondak Loj. Start on Van Hoevenberg Trail. After 1 mile, bear right at a junction on the yellow-blazed trail.

Trail: 4 miles to summit.

Elevation: 2,178 feet at trailhead to 5,114 feet at summit.

Degree of difficulty: Strenuous.

Surface and blaze: Natural forest floor, bare rock. Blue blazes for first mile, yellow blazes rest of way.

GOTHICS MOUNTAIN

[Fig. 6(11)] Old Mountain Phelps spread the story that he and the artist Frederick S. Perkins named Gothics and three other High Peaks on a summer day in 1857. The rocky arches of this mountain reminded Perkins of Gothic architecture. The rub is that a North Elba minister had used the name Gothics in a poem seven years earlier. The writer James Burnside rates the view from Gothics as the best of all the High Peaks.

From the bare summit, one looks down on Lower Ausable Lake on one side and Johns Brook Valley on the other. Marcy, Haystack, Algonquin, Colden, Saddleback—in all about 30 major peaks—can be seen. The one drawback is that the spectator can't include Gothics itself in the vistas. But anyone ascending Gothics from Lower Ausable Lake by way of Pyramid will be rewarded with a vista that includes Gothics. Some say Pyramid offers an even better view than Gothics. Though it's nearly 4,600 feet, Pyramid is not considered an independent High Peak.

Instead of retracing their ascent route, hikers can return to the lake via the Beaver Meadow Trail, reached by a right turn east of the summit. Strong hikers may opt to return by another route that leads over Armstrong and Upper Wolf Jaw mountains—for three High Peaks in one day.

Directions: Park in the Ausable Club's public lot. From the junction of NY 73 and US 9, drive north on NY 73 about 5.9 miles to a gravel road on the left, across the road from the lot for the Roaring Brook Trail into Giant Mountain Wilderness. The Ausable Club lot is on the left, right after the turn. From the north, the gravel road is on the right about 0.5 mile past the main entrance to the Ausable Club. From the lot, walk up the gravel road about 0.6 mile and turn left onto the Lake Road, a short distance before the clubhouse. Follow the Lake Road 3.3 miles to Lower Ausable Lake. The Pyramid trail, known as the Alfred E. Weld Trail, begins on the other side of the lake dam. It's 2.7 miles to the summit. One can return to the Lake Road by the Beaver Meadow Trail: leaving the summit, go northeast on the ADK Range Trail for 0.4 mile to a junction with the Beaver Meadow Trail and turn right.

Trail: 7.2 miles from lot to summit. Semiloop possible.

Elevation: About 1,350 feet at parking lot to 4,736 feet at summit.

Degree of difficulty: Strenuous.

Surface and blaze: Road, natural forest floor, bare rock. ATIS blazes.

MOUNT HAYSTACK

[Fig. 6(10)] The Marshalls regarded the view from Haystack—it looks across the wild Panther Gorge to the imposing cliffs of Marcy—as the finest of the High Peaks. A bonus is that Haystack, the state's third highest summit, is not likely to be as crowded as Marcy. A party that included Old Mountain Phelps made the first known ascent of Haystack in August 1849. To Phelps, the bare conical summit resembled a stack of hay.

There are several ways to approach Haystack. Perhaps the easiest route, about 8.9 miles, starts in the Garden and follows the Phelps Trail to the State Range Trail. A more rugged route, about 10.5 miles, starts at Elk Lake and ascends through Panther Gorge, a steep climb not recommended for backpackers.

Directions: Same as for Johns Brook Lodge (*see* page 33). Take the yellow-blazed Phelps Trail to the State Range Trail. At Bushnell Falls, bear left at the fork (this is still the Phelps Trail, though the blazes change to red). At the State Range Trail, turn left and follow blue blazes to a yellow-blazed trail on the right that leads to the summit.

Trail: 8.9 miles to summit.

Elevation: 1,520 feet at the Garden to 4,960 feet at summit.

Degree of difficulty: Strenuous.

WHITE-TAILED DEER

(Odocoileus virginianus)
The white-tailed deer may be the most popular wild animal in the U.S. When alarmed, the whitetail raises its tail, alerting other deer to possible danger.

Mount Marcy

The state's highest peak, Mount Marcy was named after former Governor William Learned Marcy.

MacIntyre Mountains

× Wright Peak

Phelps × Mountain

PHELPS BROOK

MARCY BROOK

JOHNS BROOK

ORE-BED BROOK

BUSHNELL FALLS

× Algonquin Peak

AVALANCHE LAKE

× Mount Colden

Saddleback Mountain ×

LAKE COLDEN

OPALESCENT RIVER

Little × Marcy

Mount × Marcy

SHANTY BROOK

LOWER AUSABLE LAKE

FLOWED LANDS

× Mount Haystack

Mount × Skylight

UPPER TWIN BROOK

UPPER AUSABLE LAKE

SKYLIGHT BROOK

Allen × Mountain

MARCY BROOK

SAND BROOK

DUDLEY BROOK

WEST INLET

WHITE LILLY POND

ELK LAKE

Surface and blaze: Natural forest floor, bare rock. Yellow blazes for 5.1 miles, red blazes for 2.6 miles, blue blazes for 0.5 mile, yellow blazes for final 0.6 mile.

MOUNT MARCY

[Fig. 8, Fig. 6(9)] Ebenezer Emmons, a state geologist, and several others made the first ascent of Marcy on August 5, 1837. They had begun their journey two days earlier from the McIntyre Iron Works in Tahawus, following a route that took them to Lake Colden and thence along the Opalescent River. Among those in the party was John Cheney, a famed Adirondack guide. Years later, Cheney said this of being atop Mount Marcy, the state's highest peak: "It makes a man feel what it is to have all creation under his feet." Emmons named the mountain after the governor, William Learned Marcy. A plaque placed near the summit 100 years later commemorates the first ascent.

Today, it's possible to climb Marcy and make a return trip in one day—albeit a long day. Marcy's standing as the state's highest peak makes it a popular destination, so several routes are listed below. Each description includes the number of people who registered at the trailhead in 1995. Although not all the people were going to Marcy, the numbers give an idea of the relative popularity of the trails.

From Adirondak Loj. Henry Van Hoevenberg laid out the most popular route to the summit in the 1880s; it's also the shortest: 7.4 miles. Sights along the way include Marcy Dam, Phelps Brook, and Indian Falls. Trailhead registrations: 37,028.

Directions: Same as for Adirondak Loj (*see* page 33). Take Van Hoevenberg Trail.
Trail: 7.4 miles to summit.
Elevation: 2,178 feet at trailhead to 5,344 feet at summit.
Degree of difficulty: Strenuous.
Surface and blaze: Natural forest floor, bare rock. Blue blazes.

From the Garden. Ed Phelps, the son of Old Mountain Phelps, cut a trail to Marcy from Keene Valley that follows Johns Brook and passes Bushnell Falls. The route is 9.1 miles, but if one stays at Johns Brook Lodge, it's only 5.6 miles to Marcy—an attractive option for those who don't like to rough it. Trailhead registrations: 16,330.

Directions: Same as for Johns Brook Lodge (*see* page 33).
Trail: 3.5 miles to lodge, 9.1 miles to summit.
Elevation: About 1,520 feet at the Garden to 5,344 feet at summit.
Degree of difficulty: Strenuous.
Surface and blaze: Natural forest floor, bare rock. Yellow blazes for 5.1 miles, red blazes rest of way.

From Upper Works. This scenic route follows Calamity Brook, the Flowed Lands, the Opalescent River, and Feldspar Brook, and passes tiny Lake Tear of the Clouds at 4,346 feet, the highest source of the Hudson River. Trailhead registrations: 4,793.

Directions: Same as for Flowed Lands and Hanging Spear Falls loop (*see* page 36). Park at Upper Works.

Signs like this one ask hikers to help protect arctic plants that live in fragile, high-elevation habitats.

Trail: 10.3 miles to summit.

Elevation: 1,770 feet at Upper Works to 5,344 feet at summit.

Degree of difficulty: Strenuous.

Surface and blaze: Natural forest floor, bare rock. Red blazes for first 1.8 miles, blue blazes for 2.9 miles, red blazes for 2.4 miles, yellow blazes rest of way.

From Elk Lake. The trail is longer than most, at 11 miles, but more remote, passing through Marcy Swamp, an old-growth cedar wetland, and then ascending through the rugged Panther Gorge. Trailhead registrations: 1,378.

Directions: From Northway Exit 29 in North Hudson, drive 4 miles west on Blue Ridge Road toward Newcomb and turn right onto a road marked by a sign for Elk Lake Lodge. The parking lot is on the right after 5.2 miles. Trails originating here begin on private land; they are closed during big game season from late October to early December.

Trail: 11 miles to summit.

Elevation: 1,144 feet at Elk Lake to 5,344 feet at summit.

Degree of difficulty: Strenuous.

Surface and blaze: Natural forest floor, bare rock. Blue blazes for 10.2 miles, yellow blazes to summit.

Via Great Range. The hike via the Great Range is for those who want a greater challenge: a trek from Keene Valley over seven High Peaks and two smaller summits, for a total ascent of about 9,000 feet. The journey usually takes several days with a backpack. Be warned that there are no lean-tos and only one designated campsite along the way. Except at this one site, campers must stay at least 150 feet from the trail or water. The order of the nine peaks is as follows: Rooster Comb, Hedgehog, Lower Wolf Jaw, Upper Wolf Jaw, Armstrong, Gothics, Saddleback, Basin, and Marcy.

Directions: The trail to Rooster Comb begins on private land off Interbrook Road in Keene Valley. Parking on this road is illegal, so hikers must leave their cars in town. About 0.6 mile from NY 73, Interbrook takes a sharp right over a bridge; here, instead of bearing right, walk straight ahead up a private lane; then, after passing a house on the right, take a left at the driveway of a second house.

Trail: 13.5 miles to Marcy's summit.

Elevation: About 1,120 feet at trailhead to 5,344 feet at summit.

Degree of difficulty: Strenuous.

Surface and blaze: Natural forest floor, bare rock; cables and ladders. ADK or ATIS blazes for first 8.8 miles to col between Gothics and Saddleback, blue blazes for 3.4 miles, red blazes for final 0.8 mile.

Western High Peaks

When the hermit Noah John Rondeau decided that he wanted to get away from civilization, he chose to live along the Cold River. That was in the 1920s. Times have changed, but the Western High Peaks remains remote enough to satisfy the hermit in anybody. The region lays claim to seven High Peaks, but none has an official trail. Overall, the region has far fewer trails than the Eastern High Peaks. Unlike the eastern section, the Western High Peaks is open to horseback riders.

LAKE HARRIS PUBLIC CAMPGROUND

[Fig. 9(7)] Primitive campsites are scattered throughout the Western High Peaks. Those who prefer the amenities of a campground should consider staying at Lake Harris in the town of Newcomb. One trail leads into the wilderness from the campground, or visitors can drive to nearby trailheads at Santanoni Preserve or the Upper Works.

The 89-site campground lies on the north shore of Lake Harris in the town of Newcomb, a few miles from the Adirondack Visitors Interpretive Center (*see* page 13). Once a week, staffers from the center stop by to deliver a talk on natural history. It's not uncommon for a black bear (*Ursus americanus*) to wander into the campground, so visitors are urged not to leave food and garbage lying about.

Directions: From Northway Exit 29, drive west on Blue Ridge Road and NY 28N about 21.5 miles to the campground road on the right. The campground is about 1 mile from NY 28N.

Activities: Camping, picnicking, swimming, boating, fishing.

Facilities: 89 campsites, showers, toilets, bathhouse, boat launch.

Dates: Open May through mid-Sept.

Fees: There is a charge for camping, day use, and boat and canoe rentals.

Closest town: Newcomb hamlet is about 2 miles from the center of town west on NY 28N.

For more information: Campground office, phone (518) 582-2503. For reservations, phone (800) 456-2267.

Ampersand Mountain

Those who climb to this bald summit see the best of both worlds in the Adirondacks: the High Peaks to the south and east, the lake country to the north.

1 Ampersand Mountain

To Tupper Lake

3 30

3

44

2 **3** Coreys Road

ROCK POND

PICKEREL POND

4

COLD RIVER

1 Ampersand Mountain Trailhead

2 Trail Start to Raquette Falls

3 Assembly Area for Horse Trail

4 Assembly Area for Horse Trail

5 Northville–Lake Placid Trail/ To Wanika Falls

6 Camp Santanoni

7 Lake Harris Public Campground

················· Trail

5

MOOSE POND

NEWCOMB LAKE

LONG LAKE

CATLIN LAKE

6

N

Ref: Delorme New York State

LAKE HARRIS

RICH LAKE **7**

28N

HIKING THE WESTERN HIGH PEAKS

Hikers who stick to marked trails will have to be content with relatively flat hikes, for most of the mountains in this region can be climbed only by unofficial herd paths. With a few exceptions, the destinations of the hikes that follow are ponds and lakes rather than summits.

SANTANONI PRESERVE

[Fig. 9(6)] An old gravel road leads past an abandoned farmstead and crosses two quaint stone bridges on its way to Camp Santanoni on the shores of Newcomb Lake. This magnificent log palace, built by the Pruyn family of Albany in the late 1800s, had deteriorated after the state acquired the property in 1972, but efforts are under way to restore it. Santanoni remains an outstanding example of an Adirondack Great Camp. It is on the National Register of Historic Places.

Take the footpath along the north shore of Newcomb Lake to reach a small sandy beach near a dilapidated bathhouse; it's still a good spot to swim, with a view across the water of the Santanoni Range. The path eventually leads to a lean-to toward the western end of the lake. There is another lean-to on the south shore. Tent sites also exist.

Newcomb Lake, covering 506 acres, is the largest lake in the High Peaks Wilderness. It is home to brook trout (*Salvelinus fontinalis*) and lake trout (*Salvelinus namaycush*) and possibly the endangered round whitefish (*Prosopium cylindraceum*). The use of bait fish is prohibited. Visitors can pay outfitters in Newcomb to bring in, by horsedrawn wagon, a canoe and gear.

Although the lake lies within the High Peaks Wilderness, the preserve is classified as wild forest, so mountain bikers can cycle in as far as the camp. The road also makes an excellent ski route. Equestrians may ride to the camp.

Directions: In the hamlet of Newcomb, drive 0.3 mile west from the Town Hall on NY 28N; turn right onto a road marked by a sign for the Santanoni Preserve; drive another 0.3 mile to a gate, where the trail starts.

Trail: 4.5 miles to Camp Santanoni.

Degree of difficulty: Easy with gradual climb.

Surface: Gravel road.

MOOSE POND

[Fig. 9] About 2.2 miles along the road to Camp Santanoni, the Moose Pond Horse Trail starts on the left and follows an old logging road to Moose Pond. Hikers on their way to Cold River or to the Ermine Brook slide on Santanoni Peak may want to camp at one of the tent sites here. The 185-acre cold-water pond, once part of the Pruyn family holdings, is home to brook trout (*Salvelinus fontinalis*), lake trout (*Salvelinus namaycush*), brown bullhead (*Ictalurus punctatus*), and possibly round whitefish (*Prosopium cylindraceum*). Hikers and equestrians can reach the Cold River Horse Trails by continuing north.

Santanoni Range

Santanoni got its name sometime in the first half of the nineteenth century. It comes from the Abenaki tribe's name for Saint Anthony, whom they probably learned about from French-Canadian friars.

MOUNTAIN POND

DUCK HOLE

LOWER POND

MOOSE CREEK

UPPER POND

SANTANONI BROOK

BRADLEY POND

HENDERSON LAKE

1

2

3

Santanoni Range

CALAHAN BROOK

ERMINE BROOK

N

Ref: ADK Trails of the Adirondack High Peaks Region

1 Couchsachraga Peak

2 Panther Peak

3 Santanoni Peak

.... Trail

Directions: Same as for Santanoni Preserve.

Trail: 6.7 miles to Moose Pond.

Degree of difficulty: Moderate.

Surface and blaze: Old roads.

SANTANONI RANGE

[Fig. 10] This range includes three summits in the 46ers' pantheon: Santanoni Peak [Fig. 10(3)], Panther Peak [Fig. 10(2)], and Couchsachraga Peak [Fig. 10(1)]. Santanoni is the tallest of the three, at 4,607 feet, and offers a marvelous vista that includes Wallface Mountain and Indian Pass. Both James Burnside and the Marshalls put Santanoni in the top 10 in their view ratings. The usual route to Santanoni is to take the Bradley Pond trail from Tahawus Club Road and pick up a herd path a little past the pond, about 4.3 miles from the road. The herd path eventually leads to a four-way junction atop Santanoni Ridge: left leads to Santanoni, right leads to Panther, straight leads to Couchsachraga. Hikers also can approach Santanoni from the south by way of a long slide created by a fierce rainstorm in 1985, but they must bushwack along Ermine Brook to reach the slide and another 0.5 mile after the slide to reach the summit.

Santanoni got its name sometime in the first half of the nineteenth century. It comes from the Abenaki tribe's name for Saint Anthony, whom they probably learned about from French-Canadian friars. Bob and George Marshall named Couchsachraga (kook-sa-kra-ga) after an Indian word thought to mean "dismal wilderness"—a fitting name for one of the most remote High Peaks. The Marshalls and their guide, Herb Clark, were the first to ascend Couchsachraga in 1924. Later surveys revealed that the summit falls 180 feet short of 4,000. It is the lowest High Peak.

Directions: From Northway Exit 29 in North Hudson, drive west on Blue Ridge Road about 20 miles and turn right onto the Tahawus Road. From the west: the Tahawus Road starts about 1.5 miles east of the junction of NY 28N and Blue Ridge Road. About 6 miles down Tahawus Road, bear left at the fork down a road marked by a sign that says "Marcy and the High Peaks." Park in a lot on the left 2 miles from the fork.

Trail: At least 5.8 miles to Santanoni summit.

Elevation: About 1,730 feet at trailhead to 4,607 feet at summit.

Degree of difficulty: Strenuous.

Surface and blaze: Natural forest floor.

DUCK HOLE

[Fig. 10] A logging company created this 61-acre pond by damming up a marshland in the 1870s. Today, Duck Hole is thought of as one of the prettiest spots in the Adirondack wilderness. Ringed by conifers, the pond sits in a clearing with mountains on every horizon: the Sewards to the west, the Santanonis to the south, the Sawtooth Mountains to the north, and MacNaughton Mountain to the east. The waters are home to brook trout, among other fish, and osprey and loons have been known to drop in.

There are two lean-tos at Duck Hole. The trail from the Upper Works goes through Preston Ponds Pass, the dividing line between the Hudson and St. Lawrence watersheds. It's possible to make a 14-mile loop out of this hike by returning via Bradley Pond, but that trail is not always in good shape.

Directions: Same as for Santanoni Range (*see* above) except drive 3.5 miles past the fork on Tahawus Road to the parking lot at Upper Works.

Trail: 6.9 miles to Duck Hole.

Degree of difficulty: Moderate.

Surface and blaze: Natural forest floor. Red blazes.

AMPERSAND MOUNTAIN

[Fig. 9(1)] Those who climb to this bald summit see the best of both worlds in Adirondacks: the High Peaks to the south and east, the lake country to the north. Hikers can thank Verplanck Colvin for the gorgeous views: he ordered all the trees cut on the summit in 1893 to facilitate his Adirondack Survey, and subsequent erosion and fires left the summit bare. A plaque just beyond the summit commemorates Walter Channing Rice, who manned a fire tower on Ampersand from 1915 to 1923.

While driving to the trailhead, take note of the forest at the base of Ampersand. It is one of the largest stands of old-growth hemlock (*Tsuga canadensis*), sugar maple (*Acer saccharum*), and yellow birch (*Betula alleghaniensis*) in the Adirondacks. The official trail begins with a fairly level walk through hemlock and hardwoods, but it ends with some scrambling up steep spruce slopes. After returning to the car, hikers might want to freshen up with a swim at a lovely sandy beach on Middle Saranac Lake.

Directions: From Saranac Lake village, drive west 8.1 miles on Route 3 to a lot on the right. Cross the road for the trail to the mountain. The 0.5-mile trail to the beach begins from the lot.

Trail: 2.7 miles to summit.

Elevation: 1,577 feet at road to 3,352 feet at summit.

Degree of difficulty: Strenuous.

Surface and blaze: Natural forest floor. Red blazes.

RAQUETTE FALLS

[Fig. 9(2)] North of Long Lake (*see* page 284), the Raquette River (*see* page 283) runs over a series of rapids and falls, a scenic spot visited by day hikers, campers, equestrians, canoeists, and boaters in summer and by cross-country skiers in winter. Those paddling the Adirondack Canoe Route face a 1.3-mile carry around the falls. Many canoeists have smashed their craft trying to shoot the rapids.

The hiking trail from Coreys Road, starting at the lot near Stony Creek, follows an old road along the river, though the water can be seen only in glimpses through the trees. When reaching the signpost for the canoe carry, turn right toward the river and walk about 100 yards to a small path on the right that leads to a good view of the falls. The state Department of Environmental Conservation's only outpost in the Western High Peaks is located near the falls.

Directions: From downtown Saranac Lake, drive about 12.7 miles west on NY 3 to Coreys Road on the right, then go south on Coreys Road 2.8 miles to a parking lot on the right.

Trail: 4.2 miles to falls.

Degree of difficulty: Easy.

Surface and blaze: Old road, forest floor. Part blazed with yellow horse markers.

ROCK AND PICKEREL PONDS

[Fig. 9] These pretty ponds can be reached by short paths from the south side of Coreys Road. Hikers can park in a big lot about 2.7 miles from Route 3, just past Stony Creek, and walk to the footpaths—the road is dirt here—or they can park on the roadside near the footpaths. Small signs mark both trailheads, but the trails themselves are unmarked.

The path to Rock Pond starts about 0.6 miles from the Stony Creek lot; the pond lies 0.4 miles from the road. The Pickerel Pond path begins about 0.5 mile farther up the road, from which it's only 0.3 miles to the water—short enough for a canoe carry. Rock Pond contains brook trout (*Salvelinus fontinalus*), among other fish, while Pickerel Pond contains yellow perch (*Perca flavescens*) and northern pike (*Esox lucius*). Mountain bikers can cycle the entire 5.25-mile length of Coreys Road, from Route 3 to a gate that marks the end of state land. In winter, the road is plowed as far as the Stony Creek lot. From there, the road can be easily skied.

Directions: Same as for Raquette Falls.

Trail: From lot to Rock Pond, 1 mile; to Pickerel Pond, 1.4 miles.

Degree of difficulty: Easy.

Surface: Dirt road, natural forest floor.

WANIKA FALLS

[Fig. 9(5)] Shortly after its start, the Chubb River drops over several cascades, ending in a pool deep enough for a swim. To get there, walk the first (or last) 6.7 miles of the Northville-Lake Placid Trail (*see* page 52), starting on Averyville Road, and then turn left down a short side trail that leads to a lean-to along the river. Cross the river and go upstream 100 yards for the best view of the falls. The hike is long, but it's easy terrain. There are views of mountains along the way.

Directions: From the junction of NY 73 and NY 86 in Lake Placid, drive south on NY 73 a short distance to Averyville

BLACK FLY
(Simulium spp.)
Found near running water, these biting flies are the curse of human visitors to the mountains and forests.

Road; turn right and go about 1.2 miles to the trailhead on the left. This is about 1.2 miles past a sign marking the official end of the Northville-Lake Placid Trail. There is room for more cars on the right side of the road at the top of the hill.

Trail: 6.8 miles.

Degree of difficulty: Easy to moderate.

Surface and blaze: Natural forest floor. Blue blazes.

NORTHVILLE-LAKE PLACID TRAIL

[Fig. 9(5)] This stretch of the 121-mile trail cuts through the rugged and remote Cold River country—the beloved haunt of the hermit Noah John Rondeau. It can be broken down into three sections: Long Lake to Shattuck Clearing (11.8 miles), Shattuck Clearing to Duck Hole (12 miles), and Duck Hole to Averyville Road (12 miles). This requires two overnight stays in lean-tos or tents. There are two lean-tos at Shattuck Clearing, two at Duck Hole (*see* page 49), and several others along the way.

Much of the route passes through lowlands and conifer forests in the Cold River watershed, a contrast to the higher country of the Eastern High Peaks. The second day takes hikers past a plaque marking the site of Rondeau's hermitage. On the third day, hikers can visit Wanika Falls (*see* page 51). Of course, the direction can be reversed. For a shorter car shuttle, hike from Long Lake to Duck Hole and then to the parking lot at Upper Works.

Directions: From the junction of NY 30 and NY 28N in Long Lake, drive north on NY 28N about 1.6 miles to Tarbell Road; turn left and go 0.7 mile to a parking lot on right.

Trail: 35.8 miles from Long Lake to Averyville Road.

Degree of difficulty: Easy to moderate.

Surface and blaze: Natural forest floor. Blue blazes.

HORSE TRAILS

[Fig. 9(3), Fig. 9(4)] Equestrians can ride into the heart of the wilderness on day trips or overnight excursions. In the fall, some people ride into the region to hunt. All told, there are about 50 miles of interconnecting horse trails in the Western High Peaks and adjacent Santanoni Preserve. Many of them follow old logging roads and truck trails created before the state designated the area as wilderness. Because vehicles are not allowed in the wilderness, the trails cannot be maintained as well as they once were.

Horseback riders can enter the wilderness from the Santanoni Preserve in Newcomb or Coreys Road between the villages of Saranac Lake and Tupper Lake. From Coreys Road, equestrians can ride in loops of either 12.7 miles or 32.1 miles or ride to Raquette Falls and back (*see* page 50). The longer loop, which follows some narrow paths, is not recommended for inexperienced riders. From the Santanoni Preserve, riders can go to Camp Santanoni (*see* page 47) or Moose Pond (*see* page 47). The trail to Moose Pond continues on to join the loop trails from Coreys Road. Popular destinations include Calkins Creek, Cold River, Raquette Falls, and Moose Pond.

The state Department of Environmental Conservation estimates that about 500 equestrians use the trails each year. Most use horses provided by local outfitters. All horses must have had a Coggins test before setting hoof on any state trail.

Directions: Same as for Santanoni Preserve or Raquette Falls hiking trails (*see* pages 47, 50). There are two assembly areas on Coreys Road. The second is 3.1 miles farther down the road from the Raquette Falls trailhead.

For more information: State Department of Environmental Conservation, P.O. Box 296, Route 86, Ray Brook, NY 12977. Phone (518) 897-1200. Ask for a booklet titled *Horse Trails in New York State.*

RUBY-THROATED HUMMINGBIRD (Archilochus colubris) Hummingbirds have the unique ability among birds to fly backwards or straight up or down.

COLD RIVER

[Fig. 9] Canoeists in quest of wilderness can find it on the Cold River, the longest river wholly within the High Peaks Wilderness. It starts at Duck Hole and meanders west for 14 miles before emptying into the Raquette River upstream from Raquette Falls. When water levels are medium to high, the river can be canoed for 1.5 to 2 miles from the mouth. To get to Cold River, canoeists must paddle most of Long Lake (*see* page 284) and a bit of the Raquette (*see* page 283)—all told, 10 to 11 miles.

Many campsites and lean-tos exist along the way, but because the Cold River has been classified as "wild" under the state Wild, Scenic, and Recreational Rivers Act, the lean-tos on its banks eventually may be removed.

Directions: Canoeists can put in from two beaches in the village of Long Lake on the lake's east shore. One is near the NY 30 bridge; the other at the end of Dock Road.

CHUBB RIVER

[Fig. 7] Given normal rainfall, the upper Chubb can be canoed upstream 4.5 miles from Averyville Road throughout the summer. The trip requires a 0.25-mile carry, but it is well worth it, for once on the other side of the rapids, canoeists will paddle through a big marsh with mountain vistas on either side. The marsh attracts a variety of waterfowl, such as black ducks (*Anas rubripes*) and mallards (*Anas platyrhynchos*). Sightings of bald eagles (*Haliaeetus leucocephalus*) have been reported.

Directions: From NY 73 in Lake Placid, take Averyville Road past the Northville-Lake Placid Trail parking lot to a turnoff at the top of the hill on the other side of the Chubb River bridge. A 120-yard carry trail begins on the other side of the road.

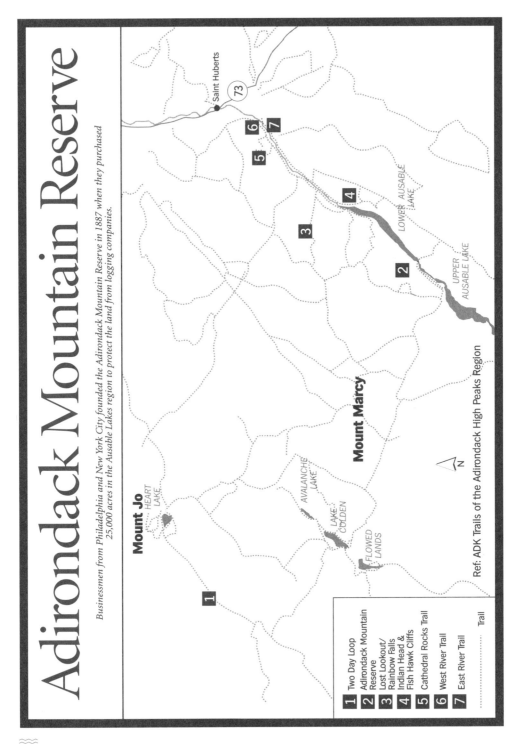

Adirondack Mountain Reserve

Businessmen from Philadelphia and New York City founded the Adirondack Mountain Reserve in 1887 when they purchased 25,000 acres in the Ausable Lakes region to protect the land from logging companies.

Saint Huberts

73

Mount Jo

HEART LAKE

LOWER AUSABLE LAKE

UPPER AUSABLE LAKE

AVALANCHE LAKE

LAKE COLDEN

FLOWED LANDS

Mount Marcy

N

Ref: ADK Trails of the Adirondack High Peaks Region

1 Two Day Loop
2 Adirondack Mountain Reserve
3 Lost Lookout/ Rainbow Falls
4 Indian Head & Fish Hawk Cliffs
5 Cathedral Rocks Trail
6 West River Trail
7 East River Trail
.... Trail

Adirondack Mountain Reserve

[Fig. 11] Businessmen from Philadelphia and New York City founded the Adirondack Mountain Reserve in 1887 when they purchased 25,000 acres in the Ausable Lakes region to protect the land from logging companies. The reserve later acquired the Ausable Club at St. Huberts, which has entertained many distinguished guests over the years, among them Mark Twain, Woodrow Wilson, Charles Lindbergh, and the naturalist John Burroughs.

By 1910, the reserve had grown to about 40,000 acres, encompassing not only both Ausable Lakes but also the summits of Mount Marcy and several other High Peaks. Since then, the reserve has sold most of its land to the state, but it still owns about 7,000 acres with some of the most breathtaking scenery in the Adirondacks. Most of the trails are open to the public, with certain restrictions: hikers are forbidden to bushwhack, camp, build fires, swim, hunt, trap, fish, or bring in pets. Upper Ausable Lake remains off limits to the public, but a few public trails pass by it.

Hikers cutting through the reserve to reach state-owned trails in the High Peaks Wilderness or Dix Mountain Wilderness usually take the quickest route possible to the trailhead. Often, this means walking up the Lake Road, which goes 3.5 miles from the Ausable Club to Lower Ausable Lake. But within the reserve are several scenic trails and destinations worth visiting for their own sake.

Directions: For all the trails described below, park in the Ausable Club's public lot. From the junction of NY 73 and US 9, drive north on NY 73 about 5.9 miles to a gravel road on the left, across the road from the lot for the Roaring Brook Trail into Giant Mountain Wilderness. The Ausable Club lot is on the left, right after the turn. From the north, the gravel road is on the right about 0.5 mile past the main entrance to the Ausable Club. From the lot, walk up the gravel road about 0.6 mile and turn left onto the Lake Road, a short distance before the clubhouse.

For more information: State Department of Environmental Conservation, P.O. Box 296, Route 86, Ray Brook, NY 12977. Phone (518) 897-1200. Ask for the leaflet titled *Hikers' Trail Map: Access to State Lands across the Property of the Adirondack Mountain Reserve.*

WEST RIVER TRAIL AND EAST RIVER TRAIL

[Fig. 11(6), Fig. 11(7)] These trails follow the Ausable River's East Branch as it winds through old forest and beaver meadows on its way from Lower Ausable Lake to Saint Huberts. The trails, located on either side of the river, are mostly level but require some climbing. They can be hiked together as a loop, but if hikers want to save time or energy, they can return by the Lake Road. Also, the loop can be shortened by crossing the Ausable at a connector trail about 1 mile before the lake.

Directions: The West River Trail, which is 3.8 miles long, begins near the watchman's hut on the Lake Road. The 3.6-mile East River Trail begins about 0.25 mile farther up the road.

Trail: 7.6-mile loop from watchman's hut. Plus 1.6-mile round-trip walk to and from car.

Degree of difficulty: Moderate.

Surface: Natural forest floor.

CATHEDRAL ROCKS AND BEAR RUN

[Fig. 11(5)] Both of these sights can be reached in a semiloop from the West River Trail. The going is steep in sections. Hikers walk along the base of a row of cliffs that ends at Cathedral Rocks, the largest among them. A short distance beyond, a trail on the right goes upward to the base of another cliff, where another right turn takes one to Bear Run. The trail climbs through a rock passageway to a ledge with a gorgeous lookout. A sign on the trail says it all: "Don't miss." The return to the West River Trail passes a waterfall on Pyramid Brook. Follow the West River Trail east 0.25 mile back to start of Cathedral Rocks Trail.

Directions: Take West River Trail about 0.6 mile to the Cathedral Rocks Trail on the right.

Trail: 3.2-mile semiloop from the watchman's hut. Plus 1.6-mile round-trip walk to and from car.

Degree of difficulty: Moderate.

Surface: Natural forest floor.

LOST LOOKOUT AND RAINBOW FALLS

[Fig. 11(3)] Toward the end of the West River Trail, a side trail leads up the side of Armstrong Mountain to Lost Lookout for great views of Lower Ausable Lake and nearby mountains. After looping back to the West River Trail, go west for a short distance to the Alfred E. Weld Trail at the outlet of Lower Ausable Lake. About 0.1 mile up the Weld trail, a short spur leads to Rainbow Falls, a beautiful 150-foot waterfall in a misty gorge.

Directions: Take West River Trail about 2.8 miles to Beaver Meadow Trail on the right; then take Beaver Meadow Trail about 0.3 mile to Lost Lookout Trail on the left.

Trail: 8.7-mile round-trip loop from watchman's hut. Plus 1.6-mile round-trip walk to and from car.

Degree of difficulty: Moderate.

Surface: Natural forest floor.

INDIAN HEAD AND FISH HAWK CLIFFS

[Fig. 11(4)] Indian Head, towering 750 feet above Lower Ausable Lake, has a gorgeous view of the Ausable Lakes and the encircling mountains. Just 0.2 mile down the trail, Fish Hawk Cliffs offers another view of the valley as well as of the jutting rock of Indian Head. The quickest route to Indian Head is via a 0.8-mile trail that starts just before the end of the Lake Road. On the way up, don't miss the Gothic Window, with its superb lookout. A more scenic route to Indian Head leaves the Lake Road after 2 miles to follow the Gill Brook Trail. The two approaches can be combined for a loop. From the parking lot, this trip is slightly more than 10 miles but entails little strenuous climbing.

Directions: Take Lake Road 2 miles to Gill Brook Trail or 3.4 miles to Indian Head Trail, both on the left.

Trail: 10-mile round-trip loop from parking lot.

Degree of difficulty: Moderate.

Surface: Road, natural forest floor.

Dix Mountain Wilderness

Nine of the 46 High Peaks lie within the Dix Mountain Wilderness south of the Adirondack Mountain Reserve. The views from the two highest, Dix and Nippletop, are rated among the best that the High Peaks have to offer. Four of the nine lack official trails but can be reached by herd paths. Fires raged over much of the area in the early 1900s, reaching the tops of Dix, Noonmark, and Round mountains, among others.

The Dix Mountain Wilderness, with about 52,000 acres, is less than a quarter of the size of the High Peak Wilderness, but it is still bigger than several other Adirondack wilderness areas. The region has 36 miles of maintained trails and three lean-tos.

For more information: State Department of Environmental Conservation, P.O. Box 296, Route 86, Ray Brook, NY 12977. Phone (518) 897-1200. The DEC publishes a leaflet titled *Trails in the High Peaks Region* that includes some trails in the Dix Mountain Wilderness. Others can be found in another DEC leaflet, *Hikers' Trail Map: Access to State Lands across the Property of the Adirondack Mountain Reserve.*

🪨 NOONMARK MOUNTAIN

[Fig. 6(23)] This is one of the world's bigger timepieces: People in Keene Valley know it's noon when the sun sits directly over the summit. The peak is one of the region's more popular destinations, for it rewards relatively little effort with a wonderful panorama of the Great Range, Giant Mountain, and Dix Mountain. Ascend Noonmark by the Henry L. Stimson Trail and return by the Felix Adler Trail and the Old Dix Trail.

Directions: Park in the Ausable Club's public lot. From the junction of NY 73 and US 9, drive north on NY 73 about 5.9 miles to a gravel road on the left, across the road from the lot for the Roaring Brook Trail into Giant Mountain Wilderness. The Ausable Club lot is on the left right after the turn. From the north, the gravel road is on the right about 0.5 mile past the main entrance to the Ausable Club. From the lot, walk up the gravel road about 0.4 mile to the Stimson Trail.

Trail: 6.2-mile loop.

Elevation: 1,381 feet at trailhead to 3,556 feet at summit.

Degree of difficulty: Moderate to difficult.

Surface and blaze: Natural forest floor.

ROUND MOUNTAIN

[Fig. 6(20)] Round Mountain is not nearly as popular as neighboring Noonmark, but it also offers good views in all directions, making it an excellent destination for those who like solitude. The artist Harold Weston notes in his book *Freedom in the Wilds* that there had been no view from Round Mountain to speak of until the 1903 fire destroyed the trees on the summit—many of them giants of 3-foot girth. Round Mountain can be climbed alone or in tandem with Noonmark. If climbing only Round Mountain, ascend by the S. Burns Weston Trail and return by the Old Dix Trail and the Stimson Trail.

Directions: Same as for Noonmark, but the Weston Trail begins 0.1 mile from the parking lot.

Trail: 5-mile loop.

Elevation: 1,280 feet at trailhead to 3,100 feet at summit.

Degree of difficulty: Moderate.

Surface: Natural forest floor.

NIPPLETOP

[Fig. 6(17)] In the 1800s, the famed guide Old Mountain Phelps insisted on calling this summit Nippletop, the name preferred by locals, as opposed to Dial, the name preferred by more fastidious hikers from out of town. Phelps won out, and the name Dial has been bestowed upon another High Peak a few miles away. Ebenezer Emmons, the state geologist, made the first ascent of Nippletop in 1837. Today there are two approaches to Nippletop. Since both start from the Lake Road, they can be combined in a rugged loop. One trail goes over Bear Den and Dial; the other climbs through Elk Pass. Nippletop's summit has fantastic views of the Dix Range, Great Range, and Mount Colvin. Both James Burnside and the Marshalls put it in the top five of their view rankings.

Directions: Same as for Noonmark. The trail over Dial, the Henry Goddard Leach Trail, begins about 1 mile down the Lake Road on the left. The trail through Elk Pass, the Gill Brook Trail, begins about 2 miles down the Lake Road.

Trail: 14.5-mile loop from parking lot.

Elevation: About 1,350 feet at road to 4,620 feet at Nippletop's summit.

Degree of difficulty: Strenuous.

Surface and blaze: Natural forest floor.

DIX MOUNTAIN

[Fig. 6(18)] Seen from the north, Dix looks as though it has been clawed by a panther: streaks of rock bared by slides run down its slopes. When Ebenezer Emmons scaled Dix in 1837, he estimated its height to be 5,200, second only to Marcy. Though Emmons erred, James Burnside ranks the view from Dix—in fact, the sixth-highest summit in the Adirondacks—as second only to Gothics's. On a clear day, it's possible to see across Lake Champlain to the Green Mountains of Vermont. Hikers should be careful not to step on the fragile alpine vegetation. There are two trails to Dix, both of them long.

FROM NY 73

The trail passes two ponds and a spruce-fir wetland and follows the North Fork of the Boquet River for a while before reaching a lean-to after about 4 miles. The paper birch along the way are a legacy of the fires in the early 1900s: These sun-loving trees thrive in openings in the forest.

Directions: From Northway Exit 30, drive north on NY 73 about 3.1 miles past the junction with US 9 to the parking lot.

Trail: 6.8 miles to summit.

Elevation: 1,657 feet at trailhead to 4,857 feet at summit.

Degree of difficulty: Strenuous.

Surface and blaze: Natural forest floor, bare rock. Blue blazes.

FROM ELK LAKE

[Fig. 6(16)] After passing several brooks and Dix Pond, the trail from Elk Lake splits a few miles before the summit. Take the trail to the left, for although a bit longer, it goes through the spectacular Hunters Pass; afterward, as this trail approaches the summit, it joins the trail from NY 73. There are two lean-tos along the Elk Lake route. Either is a good place to camp for those who want to climb the trailless High Peaks in the Dix Range—Macomb, East Dix, South Dix, and Hough. Macomb can be ascended via a slide and the other three via herd paths from Macomb. Only strong hikers should attempt all four in a day.

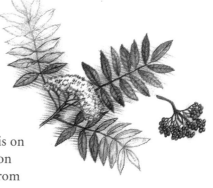

Directions: From Northway Exit 29 in North Hudson, drive 4 miles west on Blue Ridge Road toward Newcomb and turn right onto a road marked by a sign for Elk Lake Lodge. The parking lot is on the right after 5.2 miles. Trails originating here begin on private land; they are closed during big game season from late Oct. to early Dec.

Trail: 7.3 miles to summit via Hunters Pass.

Elevation: 2,057 feet at Elk Lake to 4,857 feet at summit.

Degree of difficulty: Strenuous.

MOUNTAIN ASH
(Sorbus americana)

Surface and blaze: Natural forest floor, bare rock. Red blazes for 6.9 miles, blue blazes rest of way.

Giant Mountain Wilderness

Fire swept through the Giant Mountain Wilderness in 1903, scorching the soil down to the bedrock and leaving the region's two highest summits, Giant and Rocky Peak, nearly bald. The landscape still bore the scars of fire when Bob and George Marshall climbed these peaks in the 1920s, and so the Marshalls regarded the view from the summits as rather poor. Since then, white birch, aspen, balsam fir, and red spruce have repopulated the slopes, and the views are superb.

The region's elevation rises 4,000 feet in 6 miles from US 9 near Elizabethtown to the top of Giant Mountain, the greatest change per horizontal mile of any wilderness in the Adirondacks. Whereas hearty specimens of oak, maple, basswood, and white ash grow at the lowest elevation, only stunted trees—balsam fir, red spruce, and white birch—survive at the highest. Nice stands of hemlock can be found near the Ausable River's east branch, which runs along the southwestern edge of the wilderness.

The Giant Mountain Wilderness covers about 22,100 acres and has about 12.5 miles of trails. There is only one lean-to in the region.

For more information: State Department of Environmental Conservation, P.O. Box 296, Route 86, Ray Brook, NY 12977. Phone (518) 897-1200. The DEC publishes a leaflet titled *Trails in the High Peaks Region* that includes some trails in the Giant Mountain Wilderness.

COMMON WOOD SORREL

(Oxalis montana)
From a German translation for "sour," sorrel has been used as a salad ingredient and by herbalists to treat stomach ailments and scurvy.

BAXTER MOUNTAIN

[Fig. 6(24)] This is a good climb for youngsters: short, with blueberries. The trail begins among evergreens that soon give way to beech and white birch. A steep pitch toward the end leads to a series of open ledges with views of Keene Valley, Dix Mountain, and the Great Range, including Mount Marcy. Children can hunt for blueberries on the side trails that weave among the bushes and pines on the summit. Of three trails to the top, the easiest starts on private land along NY 9N on Spruce Hill.

Directions: From NY 73 north of Keene Valley hamlet, drive 2 miles up NY 9N and park on the right a little past Hurricane Road.

Trail: 1.1 miles to summit.

Elevation: 1,670 feet at trailhead to 2,440 feet at summit.

Degree of difficulty: Moderate.

Surface and blaze: Natural forest floor. ADK blazes.

OWL MOUNTAIN LOOKOUT

[Fig. 6(27)] Located off one of the less-traveled trails to Giant Mountain, this lookout offers marvelous views of the Champlain Valley, Giant Mountain, and Rocky Peak Ridge. The route passes through a deciduous forest and crosses a few streams on its way to the rocky knob.

Directions: From NY 73 north of Keene Valley hamlet, drive 5.5 miles east on NY 9N and park at the DEC sign on the right. From NY 9 in Elizabethtown, drive 4.5 miles west; the sign will be on the left.

Trail: 2.6 miles to lookout.

Elevation: 1,100 feet at trailhead to about 2,400 feet at lookout.

Degree of difficulty: Moderate.

Surface and blaze: Natural forest floor. Red blazes.

GIANT'S WASHBOWL AND NUBBLE

[Fig. 6(21)] The Nubble is a rocky protuberance on the west flank of Giant Mountain that towers above a pond called the Giant's Washbowl. This scenic hike incorporates parts of two of the trails to Giant and two spur trails to take one over the Nubble and around the pond. There's also an overlook at Roaring Brook Falls, but hikers should not stand too close to the edge. Just above the falls is a stand of old-growth hemlocks (*Tsuga canadensis*)—some dating back four centuries. Take the Roaring Brook Trail 1.1 miles; turn right toward the Washbowl; after another 0.2 mile, turn left to climb over the Nubble; follow the Ridge Trail back to the Washbowl trail; and take that trail back to the Roaring Brook Trail.

Directions: From Northway Exit 30, drive north on NY 73 about 5.6 miles past the junction with US 9 to a lot on the right.

Trail: 4.8-mile loop.

Elevation: 1,280 feet at trailhead to 2,760 feet at Nubble.
Degree of difficulty: Moderate.
Surface and blaze: Natural forest floor. ATIS blazes.

GIANT MOUNTAIN

[Fig. 6(25)] There are several ways to get to Giant's summit, but the shortest is the Ridge Trail from NY 73. Near the start, the trail goes through a hardwood forest and past a small spring to an overlook above Chapel Pond. Soon after, it passes the Giant's Washbowl, a trout pond bordered by rock cliffs, and then climbs steeply to a series of wide-open ledges with wonderful views of the Dix Mountain Wilderness to the west and rolling hills to the south. Those who want a shorter hike can turn back here, 1.8 miles from the start. Although the bare rock of the ledges is gabbroic anorthosite, Giant's summit is mostly syenite gneiss. James Burnside ranks the view from Giant's summit as seventh best among the High Peaks. The vistas take in not only the Adirondacks but also the Champlain Valley and Vermont's Green Mountains.

Directions: From Northway Exit 30, drive north on NY 73 about about 4.1 miles past the US 9 junction to a parking area on the right. From the north, the trailhead is just past Chapel Pond.

Trail: 3 miles.
Elevation: 1,577 feet at trailhead to 4,627 feet at summit.
Degree of difficulty: Strenuous.

Surface and blaze: Natural forest floor, bare rock. ATIS blazes.

ROCKY PEAK RIDGE

[Fig. 6(34)] This rugged trek rewards the hiker with a variety of panoramic vistas along the way, from the farmhouses in the valley below to Lake Champlain in the east and the Dix Range to the southwest. Shortly before the summit is a pretty tarn, or alpine lake, nicknamed Lake Marie Louise. If hikers have lots of stamina, lots of water, and two cars, they can make an 11-mile end-to-end trek by continuing on to Giant and then descending to NY 73 by the Ridge Trail. This route is best hiked in the fall, when it's not too hot and the leaves are changing. For shorter trips, turn back at Blueberry Cobbles after 2 miles or Bald Peak after 3.9 miles.

Directions: From Northway Exit 30, drive north on NY 73 to US 9; turn right and go about 4.9 miles. From the opposite direction, the trailhead is about 1.3 miles

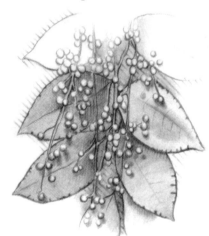

POISON SUMAC

(Toxicodendron vernix)
Poison sumac is a shrub
or a tree with 7–13
oval leaves on red stalks.

south of the New Russia Post Office.

Trail: 6.7 miles to summit.
Elevation: About 620 feet at trailhead to 4,420 feet at summit.
Degree of difficulty: Strenuous.
Surface and blaze: Natural forest floor. Yellow blazes.

Hurricane Mountain Primitive Area

Encompassing 13,499 acres, this is the second-largest parcel in the Adirondacks classified as a primitive area. It would be a candidate for wilderness classification if state officials ever decide to close an old gravel road on its northern border and remove an unmanned fire tower on Hurricane Mountain. The primitive area is sandwiched between the Giant Mountain Wilderness to the south and Jay Mountain Wilderness to the north. It has 13 miles of trails and three lean-tos. Hurricane Crag off NY 9N attracts rock climbers.

For more information: State Department of Environmental Conservation, P.O. Box 296, Route 86, Ray Brook, NY 12977. Phone (518) 897-1200.

HURRICANE MOUNTAIN

[Fig. 6(26)] Verplanck Colvin did some of his Adirondack Survey work atop this peak once he discovered its magnificent views in all directions. Of the three routes to the top, the most popular begins from NY 9N between Keene and Elizabethtown. The trail passes through hardwood and conifer forests and crosses several streams on its way to the rocky summit, denuded by fires in the early 1900s. The panorama includes the Champlain Valley to the east, Giant Mountain to the south, Mount Marcy to southwest, and Whiteface Mountain to the northwest. In August, hikers can pick blueberries while feasting their eyes on the vistas.

Directions: From NY 73 in the hamlet of Keene, drive 3.6 miles north on NY 9N. Park on the left shoulder or in a lot across the road.

Trail: 2.6 miles to summit.
Elevation: 1,694 feet to 3,694 feet at summit.
Degree of difficulty: Strenuous.
Surface and blaze: Old road, natural forest floor. Red blazes.

NUN-DA-GA-O RIDGE

[Fig. 7(17)] This little-used trail with few markers follows a rocky ridge with several vistas, ascends Weston Mountain—with great views of Marcy, Whiteface, and Hurricane—and continues to Lost Pond. There are two lean-tos along the way. Less than 0.5 mile from the start, a short detour adds Big Crow to the itinerary. More than two dozen major peaks can be discerned from Big Crow. Novice hikers can just climb

Big Crow, an easy 1.2-mile round trip. *Nun-da-ga-o* supposedly means "hill of the wind spirit" but appears to be inauthentic.

Directions: From NY 73 in Keene take East Hill Road 2.3 miles to O'Toole Road on the left, and take O'Toole Road 1.2 miles to the end to Crow Clearing.

Trail: 5.8-mile loop; if climbing Big Crow, 6.2 miles.

Elevation: About 2,215 feet to 2,800 feet at Big Crow, 2,920 feet at high point of Nun-da-ga-o Ridge.

Degree of difficulty: Moderate.

Surface and blaze: Natural forest floor, bare rock.

Jay Mountain Wilderness

[Fig. 7(18)] With only 7,100 acres, this is by far the smallest wilderness area in the Adirondacks. The gravel Glen Road separates it from the Hurricane Mountain Primitive Area. If the road ever closes, the wilderness could be expanded southward. There are no maintained trails and no lean-tos in the region, but a herd path leads to the 3,600-foot Jay Range, a lonely, wind-swept ridge adorned with cairns and glacial erratics. The panorama encompasses the High Peaks, Champlain Valley, the Green Mountains, and St. Lawrence Valley. Jay, Saddlebrook, and Slip mountains offer some of the best views.

For more information: State Department of Environmental Conservation, P.O. Box 296, Route 86, Ray Brook, NY 12977. Phone (518) 897-1200.

Directions: From NY 9N in Upper Jay, take the Upper Jay-Trumbulls Corner Road to its end, turn right and after a short distance look for yellow paint blazes and a Forest Preserve sign on the left.

Trail: About 3 miles to Jay Mountain summit.

Elevation: About 1,440 feet at start to 3,600 feet at summit.

Degree of difficulty: Strenuous.

Surface: Natural forest floor, bare rock.

Sentinel Range Wilderness

[Fig. 7] This rugged wilderness east of Lake Placid has few hiking trails, but it nonetheless offers something for everyone, from families with young children to seasoned hikers to bushwackers. Fires swept over the Sentinels in the early twentieth century, leaving many of the rocky outcrops visible today. Afterward, white birch (*Betula papyrifea*) and other pioneering hardwoods sprang up on the eastern slopes, with some conifers mixed in along the streams. Elsewhere, the forests are a mixture of hardwood and softwoods, with some pine stands on the northern ledges.

The wilderness, covering 23,252 acres, has about 14 miles of trails and lean-to. None of the trails leads to the highest peaks: Kilburn, Sentinel, and Stewart mountains, all located in the interior.

For more information: State Department of Environmental Conservation, P.O. Box 296, Route 86, Ray Brook, NY 12977. Phone (518) 897-1200.

COPPERAS POND

[Fig. 7] The lean-to at Copperas Pond is a good destination for families who want to picnic and swim. On the way, the trail winds first past Owen Pond, with a great view of Kilburn Mountain, and then past the southeastern shore of Copperas, with an awesome view of Whiteface Mountain. The outing can be extended with a short detour to Winch Pond, 0.5 mile from the main trail. The state stocks Owen with brown trout and Winch with brook trout. The use of bait fish in all the ponds is prohibited.

Directions: From the intersection of NY 76 and NY 86 in Lake Placid, drive east on NY 86 about 5 miles to the trailhead on the right. There is a second trailhead about 1 mile up the road. The distance from here to Copperas Pond is only 0.5 mile, but the trail is much steeper and less scenic. Hikers may want to spot a second car here and return by this route.

Trail: 1.3 miles to Copperas Pond.

Degree of difficulty: Easy.

Surface and blaze: Natural forest floor. Blue blazes.

PITCHOFF MOUNTAIN

[Fig. 7(21)] The open ridge has magnificent views of the Cascade Lakes and the High Peaks. Since there are two trailheads, situated 2.7 miles apart on NY 73, the best way to enjoy the vistas is on a 4.9-mile end-to-end traverse over one main and four lesser summits. Start from the western trailhead and leave a second car at the other end. For a shorter hike, just climb to Balanced Rocks, a group of boulders perched on rocky ledges about 1.6 miles from the western trailhead. The main summit lies another 0.4 mile up the trail. Pitchoff Chimney Cliff, located off NY 73 between the trailheads, has many challenging routes for rock and ice climbers. The mountain's north face, accessible from the Old Mountain Road trail, has some of the region's best ice for climbing.

Directions: If starting from the western trailhead, park in the lot for the Cascade Mountain trailhead. From Keene hamlet, drive 6.8 miles north on NY 73 to the lot on the left. From Lake Placid, the trailhead is 4.5 miles past Adirondak Loj Road. The eastern trailhead is 4.1 miles north of Keene.

Trail: 2 miles to summit.

Elevation: 2,160 feet at trailhead to 3,600 feet at summit.

Degree of difficulty: Strenuous.

Surface and blaze: Natural forest floor, bare rock. Red blazes.

NOTCH TRAILS

Either the North Notch Trail or South Notch Trail will take the hiker or skier about 3 miles through the woods to the western slopes of the Sentinel Range. There are no vistas at the end, but the walk is pleasant over easy to moderate grades. The Adirondack Mountain Club's guide to the High Peaks suggests that bushwackers climbing the 3,892-foot Kilburn Mountain, the highest in the region, make their approach from the North Notch Trail.

Directions: Both trails start from River Road outside Lake Placid. From Lake Placid, drive south on NY 73, and after crossing the Ausable River's West Branch, take a left onto River Road and go another 2 miles to reach the South Notch Trail or 3 miles to reach the North Notch Trail.

Trail: Both trails are about 3 miles.

Degree of difficulty: Moderate.

Elevation: From the road, the North Notch Trail ascends 1,200 feet, the South Notch Trail 1,100 feet.

Surface and blaze: Natural forest floor. Red blazes for both trails.

McKenzie Mountain Wilderness

Although much of this wilderness lies between the villages of Lake Placid and Saranac Lake, the ruggedness of its terrain discouraged development. Loggers did cut timber in the region, but at least 300 acres of old-growth forest—red spruce (*Picea rubens*), sugar maple (*Acer saccharum*), and yellow birch (*Betula alleghaniensis*)— survive on the eastern slope of Tamarac Mountain. A mixed forest of Adirondack hardwoods and conifers predominates throughout the wilderness, but two boreal species, balsam fir (*Abies balsamea*) and red spruce, reign on the slopes above 2,500 feet. Spruce-fir swamps are found in low-lying areas, mostly in the west.

McKenzie Mountain, at 3,861 feet, and Moose Mountain, at 3,899 feet, dominate the landscape. Two good-size ponds—McKenzie Pond, which Saranac Lake uses for drinking water, and Moose Pond—lie on the outskirts of the wilderness. Several spring-fed brooks cross the region, including Lincoln and French brooks, two trout streams that originate on nearby Esther Mountain.

The state maintains about 14 miles of trails in the 37,620-acre wilderness. Two lead to the summit of McKenzie Mountain and another leads to Haystack Mountain (not the High Peak). A trail to Whiteface Mountain cuts across the southeastern corner of the wilderness.

For more information: State Department of Environmental Conservation, P.O. Box 296, Route 86, Ray Brook, NY 12977. Phone (518) 897-1200.

MCKENZIE MOUNTAIN

[Fig. 7(5)] This trail, starting outside Lake Placid, climbs gradually for the first few miles, as it coincides with the Jackrabbit Ski Trail, but the final ascent is steep going. The trail crosses four lesser summits, each with limited views, before reaching the true summit, with ledges that open up to panoramas of Marcy, Algonquin, and other High Peaks to the south, the Saranac Lakes to the west, and Lake Placid and Whiteface Mountain to the east.

Directions: From NY 86, about 1.3 miles west of Lake Placid village, turn north on Whiteface Inn Road and go about 1.4 miles to the trailhead on the left.

Trail: 3.6 miles to summit.

Elevation: 1,921 feet at trailhead to 3,681 feet at summit.

Degree of difficulty: Strenuous.

Surface and blaze: Natural forest floor. Yellow blazes for 1.9 miles, red blazes to summit.

BAKER MOUNTAIN

[Fig. 7(2)] This small mountain is wooded on top, but its rock ledges offer views of many major peaks and several lakes. The view to the east of McKenzie Pond engulfed by wilderness is especially good. Although short, the route is steep in sections. The trail begins on a tote road but soon takes a right and climbs past an old quarry. On the way up, many side trails lead to lookouts through the trees, so parents should keep an eye on young children.

Directions: From NY 86 in Saranac Lake, turn east onto McKenzie Pond Road, left on Pine Street, and right on East Pine Street and continue to a parking area on the right at the north end of Moody Pond. The trail begins across the road.

Trail: 0.9 miles to summit.

Elevation: About 1,500 feet at trailhead to 2,452 feet at summit.

Degree of difficulty: Moderate.

Surface and blaze: Natural forest floor. Red blazes.

HAYSTACK MOUNTAIN

[Fig. 7(4)] Though not a High Peak, this Haystack has good views, too—for a lot less work. The trail also leads to an alternative route to McKenzie Mountain. The views from Haystack include the Saranac Lakes, Whiteface Mountain, and Mount Marcy.

BLACK CHERRY
(Prunus serotina)
The fallen leaves of the black cherry are highly toxic to livestock as decomposition produces cyanic acid.

Directions: From Lake Placid, drive west on NY 86 about 1.6 miles past the state Department of Environmental Conservation headquarters in Ray Brook to a large parking lot on the right. From Saranac Lake, drive east about 1.4 miles past Old Miltary Road.

Trail: 3.3 miles to summit.

Elevation: 1,638 feet at trailhead to 2,878 at summit.

Degree of difficulty: Moderate.

Surface and blaze: Natural forest floor. Blue blazes.

MOOSE POND

[Fig. 7] Although a dead-end road leads to the edge of this small lake, accessibility has not detracted from its pristine setting: The water is wholly surrounded by Forest Preserve lands. Canoeists can spend an afternoon exploring its inlets and boulder-strewn shores and gazing at the mountain scenery. Fishermen can try their luck at catching rainbow trout (*Oncorhynchus mykiss*) and landlocked salmon (*Salmo salar*), both stocked by the state. Campers will find unofficial tent sites among the cedars, hemlocks, and white birches growing along the shores. At the southern tip of the pond, Moose Creek drains into the Saranac River.

Directions: From Saranac Lake village, take NY 3 north. At Bloomingdale, NY 3 takes a sharp right and crosses a bridge; immediately after crossing the bridge, turn right onto County 18, also known as River Road, and drive 1.6 miles to an unmarked road on the right. Moose Pond is about 1.5 miles down this road. The pond is on the northwestern border of the McKenzie Pond Wilderness.

Activities: Fishing, canoeing, camping.

Facilities: Ramp for small boats.

Closest town: Bloomingdale is 2.1 miles northwest.

Jackrabbit Ski Trail

[Fig. 7(6)] Named for the legendary cross-country skier Herman "Jackrabbit" Johannsen, this Nordic trail stretches about 24 miles from the Sentinel Mountain Wilderness, east of Lake Placid, to Saranac Lake. Along the way, it passes three commercial cross-country centers that have trails that connect to the Jackrabbit. Most of the trail is of intermediate difficulty, with some sections easier or harder. A separate 9-mile section stretches from Lake Clear to the Adirondack Park Visitors Center at Paul Smiths. Eventually, the Adirondack Ski Touring Council hopes to connect the sections and extend the trail to Tupper Lake.

Most people ski only parts of the Jackrabbit, but some make end-to-end trips, staying at hotels or inns along the route. Skiers can use the trail for free in the Forest Preserve but must pay a fee if passing through any of the commercial ski centers. A day pass honored at all ski centers can be purchased.

The three ski centers on the trail are the Whiteface Club Nordic Center, Lake Placid Resort Nordic Center, and Cascade Ski Touring Center, all located in the vicinity of Lake Placid. The trail also can be reached via the Cascade trails from the Olympic trails at Mount Van Hoevenberg.

For more information: Adirondack Ski Touring Council, PO Box 843, Lake Placid, NY 12946. Phone (518) 523-1365. The council publishes a map of the ski trails.

For those who want to stick to the Forest Preserve, two routes are recommended.

OLD MOUNTAIN ROAD

[Fig. 7(22)] Starting at the Adirondack Rock and River Lodge at the eastern end of the trail, ski along an old road past beaver ponds and through a pass in the Sentinel Range with a view of the cliffs of Pitchoff Mountain's north face. The cliffs are one of the region's premier ice-climbing spots.

Directions: From NY 73 in Keene, take Alstead Hill Road to the lodge at the end.
Trail: 4.5 miles from the lodge to NY 73 near Cascade Ski Touring Center.
Degree of difficulty: Moderate.
Surface and blaze: Old road. Red blazes.

MCKENZIE POND

[Fig. 7] Starting in Saranac Lake, ski about 1.5 miles on ungroomed trails through woods and past marshes to a wilderness pond. If skiers continue, they will reach the Whiteface Club Nordic Center after a total of 5.5 miles.

Directions: From NY 86 in Ray Brook, turn north on McKenzie Pond Road and go roughly 1.5 miles to where the trail crosses the road. Blue signs mark the pulloff.
Trail: About 1.5 miles from road to McKenzie Pond.
Degree of difficulty: Moderate.
Surface: Old tote road, natural forest floor.

Meadowbrook Public Campground

[Fig. 7(3)] Located on busy NY 86 between Lake Placid and Saranac Lake, this campground makes a convenient base for day trips around the High Peaks and Saranac Lakes regions. A trail from the campground leads to the 3,088-foot Scarface Mountain, with views of the Western High Peaks and Oseetah Lake. (For hikers and mountain bikers not staying in the campground, there is another trailhead on Ray Brook Road, about 0.1 mile from NY 86 in Ray Brook.)

Directions: The campground is on NY 86 about 5 west of Lake Placid and 4.5 miles east of Saranac Lake.
Activities: Camping, picnicking, hiking.

Facilities: 62 campsites, picnic pavilion, swings, showers, toilets, trailer dump station.

Dates: Mid-May through Labor Day.

Fees: There is a charge for camping and day use.

Closest town: Saranac Lake is 4.5 miles west.

For more information: Campground office, phone (518) 891-4351. For reservations, phone (800) 456-2267.

Pine Pond Trail

[Fig. 7(23)] This popular mountain bike route goes 6.5 miles through the woods, with some ruts and muddy spots, to a sandy beach on Pine Pond. The return trip will require a long climb. In winter, the trail is used by snowmobilers and cross-country skiers.

Directions: From NY 76 in Lake Placid, take Averyville Road to the end, continuing on dirt road through a field. Bear left at a fork and park at the west end of the field.

Trail: 6.5 miles to Pine Pond.

Degree of difficulty: Moderate.

Fowlers Crossing Trails

[Fig. 7(24)] Mountain bikers can ride along 3.4 miles of interconnecting woods roads and single-track trails that lead to a variety of destinations: Oseetah Lake, Oseetah Marsh, a cedar swamp, and pine plantations. Two trails are for intermediate bikers and three for beginners. Snowmobilers use these trails in winter.

Directions: From Saranac Lake, drive east on NY 86 to a parking lot just outside the village, where the railroad tracks cross the highway.

Activities: Mountain biking.

Closest town: Saranac Lake is a short distance west on NY 86.

For more information: See *Mountain Bike Trails in the Adirondack Mountains of Essex County*, published by the Lake Placid/Essex County Visitors Bureau. Phone (518) 523-2445.

Ausable River Branches

The east and west branches of the Ausable River rise in the High Peaks and flow northeast before converging in Ausable Forks. From there, the main branch flows 22 miles to Lake Champlain, passing through Ausable Chasm and ending in an attractive marsh at the lake's edge. Only the two branches will be discussed here. Information about the main branch appears in the chapter on the Champlain Valley (*see* page 87).

WEST AUSABLE RIVER

[Fig. 7] When fishermen talk about the Ausable River, they usually mean the west branch, one of the best trout streams in the East. Trout thrive in the clean, cold water that flows off the mountains. The many rocks and boulders in the river not only aerate the water, but they also create pools where trout can hide and their prey— mayflies, stoneflies, caddisflies—can breed.

The state and Essex County do their best to uphold the river's reputation as a fly fisherman's paradise, stocking the water with more than 20,000 brown trout (*Salmo trutta*) and several hundred rainbow trout

PEREGRINE FALCON
(*Falco peregrinus*)

(*Oncorhynchus mykiss*) in one recent year. But even those who fail to catch a lunker exhilarate in the gorgeous surroundings of this mountain river. That's why the West Ausable attracts canoeists, campers, and hikers as well as fishermen.

The West Ausable proper begins its 36-mile journey as a whitewater stream at the confluence of South Meadow Brook and Marcy Brook about 1 mile from Adirondak Loj. The river settles down for a spell while meandering around Lake Placid but then plunges into serious whitewater again in the Wilmington Notch. After the Notch, the river enters a stillwater known as Lake Everest, created by a dam at Wilmington. The last 11 miles, between Wilmington and Ausable Forks, are not as accessible to the public.

WILMINGTON NOTCH

The glaciers created this narrow gorge more than 10,000 years ago when they gouged out fractured rock in a fault zone east of Lake Placid. This is where the West Ausable, hurtling over falls and rapids, earns its reputation as a nonpareil trout stream—and where canoeists can find some of the most treacherous whitewater in the Adirondacks. Motorists can catch glimpses of the stunning scenery by driving through the canyon on NY 86 between Lake Placid and Wilmington, a route that parallels the river. The Flume, one of the larger falls, can be reached by a short walk from where the highway crosses the river, about a mile east of Whiteface Mountain Ski Center. There is a pulloff just east of the bridge.

High Falls Gorge. [Fig. 7(12)] The most spectacular falls in Wilmington Notch are at High Falls Gorge, where the river drops more than 100 feet in a series of cascades over granitelike cliffs, forming potholes in the bedrock. The West Ausable sculpted the falls by eroding the anorthosite in the stream bed below them, and the tougher rock blocked the erosion from continuing farther upstream. High Falls

Gorge is a commercial tourist attraction, with hiking trails, stairs, and catwalks that lead to the base of the narrow chasm.

Directions: Drive about 7 miles east of Lake Placid on NY 86.

Activities: Nature walk (0.5 mile round trip), picnicking.

Facilities: Picnic area, restaurant, rock shop, gift shop.

Dates: Open mid-May through Columbus Day.

Fees: There is a charge for admission.

For more information: Phone (518) 946-2278 in season or (518) 946-2212 off-season.

Closest town: Wilmington is about 4 miles east.

Wilmington Notch Public Campground. [Fig. 7(15)] About 1 mile east of High Falls Gorge, the state operates a campground in a grove of birch and pine along the West Ausable. The campground opens in April, when trout season starts, so campers can fish the river right from the grounds.

Directions: From Wilmington, drive 4 miles west on NY 86. The campground is on the left.

Activities: Camping, fishing, hiking.

Facilities: 54 campsites, toilets, showers, trailer dump station.

Dates: Open April through Oct.

Fees: There is a charge for camping and day use.

Closest town: Wilmington is 4 miles east.

For more information: Campground office, phone (518) 946-7172. For reservations, phone (800) 456-2267.

FISHING THE WEST AUSABLE

Anglers can fish with success over most of the West Ausable, but they tend to congregate in the Wilmington Notch, where eddies and pools in the boulder-strewn stream create the best trout habitat. In season, fishermen often line the banks between the Conservation Monument, located on NY 86 east of Lake Placid, to the pool below the Flume. But the calmer stretch of river above the monument also has good-size trout. Other fishing spots include Lake Everest above the Wilmington dam and the pools below the dam.

A few special rules apply to the West Ausable. Fishermen must release any trout caught in a no-kill zone that stretches for 5 miles from the outlet of Holcomb Pond downstream to about 2.2 miles below the Conservation Monument. Within this zone, which is marked by signs, fishing is permitted all year, but only artificial lures may be used. In the West Ausable's tributaries, fishermen are allowed to take five extra brook trout under 8 inches, in addition to the five trout per day normally allowed by state regulations.

The brown trout taken from the West Ausable often weigh 3 to 4 four pounds and occasionally weigh up to 8 pounds. Although most fishermen come for trout, the river also holds bass, pike, and walleye.

CANOEING THE WEST AUSABLE

Most of the West Ausable can be canoed, but the whitewater stretches should be attempted only by experts. Beyond the Wilmington dam, access becomes somewhat of a problem. Over its entire course, the river drops from 2,060 feet to 550 feet, an average gradient of 0.80 percent. A state study classifies 44 percent of the river as rapids, 27 percent as having moderate current, and 29 percent as still water.

Paul Jamieson describes two possible whitewater trips above the Wilmington dam in *Adirondack Canoe Waters: North Flow*. The first starts on South Meadow Brook about 0.7 mile upstream from Marcy Brook and ends 8 miles later at the NY 73 bridge—"one of the most beautiful whitewater runs in the Adirondacks." The rapids reach Class IV intensity. The second starts at the Conservation Monument on NY 86 east of Lake Placid and ends 6.8 miles later at Lake Everest after plunging through the Wilmington Notch—"one of the most challenging of North Flow waters." The rapids reach Class VI. Both trips should be attempted only in high water.

Canoeists searching for a more placid experience can paddle the 8-mile quiet stretch between the NY 73 bridge and the Conservation Monument. Except for a carry around a cascade at the end, it's smooth going, with views of Algonquin, Whiteface, and other peaks along the way. Make sure to take out before entering the whitewater of the Notch. Flatwater enthusiasts can also put in at Lake Everest, where there are good views of Whiteface.

EAST AUSABLE RIVER

[Fig. 7]The East Ausable flows about 40 miles from Marcy Swamp through the Ausable Valley, the Keene Valley, and past the Jay Mountain Range before joining forces with the West Ausable. The Adirondack Mountain Reserve maintains hiking trails along the river in the Ausable Valley, but the public is forbidden to fish or canoe along that scenic stretch. From Saint Huberts to Ausable Forks, roads along the river provide easy access.

There is a roadside picnic spot on NY 73 across from the Marcy Airfield between the hamlets of Keene and KeeneValley. In summer, this is a good place to swim. The river has a sandy bottom in the middle, where the crystal-clear water is 4 to 5 feet deep. It's fun to swim against the gentle current and then float downstream. There is another riverside picnic area in the hamlet of Jay. A little downstream from it, the river flows under a covered bridge built in 1856, one of the oldest in the state.

FISHING THE EAST AUSABLE

Although not as famous as its cousin, the East Ausable is a decent trout stream in its own right. In one recent year, the state and Essex County stocked it with 13,280 brown, 9,800 rainbow, and 400 brook trout. Francis Betters, the author of *Fishing the Adirondacks*—and a legendary flytier—recommends fishing the pools between Hulls Falls and Keene. Because the East Ausable gets rather shallow in summer, the fishing tends to drop off in July and August.

CANOEING THE EAST AUSABLE

In the 28 miles from Saint Huberts to Ausable Forks, the East Ausable drops 550 feet for an average gradient of 0.37 percent. A state study characterizes 25 percent of this stretch as rapids, 64 percent as having moderate current, and 11 percent as stillwater. About 85 percent of the river is canoeable in medium high water.

Paul Jamieson describes several possible canoe trips on the East Ausable in *Adirondack Canoe Waters: North Flow.* In April or early May, if the water is high enough, paddlers can canoe about 4 miles from Keene Valley to Hulls Falls, encountering only Class II rapids and one short carry around a fisheries dam. A wet suit is recommended in case of a spill.

Below Hulls Falls the river enters a scenic gorge, but the canoeing becomes trickier over the next 2 miles to Keene, with rapids reaching Class III intensity and drops reaching Class V difficulty. Jamieson calls the next 6.3-mile stretch, from Keene to Upper Jay Dam, "one of the most enjoyable raceways in the northern Adirondacks," as canoeists adept enough to avoid the boulders can cruise along at 8 mph through Class I-III rapids.

Boquet River

[Fig. 6] The locals pronounce the name as either Bo-KET or Bo-KWET. The river got its name early—a landowner's diary refers to it in 1765—but its origin remains in doubt. It could be named for a British general or a French Jesuit, or the name might be a variation of *bouquet* or another French word.

The north and south forks of the Boquet River rise in the Dix Mountain Wilderness and converge near NY 73 north of Underwood; thence, the Boquet flows 47.4 miles to Lake Champlain, dropping nearly 1,200 feet in a winding course that passes through deciduous woodlands and farmlands. Ruffed grouse (*Bonasa umbellus*), black duck (*Anas rubripes*), snowshoe hare (*Lepus americanus*), river otter (*Lutra canadensis*), and bobcat (*Lynx rufus*) are among the birds and mammals that dwell near the river.

Below the forks, much of the river is canoeable, though beginners should steer clear of the worst rapids. Fishermen come in quest of salmon (*Salmo salar*), brook trout, rainbow trout, and brown trout. For hikers, Split Rock Falls is a popular destination reachable by a short walk.

SPLIT ROCK FALLS

[Fig. 6(29)] About 3.5 miles from the confluence of the forks, the Boquet tumbles over a series of falls through a narrow gorge—a lovely spot for a picnic or swim. In this stretch of river, the woods are dominated by yellow and white birch, sugar maple, cedar, hemlock, and aspen.

Directions: From NY 73 north of Underwood, drive about 2.4 miles north on US 9, following the river, to a parking lot. The falls are a short distance from the road.

▓ CANOEING THE BOQUET

A state study classifies about a third of the river as still water, about half as having moderate current, and less than a fifth as rapids. It drops from an elevation of 1,290 feet at the forks to 95 feet at Lake Champlain. In *Adirondack Canoe Waters: North Flow,* Paul Jamieson estimates that three-fourths of the river below Split Rock Falls is canoeable in spring or after a heavy rain in summer or fall.

Since roads follow the Boquet for much of its length, there are many places to put in or take out a canoe, either at bridges or state fishing-access sites.

Canoeists who don't mind Class II rapids can paddle about 11 miles from Beaver Meadow Brook, about 1.5 miles downstream from Split Rock Falls, to Elizabethtown, passing through Pleasant Valley with its splendid views of Giant Mountain. The trip requires a carry around a falls at New Russia. The 6.5-mile stretch between Elizabethtown and the Northway is more difficult, with several Class III rapids.

SUGAR MAPLE
(Acer saccharum)
Sugar maple's sap is the source of maple syrup and sugar.

From the Northway, the Boquet flows 23 miles to a salmon ladder in Willsboro. Doing the whole stretch would require several long carries. Some of the whitewater reaches Class IV intensity and should be navigated only by experts, but sections of this stretch are suitable for novices. The 2.2-mile stretch between the salmon ladder and Lake Champlain is flatwater.

▓ FISHING THE BOQUET

The Boquet is the most important tributary for Lake Champlain's landlocked salmon (*Salmo salar*). In spring and again in fall, salmon swim upstream as far as 20 miles to a falls at Wadhams, after ascending the fish ladder at Willsboro. Fish for salmon at the Willsboro Falls Pool, below the ladder, and at Wadhams Falls. The salmon are bigger in the fall.

The state stocks the Boquet not only with salmon but also with rainbow, brook, and brown trout. Fish the upper river, between Split Rock Falls and Elizabethtown, for brook trout and downstream from Elizabethtown for browns and rainbows. There are numerous fishing-access sites along the highways near the river.

Pauline Murdock Wildlife Management Area

[Fig. 6(33)] The state owns a 68.5-acre parcel on the banks of the Boquet, near Elizabethtown, that encompasses river floodplain, old pasture, and mature woods. Eastern bluebirds (*Sialia sialis*) and cedar waxwings (*Bombycilla cedrorum*) live in the floodplain, where wild grapevines and wildflowers grow. Brown and rainbow trout can be caught in this stretch of the river. A 700-yard nature trail starts at the parking lot, crosses an old canal, and winds through a forest of red pine (*Pinus resinosa*), white pine (*Pinus strobus*), hemlock (*Tsuga canadensis*), sugar maple (*Acer saccharum*), American beech (*Fagus grandiola*), and northern red oak (*Quercus rubra borealis*). Hunting, trapping, camping, and swimming are prohibited.

Directions: From US 9 just east of Elizabethtown, take County 8, also known as Elizabethtown-Wadhams Road, to a parking lot on the right.

Activities: Hiking, fishing, birdwatching.

Dates: Open year-round.

Closest town: Elizabethtown is about 0.5 mile west.

For more information: State Department of Environmental Conservation, Route 86, PO Box 296, Ray Brook, NY 12977. Phone (518) 897-1200.

Adirondack History Center

[Fig. 6(32)] This museum in an old three-story schoolhouse in Elizabethtown celebrates Essex County's past as a center of logging, farming, and mining. Lice combs, looms, spinning wheels, and cast-iron kettles are among the utilitarian artifacts on display. One room is devoted to a large collection of antique dolls. The museum also has a restored stagecoach and an Olympic bobsled.

Perhaps the museum's most unusual artifact is a fire tower, reconstructed on the premises from towers taken from Kempshall and West mountains. Visitors can climb the tower for a view of the Jay Range and surrounding countryside. The museum also has a short nature trail leading from a flower and herb garden to an old cemetery. The garden's formal design is modeled on a garden from Colonial Williamsburg.

The Brewster Library, on the museum's second floor, is open year-round by appointment. It houses a collection of resource materials—maps, photographs, census records—relating to various Adirondack communities. The Essex County Historical Society also makes its home here.

Directions: Court Street (US 9) Elizabethtown.

Facilities: Nature trail, garden, fire tower, library, gift shop.

Dates: Open mid-May to mid-Oct.

Fees: There is a charge for admission.

For more information: Adirondack History Center, Court Street, Route 9, Elizabethton, NY 12932. Phone (518) 873-6466.

John Brown Farm State Historic Site

[Fig. 7(8)] John's Brown body lies buried in the Adirondacks, near a massive boulder on his old farm in the town of North Elba, a few miles south of Lake Placid. His wife, Mary Ann Day Brown, brought the body back to the farmstead after his execution on December 2, 1859—less than two months after his unsuccessful raid on the military arsenal in Harper's Ferry, Virginia.

The fiery abolitionist had bought the 244-acre farm in 1849 from Gerrit Smith, the scion of a wealthy landowner and philanthropist, as part of a grand but doomed experiment. Smith offered tracts of land to blacks who wished to clear the land in the Adirondack wilderness for farming. Brown agreed to teach the men about agriculture. Unfortunately, the climate and terrain worked against them, and the community, nicknamed Timbucto, failed.

John Brown is buried at the John Brown Farm State Historic Site.

Frances Lee of Boston, a prominent abolitionist, had John Brown's name inscribed on the large boulder so he would never be forgotten. John Brown brought back his grandfather's tombstone from Tarrington, Connecticut, and it serves as the tombstone for John Brown and his three sons. Two sons were killed with Brown at Harper's Ferry. The two-story farmhouse has been restored and furnished in period fashion. There is a short nature trail with markers identifying trees along the way.

Directions: From Lake Placid, take NY 73 south to John Brown Road, a righthand turn near the county fairgounds.

Activities: Picnicking, hiking, cross-country skiing.

Facilities: Farm trail, a self-guided 15-minute walk.

Dates: The farmhouse is open late May to late Oct., Wednesday through Sunday. The grounds are open year-round.

Fees: None.

Closest town: Lake Placid.

For more information: John Brown Farm State Historic Site, 2 John Brown Road, Lake Placid, NY 12946. Phone (518) 523-3900.

Hudson River in Adirondack Park

The Hudson River begins as a small stream at Henderson Lake.

1 Hudson River
2 Henderson Lake

Hudson River

The Hudson River begins as a small stream—1 foot deep, 30 feet wide—flowing out of Henderson Lake amid the High Peaks and ends as a mighty river that empties into the Atlantic Ocean in New York City. Its highest source, at 4,320 feet above sea level, is Lake Tear of the Clouds on the western flank of Mount Marcy.

All told, the river travels about 269 miles. The first 96 miles—more than a third of its length—lie within the Adirondack Park. When the river leaves the park at Corinth, it is 6 feet deep and 250 feet wide.

Like other rivers, the Hudson follows the path of least resistance, cutting through bedrock that is easily eroded. Usually, the river flows along a fault, where the rock has been broken, or along a belt of soft rock, such as marble. The river's ancient course also has been altered by glacial deposits.

Near its confluence with the Indian River, the Hudson abruptly turns east to

[*Above:* The Hudson River at Newcomb]

follow an 8-mile belt of marble, sculpting the spectacular Hudson Gorge. This stretch contains the Hudson's most breathtaking scenery and most challenging whitewater, as the river rushes past 300-foot cliffs in a wild and remote part of the Adirondacks.

After leaving the gorge, the Hudson bumps into Dutton Mountain, which deflects it southward again. The river once continued southeast toward Lake George, but since a glacial moraine blocked this route about 10,000 years ago, the river today turns slightly southwest near Warrensburg.

North of Warrensburg, the Hudson has created a rare natural community known as an ice meadow. Each spring, ice floes pile up on the banks up to 10 feet thick, scouring the landscape like a miniature glacier. The ice not only cools the air, creating a microclimate, but it also delays the growing season. Several boreal plants grow in the ice meadows, such as Clinton's club brush, New England violet, and clustered sedge grass. A nature trail maintained by Warren County provides access to this part of the river (see page 187).

As early as 1758, lumbermen used the Hudson to transport timber from the Adirondacks. In the 1800s, the log drive became a rite of spring, when tens of thousands of logs would be floated down the river to Glens Falls. From Newcomb, a log could travel to Glens Falls in two days, but if it got hung up along the way, it might not get there until the next spring. The last big log drive—before trucks took over the job of the river—occurred in 1922. Finch, Pruyn & Co. continued to float 4-foot pulp logs down the Hudson until 1951.

In the 1900s, the Hudson attracted the interest of power companies. At one time or another, there were proposals to build hydroelectric dams at Lake Luzerne, in the Hudson Gorge, and near the Indian River junction. But in 1969, reacting to public outrage, the state legislature voted to prohibit dams on the Hudson from Lake Luzerne north to the river's source. Today, that entire stretch of the Hudson—about 90 miles—is classified as wild, scenic, or recreational, affording it additional protection from development.

The state owns large parcels along the river in the Hudson Gorge and in the broad valley south of Warrensburg. Fishermen and canoeists can get to the river through these lands. In addition, there are several canoe launches along highways that border or cross the river in Warren and Essex counties.

Canoeists of all abilities will find stretches of the Hudson to suit their tastes, from dangerous whitewater to gentle currents. Anglers can fish for trout in the upper reaches of the Hudson and bass farther downriver. And hikers can walk to Blue Ledge, one of the prettiest spots in the Hudson Gorge.

For more information: In Essex County, phone the State Department of Environmental Conservation's office in Ray Brook at (518) 897-1200. In Warren County or Saratoga County, phone DEC's office in Warrensburg at (518) 623-3671.

Hudson Gorge Primitive Area

The state owns more than 17,000 acres in and around the Hudson Gorge. Most of the property was acquired from 1871 to 1905 after it had been logged and abandoned for back taxes. A substantial amount of land around the gorge—including O.K. Slip Falls, one of the highest waterfalls in the Adirondacks—remains in private hands.

The Hudson Gorge Primitive Area has several low mountains, such as Starbuck and Kettle, and numerous ponds, but the main attraction is the river. In fact, the only official trail in the area leads to the river. Fishermen sometimes take unmarked paths to ponds in the region. In fall, hunters come to the area in quest of white-tailed deer (*Odocoileus virginianus*) and black bear (*Ursus americanus*).

A forest of northern hardwoods and red spruce (*Picea rubens*) grows over most of the territory. Common wildflowers include blue cohosh (*Caulophyllum thalictroides*), Canada mayflower (*Maianthemum canadense*), wild oats (*Uvularia sessilfolia*), and wood sorrel (*Oxalis montana*).

There is a 160-acre swamp of northern white cedar (*Thuja occidentalis*) just north of Kettle Mountain, about 0.5 mile south of North Woods Club Road. The cedar's presence is attributed to calcareous soils produced by the marble bedrock. One of the trees has a diameter of 40 inches. Travel in the thick swamp is difficult.

For more information: State Department of Environmental Conservation, Route 86, PO Box 296, Ray Brook, NY 12977. Phone (518) 897-1200.

BLUE LEDGE TRAIL

[Fig. 31(3)] The one marked trail in the Hudson Gorge Primitive Area leads to Blue Ledge, a 300-foot precipice carved out of marble and syenite at a bend in the river. The mossy upper section of the cliff often takes on a bluish-gray sheen, which accounts for the name.

The trail begins at Huntley Pond on North Woods Club Road. The state stocks this pond with brook trout (*Salvelinus fontinalis*). There are several primitive campsites on the northern shore.

Leaving the pond, the trail passes between two large glacial erratics, crosses a stream on a bridge, climbs a ridge where some large white pines (*Pinus strobus*) grow, and then descends to the river. Several kinds of flowers adorn the way.

The path ends across the river from Blue Ledge, which is on private land. Northern white cedars (*Thuja occidentalis*) cling to the cliffs. Ravens (*Corvus corax*) sometimes nest in the rock crevices. In the past, peregrine falcons (*Falco peregrinus*) and bald eagles (*Haliaeetus leucocephalus*) also nested at Blue Ledge.

In summer, the river here forms quiet pools where hikers can take a dip. Anglers can try their luck fishing for trout. Backpackers can camp at designated sites. The trail can be skied or snowshoed in winter.

Directions: From North Creek, drive about 10 miles north on NY 28N to North

Woods Club Road; turn left and go about 7.4 miles to a parking area on the right, near Huntley Pond. The trail begins on the other side of the road. The road may be closed during mud season in early spring. It is plowed in winter but can be rough.

Trail: 2.5 miles.
Elevation: 1,580 feet at Huntley Pond to 1,340 feet at Hudson River.
Degree of difficulty: Easy.
Surface and blaze: Natural forest floor. Blue blazes.

NORTH WOODS CLUB ROAD

[Fig. 31] The road to the Blue Ledge Trail makes an excellent mountain bike route for beginner to intermediate riders. Bikers can ride as far as Huntley Pond, more than 7 miles from NY 28N. Only the first 2 miles are paved. The road crosses the Boreas River and goes up and down several hills.

The lands owned by the North Woods Club at the end of the road are posted. The American artist Winslow Homer, who painted many Adirondack scenes, often stayed at this club in the late 1800s.

Fishermen sometimes walk south from the North Woods Club Road along the railroad tracks to the Hudson River. The tracks follow the Boreas River, which empties into the Hudson just west of Dutton Mountain. Anglers also fish the Boreas here, often walking north from the road. The state stocks the Boreas with brook trout (*Salvelinus fontinalis*) and rainbow trout (*Oncorhynchus mykiss*).

Directions: Same as for Blue Ledge (*see* page 81).
Trail: 7.4 miles from NY 28N to Huntley Pond.
Degree of difficulty: Easy to moderate.
Surface: Paved for 2 miles, dirt for 5.4 miles.

Rafting the Hudson

Those who are not whitewater canoeists can nonetheless experience the thrill of riding through the Hudson Gorge. From early April to mid-October, several companies offer rafting trips on the Hudson. Most start in the village of Indian Lake and end near the hamlet of North River, a 17-mile journey that takes about 4.5 hours.

Rafters put in on the Indian River below the Lake Abanakee dam. The town releases water from the dam to accommodate the rafts. About 7 miles from the dam, the Indian meets the Hudson. Numerous rapids—some reaching Class V intensity—are encountered on the trip. The companies provide wet suits and helmets. Customers must be at least 12 years old.

Tens of thousands of people have rafted safely through the gorge since 1979, when the first company offered the service. But any whitewater trip is not without risk: Rafters and canoeists have died from drowning or hypothermia. There are escape trails leading out of the gorge that can be used in an emergency.

Rafting trips are offered every day from early April to late June and again from early September to mid-October. In 1998, the companies began offering trips in the summer as well—on Tuesdays, Thursdays, Saturdays, and Sundays.

Several rafting companies also offer trips on the tamer stretch of the Hudson below the gorge.

For more information: Indian Lake Chamber of Commerce, Main Street, PO Box 724, Indian Lake, NY 12842. Phone (518) 648-5112. Or Warren County Tourism Department, 1340 Route 9, Lake George, NY 12845-9803. Phone (518) 761-6366 or (800) 365-1050. Ask for the leaflet *Whitewater Rafting and Canoe Access Sites.* Commercial rafting companies are listed in Appendix C.

Canoeing the Hudson

Only whitewater experts should attempt to canoe the Hudson Gorge, but intermediate and novice canoeists can find stretches of the Hudson below the gorge to match their abilities. Generally, the river gets easier as it advances southward. The following trips are divided into three categories: expert, intermediate, and novice.

For more information: See *Adirondack Canoe Waters: South and West Flow* by Alec Proskine. Many canoe access sites are listed in the leaflet *Whitewater Rafting and Canoe Access Sites.* To get a copy, contact the Warren County Tourism Department, 1340 Route 9, Lake George, NY 12845-9803. Phone (518) 761-6366 or (800) 365-1050.

EXPERT

Canoeists who venture into the Hudson Gorge can use the same put-in on the Indian River as the rafting companies and take out at North River. Generally, the 17-mile trip takes about 5 hours. For a longer trip, canoeists can put in at NY 28N in Newcomb. Allow 9 to 10 hours to cover 24 miles. It's also possible to start at the Lake Harris Public Campground in Newcomb.

The rapids in the gorge can reach Class V in high water—just one step below the most dangerous rating. In spring, one of the prime canoe seasons, the Hudson may be only 40 degrees Fahrenheit, making a wet suit a must. Several years ago, a paddler died from hypothermia after entering the gorge wearing a T-shirt and shorts.

The town of Indian Lake releases water from Lake Abanakee to accommodate commercial rafts. To ask about the release schedule, canoeists can call the town clerk's office at (518) 648-5211.

INTERMEDIATE

Canoeists will encounter plenty of Class II and Class III rapids in the 20 miles between the hamlet of North River and the stretch of river known as the Glen but nothing as challenging as those in the gorge. On the first weekend of each May, hundreds of canoeists take part in the Hudson River White Water Derby in this part of the river.

There are numerous canoe access sites along this stretch of the Hudson, including three off NY 28 in North River, one at the NY 8 bridge in Riparius, and one at the NY 28 bridge in the Glen. It's also possible to put in and take out a little upriver of the NY 28N bridge in North Creek. Thus, trips of various lengths are possible.

The distances between the major access sites and the difficulty rating of each stretch are as follows: from North River to North Creek: 5 miles, Class II rapids; from North Creek to Riparius: 8 miles, Class III rapids; and from Riparius to the Glen, 6 miles, Class III rapids. The last stretch is considered the hardest of the three. There is only one rapid in the 8.5 miles between the Glen and Thurman Station, the start of the novice section.

░ NOVICE

Beginning canoeists can handle the 15-mile flatwater stretch of the Hudson between Thurman Station, southwest of Warrensburg, and the hamlet of Lake Luzerne. Those who end their trip at Lake Luzerne must be careful to take out before the falls there.

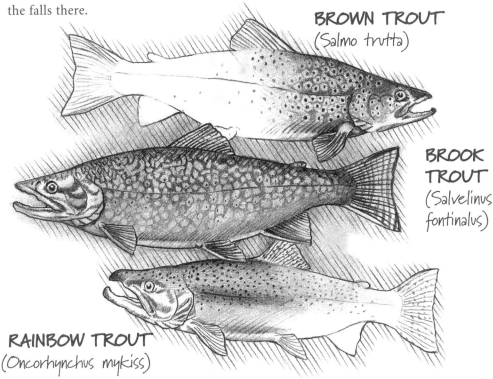

BROWN TROUT
(Salmo trutta)

BROOK TROUT
(Salvelinus fontinalus)

RAINBOW TROUT
(Oncorhynchus mykiss)

This part of the Hudson passes through a broad valley with many scenic vistas. The state owns much of the shoreline on the east side, making it possible to combine canoeing with hiking or camping. The state also owns islands where canoeists can stop to camp or have lunch. For hiking and camping opportunities, see the section on the Hudson River Recreation Area (page 185).

The Thurman Station access site is on the west bank, where County 418 crosses the river. There are two access sites in the Hudson River Recreation Area and one on River Road about 0.75 mile north of Lake Luzerne.

The approximate distances between the access sites are as follows: 5 miles from Thurman Station to the northern site in Hudson River Recreation Area, 2 miles from the northern to the southern site in the recreation area, and 8 miles from the southern site to the take-out site above Lake Luzerne.

For longer trips, put in upriver of Thurman Station at the Warren County Fish Hatchery (*see* page 187) or the Warren County Nature Trail (*see* page 187). The latter site requires a portage of about 0.4 mile.

Those ending at Lake Luzerne can get a good look at the falls from the bridge over the Hudson. Just downstream of the bridge, the Hudson meets the Sacandaga River.

Fishing the Hudson

State and county fish hatcheries stock the northern Hudson with brown trout (*Salmo trutta*) and rainbow trout (*Oncorhynchus mykiss*) in the towns of Newcomb, Minerva, and Johnsburg. The trout can best be caught between Newcomb and North River. This stretch also holds brook trout (*Salvelinus fontinalis*).

Anglers who don't mind a hike can fish for trout at Blue Ledge in the Hudson Gorge, where there are many riffles, pools, and pockets. They can also reach the Hudson by walking down the railroad tracks from North Woods Club Road (*see* page 82). Otherwise, they can reach the river at one of the canoe access sites along NY 28 in North River.

Below North River, fishermen can catch smallmouth bass (*Micropterus dolomieui*) and rock bass (*Ambloplites rupestris*) as well as an occasional trout. Some anglers like to take a canoe/float trip between Thurman Station and Lake Luzerne. This stretch can be reached at various canoe access sites. In addition, public lands border the river at the Warren County Nature Trail (*see* page 187), Warren County Fish Hatchery (*see* page 187), and Hudson River Recreation Area (*see* page 185).

Ice fishing is allowed in the Hudson in the Adirondacks.

For more information: Warren County Tourism Department, 1340 Route 9, Lake George, NY 12845-9803. Phone (518) 761-6366 or (800) 365-1050. Ask for the brochure *Grand Slam Fishing* and the leaflet *Whitewater Rafting and Canoe Access Sites.*

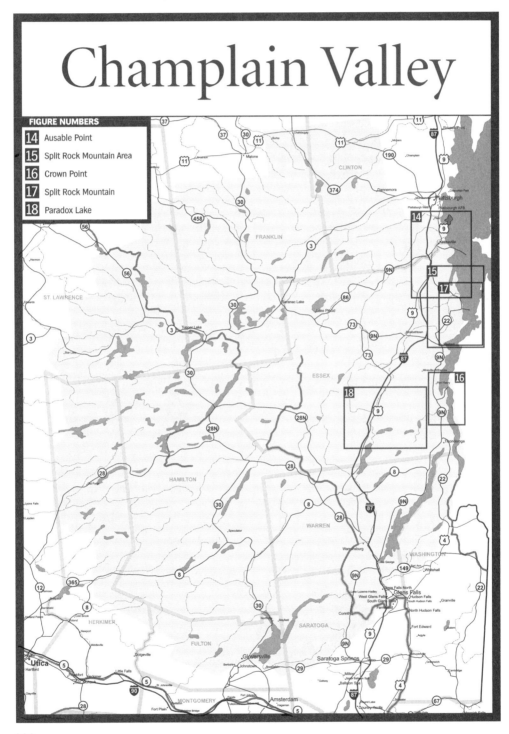

Champlain Valley

FIGURE NUMBERS

14	Ausable Point
15	Split Rock Mountain Area
16	Crown Point
17	Split Rock Mountain
18	Paradox Lake

Champlain Valley

As defined in this chapter, the Champlain Valley Region encompasses the Adirondack Park east of the Northway and north of NY 74. It includes the western shore of Lake Champlain from Ticonderoga to Valcour Island, the park's northern limit. By far, the biggest chunk of state land is the Hammond Pond Wild Forest, which lays claim to more than 40,000 acres. Poke-O-Moonshine Mountain, though it lies just west of the Northway, is included here as well, because of its great views of the lake and valley.

Lake Champlain sits between two unrelated mountain ranges, the Adirondacks and Vermont's Green Mountains. The Green Mountains, part of the Appalachians, formed about 440 million years ago when North America collided with a continent to the east in an event known as the Taconic orogeny. Although the orogeny stopped short of the Adirondack region, it created numerous block faults west of Lake

[*Above:* A view of the Champlain Valley from Coon Mountain]

Champlain. When the Adirondacks rose about 10 million years ago, large blocks of bedrock were uplifted along these faults. In one case, a ridge of billion-year-old rock runs through the valley for about 35 miles, from Ticonderoga north almost to Willsboro. Such uplifts help account for the sharp relief found in the valley.

Before the Taconic orogeny, the Adirondack region lay under a shallow sea where sediments built up to make sandstones, limestones, and dolostones. As the ocean closed, the North American plate dove under the approaching continent, creating a deep basin where shales also formed. After the Adirondacks rose about 10 million years ago, these sedimentary rocks eroded to expose the more durable metamorphic rocks beneath, but the sedimentary rocks survive in many places in the Champlain lowlands.

The Champlain Valley's most celebrated exposure of sedimentary rock is the Ausable Chasm, where the Ausable River has cut through stacks of Potsdam Sandstone, creating a narrow gorge with vertical walls up to 150 feet high. Fossil-bearing limestone can be found at Valcour Island, Willsboro Point, and Crown Point. On Isle La Motte, north of the Adirondack Park, the limestone contains fossils of one of the first coral reefs in the world—evidence that the Northeast once enjoyed a tropical climate. Elsewhere in the Adirondacks, fossils are rare.

The sedimentary rocks formed between the Cambrian and late Ordovician periods, or roughly from 530 million years ago to 440 million years ago. In contrast, the metamorphic rocks that make up the Adirondack Mountains formed more than 1 billion years ago. Despite the gap in age, they exist side by side along the lake. Within 10 miles inland, the sedimentary rocks vanish, and so the bedrock in most of the Champlain Valley covered in this chapter is metamorphic: anorthosite, gneiss, syenite, metagabbro, marble.

During the ice ages, glaciers scoured and sculpted the valley that exists today. As the last glacier retreated, about 10,000 years ago, the meltwater filled the valley to create a lake much larger than Lake Champlain. The ice had depressed the land so much that when all of it finally melted, the sea invaded the valley from the north, creating an arm of the Atlantic Ocean. Over time, the land rebounded, cutting off the sea, and the lake shrank to its current size. Beach sands can still be found at higher elevations in the valley.

At 95 feet above sea level, Lake Champlain represents the lowest elevation in the Adirondack Park. As one moves west, the terrain becomes hillier, but none of the mountains in the Champlain Valley Region reaches 3,000 feet. The climate, especially at the lower elevations, is moderate enough to support oaks and other trees usually found at more southern latitudes. For the most part, though, the trees are the same ones that grow throughout the park, such as white pine (*Pinus strobus*), hemlock (*Tsuga canadensis*), balsam fir (*Abies balsamea*), red spruce (*Picea rubens*), and the northern hardwoods.

Native Americans hunted, fished, and farmed in the valley for centuries before the arrival of Europeans. Arrowheads, pottery shards, beads, and other artifacts, some dating back 8,000 years, have been unearthed on both sides of the lake. The Indians also used the lake as a travel corridor between the St. Lawrence and the Hudson/Mohawk valleys. In 1609, Canadian Indians led Samuel de Champlain and two other Frenchmen on a canoe trip from Quebec up the St. Lawrence and Richelieu rivers to the lake.

TIMBER RATTLESNAKE
(Crotalus horridus)

For 150 years after Champlain's discovery, the French and British feuded over the lake. In 1713, the Treaty of Utrecht established Split Rock, south of Essex, as the boundary between New France and British possessions to the south. In 1734, however, the French built Fort St. Frederic, the first fort on Lake Champlain, on the peninsula at Crown Point far south of Split Rock. They built a second fort even farther south, at Ticonderoga, in 1756. The French called this fort Carillon.

The British won the struggle for New World supremacy with their victory in the French and Indian War in 1763, which gave them control of all of the Northeast and Canada. Britain built its own forts at Crown Point and Ticonderoga, both of which played a part in the Revolutionary War.

William Gilliland, an Irish soldier in the French and Indian War, founded one of the first British settlements in the Champlain Valley. After receiving a patent for 15,000 acres between Split Rock and the Boquet River, he moved there with a company of settlers in 1765. Gilliland dreamed of becoming a wealthy land baron, but he had to flee to New York City during the Revolutionary War, and his estate fell into disrepair. Eventually, he returned to the region destitute and worked as a surveyor. He died after becoming lost one winter day on Coon Mountain. Willsboro is named after this pioneer. Elizabethtown is named after his wife.

Others soon followed in Gilliland's footsteps and transformed the "howling wilderness," as he called it, into a handsome valley of farms, orchards, and charming villages. Although farms often failed elsewhere in the Adirondacks, they prospered in the Champlain Valley, thanks to the fertile soils deposited by the glacial lake and to the moderate climate. The timber and iron ore industries also flourished during the 1800s.

The many fine examples of nineteenth-century architecture in the towns along the lake attest to the success of the region's pioneers. The hamlet of Essex, founded by Gilliland, boasts one of the largest assemblages of intact pre–Civil War buildings in the country. The whole hamlet, in fact, has been put on the National Register of Historic Places.

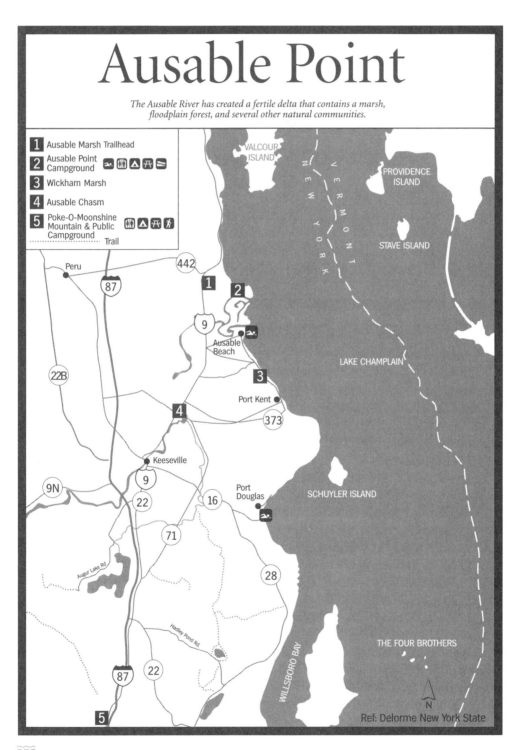

Ausable Point

*The Ausable River has created a fertile delta that contains a marsh,
floodplain forest, and several other natural communities.*

1 Ausable Marsh Trailhead
2 Ausable Point Campground
3 Wickham Marsh
4 Ausable Chasm
5 Poke-O-Moonshine Mountain & Public Campground

Trail

Peru

442

Ausable Beach

9

22B

Port Kent

373

Keeseville

9N

9

22

16

Port Douglas

71

28

Augur Lake Rd

Hadley Pond Rd

22

87

VALCOUR ISLAND

PROVIDENCE ISLAND

NEW YORK

VERMONT

STAVE ISLAND

LAKE CHAMPLAIN

SCHUYLER ISLAND

WILLSBORO BAY

THE FOUR BROTHERS

N

Ref: Delorme New York State

Although civilization is never far away in this corner of the Adirondacks, the region has its share of wild places. Old-growth trees survive along some trails in the Hammond Pond Wild Forest. Osprey fish in the marshes along Lake Champlain. Split Rock Mountain, overlooking Snake Den Harbor, is one of the last refuges in the state of the timber rattlesnake (*Crotalus horridus*). And those who climb Coon Mountain can listen to the haunting croak of the raven.

The Champlain Valley is a major flyway for migrating birds. In spring and fall, birders climb the region's hills or drive to Crown Point to watch hundreds of hawks soaring past. At other times of the year, the valley remains a bird-watcher's paradise.

For more information: State Department of Environmental Conservation, PO Box 296, Route 86, Ray Brook, NY 12977. Phone (518) 897-1200. Champlain Visitors Center, phone (518) 597-4646.

Lake Champlain

After the Great Lakes, Champlain is the sixth largest freshwater lake in the United States: 435 square miles, 120 miles long, 400 feet deep, 587 miles of shoreline, 70 islands. As impressive as that sounds, Champlain is puny by Great Lake standards: Lake Ontario, the smallest Great Lake, encompasses 7,540 square miles. By Adirondack standards, however, Champlain is indeed great: Lake George, the next biggest Adirondack lake, covers only 44 square miles.

Unlike Lake George, only part of Lake Champlain—less than a third—lies inside the Adirondack Park. For its first 35 miles or so, from Whitehall to Crown Point, the lake is so narrow that it resembles a river. North of Crown Point, the lake broadens, attaining a maximum width of 12 miles between Port Henry, New York, and Burlington, Vermont. Most of the broader part of the lake lies within Vermont. On the New York side, the park boundary ends at Valcour Island south of Plattsburgh.

In short, the Adirondack Park embraces the western shore of Lake Champlain from Whitehall to Valcour Island, about 90 miles as the crow flies. But the state owns only small pieces of the shoreline: at Ticonderoga, Putts Creek Wildlife Management Area, Crown Point, Split Rock Mountain, Wickham Marsh, Ausable Marsh, and Ausable Point. It also owns two fair-size islands, Valcour and Schuyler. With the exception of Ticonderoga, all of these places are discussed in this chapter. Ticonderoga and the lake south of Ticonderoga are discussed in the chapter on the Lake George Region (*see* page 125).

Lake Champlain can be a busy place. Several years ago, someone counted 12,425 boats in aerial photos taken over a 5-hour period one day in July. Nearly two-thirds were motorboats. About a fourth were sailboats. The rest were "other"—presumably, canoes, rowboats, and kayaks. About 14 percent of the craft were in use at the time.

So canoeists should take heed: Lake Champlain is motorboat territory. And on a windy day, the waves can reach 4 to 5 feet. Even those in small motorboats must use caution. Nonetheless, canoeists can enjoy the lake if they stay close to shore and avoid rough water.

Canoes and boats can be launched for free at state launches in Peru, Port Douglas, Port Henry, Willsboro, and Ticonderoga. Visitors can use launches at the state campgrounds at Ausable Point and Crown Point, but there is a fee for day use. Numerous marinas around the lake also offer launch facilities.

Those without boats can take one of the ferries to Vermont to enjoy the marvelous views of the Adirondacks from the water. Lake Champlain Ferries runs out of Essex, Port Kent, and Plattsburgh (phone 802-864-9804). Shorewell Ferries runs out of Ticonderoga (phone 802-897-7999).

There are several public beaches on the lake. The state beach at the Ausable Point Public Campground has a 0.25-mile of sand. Beware that the water can be quite chilly even into June.

Scuba divers say the cold water has preserved remarkably well the wrecks and relics of the French and Indian War, Revolutionary War, the War of 1812, and later periods. There is only one marked dive site on the New York side—for the *Champlain II*, a liner that ran aground in 1875—but but local dive shops can tell you where else to explore. Note that divers are forbidden to disturb wrecks or keep what they find.

Those who prefer to stay on solid ground can hike trails through marshes along the lakeshore or stroll back in time in the quaint village of Essex or marvel at the variety of birdlife at the Crown Point State Historic Site. There also are hiking possibilities just inland from the lake (*see* page 107).

For more information: State Department of Environmental Conservation, PO Box 296, Route 86, Ray Brook, NY 12977. Phone (518) 897-1200.

FISHING LAKE CHAMPLAIN

Not including Champ, the lake's legendary sea monster, Lake Champlain contains 83 species of fish, everything from tiny smelt to Atlantic salmon to huge channel catfish.

The water within the Adirondack Park can be divided into two lakes. South of Crown Point, the lake resembles a sluggish river. In these shallow waters, anglers catch walleye (*Stizostedion vitreum vitreum*), northern pike (*Esox lucius*), channel catfish (*Ictalurus punctatus*), chain pickerel (*Esox niger*), largemouth bass (*Micropterus salmoides*), smallmouth bass (*Micropterus dolomieui*), crappies, and perch.

North of Crown Point, the lake broadens and deepens. In summer, fishermen can catch cold-water species such as Atlantic salmon (*Salmo salar*), lake trout (*Salvelinus namaycush*), brown trout (*Salmo trutta*), and steelhead trout, which is a variety of rainbow trout, in the channel in the middle of the lake. The channel corresponds roughly to the New York/Vermont border. The same species are caught closer to shore during spring, fall, and winter.

The warm-water fish also can be caught in the broader lake, usually near the shore, off rocky shoals and islands, or in shallow bays.

Salmon, one of the most popular game fish, swim up the lake's streams and rivers to feed in spring, from mid-April to mid-May, and up the larger rivers to spawn in fall, from early September to mid-November. On the New York side, try fishing at these times of year around the mouths of the Ausable, Boquet, and Saranac rivers and upstream. Many anglers like to fish the Boquet below the Willsboro Fish Ladder (*see* page 99).

Other ideas on where to fish are suggested in the descriptions of specific sites on the lake.

The State of Vermont publishes an excellent booklet, the *Lake Champlain Fishing Guide*, with details on where to find fish on both sides of the lake. For a free copy, contact the Vermont Department of Fish and Wildlife, 111 West Street, Essex Junction, VT 05452; phone (802) 878-1564.

Note: Anglers need a Vermont license to fish on the Vermont side of the lake.

For more information: New York State Department of Environmental Conservation, PO Box 296, Route 86, Ray Brook, NY 12977. Phone (518) 897-1200. DEC's fishing hot line is (518) 891-5413.

▓ VALCOUR ISLAND

[Fig. 14] This charming island captures the essence of what makes Lake Champlain so special: natural beauty mixed with history. Although Valcour lies less than 5 miles from the city of Plattsburgh, it remains a wild place where wind and waves sculpt the limestone cliffs, where rare flowers bloom amid the cedars, where heron raise their young, and where deer and coyote still roam.

In 1973, the state extended the boundary of the Adirondack Park to include all of Valcour Island, so the island now represents the northern limit of the park within the Champlain Valley Region. The state, which owns all 1,100 acres of the island, maintains about 8 miles of trails, a picnic area, and 22 primitive campsites here. A nineteenth-century lighthouse on Bluff Point, on the west shore, may be visited by making an appointment with the Clinton County Historical Association. The lighthouse is on the National Register of Historic Places.

WILD LEEK (Allium tricoccum) A leafless stem grows up to 18 inches tall and holds a cluster of white, starlike flowers that bloom in midsummer.

Chazy limestone, a fossil-rich rock found in only a few places in the Champlain Valley and Canada, forms the bedrock of Valcour Island. The calcerous soils favor northern white cedar (*Thuja occidentalis*), which grows throughout the island, including in a swamp in the interior. The buds of the white cedar are one of the preferred foods of white-tailed deer (*Odocoileus virginianus*). The hardy white spruce (*Picea glauca*)—accustomed to the cold of Canada—occupies the wind-battered cliffs at the island's southern tip.

Several plants uncommon in New York can be seen on Valcour, among them ram's-head lady's slipper (*Cypripedium arietinum*) and pink lady's slipper (*Cypripedium acaule*). The island also lays claim to one of the largest rookeries for great blue heron (*Ardea herodias*) in the state. The herons often fly from the rookery, on the southern shore, to Ausable Marsh on the mainland to hunt for fish and frogs.

Valcour is about 1 mile from the state boat launch in Peru, close enough to canoe when the water is calm. There is a sandy beach and picnic area at Butterfly Bay, just north of the lighthouse. Those traveling by motorboat or sailboat will find many sheltered coves around the island suitable for mooring, such as Sloop Cove, Spoon Bay, Beauty Bay, North Bay, Bullhead Bay, and Smugglers Harbor.

The state maintains three trails on the island. The Perimeter Trail makes a 5.7-mile circuit of the island, passing numerous lookouts, coves, and beaches. From the

INDIAN CUCUMBERROOT
(*Medeola virginiana*)
This is identified by two whorls of leaves; greenish yellow flowers droop from the top whorl.

southern cliffs there is a magnificent view of the lake, the Adirondacks, and the Green Mountains. The Perimeter Trail can be picked up by walking inland after landing on the island. The 1.3-mile Royal Savage Trail cuts through the island's northern interior, and the 0.8-mile Nomad Trail cuts through the southern interior. Both trails begin and end on the Perimeter Trail. An ice storm in 1998 felled many trees and limbs on the island, so hiking off the trails may be difficult.

Camping is permitted only at the designated sites along the trails. Each site has a pit privy and picnic table. The island has no running water or electricity. There is no fee, but campers should register at the boat launch or with the island's caretaker. If the caretaker cannot be located, just set up camp, and he or she will come by.

Anglers fish the waters around Valcour's rocky shores for smallmouth bass (*Micropterus dolomieui*), northern pike (*Esox lucius*), and walleye (*Stizostedion vitreum vitreum*). Hunters visit in the fall in quest of deer. In winter, cross-country skiers ski to the island when the ice is safe.

America fought its first major naval battle off the

island, on October 11, 1776. The British had spent the summer building a fleet to attack the colonies by sailing up the lake from Canada. In a frantic race against time, the rebels built their own fleet in Whitehall to prevent or stall the invasion. That fall, the American ships hid off the western shore of Valcour Island, lying in wait for the British.

As it turns out, the Colonists were greatly outnumbered and outgunned. After a fierce battle that lasted all day, Benedict Arnold, the American commander, realized they had no hope of victory. That night, under the cover of darkness and fog, the ships slipped one by one past the British line and headed south toward the American fort at Crown Point. When day broke, the British gave chase and eventually caught up to the disabled ships. Only a few of the 15 American craft made it to Crown Point.

Although the Americans lost the battle, historians argue that the navy prevented the British from carrying out its invasion until the next year, giving the rebels time to prepare for the Battles of Saratoga. Scuba divers have located many of the relics of Arnold's fleet on the lake bottom. One of the gunboats, the *Philadelphia*, is on display at the Smithsonian Institution.

The Clinton County Historical Musuem at 48 Court Street in Plattsburgh has a diorama on the Battle of Valcour. The Lake Champlain Maritime Museum in Basin Harbor, Vermont, operates a full-scale replica of the *Philadelphia* on the lake.

The state also owns 41-acre Crab Island about 1.75 miles north of Valcour. Crab Island lies just outside the Adirondack Park.

Directions: From Plattsburgh, drive south on US 9 for 4 miles to the state boat launch in Peru. The launch has a hard-surface ramp and parking for 50 cars and trailers. It's about 1 mile to the island. Canoeists can take out at a sandy beach on Butterfly Bay north of the lighthouse or at a grassy shore on Bullhead Bay south of the lighthouse. Head inland a short ways to reach the Perimeter Trail.

Activities: Hiking, camping, picnicking, canoeing, swimming, fishing, hunting, cross-country skiing.

Facilities: Trails, picnic area, lighthouse, campsites with picnic tables and pit privies.

Dates: Open year-round.

Fees: None. Visitors to the lighthouse are asked to make a donation to the Clinton County Historical Association for its upkeep.

Closest town: Plattsburgh is about 4 miles north on US 9.

For more information: Maps of the island, showing trails and campsites, are available from the state Department of Environmental Conservation, PO Box 296, Route 86, Ray Brook, NY 12977. Phone (518) 897-1200. To visit the lighthouse, phone the Clinton County Historical Association at (518) 561-0340.

AUSABLE POINT PUBLIC CAMPGROUND

[Fig. 14(2)] Located on a spit of land at the mouth of the Ausable River, this campground boasts one of the largest state beaches in the Adirondacks: almost 0.25 mile of sand. Canoeists can launch into the river from the campground to explore the Ausable Marsh, a rich habitat for waterfowl and other birds. Nearby Dead Creek also can be explored by canoe. The campground has set aside an area near a stone jetty for windsurfing. Atlantic salmon (*Salmo salar*) can be caught in and around the Ausable when they swim upriver to feed in the spring and spawn in the fall.

Directions: From Northway Exit 35, drive east about 2.8 miles on County 442 to US 9; turn left and go about 0.3 mile to the campground entrance on the right.

Activities: Camping, picnicking, swimming, canoeing, fishing, bicycling.

Facilities: 123 campsites, sand beach with bathhouse, picnic area, playground, toilets, hot showers, car-top boat launch, windsurf area, trailer dumping station. Two campsites are accessible to the handicapped. 43 campsites have electrical hookups.

Dates: May to mid-Oct.

Fees: There is a charge for camping or day use.

Closest town: Keeseville is about 4 miles south on US 9.

For more information: Campground office, phone (518) 561-7080. For reservations, phone (800) 456-2267.

AUSABLE MARSH

[Fig. 14(1)] The Ausable River has created a fertile delta that contains a marsh, floodplain forest, and several other natural communities. The state has set aside 580 acres as a wildlife management area, constructing nest boxes for wood ducks (*Aix sponsa*) and nest platforms for osprey (*Pandion haliaetus*). Ospreys, a threatened species in New York, have bred in the marsh. Great blue heron (*Ardea herodias*) fly to the marsh from their rookery on Valcour Island, located a little north, to feed on small fish and frogs. Many other kinds of birds also frequent the marsh.

The marsh can be explored on foot or by canoe. The state has constructed a 1-mile trail that follows a man-made dike through the open marsh and a silver maple forest to the edge of the river. If canoeing, put in at the Ausable Point Public Campground (*see* page 95). The Ausable splits in two in the delta, so it's possible to travel in a loop, paddling up the north branch to the fork, down the south branch to the lake, and along the lakeshore to return to the campground. Just south of the north branch, a channel that cuts deep into the marsh is also worth exploring.

Hunting and trapping are allowed in the marsh, but no firearms may be discharged from March 1 to October 1. Swimming and camping are prohibited. Motorboats are not allowed.

Directions: From Northway Exit 35, drive east about 2.8 miles on County 442 to US 9; turn left and go about 0.3 mile to the entrance to Ausable Point Public Campground on the right, if canoeing. The campground has a canoe launch near campsite 46. If walking the marsh trail, turn right instead of left at US 9 and drive a few hundred yards to the entrance road on the left. There will be a sign.

Activities: Hiking, canoeing, bird-watching, fishing, hunting, trapping, cross-country skiing, snowshoeing.

Facilities: Hiking trail.

Dates: Open year-round.

Fees: None.

For more information: Bureau of Wildlife, State Department of Environmental Conservation, PO Box 296, Route 86, Ray Brook, NY 12977. Phone (518) 897-1291. The bureau publishes a description and map of the marsh.

Closest town: Keeseville is about 4 miles south on US 9.

WICKHAM MARSH

[Fig. 14(3)] As with nearby Ausable Marsh to the north, the state manages this marsh to improve habitat for waterfowl. The 862-acre area includes several types of natural communities, including a

FISHER
(Martes pennanti)
A boreal species, the shy fisher is an adept climber and swimmer that eats porcupines and snowshoe hares.

hardwood forest and pitch pine–oak forest. Among the birds that frequent the area are wood ducks (*Aix sponsa*), black ducks (*Anas rubripes*), mallards (*Anas platyrhynchos*), ruffed grouse (*Bonasa umbellus*), and wild turkeys (*Meleagris galloparo*).

The main trail, following red blazes, connects the marsh's two entrances. It goes past a beaver dam and a cedar plantation. Within the marsh there are several unmarked trails that follow old dirt roads. The marsh also can be explored by canoe. Hunting and trapping are allowed in season. Swimming and camping are prohibited. Motorboats also are prohibited.

Directions: From Keeseville, drive north on US 9 about 1.25 miles to County 373 on the right, just past Ausable Chasm. Drive about 1.4 miles to the first entrance, near the junction of County 17. To reach the second entrance, which is closer to the marshland, continue on County 373 to Port Kent and then turn left on Lake Street. Continue north until reaching the entrance gate. A canoe can be put into the marsh from the road near the gate. There are signs at both entrances.

Activities: Hiking, canoeing, bird-watching, fishing, hunting, trapping, cross-country skiiing, snowshoeing.

Facilities: Hiking trails.

Dates: Open year-round.

Fees: None.

Closest town: Keeseville is about 2 miles south on US 9.

For more information: Bureau of Wildlife, State Department of Environmental Conservation, PO Box 296, Route 86, Ray Brook, NY 12977. Phone (518) 897-1291. The bureau publishes a description and map of the marsh.

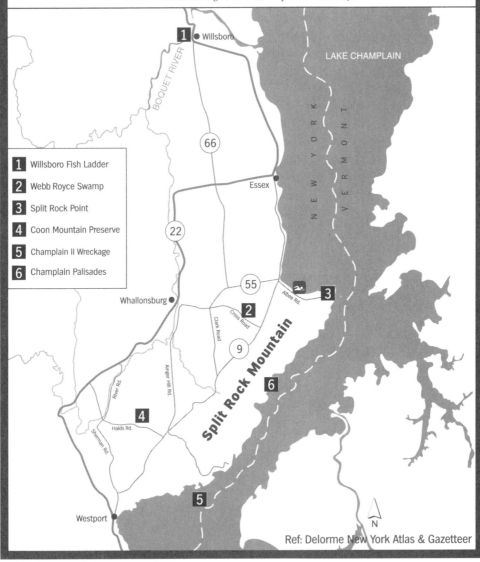

Split Rock Mountain Area

Known as the Champlain Palisades, the sheer cliffs on this wild shoreline must be counted among the lake's most spectacular scenery.

1 Willsboro

LAKE CHAMPLAIN

BOQUET RIVER

66

1 Willsboro Fish Ladder

2 Webb Royce Swamp

3 Split Rock Point

4 Coon Mountain Preserve

5 Champlain II Wreckage

6 Champlain Palisades

Essex

NEW YORK

VERMONT

22

55

Albee Rd.

3

Whallonsburg

2

Cross Road

Clark Road

9

Split Rock Mountain

Ainger Hill Rd.

6

River Rd.

4

Halds Rd.

Sherman Rd.

5

Westport

N

Ref: Delorme New York Atlas & Gazetteer

SCHUYLER ISLAND

[Fig. 14] The state owns this 178-acre island southeast of Port Kent. Schuyler has no official trails, but campsites can be found. The island gets nowhere near as much use as Valcour Island to the north. Schuyler ranks behind Valcour in its variety of birdlife, though common waterfowl such as black ducks (*Anas rubripes*) and mallards (*Anas platyrhynchos*) often can be seen here.

Anglers enjoy some success fishing for lake trout (*Salvelinus namaycush*), salmon (*Salmo salar*), and smallmouth bass (*Micropterus dolomieui*) in the vicinity of the island.

Schuyler Island is 0.5 mile from Trembleau Point, the nearest shoreline. From the nearest boat launch, in Port Douglas, the island is about 2 miles away by direct route. If taking a canoe and hugging the shore, the distance would be quite a bit longer.

Benedict Arnold stopped at Schuyler Island to mend his leaky ships and try to regroup after the Battle of Valcour Island in October 1776.

Directions: From Keeseville, take County 16 (Port Douglas Road) southeast about 3 miles to Port Douglas. There is parking for 20 cars and trailers at the hard-surface ramp.

Activities: Birdwatching, fishing.

Facilities: None.

Dates: Open year-round.

Fees: None.

Closest town: Keeseville is about 3 miles northeast on County 16 from the boat launch.

For more information: State Department of Environmental Conservation, PO Box 296, Route 86, Ray Brook, NY 12977. Phone (518) 897-1200.

WILLSBORO FISH LADDER

[Fig. 15(1), Fig. 17(1)] The state built a fish ladder on the Boquet River in 1982 to enable Atlantic salmon (*Salmo salar*) to swim to spawning grounds upstream of the dam in Willsboro. After swimming up two inclined channels, the salmon leap over an 18-inch barrier and then return to the river above the dam. The barrier prevents lamprey eels, which prey on salmon, from entering the spawning grounds.

People can watch the salmon from an observation deck above the fish ladder or through a window in one of the walls. The salmon make their spawning run in the fall, usually from early September to mid-November. The busiest time is from early October to early November. Salmon also run up the Boquet and other rivers in the spring to feed, usually from mid-April to mid-May. In spring, however, they do not advance past the dam.

Anglers fish for the salmon during both runs in the pools below the dam or in a flat-water stretch farther downstream. In fall, salmon can also be caught upstream of the NY 22 bridge in Willsboro. It is illegal to fish between the bridge and a marked boundary below the dam.

Those who want to fish the 2-mile flat-water stretch, which ends at Lake Champlain, can launch a canoe or small boat on School Street just east of the fish ladder.

Directions: From the NY 22 bridge in the hamlet of Willsboro, drive east on School Street about 0.1 mile to the fish ladder on the left. Fishermen can approach the river from School Street or from Mill Street on the opposite side of the river. On both streets, there are parking areas after the pavement ends.

Activities: Fishing, watching fish, canoeing.

Facilities: Fish ladder, car-top boat launch.

Dates: Salmon use the fish ladder in the fall.

Fees: None.

Closest town: Willsboro.

For more information: State Department of Environmental Conservation, PO Box 296, Route 86, Ray Brook, NY 12977. Phone (518) 897-1200. Ask for the leaflet *Landlocked Salmon Fishing on New York's Bouquet, Saranac, and Ausable Rivers.* DEC's fishing hotline is (518) 891-5413.

WILLSBORO BAY

[Fig. 14] Geologists believe Willsboro Bay lies in a graben created when a block of the earth's crust dropped between two faults. Most of the 4-mile-long Willsboro Point east of the bay is made of sedimentary dolostones and limestones formed roughly 440 to 480 million years ago, during the Ordovician Period, whereas the mainland to the west is metamorphic rock formed more than 1 billion years ago.

Limestone quarried at Lignonier Point, on the east side of Willsboro Point, was used in the construction of the state capitol in Albany and the Brooklyn Bridge.

With rugged hills as a backdrop, Willsboro Bay is a scenic corner of the lake to do a little fishing or canoeing. The deeper waters in the middle of the bay hold lake trout (*Salvelinus namaycush*). Anglers also have had success catching northern pike (*Esox lucius*), chain pickerel (*Esox niger*), largemouth bass (*Micropterus salmoides*), and yellow perch (*Perca flavescens*). The bay is a popular spot for ice fishing.

Directions: From NY 22 in the hamlet of Willsboro, drive north on Willsboro Point Road about 2.5 miles to Boat Launch Road and turn left.

Activities: Boating, fishing.

Facilities: Hard-surface boat ramp with pump-out facility. Parking for 100 cars and trailers.

Dates: Open year-round.

Fees: None.

Closest town: The hamlet of Willsboro is about 2.5 miles south.

For more information: State Department of Environmental Conservation, PO Box 296, Route 86, Ray Brook, NY 12977. Phone (518) 897-1200.

FOUR BROTHERS ISLANDS

[Fig. 14] The Adirondack Nature Conservancy owns four small islands, totaling 17 acres, that are nesting grounds for about 15,000 pairs of colonial water birds. The conservancy does not allow visitors to land on the islands, located about 1.5 miles east of Willsboro Point, but boaters can watch the birds from the water.

Double-crested cormorants (*Phalacrocorax auritus*) dwell on the islands from May to September. Other birds include cattle egret (*Bubulcus ibis*), black-crowned night-heron (*Nycticorax nycticorax*), great blue heron (*Ardea herodias*), herring gull (*Larus argentatus*), and great black-backed gull (*Larus marinus*). The most abundant species is the ring-billed gull (*Larus delawarensis*).

Anglers fishing off the islands have had luck catching walleye (*Stizostedion vitreum vitreum*), smallmouth bass (*Micropterus dolomieui*), and yellow perch (*Perca flavescens*).

OSPREY
(Pandion haliaetus)
Also known as the fish hawk, the osprey hovers over water before plunging in feetfirst to grasp the fish with its talons.

Directions: The closest state boat launch is on the west shore of Willsboro Point. It's roughly a 4-mile journey from either to Four Brothers. For directions to Willsboro Point, see Willsboro Bay, page 100.

Activities: Bird-watching, fishing.

Facilities: None.

Dates: The islands are not open to public.

Fees: None

Closest town: Willsboro.

For more information: Adirondack Nature Conservancy/Adironodack Land Trust, Box 65, Keene Valley, NY 12943. Phone (518) 576-2082.

🏛 HAMLET OF ESSEX

[Fig. 15] William Gilliland founded this lakeside village in 1765. Although Gilliland lost his fortune in the Revolutionary War, Essex survived and prospered as an early manufacturing center and port. The well-to-do built many fine homes in Georgian, Federal, and Greek Revival styles. Essex's heyday ended when the railroad passed it by. The population shrank, and so did capital. Rather than build new homes, the residents preserved the existing ones.

Today, Essex lays claim to one of the largest intact assemblages of pre–Civil War architecture in the nation. The entire hamlet is on the National Register of Historic Places. Essex is so quaint and free of modern-day commercialism that it almost

COMMON JUNIPER

(Juniperus communis)

Also known as dwarf juniper, the common juniper produces berries that are used as flavoring in gin.

seems like a museum village.

The Essex Community Heritage Organization publishes a leaflet describing a walking tour that passes 28 buildings, dating back to the 1780s. It also describes a driving tour of the neighboring countryside, where there are more specimens of nineteenth-century architecture. The leaflet can be obtained from the organization's office on Station Road, just up from Main Street, or from businesses in town.

Visitors might want to take a ride on the ferry that shuttles between Essex and Charlotte, Vermont, several times each day. The voyage affords a splendid view of the Adirondacks from the lake.

Directions: The tour begins at the corner of NY 22 and Main Street.

Activities: Walking tour.

Facilities: Town park.

Dates: Open year-round.

Fees: None.

For more information: Essex Community Heritage Organization, PO Box 250, Station Road, Essex, NY 12936. Phone (518) 963-7088. Ask for the leaflet titled *Essex: An Architectural Guide* (include a stamp for mailing). Also, Lake Champlain Transportation Co., King Street Dock, Burlington, VT 05401; phone (802) 864-9804.

CHAMPLAIN PALISADES/SPLIT ROCK POINT

Split Rock Mountain rises 900 feet above the water in The Narrows between Westport and Essex. Known as the Champlain Palisades [Fig. 15(6), Fig. 17(5)], the sheer cliffs on this wild shoreline must be counted among the lake's most spectacular scenery.

The Palisades formed when a block of crust—largely anorthosite and metagabbro—uplifted between two faults when the Adirondacks were created. The bedrock beneath Whallon Bay, adjacent to Split Rock Mountain, is much younger limestone. The name "Split Rock" refers to a big hunk of rock separated from the mainland by a narrow channel at the mountain's northern end.

Canoeists can reach The Narrows from Northwest Bay in the village of Westport. It's about an 8-mile trip to Split Rock, but paddlers can enjoy the Palisades without going that far. Experienced canoeists may want to round Split Rock Point [Fig. 15(3), Fig. 17(2)], and continue to Essex. To reach the point quicker, put in at the beach on Whallon Bay.

Although a paddle to The Narrows is one of the most scenic canoe trips on the lake, it holds some dangers. Not only is the water deep, but the rocky shore offers few places to land in an emergency. Do not attempt the journey unless the water is calm.

Fishermen catch lake trout (*Salvelinus namaycush*) in the deep channel of The Narrows and smallmouth bass (*Micropterus dolomieui*) in the vicinity of Split Rock Point. Atlantic salmon (*Salmo salar*) can be caught in the deeper parts of Northwest Bay. In winter, the bay is popular among ice fishermen.

Split Rock Mountain also can be explored on foot (*see* Split Rock Mountain, page 109).

Directions: The state boat launch is located on North Main Street in Westport. To get to the beach on Whallon Bay, drive south on Lake Shore Road about 2.5 miles from the hamlet of Essex and turn left on Albee Road. The beach is near the turn.

Activities: Boating, canoeing, fishing.

Facilities: Hard-surface boat ramp with parking for 35 cars and trailers.

Dates: Seasonal.

Fees: None.

CHAMPLAIN II WRECKAGE

[Fig. 15(5)] The steamer *Champlain II* carried passengers up and down the lake until it ran aground in the Narrows between Rock Harbor and Barn Rock Harbor on the night of July 16, 1875. An investigation revealed that the pilot had been taking morphine for gout. The owners salvaged much of the ship, but scuba divers can see the hull, engine mounts, and other features. This is the only marked diving site on the New York side of Lake Champlain. Divers are not allowed to disturb the wreck or remove artifacts.

Directions: Divers must register before diving on the wreck. To register, contact the Vermont Division for Historic Preservation. Look for a yellow buoy on the west side of Narrows at 44°12.36N, 73°22.58W. This is north of Westport, NY, and across from Basin Harbor, VT.

For more information: The booklet *Dive Historic Lake Champlain* describes the *Champlain II* dive site as well as six sites in Vermont. For a copy, contact the Vermont Division for Historic Preservation, National Life Building, Drawer 20, Montpelier, VT 05620-0501; phone (802) 828-3051. Copies also are available at dive shops.

BULWAGGA BAY

[Fig. 16] The large, shallow, grassy bay west of the Crown Point peninsula promises good fishing for largemouth bass (*Micropterus salmoides*), chain pickerel (*Esox niger*), northern pike (*Esox lucius*), yellow perch (*Perca flavescens*), and crappies. In winter, ice fishermen catch yellow and white perch and smelt. The bay can be reached by canoe from state boat launches in Port Henry and the Crown Point Public Campground.

A floodplain forest on the west side of the bay contains two trees rarely found in the Adirondacks, swamp white oak (*Quercus bicolor*) and black ash (*Fraxinus nigra*). It is on private land.

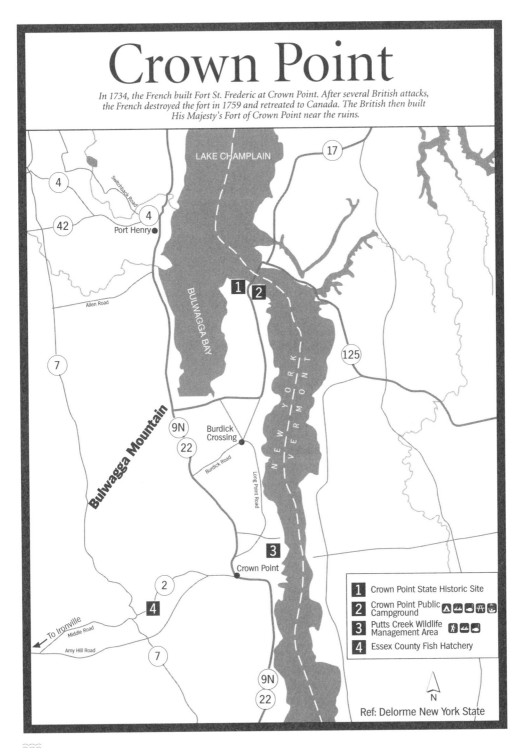

Crown Point

In 1734, the French built Fort St. Frederic at Crown Point. After several British attacks, the French destroyed the fort in 1759 and retreated to Canada. The British then built His Majesty's Fort of Crown Point near the ruins.

LAKE CHAMPLAIN

17

4

Switchback Road

4

42

Port Henry

1 2

Alien Road

BULWAGGA BAY

7

125

NEW YORK — VERMONT

Bulwagga Mountain

9N

22

Burdick Crossing

Burdick Road

Long Point Road

3

Crown Point

2

4

To Ironville

Middle Road

Amy Hill Road

7

9N

22

1 Crown Point State Historic Site

2 Crown Point Public Campground

3 Putts Creek Wildlife Management Area

4 Essex County Fish Hatchery

N

Ref: Delorme New York State

Directions: The Port Henry boat launch is located in the village off NY 9N. For the Crown Point launch, see directions to Crown Point Public Campground (*see* page 106).

Activities: Fishing, canoeing, boating.

Facilities: None.

Fees: None.

CROWN POINT STATE HISTORIC SITE

[Fig. 16(1)] Crown Point juts out between Bulwagga Bay on the west and the narrow stretch of Lake Champlain on the east. Looking north, one has a commanding view of a broad part of the lake, a glimmering expanse of water with hills rising on either side. It's easy to see why the French and British built forts here during their struggle for supremacy in the New World.

But if most people know Crown Point for its ruins, birders know it as one of the most strategic spots in the Champlain Valley to watch the annual migrations of hawks. In spring, thousands of hawks—red-shouldered (*Buteo lineatus*), red-tailed (*Buteo jamaicensis*), and broad-winged (*Buteo platypterus*), among other species— soar overhead on their way north from winter homes. Later in the spring, various passerine birds travel the same route. The birds also can be seen in the fall on their way back south.

At other times of year, Crown Point remains a fantastic place for birding. Swallows, flycatchers, sparrows, and warblers flit back and forth over the grounds. Osprey (*Pandion haliaetus*), kestrel (*Falco sparverius*), killdeer (*Charadrinus*), and turkey vulture (*Cathartes aura*) also can be observed. Peregrine falcons (*Falco peregrinus*) nested beneath the Champlain Bridge one recent spring. All told, about 175 species have been observed at Crown Point. So keep your eyes and ears open while strolling among the stone ruins.

In 1734, the French built Fort St. Frederic at Crown Point even though Britain claimed title to the land under the Treaty of Utrecht. After several British attacks, the French destroyed the fort in 1759 and retreated to Canada. The British then built His Majesty's Fort of Crown Point near the ruins. In 1775, a band of patriots took over the fort without bloodshed, but the Americans abandoned it to the British the next year.

Crown Point's history is set forth in exhibits at the visitor center and signs on the interpretative trail. Inside the earthen ramparts of the British fort, look for the old graffiti etched into the limestone bedrock—written testimony to the enduring popularity of these ruins. Look also for the fox holes in the ramparts: they are the burrows of the fort's latest occupants, red fox (*Vulpus fulva*).

Directions: From Ticonderoga, drive north on NY 9N about 10 miles to NY 903; turn right and go about 4 miles to the entrance on the left.

Activities: Exploring ruins, picnicking, bird-watching, cross-country skiing.

Facilities: Visitor center, interpretative trails, picnic pavilion.

Dates: Mid-May through Oct. The grounds are accessible year-round.

Fees: None.

Closest town: Port Henry is about 8 miles away by road.

For more information: Crown Point State Historic Site, R.D. 1, Box 219, Crown Point, NY 12928. Phone (518) 597-4666. Ask for the leaflet on Crown Point's history and the site's bird list.

CROWN POINT PUBLIC CAMPGROUND

[Fig. 16(2)] The campground is located across the road from the Crown Point State Historic Site, just south of the Champlain Bridge leading to Vermont. A steamboat pier built at the campground in 1929 is a popular place to fish for largemouth bass (*Micropterus salmoides*), smallmouth bass (*Micropterus dolomieui*), northern pike (*Esox lucius*), and panfish. The bridge abutments also are good places to fish.

Boats and canoes can be launched at the campground. Canoeists might want to explore the riverlike stretch of lake south of Crown Point or Bulwagga Bay west of the point. Both places offer good fishing for warm-water species.

Standing near the pier, the Champlain Memorial Lighthouse commemorates Samuel de Champlain's discovery of the lake in 1609. A small earthworks built by Colonial soldiers retreating from Quebec in 1776 and the ruins of several redoubts also can be found at the campground.

Directions: From Ticonderoga, drive north on NY 9N about 10 miles to NY 903; turn right and go about 4 miles to the entrance on the left.

Activities: Camping, picnicking, boating, canoeing, fishing.

Facilities: 66 campsites, picnic area, boat ramp, hot showers, trailer dump station. Campsites are accessible to handicapped.

Dates: Apr. to mid-Oct.

Fees: There is a charge for camping or day use.

Closest town: Port Henry is about 2 miles by water and 8 miles by road.

For more information: Campground office, phone (518) 597-3603. For reservations, phone (800) 456-2267.

PUTTS CREEK WILDLIFE MANAGEMENT AREA

[Fig. 16(3)] The state owns about 113 acres of marsh and woodland near the mouth of Putnam Creek where visitors can see a variety of waterfowl and songbirds. The Department of Environmental Conservation has erected nest boxes in the marsh for wood ducks (*Aix sponsa*). Other birds that visit the area include the rare least bittern (*Ixobrychus exilis*), Virginia rail (*Rallus limicola*), northern oriole (*Icterus galbula*), red-eyed vireo (*Vireo olivaceus*), and catbird (*Dumetella carolinensis*).

A trail leads to three scenic views of the marsh. Visitors may be able to see muskrat (*Ondatra zibethicus*), beaver (*Castor canadensis*), and mink (*Mustela vison*). The waters are home to northern pike, bass, bullheads, and panfish. In spring and fall, steelhead trout run up Putnam Creek from Lake Champlain. The marsh can be reached by canoe from the lake. Hunting and trapping are allowed in season. Swimming and camping are prohibited.

Directions: From Ticonderoga, drive north on NY 9N/22. After passing through the hamlet of Crown Point, turn right on Lake Road; go about 0.5 mile to Russell Street; turn right and go about 300 yards. Park on the right side of the road. Enter the state land through a 30-foot right-of-way, which is marked only by two yellow iron pipes. If you drive over the railroad tracks, you've gone too far. If coming by canoe, follow the directions to Crown Point Public Campground (*see* page 106).

Activities: Hiking, canoeing, bird-watching, fishing, hunting, trapping, cross-country skiing, snowshoeing.

Facilities: A hiking trail (an easy 0.5-mile loop).

Dates: Open year-round.

Fees: None.

For more information: Bureau of Wildlife, State Department of Environmental Conservation, PO Box 296, Route 86, Ray Brook, NY 12977. Phone (518) 897-1291.

Closest town: The hamlet of Crown Point is about 1 mile south.

Hiking the Champlain Valley

The five hikes described below enable visitors to explore the territory just inland from Lake Champlain on lands owned by the state or Adirondack Nature Conservancy. Three of the hikes end on summits with great views of the lake, the valley, and the High Peaks. These peaks are good places to watch the migration of hawks in spring and fall. The Split Rock Mountain hike ends at a cliff overlooking the lake. The last leads to one of the region's premier bird-watching spots.

POKE-O-MOONSHINE MOUNTAIN

[Fig. 14(5)] Travelers unfamiliar with the art of rock climbing may do a double-take while driving past Poke-O-Moonshine on the Northway or US 9 on a summer's day: Is that speck of color halfway up that vertical cliff really a person? Yes, it is. For Poke-O-Moonshine is a rock climber's paradise. Don Mellor notes in *Climbing in the Adirondacks:* "Its steep walls, clean cracks, and abundant natural lines make it a crag to rival any in the East." So far, climbers have identified more than 50 routes up its various precipices, including some of the hardest the Adirondacks have to offer.

The cliffs also attract ravens (*Corvus corax*) and peregrine falcons (*Falco peregrinus*), which nest on its high ledges. Poke-O rises nearly 1,000 feet above the surrounding terrain, a giant mass of granitic gneiss shot through with sills and dikes of diabase, gabbro, and other rock that weathered faster than the gneiss. Many of the rock-climbing routes follow these eroded cracks.

For hikers, there is a trail that leads to a fire tower on the summit. The tower is

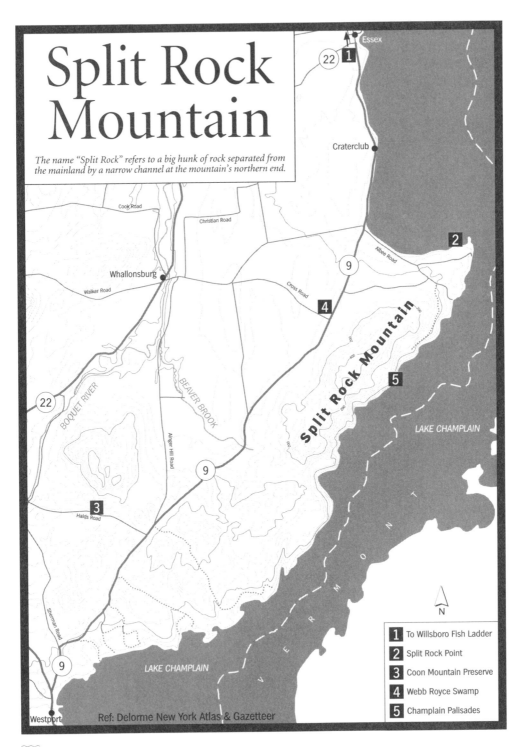

Split Rock Mountain

The name "Split Rock" refers to a big hunk of rock separated from the mainland by a narrow channel at the mountain's northern end.

Essex

Craterclub

Cook Road

Christian Road

Albee Road

Whallonsburg

Walker Road

Cross Road

Split Rock Mountain

BOQUET RIVER

BEAVER BROOK

Anger Hill Road

LAKE CHAMPLAIN

V E R M O N T

Halds Road

Sherman Road

LAKE CHAMPLAIN

Westport

Ref: Delorme New York Atlas & Gazetteer

N

1 To Willsboro Fish Ladder
2 Split Rock Point
3 Coon Mountain Preserve
4 Webb Royce Swamp
5 Champlain Palisades

not in great shape, but there are plans to restore it. In any case, you do not need to go up it to enjoy the wonderful views of the High Peaks on one side and Lake Champlain on the other. Whiteface Mountain stands out directly west. The trail climbs steeply through a largely hardwood forest, passing numerous boulders and rock walls, to the stone chimney and foundations of a vanished ranger cabin. A path to the left goes to a lean-to. From the foundations, the trail leads to an open ledge, passing a stand of red pines (*Pinus rubens*), before beginning the final ascent.

Hikers may see an inordinate amount of fallen trees and branches in the woods—the aftermath of an ice storm that hit the northern Adirondacks in 1998. In spring, many wildflowers adorn the trail, among them red trillium (*Trillium erectum*), Dutchman's breeches (*Dicentra cucullaria*), blue cohosh (*Caulophyllum thalictroides*), Carolina spring beauty (*Claytonia caroliniana*), and wild oats (*Uvularia sessilfolia*).

Directions: From Northway Exit 33, drive 3.1 miles south on US 9 to the state campground on the right. If coming from the south, the campground is about 15 miles north of the hamlet of Elizabethtown. The trail begins near the highway on the south side of the campground.

Trail: 1.2 miles to summit.

Elevation: 900 feet to 2,180 feet.

Degree of difficulty: Moderate.

Surface and blaze: Natural forest floor. Red blazes.

Closest town: Keeseville is about 6 miles north on US 9.

POKE-O-MOONSHINE PUBLIC CAMPGROUND

The campground lies along US 9 at the base of Poke-O-Moonshine Mountain. It's rather spartan—there's not much to do besides climb the mountain—but its location makes it popular among rock climbers. Take note of the enormous boulder, about 25 feet high, resting on the ground not far from the entrance.

Directions: See Poke-O-Moonshine Mountain, page 107.

Activities: Hiking, rock climbing, picnicking.

Facilities: 25 sites for trailers and tents. Showers.

Dates: Mid-May to early Sept.

Fees: There is a fee for camping and day use.

Closest town: Keeseville is 6 miles north on US 9.

For more information: Campground office, phone (518) 834-9045. For reservations, phone (800) 456-2267.

SPLIT ROCK MOUNTAIN

[Fig. 17] The state owns about 3,000 acres of Split Rock Mountain, including 4.3 miles of shoreline where the Champlain Palisades rise dramatically out of the water. This is the longest stretch of undeveloped shore on the New York side.

The Department of Environmental Conservation is developing a plan for Split Rock Mountain, but in the meantime, hikers can explore the tract along old logging roads. An ice storm felled countless trees and limbs in the area in 1998, so bush-whacking will not be easy.

The DEC has designated one of the roads a snowmobile trail. The trail ends at a cobble beach on Louis Clearing Bay, giving ice fishermen access to the lake. Hikers also can take this trail to the shore or veer off to a fabulous lookout from cliffs about 400 feet above Snake Den Harbor.

From the parking lot, follow the logging road past a creek and hemlock trees (*Tsuga canadensis*) on the right. Continue straight at junctions with a road on the right at 0.3 mile and with a road on the left a short distance ahead. The road soon passes old stone walls hidden in the woods and later swings left. Go straight until the road starts a steep descent to the shore, then look for a path leading to the right. Take this 0.1 mile to the lookout. The shore is only 0.3 mile from the turn, so if hikers are unsure whether or not they are at the correct turn, they can walk to the shore first, or at least continue far enough to see the water.

The cliffs look straight down at Snake Den Harbor and southeast across the lake to Vermont farmland and the Green Mountains beyond. Serviceberry trees and junipers cling to the rocky ledges. In spring, look for blooms of Dutchman's breeches (*Dicentra cucullaria*).

Split Rock Mountain is thought to be the northernmost habitat of the timber rattlesnake (*Crotalus horridus*) in the East, but the snakes are rarely seen.

Directions: From Northway Exit 31, drive east on NY 9N for about 4.3 miles to NY 22 in Westport; turn left and go about 0.5 mile to Lake Shore Drive; turn right and go 4.1 miles to a parking lot on the right.

Trail: About 1.6 miles to cliffs.

Elevation: 310 feet to 420 feet at cliffs above Snake Den Harbor.

Degree of difficulty: Easy.

Surface: Old tote road.

For more information: State Department of Environmental Conservation, PO Box 296, Route 86, Ray Brook, NY 12977. Phone (518) 897-1200.

WEBB ROYCE SWAMP

[Fig. 17(4)] In 1994, the state acquired about 305 acres of prime bird land across the road from Split Rock Mountain. So many species frequent the Webb Royce Swamp and its environs that birders call this locale "the magic triangle," a reference to the three roads that border it. No official trails cross the state land, but visitors can walk down an informal path to the cattails on the edge of a marsh. It's an easy hike of approximately 0.5 mile.

Among the birds that can be seen are osprey (*Pandion haliaetus*), blue-winged teal (*Anas discors*), Virginia rail (*Rallus limicola*), great egret (*Casmerodius albus*), black-crowned night-heron (*Nycticorax nycticorax*), great blue heron (*Ardea herodias*), pintail (*Anas acuta*), black duck (*Anas rubripes*), mallard (*Anas platyrhynchos*),

Canada goose (*Branta canadensis*), and great horned owl (*Bubo virginianus*).

The Webb Royce land contains a variety of wetland communites, including a deciduous swamp of silver maple (*Acer saccharinum*) and swamp white oak (*Quercus bicolor*). The latter species is rare in the Adirondacks. The wetlands are surrounded by cornfields and hayfields.

Directions: From Northway Exit 31, drive east on NY 9N for 4.3 miles to NY 22 in Westport; turn left and go about 0.5 mile to Lake Shore Drive; turn right and go about 5.1 miles to Cross Road; turn left and go approximately 0.5 mile to an unmarked path on the right.

Activities: Birdwatching.

Facilities: None.

Dates: Open year-round.

Fees: None

Closest town: Westport is about 5 miles west on Lake Shore Drive.

For more information: State Department of Environmental Conservation, PO Box 296, Route 86, Ray Brook, NY 12977. Phone (518) 897-1200.

COON MOUNTAIN PRESERVE

[Fig. 15(4), Fig. 17(3)] Coon Mountain is a monadnock, or solitary mountain, of anorthosite rising from the valley floor a few miles from Lake Champlain. The Adirondack Nature Conservancy and Adirondack Land Trust, owners of the 246-acre preserve, have laid out an interesting trail that leads to a summit overlooking the Champlain Valley and the lake. It's a good place to watch for migrating hawks in spring and fall.

The trail begins by following an old logging road a short ways, passing through a stand of hemlock (*Tsuga canadensis*), and then climbs through a talus-filled ravine beneath sheer cliffs. Porcupines live among the jumbled rocks. While ascending the ravine, turn back for a glimpse of the lake. The trail turns left at the end of the ravine and soon reaches a ridge that follows a natural stone wall covered with peeling rock lichen.

From the summit, hikers can see the High Peaks to the west and Vermont's Green Mountains to the east, but just as intriguing are the smaller summits, such as Raven Hill and Mount Discovery, that stand out on the plain like humps on a camel. Listen for the croaking of ravens (*Covus corax*) that nest on the cliffs.

Many wildflowers grow along the trail, among them blue cohosh (*Caulophyllum thalictroides*), red trillium (*Trillium erectum*), Dutchman's breeches (*Dicentra cucullaria*), jewelweed (*Impatiens capenis*), and Herb Robert (*Granium robertianum*). Thanks to the valley's mild climate, southern trees such as red oak (*Quercus rubra*), white oak (*Quercus alba*), and shagbark hickory (*Corya ovata*) flourish here along with the more typical Adirondack hardwoods. Dwarf juniper (*Juniperus communis*) grows on the summit.

A leaflet available at the trailhead points out that William Gilliland, one of the valley's pioneers, died on Coon Mountain in the winter of 1796 after becoming lost on a hike.

Directions: From Northway Exit 31, drive east on NY 9N for about 4.3 miles to NY 22 in Westport; turn left and go about 0.5 mile to Lakeshore Drive; turn right and go 2.6 miles to Halds Road; turn left and go 0.9 mile to a parking lot on the right, where the trail begins.

Trail: About 1 mile to summit.

Elevation: About 400 feet to about 980 feet.

Degree of difficulty: Easy to moderate.

Surface and blaze: Natural forest floor, talus. Red blazes.

For more information: Adirondack Nature Conservancy and Adirondack Land Trust, Box 65, Keene Valley, NY 12943. Phone (518) 576-2082.

BELFRY MOUNTAIN

[Fig. 6(30)] No hike in the Adirondacks offers such a magnificent panorama for such little effort. A short gravel road ends at a fire tower from which hikers can look out at the High Peaks, Champlain Valley, and Green Mountains. In spring and fall, migrating hawks can be seen passing through the valley. Even without the tower, the views are superb from the grassy summit. Serviceberry trees and several kinds of wildflowers, such as wild columbine (*Aquilegia canadensis*) and early saxifrage (*Saxifraga virginiensis*), bloom on the summit in spring.

Directions: From Northway Exit 30, go about a hundred yards south on US 9 and turn left onto County 6; go east for 8.2 miles to a four-way stop near Roe Pond; turn left onto County 70 and go uphill for 0.6 mile. Park on the side of the road opposite a large yellow gate. The trail begins on the other side of the gate. From Port Henry, take County 4 west to Moriah Center, pick up County 70 there and head north.

Trail: 0.4 mile.

Elevation: 1,700 feet to 1,820 feet.

Degree of difficulty: Easy.

Surface and blaze: Gravel road. Red blazes.

Ausable Chasm

[Fig. 14(4)] The Ausable Chasm has been a tourist attraction since 1870, but it intrigued European settlers long before then. William Gilliland visited the chasm in 1765 and described it as "a most curious canal; this is prodigous rock." Five years earlier, Maj. John Howe explored the chasm on ropes.

The Ausable River carved the chasm after the last ice age, cutting through layers of sandstone to create a narrow gorge with walls up to 150 feet high. The sandstone formed more than 500 million years ago in the Cambrian Period when the Potsdam Sea covered the Adirondack region. Mud cracks and ripple marks can be observed in the stone. Patrons can walk along a trail that follows the rim of the 1.5-mile chasm or ride a raft, tube, or kayak down the river. There also are guided boat tours. The company that owns the chasm also runs a campground across the road.

EASTERN CHIPMUNK
(Tamias striatus)
Chipmunks live in underground burrows up to 12 feet long.

Good views can be had for free from the US 9 bridge spanning the chasm. There is a parking lot on the west side of the bridge.

Directions: From Northway Exit 34 near Keeseville, drive east on NY 9 for 1.5 miles to US 9; turn left and go 1.5 miles to the chasm.

Activities: Hiking, picnicking, rafting, tubing, kayaking.
Facilities: Trails, picnic area, playground, gift shop, restaurant.
Dates: Mid-May to early Oct.
Fees: There is a charge for admission.
For more information: Ausable Chasm, phone (800) 537-1211.

Essex County Fish Hatchery

[Fig. 16(4)] Essex County raises rainbow trout (*Oncorhynchus mykiss*), brook trout (*Salvelinus fontinalis*), and brown trout (*Salmo trutta*) in a hatchery along Putnam Creek in the town of Crown Point. The hatchery releases about 50,000 trout each year into the county's rivers, ponds, and lakes. The fish can be seen in concrete ponds and runways at the hatchery.

Directions: From Northway Exit 28, drive east on NY 74 about 12 miles to Corduroy Road, where there is a sign for the hatchery; turn left and drive about 4.8 miles to a fork; bear left and continue another 3 miles to the hamlet of Crown Point Center and look for the hatchery's entrance road on the right. If coming from Port Henry or Ticonderoga, take NY 9N to the four-way intersection in the hamlet of Crown Point, where there is a sign for the hatchery, and drive west about 2 miles to Crown Point Center. The hatchery road will be on the left.

Activities: Looking at fish.
Facilities: Concrete fish ponds and runways.
Dates: Open year-round.
Fees: There is a charge for admission.

Closest town: The hamlet of Crown Point is about 2 miles east.

For more information: Essex County Fisheries Department, PO Box 501, Crown Point, NY 12928. Phone (518) 597-3844.

Ironville

[Fig. 18(4)] In 1828, Allen Penfield opened an iron mine in the hills in the town of Crown Point and made enough money to build a handsome Federal-style home that today houses the Penfield Homestead Musuem. Penfield's home and several other nineteenth-century buildings at this country crossroads constitute the Ironville Historic District, which is on the National Register of Historic Places.

Penfield's mine produced high-quality iron that was used to armor the *Monitor*, the Civil War battleship, and to make steel for the Brooklyn Bridge. The museum has several exhibits on the iron industry, including samples of slag, the mine's glossy waste product, but it also showcases artifacts of everyday life in the 1800s. The house itself is a curiosity, featuring biblical passages above bedroom doorways and a painted floor in the nursery. On the grounds are the remains of an iron forge.

Penfield Pond, across the road, is owned by the Penfield Foundation. The pond is stocked with trout, bass, bullhead, and northern pike. The museum sells fishing and boating permits. Canoes and rowboats can be put in the pond at a grassy launch. Gasoline engines are not allowed on the water. There is a picnic table near the launch site.

East of the pond, Putnam Creek rushes through a rocky gorge. Visitors can see the gorge by walking 100 yards or so down Peasley Road, a dirt road that starts just east of the Penfield Museum. For a longer hike, turn right a little past the gorge to follow a rough dirt road through the woods east of Penfield Pond. The road is a good route for mountain bike riding or cross-country skiing. After about 2 miles, the road ends at Warner Hill Road.

Directions: From Ticonderoga, drive north on NY 9N to the four-way intersection in the hamlet of Crown Point; turn left on County 2 and go about 0.5 mile to a fork; bear left onto County 47 and go about 6 miles to Ironville.

Activities: Hiking, canoeing, fishing.

Facilities: Museum, small-boat launch, picnic table.

Dates: May 15-Oct. 15.

Fees: A donation is requested for admission to the museum. There is a charge for fishing and boating.

Closest town: Crown Point hamlet is about 6.2 miles east.

For more information: Penfield Homestead Museum, Ironville Road, Crown Point, NY 12928. Phone (518) 597-3804.

Hammond Pond Wild Forest

Most of the state land in the Champlain Valley Region belongs to the Hammond Pond Wild Forest, which encompasses more than 40,000 acres. For the most part, these lands lie in the western part of the region, east of the Northway and north of NY 74. Several public roads cross through the wild forest, making access easy.

With its numerous ponds, the Hammond Pond Wild Forest appeals more to the fisherman than to the mountain climber. All told, there are 32 bodies of water within its boundaries. Many formed as kettle ponds after huge blocks of ice, left behind by the retreating glacier about 10,000 years ago, became surrounded by till deposited by glacial meltwater. When the blocks melted, they left depressions that filled with water. Several of the ponds are trout waters where anglers are forbidden to use bait fish.

The mountains in the Hammond Pond Wild Forest are smallish and nearly all lack official trails. The highest is Hail Mountain, at 2,680 feet. Other high summits include Owl Pate, at 2,340 feet, and Bald Peak, at 2,320 feet. Hikers can get to them only by a bushwhack. As matter of fact, the only mountain with an official trail is Peaked Hill in the southern part of the wild forest, and that trailhead is reachable only by canoe or boat.

There are about 20 miles of marked trails, many following old logging roads. Since most lead to ponds, not summits, the trails will delight those who enjoy relatively easy walks through the woods. In winter, many of the trails are skiable. Some double as snowmobile trails. The only lean-tos are at Moose Mountain Pond and Eagle Lake's Crown Point Bay.

In the 1800s, the lands that now constitute the Hammond Pond Wild Forest were logged heavily, initially only for softwoods, which were floated

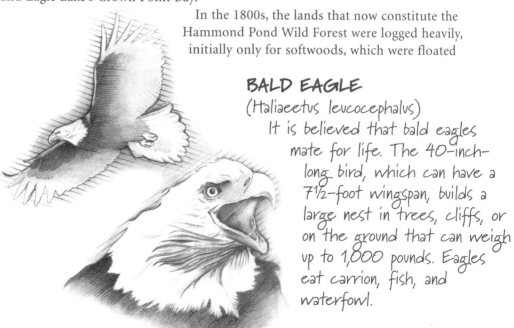

BALD EAGLE

(Haliaeetus leucocephalus)
It is believed that bald eagles mate for life. The 40-inch-long bird, which can have a 7½-foot wingspan, builds a large nest in trees, cliffs, or on the ground that can weigh up to 1,000 pounds. Eagles eat carrion, fish, and waterfowl.

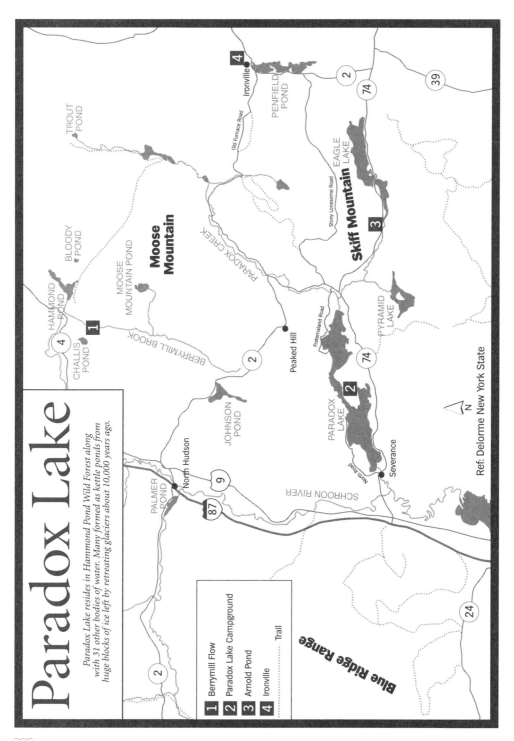

Paradox Lake

Paradox Lake resides in Hammond Pond Wild Forest along with 31 other bodies of water. Many formed as kettle ponds from huge blocks of ice left by retreating glaciers about 10,000 years ago.

1 Berrymill Flow
2 Paradox Lake Campground
3 Arnold Pond
4 Ironville
········ Trail

TROUT POND

BLOODY POND

HAMMOND POND

CHALLIS POND

Moose Mountain

MOOSE MOUNTAIN POND

BERRYMILL BROOK

PARADOX CREEK

Peaked Hill

JOHNSON POND

PALMER POND

North Hudson

SCHROON RIVER

PARADOX LAKE

PYRAMID LAKE

Skiff Mountain

EAGLE LAKE

PENFIELD POND

Ironville

Old Furnace Road

Stony Lonesome Road

Fraternaland Road

North Road

Severance

Blue Ridge Range

Ref: Delorme New York State

N

down the Schroon and Boquet rivers. After several iron mines opened in the Champlain Valley, loggers clear-cut large tracts for charcoal to feed the smelters. They also cut down hemlocks for tanneries, which used the tannin found in the bark. The timber and ore industries peaked in the 1880s and fell into decline once the necessary resources became scarce.

By 1850, the forest had been cut so much that the iron companies started importing coal for the smelters. As the iron companies and other owners abandoned their denuded lands, the state acquired the properties for back taxes. Today, these lands make up the bulk of the wild forest.

The woods have rebounded strongly since falling into state hands. The most typical forest is a mixture of white pine (*Pinus strobus*) and northern hardwoods. In steep valleys and on moist slopes, especially northern slopes, hemlock (*Tsuga canadensis*) often replaces or joins the pine. Southern trees such as red oak (*Quercus rubra borealis*) and white oak (*Quercus alba*) can be found on southern hillsides, often on dry ridges. Some old-growth pine, hemlock, and yellow birch (*Betula alleghaniensis*) survive on the trails to Hammond Pond and Berrymill Flow. Many of these trees have diameters greater than 3 feet.

For more information: State Department of Environmental Conservation, PO Box 296, Route 86, Ray Brook, NY 12977. Phone (518) 897-1200. DEC's leaflet *Trails in the Schroon Lake Region* includes five trails in the Hammond Pond Wild Forest.

PARADOX LAKE PUBLIC CAMPGROUND
[Fig. 18(2)] Paradox Lake, lying on the southern fringes of the Hammond Pond Wild Forest, drains into the Schroon River, but in spring the flow of its outlet sometimes reverses until the water table falls to its normal level. And this accounts for the lake's name: it comes from an Indian word—now anglicized—meaning "water running backward."

The state has a campground on the south shore of the narrowest part of the lake. Since the lake stretches more than 4 miles, it attracts a good number of boaters and fishermen. Most of the shoreline remains in private hands.

The lake supports a two-story fishery. The state stocks it with rainbow trout (*Oncorhynchus mykiss*) and lake trout (*Salvelinus namaycush*). Other fish include largemouth bass (*Micropterus salmoides*), smallmouth bass (*Micropterus dolomieui*), and northern pike (*Esox lucius*). Boats and canoes can be rented and/or launched at the campground.

Only a few official trails in the vicinity lead into the Hammond Pond Wild Forest. However, visitors will find plenty of other hiking opportunities in the nearby Pharaoh Lake Wilderness, located south of NY 74 (*see* Pharaoh Lake Wilderness, page 149).

Directions: From Northway Exit 28, take NY 74 east for about 3.6 miles to an entrance on the left. From the east, the entrance is located on the right about 4.5

miles past the state fishing access site on Eagle Lake.

Activities: Camping, boating, fishing, hiking, picnicking, swimming.

Facilities: 58 campsites, boat launch, picnic area, sand beach, playground, hot showers, toilets, trailer dump station, canoe and boat rentals.

Date: May through mid-Oct.

Fees: There is a charge for camping or day use.

Closest town: Schroon Lake village is about 3 miles west.

For more information: Campground office, phone (518) 532-7451. For reservations, phone (800) 456-2267.

PEAKED HILL

[Fig. 18] For a small mountain, Peaked Hill packs in much adventure. Hikers can get to the trailhead on the north shore of Paradox Lake only by water. Canoes and boats can be launched from Paradox Lake Public Campground on the opposite shore. The little-used trail climbs through a mixed wood to Peaked Pond, where anglers can fish for smallmouth bass (*Micropterus dolomieui*) and yellow perch (*Perca flavescens*). From the pond, the trail enters a ravine before ascending to the summit, with good views of Paradox and Schroon lakes, the Pharaoh Lake Wilderness, and peaks to the southwest.

Directions: See Paradox Lake Public Campground, above. If putting in a canoe at the boat launch, paddle northwest to the start of The Narrows and then cross. It's about a 0.5-mile trip.

Trail: 1 mile to Peaked Pond, 2.2 miles to summit.

Elevation: 800 feet to about 1,900 feet.

Degree of difficulty: Moderate.

Surface and blaze: Natural forest floor. Blue blazes.

ARNOLD POND AND SKIFF MOUNTAIN

[Fig. 18(3)] The trail to Arnold Pond is short but steep and rocky—a good test of youngsters eager to tackle tougher climbs. The route passes through a mixed wood up a hillside strewn with small boulders, passing a lookout along the way that offers a glimpse of the mountains in the Pharaoh Lake Wilderness to the south.

In spring, violets, wild oats (*Uvularia sessilfolia*), early saxifrage (*Saxifraga virginiensis*), and miterwort (*Mitella diphylla*) bloom in the woods. The small pond lies at the bottom of steep cliffs, with talus piled along its northern shore. Ravens sometimes circle above the cliffs, while great blue herons sometimes visit the marshy shores.

Although the official trail ends at the pond, a well-trodden path marked by cairns continues up the mountain. From above, there are excellent views of the peaks to southeast, south, and west. The summit is an attractive blend of woods, grassy patches, and slabs of bedrock. Colorful lichens and veins of quartz adorn the rock. On the way up, look for wild columbine (*Aquilegia canadensis*) in spring. To take the trail to the summit, turn left upon reaching the pond.

Directions: From Northway Exit 28, drive east on NY 74 about 7.9 miles to a parking lot on the right for Glidden Marsh and other destinations in the Pharaoh Mountain Wilderness. The trail to Arnold Pond begins on the other side of the road about 100 yards west of the lot. If coming from the east, the lot will be on the left 1 mile or so past the state fishing access site on Eagle Lake.

Trail: 0.3 mile to Arnold Pond, about 1 mile to summit.

Elevation: 953 feet to 1,300 feet at pond or about 1,850 feet at summit.

Degree of difficulty: Moderate.

Surface and blaze: Natural forest floor. Blue blazes to pond. Cairns thereafter.

BROWNHEADED COWBIRD
(Molothrus ater)
The cowbird lays its eggs in the nests of other birds that feed the newly hatched intruder until it can fly.

🦌 EAGLE LAKE

[Fig. 18] Although private land surrounds most of this pretty lake just east of Skiff Mountain, the state maintains picnic sites and a lean-to near Crown Point Bay on the northeastern shore, reachable only by water. Primitive campsites also can be found there. Boats can be put in at a state launch on the south side of NY 74, which cuts across the lake on a causeway. From the launch, it's about a 2.5-mile trip to the campsites, which are north of NY 74.

The state and Essex County stock the lake with brown trout (*Salmo trutta*). Anglers may keep up to five trout of any size. Ice fishing is permitted.

Directions: From Northway Exit 28, drive east 9.1 miles on NY 74 to the launch on the right.

Activities: Camping, canoeing, boating, fishing, picnicking, swimming.

Facilities: Beach boat launch with parking for six cars and trailers, picnic tables, pit privies, lean-to, primitive campsites.

Fees: None.

Closest town: Schroon Lake is about 9 miles west on NY 74.

For more information: State Department of Environmental Conservation, PO Box 296, Route 86, Ray Brook, NY 12977. Phone (518) 897-1200.

🦌 CHALLIS POND

[Fig. 18] Since it is less than 1 mile from the road, Challis Pond is a fairly popular destination of fishermen and day hikers. The trail to the pond winds through a dark forest of hemlock (*Tsuga canadensis*), white pine (*Strobus pinus*), and cedar to a pond encircled by wooded hills. In spring, red trillium (*Trillium erectum*) blooms along the path. About halfway to the pond, you may glimpse a waterfall through the trees on the right, where the outlet from the pond spills over a natural rock wall about 12 feet high. Yellow pond lily (*Nuphar variegatum*) and pickerelweed (*Pontederia cordata*) flourish along the edges of the 12-acre pond. The state stocks the water with brook trout (*Salvelinus fontinalis*). Anglers are forbidden to use bait fish.

Directions: From Northway Exit 29, drive about 0.4 mile east to US 9; turn left and go 2.6 miles; turn right at the sign for Port Henry and take another right after 0.3 mile. The trailhead is on the right after another 2.9 miles. Either park here along the road or continue another 0.1 mile to a lot on the right.

Trail: 0.6 mile to pond.

Degree of difficulty: Easy.

Elevation: 950 feet to 1,150 feet.

Surface and blaze: Natural forest floor. Red blazes.

BERRYMILL FLOW AND MOOSE MOUNTAIN POND

[Fig. 18(1)] At Berrymill Flow, once the site of a sawmill, a grassy marsh stretches for more than 1 mile behind the remnants of a broken beaver dam. The Berrymill Brook meanders lackadaisically through the marsh before forming a pool at the dam. The whole scene is framed by forested mountains. Bird-watchers should bring their binoculars. And their cameras.

The trail follows an old tote road that for much of the way parallels the brook, at one point passing a small waterfall. Evergreens such as white pine (*Strobus pinus*), hemlock (*Tsuga canadensis*), balsam fir (*Abies balsamea*), and cedar dominate the woods. Yellow violets, red trillium (*Trillium erectum*), wild oats (*Uvularia sessilfolia*), hobblebush (*Viburnum alnifolium*), and early fly honeysuckle (*Lonicera canadensis*) bloom along the trail in spring.

After reaching the still water, the trail crosses the brook and follows the edge of the flow for a while before turning east for the 38-acre Moose Mountain Pond. A lean-to on the eastern shore looks across the pond to Moose Mountain and Owl Pate. It's a good place to stay if you're fishing for the brook trout (*Salvelinus fontinalis*) stocked by the state. The use of bait fish is prohibited.

Directions: From Exit 29, drive about 0.4 mile east to US 9; turn left and go 2.6 miles; turn right at the sign for Port Henry and take another right after 0.3 miles; go 3 miles to a parking lot on the right, where the trail begins.

Trail: 1.5 miles to Berrymill Flow, 3.2 miles to Moose Mountain Pond.

Elevation: 950 feet at trailhead to 1,090 feet at Berrymill Flow and 1,265 feet at Moose Mountain Pond.

Degree of difficulty: Easy.

Surface and blaze: Old tote road, natural forest floor. Blue blazes.

🟫 HAMMOND POND AND BLOODY POND

[Fig. 18] An old tote road passes through a dark forest of large pines and hemlocks (*Tsuga canadensis*) to a wooden spillway at the outlet of Hammond Pond. A grassy area here with slabs of bedrock makes an attractive picnic spot. For much of the way to the pond, the trail follows Black Brook, which at one point wanders through a marsh where hikers may see a great blue heron (*Ardea herodias*). Hobblebush (*Viburnum alnifolium*) and early fly honeysuckle (*Lonicera canadensis*) grow along the trail. The shallow pond is inhabited by warm-water fish such as northern pike (*Esox lucius*).

The tote road forks after about 0.75 mile. Bear left to go to the spillway. Bear right to go to Bloody Pond. The road to the right passes the southern edge of Hammond Pond, where ducks often congregate, and then crosses Black Brook on a wooden bridge. After crossing a second creek, turn left on an unofficial trail marked by yellow paint daubs. The trail goes past an interesting waterfall in spring and climbs through a rock cleft on its way to Bloody Pond, about 0.2 mile away.

Trailing arbutus (*Epigaea repens*), a protected wildflower, and leatherleaf (*Chamaedaphne calyculata*) bloom along the shore. The state stocks the 6-acre pond with brook trout (*Salvelinus fontinalis*). Anglers are forbidden to use bait fish.

Directions: See Berrymill Flow and Moose Mountain Pond, page 120.

Trail: 1 mile to Hammond Pond, 1.9 to Bloody Pond.

Elevation: 950 feet to 1,100 feet at Hammond Pond.

Degree of difficulty: Easy.

Surface and blaze: Old tote road, natural forest floor. Red blazes to Hammond Pond. Yellow blazes to Bloody Pond.

🟫 TROUT POND

[Fig. 18] The trail to Trout Pond from County 4 has much to hold one's interest. Not far from the start, hikers encounter a large beaver dam that has created a pond visited by mallards (*Anas platyrhynchos*) and other waterfowl. Dead trees, toppled and still upright, line the mucky shore—an eerie scene of devastation. The trail continues through a dark evergreen forest, the haunt of a barred owl (*Strix varia*), passes a few swamps, and crosses a stream that gurgles merrily among the ferns and mossy rocks. Red trillium (*Trillium erectum*), wild oats (*Uvularia sessifolia*), and early fly honeysuckle (*Lonicera canadensis*) bloom in spring along the path.

Trout Pond is not exclusively a trout pond: it also contains bullheads (*Ictalurus nebulosus*) and golden shiners (*Notemigonous crysoleucas*). Hikers can continue on the trail to Round Pond, East Mill Flow, and Sharp Bridge Public Campground. The campground is 5.2 miles from the trailhead.

Directions: From Northway Exit 29, drive about 0.4 mile east to US 9; turn left and go 2.6 miles; turn right at the sign for Port Henry and take another right onto County 4 (the Moriah Road) after 0.3 miles; go 6.3 miles to a parking lot on the left, where the trail begins.

GREAT HORNED OWL

(Bubo virginianus)
This owl, growing to 2 feet in height, will prey on medium sized mammals or birds, including waterfowl, grouse, skunks and porcupines.

Trail: 1.3 miles to Trout Pond, 2.5 miles to Round Pond, 5.2 miles to campground.
Degree of difficulty: Easy.
Surface and blaze: Natural forest floor. Red blazes.

SHARP BRIDGE PUBLIC CAMPGROUND

[Fig. 6(28)] Located amid large white pines on the banks of the upper Schroon River, Sharp Bridge is one of the oldest state campgrounds in the Adirondacks. It opened in 1920 with a single campsite.

The Schroon, which starts just 3 miles upstream, is too low to canoe at the campground, except perhaps in early spring. The river is stocked with brook trout (*Salvelinus fontinalis*) and brown trout (*Salmo trutta*). The hiking trail to East Mill Flow begins at the campground.

Directions: From Northway Exit 29, drive about 0.4 mile east to US 9; turn left and go about 8 miles north to the Sharp Bridge Public Campground on the right. From Northway Exit 30, drive about 6 miles south on US 9 to the campground.

Activities: Camping, hiking, fishing, cross-country skiing, snowshoeing.

Facilities: 40 campsites, picnic area, hiking trail, area, showers, trailer dump station.

Dates: Open late May through Labor Day.

Fees: There is a charge for camping or day use.

Closest town: North Hudson is about 8 miles south on US 9.

For more information: Campground office, phone (518) 532-7538. For reservations, phone (800) 456-2267.

EAST MILL FLOW

[Fig. 6(28)] Starting at the Sharp Bridge Public Campground, this trail follows the Schroon River at the outset and passes by many huge white pines (*Strobus pinus*) on its way to a big beaver dam on East Mill Brook. Hikers can walk up to the dam from either shore for a close look at the beavers' work, which has created an attractive pond bordered by rock walls.

Evergreens dominate the forest for most of the route, and often a carpet of needles softens the path. In spring, red trillium (*Trillium erectum*) blooms in abundance. Other wildflowers found along the trail include blue cohosh (*Caulophyllum thalictroides*), wild oats (*Uvularia sessilfolia*), miterwort (*Mitella diphylla*), and trailing arbutus (*Epigaea repens*). Look also for early fly honeysuckle (*Lonicera canadensis*). A small wooden bridge spans East Mill Brook. On the other side, the trail continues to Round Pond and Trout Pond, ending at the Moriah Road.

Directions: From Northway Exit 29, drive about 0.4 mile east to US 9; turn left and go about 8 miles north to the Sharp Bridge Public Campground on the right. From Northway Exit 30, drive about 6 miles south on US 9 to the campground. Park on the left upon entering the grounds. To reach the trailhead, walk along the campground road beside the river.

Trail: 2.7 miles to the flow, 3.9 miles to Round Pond, 5.2 miles to the Moriah Road.

Degree of difficulty: Easy.

Surface and blaze: Old woods road, natural forest floor. Red blazes.

Lincoln Pond Public Campground

[Fig. 6(31)] This campground lies north of the contiguous state lands that make up the bulk of the Hammond Pond Wild Forest. Although Lincoln Pond can hardly be called wild—a causeway carrying County 7 bisects it—the state owns the shore and woods on the western side. For those seeking privacy, the campground has several campsites located on the more remote parts of the pond.

The state stocks Lincoln Pond with tiger muskellunge (*Esox masquinongy*). Other species found in the pond include smallmouth bass (*Micropterus dolomieui*), yellow perch (*Perca flavescens*), and bullhead. Anglers sometimes fish from the causeway. The campground rents rowboats and canoes.

Directions: From the junction of NY 9N and US 9 in Elizabethtown, drive east on NY 9 about 0.5 mile to Lincoln Pond Road; turn right and go to the entrance on the right. The campground is about 6 miles from Elizabethtown.

Activities: Camping, picnicking, swimming, canoeing, fishing.

Facilities: 35 campsites, picnic area, playground, beach, car-top boat launch, hot showers, trailer dump station. Campsites are accessible to the handicapped.

Dates: May through Labor Day.

Fees: There is a charge for camping or day use.

Closest town: Elizabethtown is about 6 miles north.

For more information: Campground office, phone (518) 942-5292. For reservations, phone (800) 456-2267.

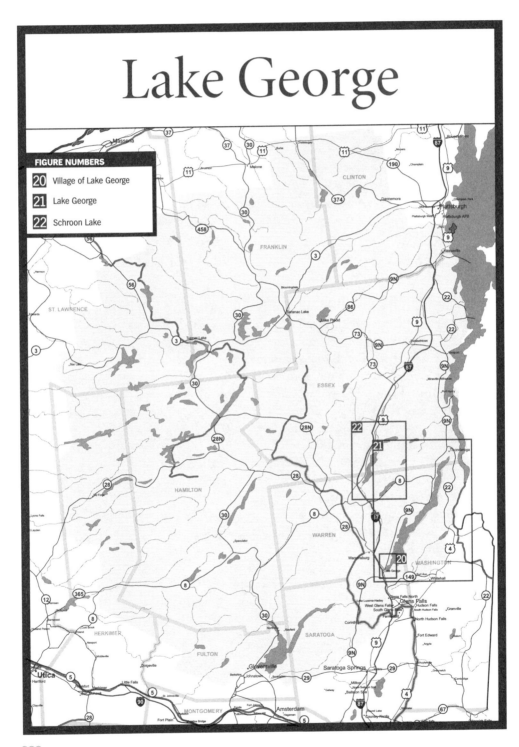

Lake George

FIGURE NUMBERS

20 Village of Lake George

21 Lake George

22 Schroon Lake

Lake George

Lake George's fame as a place of rugged splendor and as the setting of historic battles made it one of the first tourist spots of the early republic, attracting such notable visitors as Thomas Jefferson, who commented on its limpid waters, James Madison, and the historian Francis Parkman. In the latter 1800s, it evolved into a resort for the wealthy, many of whom built lavish estates along its shores. Nowadays, the region is a playground for everyone from the jet-skier to the backcountry camper.

As defined in this chapter, the Lake George region encompasses the southeastern corner of the Adirondack Park, bounded by the Northway to the west and by NY 74 to the north. It includes two large chunks of state land: the Lake George Wild Forest, which is bisected by the lake, and the Pharaoh Lake Wilderness, located east of Schroon Lake. There are some other large waterways in the region, such as Schroon

[*Above:* Sailing is popular on Lake George]

Lake and Brant Lake, but none compares with Lake George.

Despite the development along some of its shoreline, Lake George has not lost its singular beauty. The lake, the largest wholly within the Adirondack Park, stretches 32 miles from the village of Lake George northward to La Chute River near Ticonderoga. Hemmed in by rocky slopes and sheer cliffs, the narrow water at times resembles a Norwegian fjord. Dozens of islands—most congregated in The Narrows that separates the north and south basins—add a final touch to a spectacular landscape.

Lake George owes its existence to two geological accidents. Sometime after the late Ordovician Period, about 450 million years ago, shifts in the Earth's crust along faults in the region caused large chunks of bedrock to sink, forming a valley known as a *graben*—German for "grave." Before the ice ages, two rivers ran in opposite directions through the valley. One flowed south from Northwest Bay to an outlet near Dunham's Bay. The other rose in high ground now occupied by The Narrows and flowed north. The glaciers, besides scouring the valley walls, cleared out The Narrows and, upon melting, deposited debris that dammed the river at the southern end of the graben. The water backed up to form Lake George and carved a new outlet in the north. Many of the islands in The Narrows are the scattered remnants of the former high ground.

White pine (*Pinus strobus*) and northern red oak (*Quercus rubra borealis*) grow here in greater abundance than in most other parts of the park, thanks to a more moderate climate. Way back in 1749, the Swedish naturalist Peter Kalm observed that "the white pine throve in this region and grew to an unusual height." The British took note of the pines, too, for they cut down the tallest and straightest of them to make ship masts for the Royal Navy. A similar practice in New England created such resentment that Colonists adopted the pine tree as one of the symbols of the Revolution.

The oak-pine-hickory forest on Tongue Mountain—a peninsula that juts out between Northwest Bay and The Narrows—has been identified as the largest forest of its kind in the park. Pines also can be found in abundance throughout the Champlain Valley to the north, but the oaks become more scarce as latitude increases. The more common Adirondack trees also grow around Lake George, including sugar maple (*Acer saccharum*), yellow birch (*Betula alleghaniensis*), hemlock (*Tsuga canadensis*), balsam fir (*Abies balsamea*), and red spruce (*Picea rubens*). Nearly all of the forest was cleared or logged in the past, but it has grown back nicely.

By and large, the fauna of the woods in the Lake George Region is the same as elsewhere in the Adirondacks. The biggest exception is the timber rattlesnake (*Crotalus horridus*) that dwells among rocky ledges along Lake George and Lake Champlain. The rattler is most abundant on Tongue Mountain, but even there it is rarely seen by hikers. The steep mountains also have proven to be suitable habitat for peregrine falcons (*Falco peregrinus*) and ravens (*Corvus corax*), two birds that have made a comeback of late in the Adirondacks. Occasionally, bald eagles (*Haliaeetus leucocephalus*) have been spotted above the lake, leading to speculation that they are nesting somewhere in the

Pharaoh Lake Wilderness. Moose (*Alces alces*), which also are returning to the park, often pass through the region in their wanderings from nearby Vermont, sometimes swimming from the east shore to west. There are plenty of white-tailed deer (*Odocoileus virginianus*) in the area and some black bear (*Ursus americanus*). But the bear's range peters out on the east side of Lake George, a fact borne out by hunting statistics: Although hunters bag bear fairly regularly in the woods on the west side of the lake, they managed to kill only one in 10 years on the east side.

Visitors will see evidence of beavers, like this gnawed log, in the Lake George Region.

Before the arrival of Europeans, Native Americans came to Lake George to hunt and fish. It's possible that some stayed year-round, but archaeologists have not found evidence of permanent settlements. Arrowheads, net sinkers, scrapers, and other artifacts dating back more than a thousand years have been dug up at an ancient campsite on Assembly Point, a long peninsula northeast of the village of Lake George. Artifacts have been found at other shoreline sites as well. The Indians also used the lake to travel between the Hudson River valley and Lake Champlain, a route that later became a bone of contention between the French and English.

The Iroquois called Lake George *Andiatarocte*, meaning "where the lake is shut in." The Jesuit missionary Father Isaac Jogues, the first white man to set eyes on the lake, christened it Lac du Saint Sacrement in 1646. Jogues was on his way to serve as ambassador to the Mohawks, one of the Iroquois tribes. He volunteered for the job even though the Mohawks had kept him captive four years earlier. This time, they killed him. There is a statue of Jogues in Lake George Battlefield Park.

Sir William Johnson, who married a Mohawk, renamed the water Lake George in honor of the reigning British monarch after British troops fought off the French there in 1755. Johnson built Fort William Henry near the site, but the French captured the fort two years later and their Indian allies massacred many of its inhabitants. James Fenimore Cooper gives a fictional account of the siege in his novel *The Last of the Mohicans.* Cooper later tried to get the lake's name changed to Horicon, after an Indian tribe. Though he failed, there is a town of Horicon in the vicinity of Schroon Lake.

Lake George continued to be a battleground throughout the French and Indian War and the Revolution. Although the region attracted visitors and settlers right after the Revolution, the tourist trade really boomed after the Civil War. Fancy hotels catered to the wealthy, and steamships ferried sightseers around the lake. Soon, mansions cropped up along the shore between Lake George village and Bolton

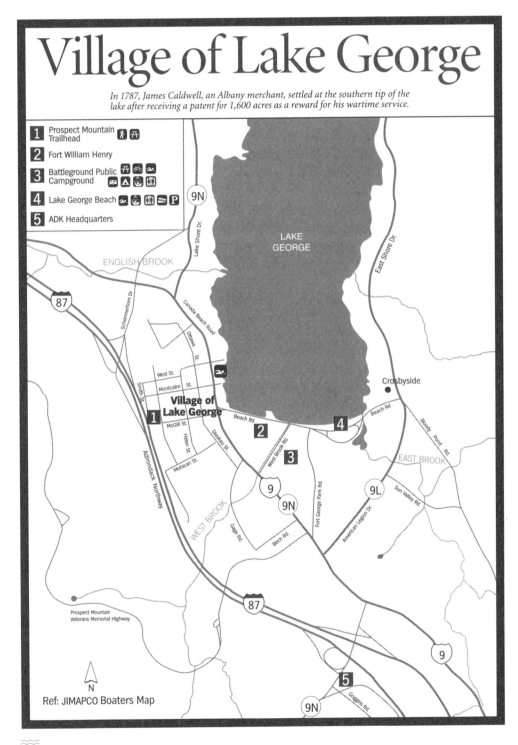

Village of Lake George

In 1787, James Caldwell, an Albany merchant, settled at the southern tip of the lake after receiving a patent for 1,600 acres as a reward for his wartime service.

1 Prospect Mountain Trailhead

2 Fort William Henry

3 Battleground Public Campground

4 Lake George Beach

5 ADK Headquarters

LAKE GEORGE

Village of Lake George

Crosbyside

EAST BROOK

ENGLISH BROOK

WEST BROOK

Lake Shore Dr.
East Shore Dr.
Canada Beach Road
Schermerhorn Dr
Ottawa St.
West St.
Smith St.
Montcalm St.
McGill St.
Helen St.
Mohican St.
Diesau St.
Beach Rd
West Brook Rd
Beach Rd
Bloody Pond Rd.
Fort George Park Rd.
American Legion Dr.
Sun Valley Rd
Gage Rd.
Birch Rd.
Adirondack Northway
Goggins Rd.

Prospect Mountain Veterans Memorial Highway

N

Ref: JIMAPCO Boaters Map

Landing—a 10-mile strip nicknamed Millionaires' Row. Its summertime denizens included Alfred S. Ochs, the publisher of *The New York Times;* Charles Evans Hughes, the nation's chief justice; and the painter Georgia O'Keeffe and her soul mate, the photographer Alfred Stieglitz. In time, as the middle classes flocked to the lake in greater numbers, the mansions of Millionaires' Row gave way to the motels of today.

Few regions of the country offer so much in the way of history and scenic beauty. There is something for every lover of the outdoors. You can hike up a 2,600-foot mountain, camp on an island, canoe through a marsh, ride a horse through the woods, fish for salmon and trout, scuba-dive to look at 240-year-old shipwrecks, walk amid historic ruins, or just relax on a sandy beach.

For more information: State Department of Environmental Conservation, PO Box 232, Hudson Street Extension, Warrensburg, NY, 12885. Phone (518) 623-3671.

Lake George: The Village

Before the Revolution, a few pioneers had built log cabins around Lake George, but these had to be abandoned during the war. In 1787, James Caldwell, an Albany merchant, settled at the southern tip of the lake after receiving a patent for 1,600 acres as a reward for his wartime service. His family built an iron forge and grist mill and leased or sold land to other settlers. The community, known as Caldwell for decades, adopted the name Lake George when it was incorporated as a village in 1903. Tourism has been the main business of Lake George since the 1800s. As early as 1817, Caldwell and some associates built a steamboat to take visitors around the lake, starting a tradition that continues to this day.

PROSPECT MOUNTAIN

[Fig. 20(1)] At the turn of the century, the Prospect Mountain House occupied this summit, and a funicular railway ran to the top from the village. Today, those who want a quick introduction to the region can drive to the summit on a 5.5-mile toll road, the Prospect Mountain Veterans Memorial Highway. Visitors can park 100 feet below the summit and walk the rest of the way or take a free shuttle. The sweeping views take in Lake George and Vermont's Green Mountains to the east, the High Peaks to the north, and on an especially clear day, the Catskills far to the south, beyond the skyscrapers of the Empire State Plaza in Albany. Hikers can climb to the top from the village via a 1.7-mile trail. It is somewhat steep and rocky, but thousands make the climb each year. Dogs are not allowed on the summit. In winter, snowmobilers can ride up the highway as far as the parking lot.

Directions: The summit actually lies just west of the village limits in the town of Lake George. From Northway Exit 21, take NY 9N east a few hundred yards to US 9; go north on US 9 about 0.5 mile to the Veterans Memorial Highway. If hiking, continue on US 9 another mile into the village, turn left onto Montcalm Street, drive several blocks to the end, turn right on Cooper Street, left on West Street, and left on Smith Street, where there is a parking area.

Facilities: Self-guided nature trail on summit. Picnic tables. "Viewmobile" shuttles.

Activities: Hiking, picnicking.

Dates: The highway is open to automobiles from late May to late Oct.

Fees: There is a toll for automobiles.

Closest town: The village of Lake George lies just east of the mountain.

LAKE GEORGE BATTLEGROUND PUBLIC CAMPGROUND AND BATTLEFIELD PARK

[Fig. 20(3)] The state operates a campground and park just southwest of the village. The campground has 68 sites for tents or trailers. Campers must pay an extra fee to swim at nearby Lake George Beach. Battlefield Park, located next to the campground, has picnic facilities for day use. Also on the grounds are the ruins of Fort George, the successor to Fort William Henry, and memorials to Father Isaac Jogues, the Jesuit martyr; Sir William Johnson, the Colonial general; and King Hendrick, the Mohawk chief who was Johnson's ally. The 9-mile Warren County Bikeway, which ends in Glens Falls, bisects the park.

Directions: From Northway Exit 21, take US 9 north about 1 mile to the campground on the right.

Activities: Camping, picnicking, sightseeing, bicycling, swimming.

Facilities: 68 tent and trailer sites, showers, toilets, trailer dump station.

Dates: Open from early May through Columbus Day.

Fees: There is a charge for camping and swimming at Lake George Beach.

Closest town: Lake George village is 0.25 mile west.

WOOD FROG
(Rana sylvatica)

LAKE GEORGE BEACH

[Fig. 20(4)] During the last ice age, a glacial stream flowed northward into proto-Lake George, depositing the sands that make up Lake George Beach. On hot summer days, this large strand will be crowded with sunbathers and swimmers. Handicapped swimmers have exclusive use of a concrete boat launch at the beach from Memorial Day weekend until a week after Labor Day. Boaters may use it at other times of the year. There is another beach at Shepard Memorial Park on Canada Street in the heart of the village.

Directions: From US 9 in Lake George, drive east on Beach Road about 0.25 mile past the village limit.

Activities: Swimming, boating.
Facilities: Showers, bathrooms, boat launch, parking lot.
Dates:
Fees: There is a charge for using the beach.
Closest town: Lake George village.

FORT WILLIAM HENRY

[Fig. 20(2)] Visitors to this massive log-and-earth bastion, named after a son of King George III, can watch soldiers in eighteenth-century uniforms demonstrate the fine arts of molding a musket ball, tossing a grenadier bomb, or shooting off an old cannon. The fort hands out musket balls to youngsters as souvenirs.

Rebuilt in the 1950s, Fort William Henry figured prominently in the French and Indian War. As tensions between the British and French escalated in 1755, Sir William Johnson and his troops cut a path through the wilderness from Fort Edward on the Hudson River north to Lac du St. Sacrement. Upon arrival, he renamed the water Lake George, claiming it for Britain. That fall, three brutal skirmishes, collectively known as the Battle of Lake George, prompted the British to build the fort at the southern end of the lake.

Led by the Marquis de Montcalm, the French captured the fort in the summer of 1757. The English surrendered under a promise of safe passage, only to be slaughtered by Algonquin and Huron warriors who were allies of the French—an atrocity that inspired James Fenimore Cooper to write *The Last of the Mohicans*. The fort shows the 1936 film classic based on the novel every hour.

The fort exhibits thousands of artifacts found buried in the sand during the restoration: cannons, rifles, coins, belt buckles, surgical instruments, pottery shards, and, of course, musket balls. There also are human and animal skeletons on display.

Directions: From Northway Exit 21, drive east to NY 9; turn left and drive about 0.75 mile to the entrance on the right. There is another entrance on Beach Road.

Dates: Open daily from May to mid-Oct.

Fees: There is a charge for admission.

For more information: Phone (518) 668-5471.

ADIRONDACK MOUNTAIN CLUB HEADQUARTERS

[Fig. 20(5)] Although its lodges and campgrounds are in the High Peaks, the hiking club—popularly known as ADK—has its headquarters at 814 Goggins Road outside the village of Lake George. The club keeps exhibits there year-round and sponsors lectures on Adirondack subjects and workshops on outdoors skills. It's a good place to drop by if you have any questions about the Lake George Region or any other part of the Adirondacks. Trail guides and other books published by ADK can be bought here.

Directions: From Northway Exit 21, drive west less than 1 mile on NY 9N to

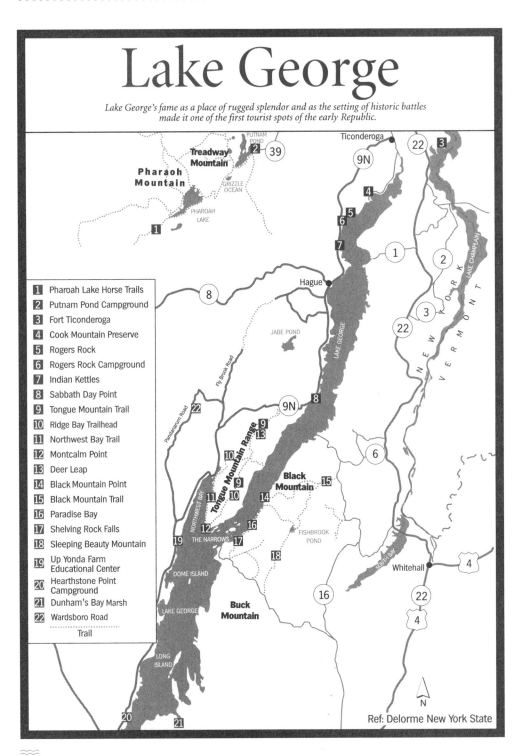

Lake George

*Lake George's fame as a place of rugged splendor and as the setting of historic battles
made it one of the first tourist spots of the early Republic.*

1 Pharoah Lake Horse Trails
2 Putnam Pond Campground
3 Fort Ticonderoga
4 Cook Mountain Preserve
5 Rogers Rock
6 Rogers Rock Campground
7 Indian Kettles
8 Sabbath Day Point
9 Tongue Mountain Trail
10 Ridge Bay Trailhead
11 Northwest Bay Trail
12 Montcalm Point
13 Deer Leap
14 Black Mountain Point
15 Black Mountain Trail
16 Paradise Bay
17 Shelving Rock Falls
18 Sleeping Beauty Mountain
19 Up Yonda Farm
    Educational Center
20 Hearthstone Point
    Campground
21 Dunham's Bay Marsh
22 Wardsboro Road
    Trail

Ref: Delorme New York State

Goggins Road and take a left. The ADK parking lot is on the left a few hundred feet down the road.

For more information: Adirondack Mountain Club, 814 Goggins Road, Lake George, NY 12845-4117. Phone (518) 668-4447.

Lake George: The Lake

Looking down on Lake George from a nearby peak on a summer's day, a hiker can see many different kinds of vessel plying the water, from kayaks to steamboats and everything in between. And this variety is mirrored in the variety of activities pursued on and along the lake: People can be seen sailing, fishing, swimming, scuba-diving, water skiing, hiking the shoreline, picnicking on the islands, even soaring above it all with a parasail.

Adirondack Mountain Club

The Adirondack Mountain Club (ADK) began in 1922 with the mission of improving the hiking trails in the Adirondack Park. Within six months, the club had built the 133-mile Northville-Lake Placid Trail, now used by thousands of hikers each year, and the club has been going strong ever since. ADK not only maintains trails, but it also publishes books on the Adirondacks, including a series of guidebooks with maps, sponsors natural history lectures and outdoors workshops, and lobbies for land conservation and environmental protection. It played a big role in the state's acquisition of the William C. Whitney Area in 1998. The club owns and operates the Adirondak Loj and Johns Brook Lodge on the edge of the High Peaks Wilderness. ADK's success and industry perhaps is not surprising, given its pedigree: its charter members included Bob Marshall, one of the founders of the Wilderness Society; Gifford Pinchot, the first chief of the U.S. Forest Service; and Franklin Delano Roosevelt. Membership has grown to 22,000. The club chose the abbreviation ADK—short for Adirondack—to distinguish itself from the Appalachian Mountain Club.

For more information: Adirondack Mountain Club, 814 Goggins Road, Lake George, NY 12845-4117. Phone (518) 668-4447.

LAKE GEORGE ISLANDS PUBLIC CAMPGROUND

The Lake George islands, with their fanciful names and many legends, have long fascinated tourists. More often than not, a story lies behind each island's name. Diamond Island is where visitors could dig up quartz "diamonds" while the supply lasted. Tea Island is where guests at the early hotels were taken for afternoon tea. Prisoners Island is where the British kept 148 French captives for a few days in 1758. And as for As You Were Island—well, it seems that one day a hunter's musket misfired as he took aim at a deer, and while priming the gun for another shot, he commanded the animal to remain "as you were."

Folklore says there are 365 islands, one for each day of the year, but the actual tally is probably much less. The campground brochure lists 147 owned by the state and 32 in private hands, for a total of 179. Whatever their number, the state recognized the islands' value early on, enacting a law in 1878 that decreed all islands not already privately owned to be public property and forbade their future sale. An 1893 law added all the islands to the nascent Adirondack Park, even though the park's boundary did not then extend to Lake George.

The Lake George Islands Public Campground is the fruit of these forward-looking laws. Here it's possible for Everyman to be the lord of his own small island—for up to two weeks (although most of the islands have several campsites). The campground also maintains campsites on a remote stretch of mainland accessible by boat. Trails on this part of the mainland, which are open to everyone, lead into the surrounding mountains and along the undeveloped shoreline.

All told, the campground has 362 campsites on 44 islands and 25 on the mainland. Forty-two of the sites are for large boats with sleeping quarters. All the sites have a dock, fireplace, picnic table, and toilet. No drinking water is available, but there are two springs on the mainland and bottled water is sold at a store on Glen Island. The store also sells firewood, which is scarce on the islands. No dogs are allowed.

The campground is divided into three sections, each with its own ranger headquarters. In the southern section, all 90 campsites are on Long Island. The central section, extending from Long Island into The Narrows, has 212 sites scattered over 26 islands and the mainland. The northern section has 85 sites scattered over 17 islands. The headquarters are located on Long Island, Glen Island, and Narrow Island.

For day trippers, the campground maintains 116 picnic sites on eight islands and on the lakeshore. Permits are required for these as well as the campsites. No permit is required for hikers who want only to walk the trails.

Canoeists should beware that reaching the appropriate ranger headquarters and island campsites may require a paddle of several miles. Some may prefer to pay a marina to tow their canoe and gear to the ranger headquarters and paddle from there.

Directions: There are many marinas where, for a fee, campers can park their cars and launch their boats. From the marina, campers should go the appropriate ranger station to sign in.

Facilities: 387 campsites, including 42 cruiser sites; 116 day-use sites; 9 picnic shelters. Ranger headquarters on Long Island, Glen Island, and Narrow Island. Store on Glen Island.

Activities: Camping, picnicking, hiking, boating, swimming.

Dates: Campground open mid-May to mid-September. Day users must leave by 9 p.m.

Fees: There is a charge for camping and picnicking.

For more information: The campground pamphlet includes a map of the islands. For a copy, contact the state Department of Environmental Conservation at PO Box 232, Hudson Street Extension, Warrensburg, NY 12885; phone (518) 623-3671. The phone numbers of the three ranger headquarters are as follows: Long Island, (518)

656-9426; Glen Island, (518) 644-9696; Narrow Island, (518) 499-1288. For reservations, phone (800) 456-2267.

⊞ BOATING ON LAKE GEORGE

Boats can be launched or rented at numerous marinas around the lake. In addition, there are public-owned boat ramps at Lake George Beach, the town beach and Rogers Rock Public Campground in Hague, and Mossy Point in the town of Ticonderoga. Small boats also can be launched at a state site on NY 9N in Bolton near Northwest Bay.

The Lake George Park Commission requires most boats to be registered before being used on the lake. The exceptions are motorboats with less than 10 horsepower and nonmechanized craft less than 18 feet long. The registration fee, which varies with the size of the boat, can be paid at the commission's office or at a number of marinas, stores, campgrounds, and municipal offices in the region. For information about registration and other special boating regulations, phone the commission at (518) 668-9347.

Lake George boaters will find many bays and islands to explore and scenic vistas to enjoy. The quick tour that follows is meant only to whet the appetite:

DOME ISLAND

[Fig. 21] The Eastern New York Nature Conservancy keeps this island as a nature sanctuary and forbids people to visit, but it's worth a close look. Old-growth specimens of northern red oak (*Quercus rubra borealis*), hemlock (*Tsuga canadensis*), and American beech (*Fagus grandifolia*), among other species, cover most of the island, and white cedars (*Thuja occidentalis*) line its steep banks. Among the birds that live on the island are cedar waxwings (*Bombycilla cedrorum*), spotted sandpipers (*Actitus macularis*), herring gulls (*Larus argentatus*), and several types of woodpeckers. The island lies a few miles south of Montcalm Point at the tip of Tongue Mountain.

MONTCALM POINT

[Fig. 21(12)] The state keeps a dock at the point of Tongue Mountain, located about 11.25 miles from Lake George villlage. Boaters can stop here for a swim or take one of two trails on the Tongue Mountain peninsula. One leads to the Tongue Mountain ridge, where there are great views of the lake. The other follows the shore of Northwest Bay.

THE NARROWS

[Fig. 21] The Narrows begin after

HOBBLEBUSH
(Viburnum alnifolium)
With white flower clusters and dark purple berries, this viburnum is a treasured ornamental plant.

Legend of Rogers Rock

One winter day in 1758, Robert Rogers and his Rangers ambushed a party of French soldiers and Indian allies traveling along the frozen Trout Brook, south of Ticonderoga. As it turned out, a much larger French contingent was nearby, and it soon attacked and routed the Rangers. Rogers himself, as the story goes, retreated to the brink of Bald Mountain, a 500-foot precipice that rises out of Lake George. After hurling his knapsack over the cliff, he put his snowshoes on backward and walked away from the precipice—thus making it appear he had gone over the edge. He then scrambled down an easier route and joined the survivors of his band on the lake. (Another account says he slid down the precipice itself.) When the Indians reached the cliff, seeing the tracks and Rogers on the ice below, they assumed he was in the good graces of the Great Spirit and let him go. The story is apocryphal, as Rogers does not mention the incident in his journal, but it nonetheless spread quickly; less than 10 years later a land petition referred to the cliff as "Rodgers' [sic] Leap." Today the hill is called Rogers Rock and the precipice Rogers Slide.

Montcalm Point. Go slow while navigating among the islands so you'll have more time to soak in the gorgeous scenery. Glen Island, near the start of The Narrows, has a store and ranger headquarters.

PARADISE BAY

[Fig. 21(16)] This is one of the loveliest and most popular coves on the lake. It's tucked behind Sarah Island on the east of The Narrows, about 1.25 miles north of Glen Island. Boats are not allowed to anchor or moor in the bay from May 15 to September 15, but two boats can tie up to a state dock there.

BLACK MOUNTAIN POINT

[Fig. 21(14)] Boaters can dock here for a picnic or a hike. Trails lead along the shore and up Black Mountain. A permit from the Glen Island ranger station is required for a picnic. Black Mountain Point is on the east side of The Narrows, about 2.5 miles north of Glen Island.

SABBATH DAY POINT

[Fig. 21(8)] The nineteenth-century writer S.G.W. Benjamin regarded the views from here as the finest on the lake. One can look south toward The Narrows or north toward Anthony's Nose and a wider part of the lake. The point is on the west shore about 1.25 miles north of the Narrow Island ranger station.

INDIAN KETTLES

[Fig. 21(7)] Pebbles swirling in the turbulent waters of the melting glacier, about 10,000 years ago, wore potholes in a rocky spit on the west side of the lake, opposite Anthony's Nose. The name, which dates back at least to the early 1800s, arises from the belief that Native Americans used the potholes to grind corn. Indian Kettles is located about 2 miles north of the hamlet of Hague.

ROGERS ROCK

[Fig. 21(5)] Like Anthony's Nose, Rogers Rock rises straight out of the lake. It's named for Robert Rogers, the daredevil leader of Rogers Rangers in the French and Indian War. Rogers supposedly escaped some Indians by sliding down the precipice. Rogers Rock is located on the west shore about 1.75 miles north of Indian Kettles. A trail to the brink starts at Rogers Rock Public Campground (*see* Rogers Rock Public Campground, page 140).

For more information: For a free boating map and information about marinas, phone the Warren County tourism office at (800) 958-4748. JIMAPCO, Inc. sells a multicolored, waterproof boating map. Phone (518) 899-5091.

CANOEING ON LAKE GEORGE

Lake George is not the best place for canoes, given all the powerboats on the water and the constant threat of wind-whipped waves. Those who do venture forth in a canoe would be well advised to stick close to shore or go out in the early morning when the waters are quiet. Also, keep in mind that the Lake George Park Commission's rules for boaters also apply to canoeists.

With those caveats out of the way, here are some suggestions for canoeing on Lake George:

DUNHAM'S BAY MARSH

[Fig. 21(21)] More than 1,000 acres of marsh, fen, and swamp—one of the largest wetlands in the Adirondacks—lie in the southeastern corner of the lake. A rich diversity of animals and birds, including ducks, heron, otter, and mink, lives among the cattails and marsh grass. The state, which owns most of the wetland, does not allow motorboats, but canoeists can explore the marsh by paddling up a meandering outlet that flows under NY 9L into Dunham's Bay.

Directions: From Lake George village, drive east on NY 9L to Dunham's Bay Docks and Marina.

Fees: There is a charge for parking at the marina.

Closest town: Lake George village.

NORTHWEST BAY

[Fig. 21] After putting in at Northwest Bay Brook, canoeists will paddle through a lush marsh, home to great blue heron (*Ardea herodias*) and beaver (*Castor canadensis*), before emerging into Northwest Bay. Tongue Mountain looms over the bay to the east. The state owns nearly all of the Tongue Mountain peninsula, except for a few small inholdings, so feel free to pull up to the shore at any time. A trail follows the shore to Montcalm Point at the tip of the peninsula. Timber rattlesnakes (*Crotalus horridus*) dwell in the area, but they are rarely seen. The snake is on the state's list of endangered species.

Directions: From Northway Exit 24, drive east 5 miles on County 11 to NY 9N, then north 4.3 miles on NY 9N to a state fishing-access site on the right.

THE NARROWS

[Fig. 21] Canoeists can reach the scenic Narrows in a short time after putting in on the east shore of the lake a little north of Shelving Rock Bay. Once in The Narrows, they can paddle among the islands or continue up the shore. North of Pearl Point, where The Narrows begins, the shoreline is state-owned and a trail follows it.

Directions: From Northway Exit 20, drive north on US 9 about 0.5 mile to NY 149; east on NY 149 about 6.3 miles to Buttermilk Falls Road on the left. This road turns into Sly Pond Road after about 3 miles and Shelving Rock Road after about 9 miles. Park toward the end of the road, about 12.8 miles from NY 149. A trail that begins about 0.2 mile farther down the road, near the gate to the Knapp home, leads to the lake. Overnight parking is prohibited here.

FISHING AT LAKE GEORGE

The lake offers good fishing most of the year, including winter once the water freezes. Lake George is a two-story fishery, with landlocked salmon (*Salmo salar*) and lake trout (*Salvelinus namaycush*) dwelling in the colder depths and largemouth bass (*Microptera salmoides*), smallmouth bass (*Microptera dolomieui*), northern pike (*Esox lucius*), chain pickerel (*Esox niger*), and panfish dwelling in warmer water.

The bass fishing is especially good, but many fishermen enjoy the challenge of reeling in a feisty salmon. The salmon average 3 to 4 pounds but can weigh more than 9 pounds. In the early spring, the salmon and lake trout can be found a few hundred yards off shore, feeding near smelt streams. As the lake warms up, they move into deeper waters. After the lake cools in the fall, they again can be found closer to shore. The state stocks the lake with thousands of salmon each year. There is no closed season for salmon or lake trout.

Bass fishermen have the best luck in June and July. The smallmouth average 2 to 3 pounds and the largemouth 3 to 4 pounds. The best times to catch northern pike are late spring to early summer and the fall. The pike average 4 to 7 pounds but can weigh up to 20 pounds.

The lake usually freezes over by January, but fishermen should check on ice conditions before venturing out. Winter fishermen have luck with a variety of species, including salmon, lake trout, pike, and jack perch.

The use of smelt, dead or alive, as bait is forbidden in Lake George. Fishermen may keep two salmon (minimum size 18 inches), two lake trout (minimum size 23 inches), and up to five other trout of any size.

For more information: Warren County publishes a guide called *Grand Slam Fishing* that offers many tips for fishing in Lake George as well as other lakes and rivers in the county. To get a copy, phone the county tourism office at (800) 958-4748. The state Department of Environmental Conservation has a fishing hot line: (518) 623-3682.

SUBMERGED HERITAGE PRESERVE

Not all Lake George artifacts are locked up in a museum. Some are at the bottom of the lake, visible only to the fishes and scuba divers: seven bateaux and a gunship from the French and Indian War and a motorboat from the turn of the century. The state keeps mooring buoys at each of the three sites. Only one boat may moor at a time. Divers are not allowed to touch the relics.

BOREAL CHICKADEE
(Parus hudsonicus)
This brown-capped bird sings its "chick-a-dee" in a buzzy voice.

The seven bateaux, known as the Sunken Fleet of 1758, are located about 150 feet west of the Wiawaka Holiday House. The British intentionally scuttled these and similar boats to prevent the French from capturing them. This is an intermediate dive in 25 to 40 feet of water.

The *Land Tortoise,* a gunship known as a radeau, is located about 2,500 feet northeast of Tea Island. The British also scuttled this ship in 1758, but they were unable to recover it the following spring. This is an advanced dive in 105 to 107 feet of water. Divers must register at Million Dollar Beach.

The motorboat *Forward,* built in 1906, is located about 2,500 feet southeast of Diamond Island. Owned by a wealthy family, it is thought to have been one of the first gasoline-powered boats on the lake. This is an intermediate dive in 35 to 40 feet of water.

For more information: The state Department of Environmental Conservation publishes a pamphlet on each site. Phone the Ray Brook office at (518) 897-1200.

HEARTHSTONE POINT PUBLIC CAMPGROUND

[Fig. 21(20)] This campground, opened by the state in 1927, encompasses about 99 acres on the west shore of the lake, about 2 miles north of Lake George village.

Directions: From Northway Exit 22, drive east to NY 9N, then north on NY 9N for 2 miles. It's on the right.

Activities: Swimming, fishing.

Facilities: 251 tent and trailer sites, toilets, showers, trailer dump station, sand beach. The beach and gazebo are accessible to the handicapped.

Dates: Open mid-May through Labor Day.

Fees: There is a charge for camping or day use.

For more information: Phone the campground at (518) 668-5193. For reservations, phone (800)-456-2267.

Closest town: Lake George village is a few miles south.

ROGERS ROCK PUBLIC CAMPGROUND

[Fig. 21(6)] Those staying at this campground in the northern end of Lake George will want to be sure to walk the trail to the top of Rogers Rock for a great view of the southern Adirondacks and Vermont and the chance to see ravens sailing above the lake. The trail is open to other hikers as well, but the campground charges a day-use fee. Although only 1.1 miles, the trail is quite steep. It begins near campsite 184.

Eleven of the 321 camping sites are on the Waltonian Islands, named for Izaak Walton, who wrote *The Compleat Angler, or the Contemplative Man's Recreation* in 1653. The campground has set aside two areas on the mainland for groups of 35 to 60 people.

Directions: From Northway Exit 25, drive east on NY 8 to Hague to NY 9N, then north 3 miles on NY 9N. It's on the right.

Activities: Swimming, bicycling, fishing, boating, hiking.

Facilities: 321 campsites, including 11 on islands; picnic areas and pavilions; toilets and showers; boat launch, mooring buoys, and boat pumpout station; sand beach with bathhouse; trailer dump station.

Dates: Open early May through Columbus Day.

Fees: There is a charge for camping or day use.

Closest town: Hague is 3 miles south.

For more information: Phone the campground at (518) 585-6746. For reservations, phone (800)-456-2267.

Lake George Wild Forest

In the nineteenth century, most of the land around Lake George was either logged or cleared for farming. Once the land had been logged over, it sometimes was abandoned, and so by 1900, the state had acquired 3,700 acres through tax foreclosures. Today, the Lake George Wild Forest encompasses about 54,000 acres on both sides of the water with more than 100 miles of trails.

The more detailed discussion that follows divides the Lake George Wild Forest into three sections: East Shore, Tongue Mountain Range, and Northern Section.

For more information: State Department of Environmental Conservation, PO Box 232, Hudson Street Extension, Warrensburg, NY, 12885. Phone (518) 623-3671. Ask for the leaflet titled *Trails in the Lake George Region*.

EAST SHORE

The state obtained a big chunk of its 20,550 acres on the east side of the lake when it purchased the Knapp estate in 1941. George O. Knapp, the vice president of Union Carbide, had built a palatial summer home near Shelving Rock Mountain in the early

1900s and bought up much of the land in the vicinity, eventually acquiring several miles of shoreline. Some of the former owners continued to live on the land and work for the estate. Lilacs, grapevines, and daffodils still grow here and there in the forest— reminders of the old days. The estate's many carriage roads today serve as horse trails.

Woods in various stages of succession cover the landscape. Near the shoreline, oaks and pines often flourish together, but as elevation increases, northern hardwoods such as beech (*Fagus grandifolia*), yellow birch (*Betula alleghaniensis*), and sugar maple (*Acer saccharum*) start to take over, with white pine (*Pinus strobus*) mixed in. On higher slopes, red spruce (*Picea rubens*) and hemlock (*Tsuga canadensis*) replace the pine. Hemlocks also can be found in pure stands in moist coves. Near the top of Black Mountain, the region's tallest peak, there is a spruce-fir forest.

The eastern shore has about 72 miles of trails. Hikers can walk along the lake for a close-up view of the water and its islands or climb to a summit for a panoramic view from above. The peaks of Black, Buck, Shelving Rock, and Sleeping Beauty mountains all have marvelous vistas. Trails also lead through the forest to several pretty ponds, five of which have lean-tos. In trout season, fishermen often try their luck at Fishbrook Pond or Greenland Pond. About 41 miles of trails are open to horses and 39 miles are open to snowmobiles. Many trails are also suitable for mountain biking, cross-country skiing, and snowshoeing.

BUCK MOUNTAIN

[Fig. 21] This popular peak can be climbed from Pilot Knob or Shelving Rock Road for a view of Lake George and nearby mountains. On a clear day, it's possible to see the High Peaks. The 3.3-mile Pilot Knob trail is longer but more scenic, with several vistas of the lake en route. Both trails can be snowshoed, but crampons might be needed in spots.

Directions: For Pilot Knob, from Northway Exit 20, drive north on US 9 about 0.5 mile to NY 149; east on NY 149 about 4.7 miles to NY 9L; and north on NY 9L about 4.9 miles to Pilot Knob Road. Take a right at the sign and drive another 3.5 miles to the trailhead. For Shelving Rock Road, continue east on NY 149 past the NY 9L junction about 1.6 miles to Buttermilk Falls Road on the left. This road turns into Sly Pond Road after about 3 miles and Shelving Rock Road after about 9 miles. The Buck Mountain trail begins 10.7 miles from NY 149.

Trail: The summit is 3.3 miles from Pilot Knob or 2.3 miles from Shelving Rock Road.

Elevation: From 330 feet at Pilot Knob or 1,200 feet

The American bittern blends in with the reeds of its swamp habitat.

at Shelving Rock Road to 2,330 feet at summit.

Degree of difficulty: Moderate.

Surface and blaze: Forest floor with rocky sections. Yellow blazes.

BLACK MOUNTAIN

[Fig. 21(15)] The region's highest summit offers a view of all Lake George except The Narrows, which is blocked by other mountains. Timber rattlesnakes (*Crotalus horridus*) den near the summit. It's best to climb Black in a loop that takes one past Lapland Pond, where herons (*Ardea herodias*) live, and the pair of Black Mountain Ponds on the way up. Hikers with boats can reach the summit by another trail that starts on the lakeshore. There is a communications antenna and unmanned fire tower on the summit. The tower is not open to the public.

Directions: From Northway Exit 20, drive north on US 9 about 0.5 mile to NY 149; east on NY 149 to US 4 in Fort Ann village; north on US 4 to NY 22; north on NY 22 to Huletts Landing Road; west on Huletts Landing Road to Pike Brook Road, about 2.7 miles down on the left. The trailhead is 0.8 mile down the road. From Northway Exit 28, drive east on NY 74 to NY 22, near Ticonderoga village, and south on NY 22 to Huletts Landing Road.

Trail: 6.4-mile loop.

Elevation: 1,600 feet at trailhead to 2,646 feet at summit.

Degree of difficulty: Strenuous.

Surface and blaze: Forest floor, some rocky sections. Red blazes for first mile; blue blazes to Lapland Pond; yellow blazes past Black Mountain Ponds to junction with trail from lakeshore; red blazes to summit; return by red-blazed trail on opposite side of summit.

SLEEPING BEAUTY MOUNTAIN

[Fig. 21(18)] The rocky cliffs of the aptly named Sleeping Beauty Mountain look out over Lake George's southern basin, with a good view of the Tongue Mountain Range cleaving the waters to form Northwest Bay and The Narrows. The trail begins at the Hogtown trailhead, the main trailhead for the region, and follows an old carriage road past the stone foundations of a farmhouse at Dacy Clearing. Eventually, a foot trail leads away from the road and curls around the back of the mountain. The junction is marked by a sign.

Directions: See directions to Shelving Rock Road under Buck Mountain page 141. The Hogtown trailhead is 10.2 miles from NY 149.

Trail: 3.4 miles to summit.

Elevation: 1,309 feet at trailhead to 2,347 feet on summit.

Degree of difficulty: Moderate.

Surface and blaze: Old carriage roads, forest floor.

SHELVING ROCK FALLS

[Fig. 21(17)] This trail follows a scenic stretch of Lake George shoreline that attracts a good many picnickers and backpackers in summer and ends at a rocky waterfall where the Knapp estate's powerhouse was located. Waterfowl sometimes can be seen in a wetland at Shelving Rock Bay. Beware that the top of the falls is very slippery and several accidents have occurred there. To return, hikers can retrace their steps or take one of several side trails back to Shelving Rock Road.

Directions: See directions to Shelving Rock Road under Buck Mountain, page 141. Park toward the end of the road, about 12.8 miles from NY 149. The trail begins about 0.2 mile farther down the road, before the gate to the remaining Knapp property.

Trail: 1.6 miles to falls.

Degree of difficulty: Easy.

Surface: Natural forest floor.

FISHBROOK POND

[Fig. 21] Stocked with brook trout (*Salvelinus fontinalis*) and rainbow trout (*Oncoryhncus mykiss*), this is one of the region's more popular ponds for fishing. Bullheads also live in the pond. At 32 acres, it's also the largest pond in this part of the Lake George Wild Forest—a good place to swim or camp. If camping, Fishbrook Pond makes a good base from which to explore nearby peaks and ponds, as trails radiate from it in all directions. Fishermen might also want to try their luck at Lapland, Greenland, Bumps, and Upper Black Mountain ponds, all of which are stocked with brook trout. There are two lean-tos at Fishbrook Pond and one each at Greenland, Lapland, and Upper Black Mountain ponds.

Directions: See directions to Black Mountain trailhead on Pike Brook Road, page 142.

Trail: 4 miles to Fishbrook Pond, passing Lapland and Millman ponds en route.

Elevation: 1,600 feet at trailhead to 1,836 feet at Fishbrook Pond.

Degree of difficulty: Easy.

Surface and blaze: Natural forest floor. Red blazes for first mile, blue blazes rest of way.

HORSE TRAILS

Equestrians can ride through the forest along old carriage and woods roads to many of the most beautiful spots in the Eastern Lake George Wild Forest, including mountain vistas, the lakeshore, and interior ponds. The 41.25 miles of trails—also used by hikers—allow for a variety of loops from three starting points, including the Hogtown trailhead, the main trailhead on Shelving Rock Road. (*See* Sleeping Beauty Mountain, page 142.)

For more information: The state Department of Environmental Conservation publishes a booklet titled *Horse Trails in New York State* in addition to the pamphlet *Trails in the Lake George Region.* Phone DEC's Warrensburg office at (518) 623-3671.

SNOWMOBILE TRAILS

The 38.6 miles of snowmobile routes, marked by round orange disks, often coincide with horse trails, enabling snowmobilers to ride deep into the forest or along the lake. One trail goes up Black Mountain. Starting points include the Hogtown trailhead (*see* Sleeping Beauty Mountain, page 142) and Black Mountain trailhead (*see* Black Mountain, page 142).

For more information: Get the state Department of Environmental Conservation booklet *Snowmobiling in New York State.* Phone DEC's Warrensburg office at (518) 623-3671.

▓ TONGUE MOUNTAIN RANGE

[Fig. 21] A series of midsize peaks forms the spine of a large peninsula that juts into Lake George between The Narrows and Northwest Bay. On both sides of the peninsula, the Earth's crust sank along faults sometime after the late Ordovician Period, creating valleys that filled with water when the glaciers created Lake George. Hikers who walk along the ridge are rewarded with numerous vistas of the lake and its islands and the mountains on the east shore.

Oak-pine forests—uncommon in most of the Adirondacks—cover much of the range, but hemlocks (*Tsuga canadensis*) can be found in shady glens. Tongue Mountain is known for its abundance and variety of wildflowers, such as trailing arbutus (*Epigaea repens*), Canada mayflower (*Maianthemum canadense*), bunchberry (*Cornus canadensis*), and wild sarsaparilla (*Aralia nudicaulis*). Periodic ground fires on the dry, rocky terrain help flowers by clearing away the understory and giving them space to grow. Hike the Tongue in early May to see the flowers in full bloom. Timber rattlesnakes (*Crotalus horridus*) hang out among the ridge's rocky ledges, but people seldom see them. Nonetheless, hikers should be careful where they step and place their hands.

Tongue Mountain has about 20 miles of trails but few possibilities for loops. There only two roadside trailheads, both off NY 9N. The trails also can be reached by water at Montcalm Point and Five Mile Point. Snowmobiles and horses are not allowed on Tongue Mountain, but bicycles are.

TONGUE MOUNTAIN TRAIL

[Fig. 21(9)] Most people will want to hike only sections of this trail, a rugged traverse over several peaks that ends at Montcalm Point, 5.4 miles from the nearest road. Those who want to do it all can leave a second car at Clay Meadow and return there by way of the Northwest Bay Trail—a total hike of 17 miles. Since there are two lean-tos along the way, the trek can be broken into two days. Hikers should carry plenty of water, because the ridge is dry. Of the many scenic views, those at Five Mile Mountain, French Point Mountain, and First Peak are especially spectacular. Advanced mountain bikers can ride the trail as far as Five Mile Mountain.

Directions: From Northway Exit 24, go 5 miles east to NY 9N, turn left, and go 7.7 miles to a parking lot on the left. The trail begins across the road. After the hike, drive a short distance down the road to a pulloff on the right with a vista of Lake George.

Trail: 11.2 miles from trailhead to Montcalm Point.

Elevation: 1,065 feet at trailhead, 2,256 feet at Five Mile Mountain, 320 feet at lakeshore.

Degree of difficulty: Strenuous.

Surface and blaze: Forest floor, with rocky sections. Blue blazes.

DEER LEAP

[Fig. 21(13)] Legend has it that a deer pursued by a hunter to the edge of this precipice overlooking The Narrows leapt to its death on the rocks below. The trail to Deer Leap is a 1.1-mile spur off the Tongue Mountain Trail. The lookout offers a good view of northern Lake George. Black Mountain, the region's highest summit, stands out as one looks south across the water. This is an easy snowshoe trip in winter.

Directions: Same as for Tongue Mountain Trail.

Trail: 1.7 miles one-way.

Elevation: 1,065 feet at trailhead to 1,100 feet at Deer Leap.

Degree of difficulty: Easy.

Surface and blaze: Forest floor. Blue blazes for first .6 mile, yellow blazes rest of way.

NORTHWEST BAY TRAIL

[Fig. 21(11)] The Civilian Conservation Corps originally built this as a horse trail. It follows the shore of Northwest Bay from Clay Meadow to Montcalm Point, passing through a pine plantation, marshes, streams, and hemlock glens. Great blue herons (*Ardea herodias*) sometimes can be seen in Northwest Bay. There are good places to swim along the way and at the point, where there is a dock. Montcalm Point has a magnificent view of The Narrows and its islands and the mountains to the east. Dome Island, owned by The Nature Conservancy, is to the south. Intermediate mountain bikers can take the trail, but they may have to walk their bikes in sections.

Directions: From Northway Exit 24, go 5 miles east to NY 9N; turn left and go 4.7 miles to the Clay Meadow parking lot on the left, about 100 feet past the trailhead.

Trail: 5.4 miles from Clay Meadow to Montcalm Point.

Degree of difficulty: Moderate.

Surface and blaze: Natural forest floor. Blue blazes.

RIDGE AND BAY LOOP

[Fig. 21(10)] This is the shortest loop possible, sticking to official trails: From Clay Meadow, hike 2 miles east to the Tongue Mountain Trail, then 7 miles south to Montcalm Point, and finally 5.4 miles north on the Northwest Bay Trail to return to

BEE BALM
(Monarda didyma)
Used to produce a medicinal tea by Native Americans, bee balm is seldom visited by bees, but instead is usually pollinated by hummingbirds.

Clay Meadow. The hike combines the best of the ridge and shore trails. To reach the ridge, start up the Five Mile Point Trail, bearing left at the junction about 0.4 mile from the trailhead. The way right is the Northwest Bay Trail, the return route.

Directions: Same as for Northwest Bay Trail.

Trail: 14.4-mile loop.

Elevation: About 420 feet at Clay Meadow, 1,813 feet at Fifth Peak, 320 feet at Lake George.

Degree of difficulty: Strenuous.

Surface and blaze: Natural forest floor, with rocky sections. Blue blazes for first 0.4 mile, red blazes to Tongue Mountain ridge, blue blazes to Montcalm Point and on return to Clay Meadow.

▓ NORTHERN SECTION

A large piece of the Lake George Wild Forest lies north of Tongue Mountain, on the other side of NY 9N. Most of the land was logged or farmed in the past—it's still possible to come across an apple tree or stone wall in the woods—but the forest has long since grown back.

The Bolton Civilian Conservation Corps camp was located in this region from 1937 to 1941. The men from the camp built campgrounds and ranger stations around Lake George and planted several stands of pine and spruce.

Several trails in this section lead to ponds popular with fishermen. There are also snowmobile and mountain bike routes.

JABE POND

[Fig. 21] A dirt road leads to within 300 feet of this 1-mile-long pond ringed by wooded mountains, making it a good destination for canoeists and for families with young children. Beware, however, that the road is rough and usually closes during spring mud season.

Anglers come here for the brown trout (*Salmo trutta*) stocked by the state. Fishermen are allowed to keep up to three trout (minimum size 12 inches). Only artificial lures are permitted.

There are several good campsites along the shore. Canoeists may want to explore the island at the southern end of the pond. The 1-mile dirt road to the pond is a good route for a mountain bike.

Directions: From Northway Exit 24, drive 5 miles east to NY 9N; north on NY 9N to Split Rock Road, located on the left about 1.5 miles north of Silver Bay; and west on Split Rock Road about 1.8 miles to the dirt road leading to Jabe Pond.

Activities: Fishing, canoeing, camping, mountain bike riding.

Fees: None.

Closest town: Hague is about 4 miles north.

WARDSBORO ROAD

[Fig. 21(22)] This old dirt road and trail through a pleasant wood is suitable for hiking, mountain biking, skiing, or snowshoeing. It also is a snowmobile route. The suggested turnaround is at a trail junction about 3.5 miles from the start.

Directions: From Northway Exit 24, go east 5 miles to NY 9N, north 6 miles to Pandanarum Road on the left, 1.8 miles to Wardsboro Road on the right, and 3.4 miles to the trailhead near an old cemetery.

Trail: 3.5 miles one-way.

Elevation: About 500 feet at cemetery, about 1,340 at high point.

Degree of difficulty: Easy.

Surface: Old woods road, some wet areas.

COMMON LOON
(Gavia immer)
The loon can swim long distances underwater or with its eyes and bill under the surface before diving below.

Cook Mountain Preserve

[Fig. 21(4)] The Adirondack Nature Conservancy and Lake George Basin Conservancy own this 200-acre preserve in the town of Ticonderoga. A trail through a wood of red oak (*Quercus rubra borealis*), American beech (*Fagus grandifolia*), and sugar maple (*Acer saccharum*) leads to a ridge on Cook Mountain with good views of northern Lake George, including Anthony's Nose and Rogers Rock, as well as Lake Champlain and Vermont's Green Mountains.

Directions: From monument and traffic circle on NY 9N in the village of Ticonderoga, drive south on Lord Howe Street for 0.75 mile to T intersection at Alexandria Street. Take a left, then a quick right onto Baldwin Road. The trailhead is 1.5 miles down on the right.

Trail: 1.3 miles to summit.

Elevation: 335 feet on Baldwin Road to 1,230 feet at summit.

Degree of difficulty: Moderate.

Surface and blaze: Old woods road, forest floor. Red blazes.

Ticonderoga

The modern village of Ticonderoga sits on La Chute River, a short, cascading stream that drains Lake George into Lake Champlain. Most people associate the village with the eighteenth-century fort that lies just outside its borders, but there are two other museums here that might appeal to history buffs. The Ticonderoga Heritage Museum, next to Bicentennial Park, focuses on the region's industrial history. The Hancock House, a replica of John Hancock's house in Boston, focuses on social history. Visitors can pick up a map at the Hancock House for a self-guided tour of the village. Both are open year-round, but hours vary seasonally.

Visitors also can take a self-guided tour of La Chute River. The river, which falls 230 feet in just 3.5 miles, has for centuries provided power for sawmills, paper mills, and other industries. The 0.25-mile trail starts at Bicentennial Park and ends at Richards Island Dam. Maps can be obtained at the Heritage Museum, Ticonderoga Chamber of Commerce, or Black Watch Memorial Library. Fishing is permitted in the river, which is stocked with rainbow trout (*Oncorhynchus mykiss*).

FORT TICONDEROGA

[Fig. 21(3)] The French built a fort overlooking the Lake Champlain Narrows in 1755, when they were engaged in a struggle with the British for supremacy of the New World. They named it Carillon, because the cascades of the nearby La Chute sounded like chimes. Lord Jeffrey Amherst captured Carillon in 1759, but not before the French blew up much of it. Amherst rebuilt the stone fort and renamed it Ticonderoga—a Mohawk word meaning "place between great waters."

By May 1775, the British had made a new enemy: the American Colonies. That month, Ethan Allen, Benedict Arnold, and the Green Mountain Boys made a daring raid and captured the fort "in the name of the great Jehovah and the Continental Congress." This victory, coming just three weeks after the battles at Lexington and Concord, helped to fire up the Colonists' resolve. Cannon from the fort were hauled by sledges to Boston, where they were turned against the British.

In 1777, Gen. John "Gentleman Johnny" Burgoyne reclaimed Ticonderoga for the British by placing cannons on Mount Defiance, a steep embankment overlooking the bastion. After the Americans won the war, the fort was abandoned, but it became a tourist spot early on, attracting such notables as Thomas Jefferson and the historian Francis Parkman.

Military artifacts from two wars, including powder horns, weapons, and cannons, as well as surgeon's kits, maps, books, and personal portraits and letters are on display. Under the barracks are the great ovens where each day thousands of loaves of bread were baked to nourish the armies.

Events scheduled throughout the summer include a war encampment, a fife and drum corps muster, and demonstrations of black powder shooting and cannon firing. Cruises across Lake Champlain on the *Carillon* are available.

Mount Defiance is on fort property. A short, steep climb to the top opens up a panoramic view of the fort, lake, and surrounding countryside. The Kings Garden showcases flowers and other plants.

Directions: From Northway Exit 28, drive 18 miles east on Route 74 to the fort.
Activities: Picnicking, hiking.

Facilities: Restaurant, museum shop.
Dates: Open daily from early June through late Oct.
Fees: There is a charge for admission except for children under age 7.
For more information: Phone (518) 585-2821.

Pharaoh Lake Wilderness

The 46,283-acre Pharaoh Lake Wilderness, located a short distance from the Northway, has long been a favorite haunt of hikers and fishermen from the Albany area to the south. Pharaoh Mountain, at 2,551 feet, dominates this landscape of rolling hills and glacial ponds.

Pharaoh Lake, with its six lean-tos and dozens of tent sites, is the most popular destination of overnight campers. On busy weekends, up to 300 campers have been counted along its shores. Those in search of solitude might want to hike to one of the many smaller ponds. Most of them can be reached by the nearly 70 miles of trails that crisscross the wilderness. Lean-tos also exist at Tubmill Marsh, Oxshoe Pond, Lilypad Pond, Rock Pond, Little Rock Pond, Grizzle Ocean, Clear Pond, and Berrymill Pond. Tent sites are scattered throughout the region.

For the best vistas, hikers can take trails to the summit of Pharaoh Mountain or Treadway Mountain. Some of the cliffs in the wilderness make good rock climbs.

Although the mountains of the Pharaoh Lake Wilderness are not huge, the terrain was rugged enough to discourage settlement. Except for a few farms, sporting lodges, and mines—mostly on the fringes of the wilderness—the region's main business was logging. The loggers first cut down the white pine (*Pinus strobus*), the most valuable timber, and then turned their attention to hemlock (*Tsuga canadensis*), whose bark was used in tanning. When iron mines created a demand for charcoal, and thus for trees of all kinds, the loggers laid bare whole hillsides. Traces of farms, sawmills, and mines can still be found in the woods.

In the early 1900s, fires swept through much of the region, leaving nothing but rock on some summits. The fires and the logging left almost no virgin timber. The woods have since grown back, but they are in transition, slowly progressing toward a climax forest. Pioneer hardwoods, such as red maple (*Acer rubrum*), paper birch (*Betula papyrifea*), quaking aspen (*Populus tremuloides*), and pin cherry (*Prunus pensylvanica*), dominate much of the woods, but in some places—between Grizzle Ocean and Putnam Pond, for example—these have been succeeded by more shade-tolerant hardwoods, such as sugar maple (*Acer saccharum*), yellow birch (*Betula alleghaniensis*), and beech (*Fagus grandifola*). Several other types of forests can be found here: pine-oak on fertile southern slopes, mixed pine on dry ridges and along shores, hemlock along streams and in narrow valleys, and spruce-fir in moist lowlands and on the upper slopes. Also, stands of red, white, and Scotch pines and

Norway spruce were planted in a few places before 1940.

The usual Adirondack mammals make their home in the region, including white-tailed deer (*Odocoileus virginianus*), black bear (*Ursus americanus*), beaver (*Castor canadensis*), otter (*Lutra canadensis*), fisher (*Martes pennanti*), marten (*Martes americana*), bobcat (*Lynx rufus*), and an occasional moose (*Alces alces*). In winter, the deer tend to concentrate in spruce-fir forests in the southern sector of the wilderness. About 140 species of birds live here, including wild turkeys (*Meleagris gallopavo*), ravens (*Corvus corax*), ruffed grouse (*Bonasa umbellus*), and various kinds of ducks, hawks, and owls. Osprey (*Pandion haliaetus*) and loons (*Gavia immer*) are less common but have been sighted. Brook trout (*Salvelinus fontinalis*) are stocked in about half of the 41 ponds.

For more information: The state Department of Environmental Conservation publishes a pamphlet titled *Trails in the Schroon Lake Region*. Contact DEC at PO Box 232, Hudson Street Extension, Warrensburg, NY 12885. Phone (518) 623-3671.

PUTNAM POND PUBLIC CAMPGROUND

[Fig. 21(2)] From this base on the eastern edge of the Pharaoh Lake Wilderness, hikers can explore the surrounding mountains by day and enjoy the comforts of a state campground at night. For day trippers, too, the campground is the most convenient starting point for hikes to Treadway Mountain and several ponds.

Canoeists can spend hours exploring the coves and islands of the 1-mile-long Putnam Pond, a haunt of common loons (*Gavia immer*) and wood ducks (*Aix sponsa*). Hemlocks (*Tsuga canadensis*), white cedars (*Thuja canadensis*), paper birch (*Betula payrifea*), and red pine (*Pinus resinosa*) grow along the boulder-strewn shores. Paddlers can cross the pond to reach isolated campsites or pick up foot trails that lead to the interior of the wilderness.

The pond is stocked with tiger muskies (*Esox masquinongy*), but smallmouth bass (*Micropterus dolomieui*), yellow perch (*Perca flavescens*), and northern pike (*Esox lucius*) also can be caught.

Canoes and rowboats can be rented at the campground. There is a sandy beach on the pond.

Directions: From Northway Exit 28, drive east about 9 miles on NY 74. The entrance is on the right.

Activities: Camping, hiking, swimming, fishing, boating, picnicking, bicycling.

Facilities: 61 campsites, picnic shelter, beach, showers, dumping station. There is a handicapped-accessible site.

DEER MOUSE
(*Peromyscus maniculatus*)

Dates and hours: Open late May through Labor Day.

Fees: There is a charge for camping and day use.

For more information: To reach the campground office, phone (518) 585-7280. For reservations, phone (800) 456-2267.

TREADWAY MOUNTAIN

[Fig. 21] Here's a great hike that combines canoeing with climbing. After putting in at the state campground, paddle about 0.75 mile across Putnam Pond to a trail that leads to an open summit with wonderful views of Pharaoh Mountain, Glidden Marsh, and Schroon Lake to the west, the Lake George mountains to the south, and the High Peaks to the northwest. From the west shore of the pond, the 2.3-mile trail skirts a wetland beside a small trout pond and then climbs through hemlocks and hardwoods to several rocky knobs denuded by fires in the early 1900s. Trailing arbutus (*Epigaea repens*) and blueberries grow near the summit. It is possible to walk around the southern end of the pond to the summit trail, but this adds 3.2 miles to the round trip.

Directions: Start at Putnam Pond Public Campground. Paddle southwest to trailhead. Canoes and rowboats can be rented at the campground.

Trail: After a 0.75-mile paddle, it's 2.3 miles from shore to summit. If hiking the whole way, it's 3.9 miles from campground to summit.

Elevation: 1,308 feet at Putnam Pond to 2,240 feet on summit.

Degree of difficulty: Moderate.

Surface and blaze: Natural forest floor, bare rock. If starting from west shore, blue blazes for first 0.4 mile and red blazes the rest of the way. Otherwise, yellow blazes for first 1.4 miles, blue blazes for next 0.4 mile, red blazes the rest of the way.

GRIZZLE OCEAN

[Fig. 21] A logger named Grizzle once boasted so much about the fish he caught in this pond that his friends joked that it must be an ocean. Well, 19 acres don't make an ocean, but it's no exaggeration to say this conifer-ringed water is a picturesque place to camp, fish, and swim. There is a lean-to on the northeastern shore, set back among pines, but it often is full on summer weekends. The state stocks the pond with brook trout. A 1.6-mile trail circles the pond.

Directions: Start at Putnam Pond Public Campground. The Grizzle Ocean Trail passes by the south end of the pond.

Trail: 1.8 miles from campground to lean-to.

Elevation: 1,308 feet at Putnam Pond to 1,475 feet at Grizzle Ocean.

Degree of difficulty: Easy.

Surface and blaze: Natural forest floor. Yellow blazes for 1.6 miles, blue blazes to lean-to.

▒ PHARAOH LAKE

[Fig. 21] Covering 441 acres, this is one of the largest lakes in the Adirondacks wholly surrounded by land designated as wilderness. Several rocky ledges and bluffs overlook the lake, and white cedars (*Thuja canadensis*), hemlocks (*Tsuga canadensis*), and white pines (*Pinus strobus*) grow along the shores. The view from the east shore, looking across the water to Pharaoh Mountain, is especially scenic.

CEDAR WAXWING (*Bombycilla cedrorum*)

The state stocks the water with brook trout (*Salvelinus fontinalis*), but lake trout (*Salvelinus namaycush*), smallmouth bass (*Micropterus dolomieui*), brown bullheads (*Ictalurus nebulosus*), yellow perch (*Perca flavescens*), golden shiners (*Notemigonus crysoleucas*), common shiners (*Notropis cornutus*), and pumpkin-seeds (*Lepomis gibbosus*) also live in the lake.

The trail from Mill Brook leads past a marsh and through a pine plantation, hemlocks, and mixed hard-woods to a junction just before the lake. Here, the trail to the left leads to the two lean-tos on the west shore and, eventually, to the summit of Pharaoh Mountain. Take a right to go along the more scenic east shore, where trailing arbutus (*Epigaea repens*) and blueberries grow. The two trails do not encircle the lake, but an unofficial path on the northwestern shore connects them.

Those who stay at Pharaoh Lake for a few days can explore other parts of the wilderness by taking the other trails that lead to the lake.

This trail makes an excellent cross-country ski trip.

Directions: From Northway Exit 25, drive east on NY 8 to Palisades Road, at northern end of Brant Lake, and take a left; go 1.6 miles to Beaver Pond Road and take a right; go 1.1 miles to Pharaoh Lake Road on the right; and go 0.3 mile to the wilderness boundary. It's a 1.1-mile walk down the road to the trailhead at Mill Brook. Note: It's possible to drive to Mill Brook, but the road is rough. Although it's illegal to drive past the wilderness boundary, the state has not been enforcing the law in this instance. That could change.

Trail: 3.6 miles from wilderness boundary (or 2.5 miles from Mill Brook) to Pharaoh Lake.

Degree of difficulty: Easy.

Elevation: About 925 feet at Mill Brook to 1,146 feet at lake.

Surface and blaze: Old tote road, natural forest floor. Blue blazes.

▒ PHARAOH MOUNTAIN

[Fig. 21] The highest peak in the Pharaoh Lake Wilderness looks down upon a rugged countryside dotted with lakes and ponds. From the summit, hikers can enjoy superb views of the High Peaks, Green Mountains, Lake George's mountains, and Lake Champlain.

Starting at Crane Pond, the trail leads through an evergreen forest past Glidden Marsh, home to great blue heron (*Ardea herodias*), and climbs up the mountain's north slope. Because fire ravaged the summit in the early twentieth century, hikers find themselves walking on bare rock past scrubby trees before reaching the summit. The exposed bedrock is mostly granitic gneiss. Look for red bits of garnet.

Directions: From Northway Exit 28, take US 9 south to Alder Meadow Road; turn left and go 2.2 miles to a fork; bear left and go 0.4 mile to the parking lot at the wilderness boundary. It's a 2-mile walk to Crane Pond Outlet, where the trail to Pharaoh Mountain begins. Note: It's possible to drive the two miles to Crane Pond, but the road is rough. Although it's illegal to drive past the wilderness boundary, the state has not been enforcing the law in this instance. That could change.

Trail: 4.9 miles from wilderness boundary (or 2.9 miles from Crane Pond Outlet) to summit.

Elevation: 1,081 feet at Crane Pond to 2,551 feet at summit.

Degree of difficulty: Moderate.

Surface and blaze: Dirt road, natural forest floor, bare rock. Red blazes from Crane Pond.

Red Eft

The red eft may be only a few inches long, but its bright reddish-orange skin makes it stand out among the green and brown hues of the forest. The red eft is the terrestrial form of the red-spotted newt (*Notophthalmus viridescens viridescens*), a subspecies of the Eastern newt. These newts are born in ponds and lakes in spring, but within two to three months, they develop lungs and leave the water to live on land. They eat insects, slugs, earthworms, and other invertebrates. Because red efts need moisture, which they absorb through their skin, they usually forage underground, but on rainy and humid days they venture to the surface. This is the time to look for them. Red efts hibernate in winter. After five years or so, they return to water, where they live several more years as aquatic newts. Their lungs continue to function, but red efts also undergo changes that enable them to absorb oxygen through their skin and the lining of their mouths. They also develop keeled tails to help in swimming. In this stage, the newts are an olive green or yellow with red spots.

PHARAOH LAKE HORSE TRAILS

[Fig. 21(1), Fig. 22(3)] Two trails in the wilderness are open to horses. One is the trail from Mill Brook to Pharaoh Lake described earlier (*see* page 152). The other is the 10.1-mile Sucker Brook Trail, which also leads to Pharaoh Lake, where it meets the first trail. The Sucker Brook Trail follows an old road through a variety of woods and passes the stone ruins of a farmhouse. The trail is also suitable for walking, but it

Acid Rain

Acid rain forms when sulfur dioxide and nitrous oxides emitted by power plants, factories, and automobiles mix with water vapor to create sulfuric and nitric acids. The Adirondacks are especially hard hit because prevailing winds carry the pollution to the mountains from the industrial Ohio Valley. It's estimated that 500 out of 2,800 lakes and ponds in the Adirondacks no longer support the fish and plants that they once did. More than 200 lakes are completely devoid of fish. The acid leaches toxic metals such as mercury and aluminum from the earth. The metals accumulate in the water and damage gills, so the fish suffocate. Fish eggs often fail to hatch in acidified waters. Acid rain also has been blamed for the deaths of trees, especially red spruce on upper slopes. The term *acid rain* is something of a misnomer, for acid fog and dry deposition do as much damage as rain. One of the worst pollution events is acid shock, when the snows melt in spring and swell streams, ponds, and lakes with acidic waters. Usually, about 27 percent of Adirondack lakes have a pH under 5.0—the level at which most fish cannot long survive. After acid shock, the number rises to 58 percent for several weeks.

gets little use from either riders or hikers. The first few miles are good skiing.

The following information is for the Sucker Brook Trail.

Directions: From the hamlet of Adirondack on the east shore of Schroon Lake, drive 0.5 mile on Beaver Pond Road to a fork; bear left and go 0.2 mile to a T-intersection; turn left and go 0.6 mile to a parking area.

Trail: 10.1 miles

Degree of difficulty: Easy (for hikers).

Elevation: 880 feet at trailhead to 1,146 feet at lake.

Surface and blaze: Old woods road, natural forest floor. Yellow blazes.

For more information: The state Department of Environmental Conservation publishes a booklet *Horse Trails in New York State*. Phone (518) 623-3671.

South Bay and Lake Champlain Narrows

[Fig. 21] On a map, the lower reaches of Lake Champlain appear as a narrow ribbon of water east of Lake George, resembling a river more than a lake. Near Whitehall, the lake ends at the Champlain Canal, which goes to the Hudson River. A few miles before Whitehall, Lake Champlain meets South Bay, a pondlike body of water hemmed in by wooded hills and rocky cliffs.

Long-distance canoeists can paddle up the Champlain Narrows as far as Ticonderoga, Crown Point, or points north, but most canoeists probably would be content to spend an afternoon exploring South Bay, a home to great blue heron. For the most scenic route, paddle along the western shore, past numerous small inlets with yellow pond lilies (*Nuphar variegatum*), pickerelweed (*Pontederia cordata*), and cattails (*Typha latifolia*), to a large marsh at the southern tip where South Bay Creek comes in. The inlets are good places to fish for yellow perch (*Perca flavescens*).

Two exotic species, Eurasian water milfoil and water chestnut (*Trapa natans*), have invaded South Bay. All boaters should be careful to avoid bringing in these plants on the bottoms of their craft.

Canoeists who disembark on the shores should be aware that timber rattlesnakes (*Crotalus horridus*) are believed to dwell on the rocky ledges around South Bay.

Ice fishing is allowed at South Bay and along the Champlain Narrows. Regardless of the season, anglers must have a Vermont license to fish on the eastern side of the Narrows, since the New York/Vermont border runs down its middle. The species found in the Narrows include yellow perch, northern pike (*Esox lucius*), channel catfish (*Ictalurus punctatus*), and black crappies (*Pomoxis nigromaculatus*).

Canoeists who want to explore The Narrows and its marshes should beware that virtually no state land lies along its shore between South Bay and the Crown Point Public Campground, a stretch of roughly 35 miles. Paul Jamieson notes in *Adirondack Canoe Waters: North Flow* that long-distance canoeists may have to camp between the shoreline and railroad tracks.

Directions: From the village of Whitehall, drive north on NY 22 a few miles to a bridge over the northern end of South Bay; soon after crossing the bridge, turn right to a state boat ramp. The paddle from the ramp to the marsh is about 3.5 miles.

Activities: Canoeing, boating, fishing.

Facilities: Boat ramp.

Dates: Open year-round.

Fees: None.

Closest town: The village of Whitehall is a few miles southeast.

Brant Lake

[Fig. 22] Although surrounded by private land, this 5-mile-long lake remains accessible to canoeists and boaters by a hard-surface ramp at its southern tip. The state stocks the lake with brown trout (*Salmo trutta*), which typically weigh 2 to 3 pounds when caught but can weigh as much as 5. Brant Lake also holds largemouth bass (*Micropterus salmoides*), smallmouth bass (*Micropterus dolomieui*), pickerel (*Esox americanus*), bullheads, and panfish. Ice fishing for trout is allowed. Brant Lake is located between Schroon Lake and Lake George in the town of Horicon.

Directions: From Northway Exit 25, drive east about 3 miles on NY 8 to the boat launch on the left.

Activities: Canoeing, boating, fishing.

Facilities: Boat ramp.

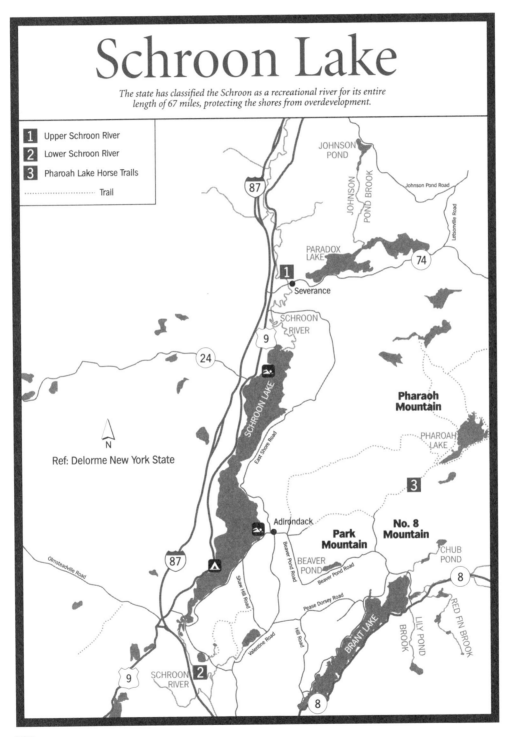

Schroon Lake

The state has classified the Schroon as a recreational river for its entire length of 67 miles, protecting the shores from overdevelopment.

1 Upper Schroon River

2 Lower Schroon River

3 Pharoah Lake Horse Trails

·················· Trail

JOHNSON POND

JOHNSON POND BROOK

Johnson Pond Road

Letsonville Road

87

PARADOX LAKE

74

1 Severance

SCHROON RIVER

9

24

SCHROON LAKE

East Shore Road

N

Ref: Delorme New York State

Pharaoh Mountain

PHAROAH LAKE

3

Adirondack

Park Mountain

No. 8 Mountain

CHUB POND

Olmsteadville Road

87

Beaver Pond Road

BEAVER POND

Beaver Pond Road

8

Shaw Hill Road

Pease Dorsey Road

RED FIN BROOK

Valentine Road

Hill Road

BRANT LAKE

LILY POND BROOK

9

SCHROON RIVER

2

8

Dates: Open year-round.
Fees: None.
Closest town: Brant Lake hamlet is a little south of the lake.

Schroon River and Schroon Lake

The Schroon River looks like a piece of blue string dropped haphazardly on the map: it's so bunched up and squiggly in places that it seems to be going in three directions at once. The river exhibits its fickleness again for 9 miles in its midlife transformation into a lake—the 10th largest in the Adirondacks, not counting Lake Champlain. One thing the Schroon is not is boring: it's got rocky chutes and marshy meanders, brook trout (*Salwelinus fontinalis*) and landlocked salmon (*Salmo salar*), osprey (*Pandion haliaetus*) and red-winged blackbirds (*Agelaius phoeniceus*).

The state has classified the Schroon as a recreational river for its entire length of 67 miles, protecting the shores from overdevelopment. Since the river is never far from main roads, canoeists and fishermen can get to it easily. The river is stocked with salmon, brook trout, brown trout (*Salmo trutta*), rainbow trout (*Oncorhynchus mykiss*).

From a broken dam at Deadwater Pond in North Hudson, the river flows south to the Hudson below Warrensburg. It can be divided into three sections: the upper Schroon, stretching about 27 miles to Schroon Lake; the lake; and the lower Schroon, stretching about 30 miles from the lake to the Hudson.

UPPER SCHROON

[Fig. 22(1)] The Schroon begins its journey flowing past white cedar (*Thuja occidentalis*), white pine (*Pinus strobus*), balsam fir (*Abies balsamea*), and various hardwoods in what often seems to be a wilderness setting—though the highway is not far away. Except in spring or other times of high water, the first 9 miles are not canoeable.

Those who do canoe the upper reaches can put in at the Sharp Bridge Public Campground on US 9 in North Hudson. If the water is not high enough there, try starting at the Blue Ridge Road bridge, near Northway Exit 29. The rapids between the campground and Schroon Falls, about 12.5 miles downstream, reach Class II intensity.

Below the falls the river is more peaceful as it meanders south toward the lake. For a pleasant flatwater journey through oxbows and a swamp, put in at NY 74 north of the lake in the town of Schroon. From there, it's just 2 miles to the lake, as the hawk flies, but the river's twisty course makes the trip 3.5 miles long.

SCHROON LAKE

[Fig. 22] This 4,230-acre lake just west of the Pharaoh Lake Wilderness attracts many salmon fishermen, especially during the smelt runs of early spring. The lake is stocked with brown trout, brook trout, and lake trout (*Salvelinus namaycush*) as well as salmon. Other species found include largemouth bass (*Micropterus salmoides*), smallmouth bass (*Micropterus dolomieui*), northern pike (*Esox lucius*), and pickerel (*Esox americanus*). Ice fishing for trout and salmon is allowed.

Boats can be launched at a state hard-surface ramp at the southern end of the lake off County 62 just north of Pottersville. There is parking for 49 cars and trailers. Canoes and small boats also can be launched at the Eagle Point Public Campground on the lake's west shore and at the public beach in the village of Schroon Lake.

THE EAGLE POINT PUBLIC CAMPGROUND.

Directions: From Northway Exit 26, drive north on US 9 for about 2 miles to the campground on the right.

Activities: Camping, picnicking, fishing, boating.

Facilities: 72 campsites, picnic area, boat launch, beach, showers, toilets, trailer dump station. The beach is accessible to the handicapped.

Dates: Open May through Labor Day.

QUEEN ANNE'S LACE
(Daucus carota)
A very common wildflower found across North America from Alaska to Mexico. Growing to 5 feet tall, the flowers are creamy white with a single dark flower in the center.

Fees: There is a charge for camping or day use.

Closest town: Pottersville is a few miles south.

For more information: Phone the campground at (518) 494-2220. For reservations, phone (800) 456-2267.

LOWER SCHROON

[Fig. 22(2)] The first 4 miles of the Schroon south of the lake make an excellent flatwater paddle, as the river winds through the vast Jenks Swamp. Canoeists can put in at the state boat launch at the southern end of Schroon Lake. They can either return to the starting point or, if using a two-car shuttle, take out at the bridge before the Starbuckville Dam on Schroon River Road, about 5.5 miles from the launch.

Below the dam, the Schroon is full of rapids for several miles, often reaching Class II or III intensity, but the river calms down again for the last 10 miles to Warrensburg, winding through a series of oxbows. Canoeists should be careful not to venture beyond the US 9 bridge in Warrensburg, for two dams lie downstream.

Up Yonda Farm Environmental Education Center

[Fig. 21(19)] A seasonal butterfly garden, a beehive, and a rustic museum (with a large diorama catching native animals in midprowl) are among the exhibits at this 68-acre educational center in Bolton Landing. There also is a self-guided nature trail that meanders 0.25-mile through white pines and over an intermittent stream and a pond, stocked with noisy frogs. Throughout the year, the center offers lectures and slide shows on a slew of topics, including nature crafts, backyard birds, maple sugar basics, and aquatic adventures.

Directions: From Northway Exit 24, drive east on County 11 for 5 miles to its end. Turn right onto NY 9N and go for 0.5 mile to Up Yonda Farm on the right.

Activities: Hiking, educational lectures and exhibits.

Facilities: Museum, nature trail.

Dates: Year-round, daily from 9 a.m. to 4 p.m.

Fees: There is a charge for admission.

For more information: Phone (518) 644-9767.

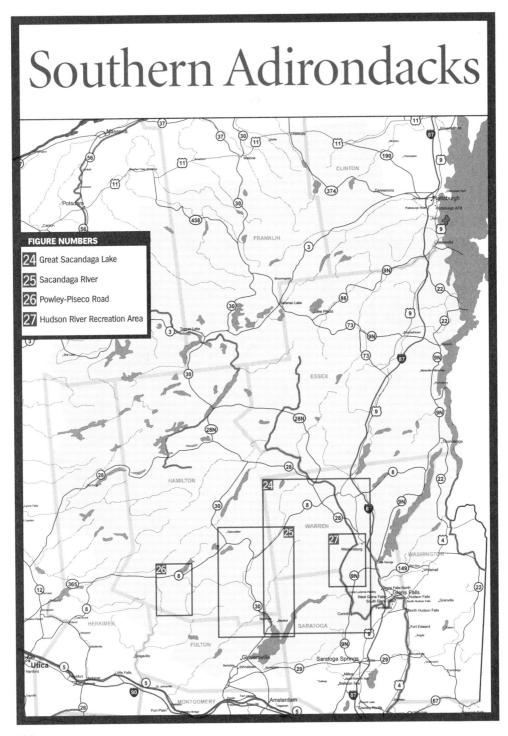

Southern Adirondacks

FIGURE NUMBERS

24 Great Sacandaga Lake

25 Sacandaga River

26 Powley-Piseco Road

27 Hudson River Recreation Area

Southern Adirondacks

The Southern Adirondacks Region, as defined in this chapter, encompasses all of the Adirondack Park south of NY 8 and west of the Northway. The region includes the Great Sacandaga Lake, the third largest lake in the park; several hundred thousand acres of Forest Preserve, crisscrossed with hiking trails and dotted with small lakes and ponds; and four state campgrounds. The Sacandaga River begins and ends in the Southern Adirondacks. The Hudson and Schroon rivers pass through it as well, but they are discussed in other chapters.

Rolling hills and small mountains make up most of the terrain. Few peaks rise above 3,000 feet. Crane Mountain, the highest peak with a trail, is 3,254 feet—about 2,100 feet shorter than Mount Marcy, the state's highest mountain. Still, hikers will get a good workout climbing Crane or one of the region's other big summits, such as Hadley Mountain and Mount Blue.

[*Above:* The Sacandaga River]

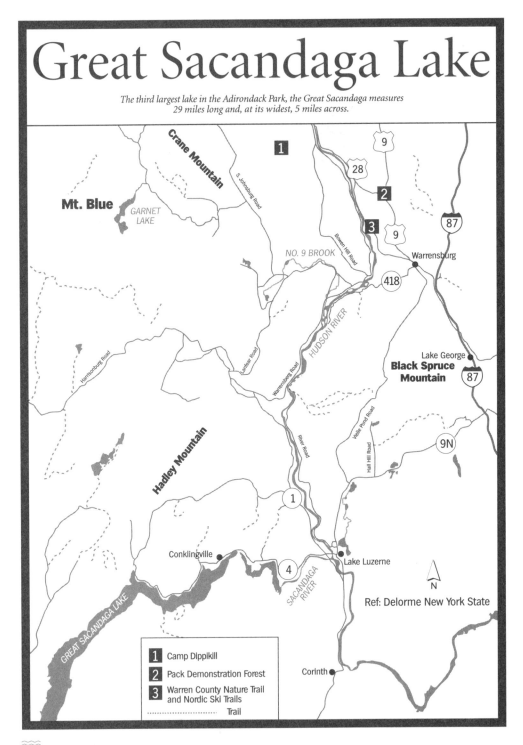

Great Sacandaga Lake

*The third largest lake in the Adirondack Park, the Great Sacandaga measures
29 miles long and, at its widest, 5 miles across.*

1 Camp Dippikill

2 Pack Demonstration Forest

3 Warren County Nature Trail
and Nordic Ski Trails

.... Trail

Ref: Delorme New York State

Various gneisses constitute the bulk of the bedrock. Gneiss, a coarse-grained metamorphic rock, often is characterized by alternating light and dark streaks. Anorthosite, the durable rock so common in the High Peaks, crops up in places. Both rocks formed deep in the earth more than 1 billion years ago. Limestone and dolostone—younger but softer rocks—survive in valleys that protected them from erosion.

The forests differ little from those elsewhere in the Adirondacks, except that in many places oak grows alongside the usual Adirondack hardwoods. This is due to a slightly milder climate. The animals, too, are the same as those found elsewhere, with a notable exception: bald eagles (*Haliaeetus leucocephalus*) often winter at Great Sacandaga Lake. And one recent spring, a cow moose (*Alces alces*) gave birth in woods just south of the lake—another sign that the species is making a comeback in the Adirondacks.

Since the southern region is not far from early European settlements in the Mohawk and Hudson valleys, it comes as no surprise that the land was logged heavily in the 1800s and early 1900s. Lumberjacks floated softwood logs down the Sacandaga, Schroon, and Hudson rivers to the big boom at Glens Falls or to local sawmills. Bark from hemlock trees was hauled to nearby tanneries for its tannin. Even today, many private woodlots are cut for timber. Nevertheless, stands of old-growth forest survive within reach of the day hiker.

Before the Europeans arrived, Native Americans had built villages just south of the Adirondacks. One such village, Garoga, lent its name to the hamlet of Caroga Lake. Evidently, Indians did not live year-round in the Southern Adirondacks, but they did hunt and fish in the region. They also traveled through the Sacandaga Valley to reach Lake George and Lake Champlain. A military road built in the early 1800s followed an old Indian trail from Fish House on the Sacandaga River north to Raquette Lake.

For more information: The state Department of Environmental Conservation keeps offices in Northville and Warrensburg. The Northville office's address is 701 S. Main Street, Northville, NY 12134; phone (518) 863-4545. The Warrensburg office's address is PO Box 220, Hudson Street Extension, Warrensburg, NY 12885; phone (518) 623-3671.

Great Sacandaga Lake

[Fig. 24] New York State created the Great Sacandaga Lake by damming the Sacandaga River at Conklingville in 1930, with the aim of preventing floods along the Hudson. The two rivers meet near the village of Lake Luzerne. Before the dam, spring floods often wreaked havoc in communities downriver of the village, leaving streets underwater and forcing factories to close. Today, the Sacandaga's flow—and the level of the lake—is controlled by Hudson River-Black River Regulating District.

The third largest lake in the Adirondack Park, the Great Sacandaga measures 29 miles long and, at its widest, 5 miles across. It has an average depth of 40 feet. Although nearly as large as Lake George, the Great Sacandaga lacks the glamour of its

Brook Trout

Fishery biologists believe that brook trout (*Salvelinus fontinalis*) populated the Adirondacks soon after the retreat of the glacier more than 10,000 years ago. The meltwaters enabled trout to reach ponds and lakes that became isolated when the waters receded. Over the centuries, the trout developed into separate strains. Europeans unwittingly decimated the trout population by introducing exotic species, such as pike and perch, into trout waters. These fish compete with trout for food and eat their eggs. Today, only a half-dozen strains carry on the bloodlines of the aboriginal trout. One of these is the Little Tupper trout. The Little Tupper looks like a paler version of the familiar brook trout: the reds and greens are not as intense. It has adapted well to life in Little Tupper Lake which is rather shallow and warm for trout, and the Little Tupper often grows to twice the size of normal brookies. The State Department of Environmental Conservation has bred Little Tupper in hatcheries and released them into ponds around the Adirondacks. Most hatchery trout, however, are a cross between Temiscamie trout, a wild Canadian variety, and mongrel domestic trout. This trout resists diseases that can afflict fish in crowded hatcheries and retains enough instinct to survive in the wild. Most trout caught in the Adirondacks are this hybrid.

its historic counterpart. Here you will find no majestic cliffs rising out of the water and no charming archipelagos. But the Great Sacandaga does have compensations: It is less crowded and more laid back than the famed Queen of Lakes.

Like Lake George, the Great Sacandaga occupies a *graben,* a valley created when a large chunk of crust drops between two faults. The hills on either side are made largely of gneisses formed deep in the earth about a billion years ago.

The natural history of the Great Sacandaga begins not in 1930 but in the Wisconsin Ice Age. Before the arrival of the glaciers, the Sacandaga River flowed south out of the Adirondacks to the Mohawk River. When the last glaciers melted, they left a moraine—a ridge of rock, silt, and sand—that blocked the Sacandaga. The river backed up, creating a lake similar to the reservoir of today. As the waters rose, they spilled into a rocky gorge near the site of the modern dam and carved a channel to the Hudson. Over the centuries, the outlet cut deeper into the gorge, lowering the level of the lake until only a river remained.

The 1,100-foot dam at Conklingville, designed by Edward Haynes Sargent, holds back 283 billion gallons of water. The regulating district closes the dam each spring to fill up the reservoir. Throughout the summer, it releases water to generate electricity and to ensure an adequate flow in the Hudson. When the lake level drops far enough, the foundations, stone walls, and roads of the old river communities can be seen around the margins of the lake. In recent years, the district has taken steps to keep the lake level high throughout the summer.

Motorists can get a great view of the lake from the road across the dam. There is an even better view just east of the dam at a pulloff on North Shore Road. Both are good places to look for bald eagles (*Haliaeetus leucocephalus*) that sometimes winter at the eastern end of the lake.

Since its birth, the lake has been popular among fishermen and boaters. In 1940, a fisherman pulled out a northern pike (*Esox lucius*) that weighed 46 pounds 2 ounces—which stood as a world record for nearly four decades. The lake also holds walleyes (*Stizostedion vitreum vitreum*), largemouth bass (*Micropterus salmoides*), smallmouth bass (*Micropterus dolomieui*), and rock bass (*Ambloplites rupestris*). In addition, a fishermen's association stocks the lake each year with brown trout (*Salmo trutta*), rainbow trout (*Oncorhynchus mykiss*), and Donaldson trout, a hybrid from the West. Ice fishing is permitted.

The state maintains four boat launches on the lake: at Northampton Beach Public Campground; off NY 30 just north of Northville; off South Shore Road five miles north of the hamlet of Edinburg, and in Broadalbin. The campground and several towns have beaches.

For more information: State Department of Environmental Conservation at 701 S. Main Street, Northville, NY 12134. Phone (518) 863-4545. *The Sacandaga Story: A Valley of Yesteryear* by Larry Hart tells the story of the Sacandaga River valley before the reservoir.

NORTHAMPTON BEACH PUBLIC CAMPGROUND

[Fig. 25(7)] The only state campground on the Great Sacandaga lies on the northwestern shore between Mayfield and Northville. Some campsites are unavailable during times of high water.

Directions: From Northville, drive south on NY 30 about 2.6 miles and turn left at the sign for the campground. The campground is reached about 2 miles after the turn. From the south, the turn is 8.2 miles past the junction of NY 30 and NY 30A in Mayfield.

Activities: Swimming, fishing, boating, sailing, canoeing.

Facilities: 224 campsites, picnic area, sand beach, playground, boat launch, toilets, hot showers, trailer dump station. Some campsites are accessible to the handicapped.

Dates: Open early May through mid-Oct.

Fees: There is a charge for camping or day use.

Closest town: Northville is about 2.7 miles north.

For more information: Campground office, phone (518) 863-6000. For reservations, phone (800) 456-2267.

WOOD DUCK
(*Aix sponsa*)

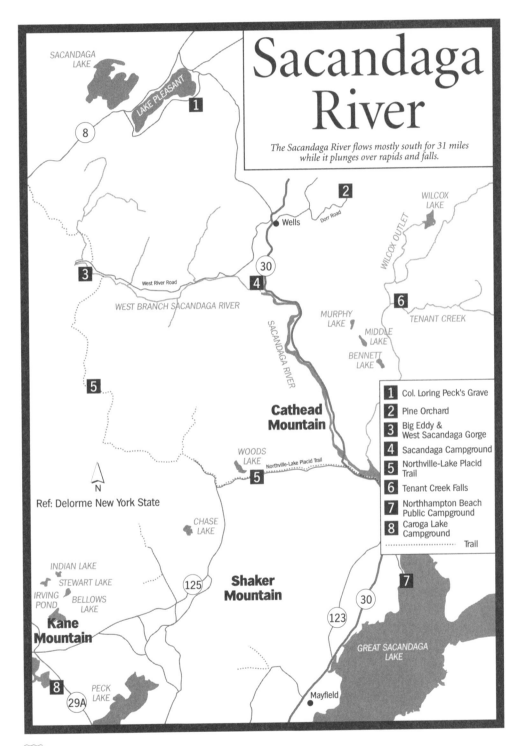

Sacandaga River

The Sacandaga River flows mostly south for 31 miles while it plunges over rapids and falls.

SACANDAGA LAKE

LAKE PLEASANT

1

8

2

WILCOX LAKE

Wells

Dorr Road

WILCOX OUTLET

30

3

West River Road

4

6

TENANT CREEK

WEST BRANCH SACANDAGA RIVER

MURPHY LAKE

SACANDAGA RIVER

MIDDLE LAKE

BENNETT LAKE

5

Cathead Mountain

WOODS LAKE

Northville-Lake Placid Trail

5

N

Ref: Delorme New York State

CHASE LAKE

1 Col. Loring Peck's Grave
2 Pine Orchard
3 Big Eddy & West Sacandaga Gorge
4 Sacandaga Campground
5 Northville-Lake Placid Trail
6 Tenant Creek Falls
7 Northhampton Beach Public Campground
8 Caroga Lake Campground
·········· Trail

INDIAN LAKE

STEWART LAKE

IRVING POND

BELLOWS LAKE

125

Shaker Mountain

7

30

Kane Mountain

123

GREAT SACANDAGA LAKE

8

PECK LAKE

29A

Mayfield

Sacandaga River

[Fig. 25] From Lake Pleasant, the Sacandaga flows mostly south for 31 miles before reaching the Great Sacandaga. In places, the river plunges over rapids and falls impassable by canoe, but it offers plenty of opportunities for both flat-water and white-water enthusiasts. Anglers fish the Sacandaga for the brook trout (*Salvelinus fontinalis*) and brown trout (*Salmo trutta*) stocked by the state.

Flat-water canoeists enjoy paddling the first 4 miles of the Sacandaga, as it meanders through swampy lowlands with frequent views of surrounding mountains. The sandy channel widens when the Kunjamuk River enters from the north (*see* page 208). Be sure to turn around or exit before entering the rapids, which are a prelude to Christine Falls and Austin Falls.

Between Austin Falls and Augur Falls, the Sacandaga winds through another lowland known as Augur Flats, a great place to see wildlife. From the put-in, it's possible to canoe a few miles upstream, though downed trees can get in the way. Do not paddle downstream from the put-in, for that way leads to Augur Falls. If canoeing the flats, though, be sure to take the short walk to see the falls and the lovely gorge (*see* page 194).

Below Augur Falls, whitewater canoeists can enjoy a run of about 4.5 miles to Lake Algonquin. The rapids in this stretch reach Class III intensity, according to Alec Proskine in *Adirondack Canoe Waters: South Flow*. From the dam at the south end of the lake, it's another 14 miles to Great Sacandaga Lake. This stretch, too, may be suitable for whitewater canoeing in spring, but it is quite dry in summer. Since NY 30 parallels the river, access is easy. The rapids reach Class II intensity.

The hamlet of Wells is built around Lake Algonquin, whose dam backs up the Sacandaga for 1.5 miles. Canoes can be launched at the town beach at the north end of the lake. Motorboats also use the water. Besides trout, fish living in the lake include chain pickerel (*Esox niger*), pumpkinseed (*Lepomis gibbosus*), and yellow perch (*Perca flavescens*). Ice fishing is permitted.

Directions: If canoeing the start of the Sacandaga, put in at the launch where NY 30 crosses the river in Speculator. The take-out or alternative put-in is a dirt parking lot on the east side of NY 30 about 1.5 miles south of the bridge. If canoeing Augur Flats, from the junction of NY 30 and NY 8 outside the hamlet of Wells, drive north on NY 30 about 1 mile to a dirt road on the right; bear left after the turn to reach the river. If canoeing the whitewater stretch below Augur Falls to Lake Algonquin, put in at the junction of NY 30 and NY 8. If canoeing the lower stretch, put in just below the Lake Algonquin dam or at Sacandaga Public Campground (*see* page 168). Possible take-outs below the campground include the Town Hall at Hope, the NY 30 bridge in Hope, and the boat launch off NY 30 on the Great Sacandaga Lake near Northville.

For more information: Contact the local office of the state Department of Environmental Conservation at 701 S. Main Street, Northville, NY 12134. Phone (518) 863-4545.

SACANDAGA PUBLIC CAMPGROUND

[Fig. 25(4)] Long before the state opened a campground at the junction of the Sacandaga and West Sacandaga rivers, wayfarers found the Forks—its local name—a pleasant place to camp for the night. The state campground opened in the 1920s. Many of the campsites are on a tongue of land between the two rivers. In spring, the campground is popular with trout fishermen.

Directions: From Northville, drive 12.5 miles north on NY 30 to the entrance on the left. If coming from the north, the entrance is 2.6 miles south of the hamlet of Wells.

Activities: Camping, picnicking, fishing, canoeing.

Facilities: 143 campsites, two picnic areas, toilets, hot showers, trailer dump station, pay telephone. Some of the campsites and other facilities are accessible to the handicapped.

Dates: Open mid-May through Labor Day.

Fees: There is a fee for camping or day use.

Closest town: The hamlet of Wells is 2.6 miles north.

For more information: Campground office, (518) 924-4121. For reservations, phone (800) 456-2267.

RAFTING ON THE SACANDAGA

East of the Great Sacandaga Lake, the Sacandaga becomes a river again. Several commercial outfitters offer raft and tube rides down the last 4 miles to the confluence with the Hudson. This stretch can also be navigated by canoe or kayak, but keep in mind that the rapids reach Class III.

River trips are possible only when Niagara Mohawk Power Corp. releases water from the Stewart Dam, which is located below the bigger dam at Conklingville. By agreement with the outfitters, the utility releases water daily from Memorial Day through Columbus Day. Outside those dates, the releases are unpredictable.

Most outfitters put in their craft on Niagara Mohawk land near the dam and take out at the Sacandaga Outdoors Center near the village of Lake Luzerne. Those who wish to put in their own craft at the site can pay the center for a shuttle service. The center is an outfitter that also manages the property.

For more information: Sacandaga Outdoors Center, 304 Old Corinth, Hadley, NY 12835. Phone (518) 696-5710. Other outfitters are listed in Appendix C.

Wilcox Lake Wild Forest

Although the state has not reckoned the exact acreage of the Wilcox Lake Wild Forest, it encompasses more territory than several wilderness areas in the Adirondack Park. The region, located north of Great Sacandaga Lake, offers a variety of hikes, ranging from short walks to treks of 15 miles or more.

Many of the trails follow old logging roads, often leading past ponds and lakes. Since the trails are fairly flat, they also attract cross-country skiers. Many trails double as snowmobile routes. The wild forest also offers some of the most challenging climbs in the Southern Adirondacks.

For more information: The state Department of Environmental Conservation has offices in Northville and Warrensburg. For questions on Hamilton and Fulton counties, contact the Northville office at 701 S. Main Street, Northville, NY 12134; phone (518) 863-4545. For questions on Warren County, contact the Warrensburg office at address is PO Box 220, Hudson Street Extension, Warrensburg, NY 12885; phone (518) 623-3671.

HADLEY MOUNTAIN

[Fig. 24] This rocky summit overlooking Great Sacandaga Lake offers one of the best panoramas in the Southern Adirondacks. The mountain's forest burned several times in the early 1900s, which accounts for the large amount of paper birch (*Betula papyrifea*), a pioneer species, growing on the slopes. The trail passes through a stand of large old hemlock (*Tsuga canadensis*) at the start but soon enters a hardwood forest with striped maple (*Acer pensylvanicum*) in the understory.

In places, the trail resembles a natural sidewalk where it has been worn down to the smooth bedrock—gneiss mixed with quartz, hornblende, and biotite. Near the summit, hikers leave the woods to walk along an open ridge with vistas to the south and west. The fire tower at the top has been restored. Great views can be had even without climbing the tower.

Directions: From Lake Luzerne, take Bridge Road over the Hudson River and continue west along the northern shore of the Sacandaga River and Great Sacandaga Lake for 20 miles to Hadley Hill Road in Day; turn right and go 5.6 miles to a road on the left. The trailhead is 1.4 miles down this road on the left.

Trail: 1.8 miles to summit.

Elevation: From 1,150 feet to 2,675 feet.

Degree of difficulty: Moderate.

Surface and blaze: Natural forest floor, bare rock. Red blazes.

CRANE MOUNTAIN

[Fig. 24] The dome of Crane Mountain rises 2,000 feet above the valley floor northwest of Warrensburg, affording hikers a superb vista of the Southern Adirondacks from its windswept ledges. The trail is not for little children, as it requires some scrambling over bare rock and, in a couple of places, climbing wooden ladders. The trail passes through a forest of hardwoods mixed with hemlock (*Tsuga canadensis*) and balsam fir (*Abies balsamea*).

The battered evergreens on the summit ledges show evidence of flagging: the branches facing the wind have died, leaving only the leeward side of the trees green.

On the northwestern side, the summit looks down on Crane Mountain Pond. Hikers who return to the trailhead by an alternative route that leads past this pretty pond might want to take a dip. The state stocks the 13-acre water with brook trout. Anglers are prohibited from using baitfish.

Directions: Beware that the road names and signs in rural Warren County can be confusing. From Northway Exit 23 at Warrensburg, drive west a short distance to US 9; turn right and go about 0.8 mile to NY 418; turn left and go about 4.9 miles to a T-intersection just after crossing the Hudson River; turn left and then make a quick right; go about 1 mile to another T-intersection; turn right and go 0.9 mile to the Glen-Athol Road on the right, which eventually leads into Pleasant Valley Road (or just Valley Road); turn right on the Glen-Athol Road and continue straight on it and the Valley Road for 6.4 miles to Garnet Lake Road; turn left and go about 1.4 miles to a dirt road on the right. The trailhead is approximately 2 miles down this road, which can be rough going. From the north, Garnet Lake Road can be reached by driving south from NY 8 in Johnsburg on the South Johnsburg Road.

Trail: 1.4 miles to summit.

Elevation: 2,100 feet to 3,254 feet.

Degree of difficulty: Moderate.

Surface and blaze: Natural forest floor. Red blazes.

GARNET LAKE AND MOUNT BLUE

[Fig. 24] Although camps line the shores at its northern end, Garnet Lake lies mostly within the Forest Preserve. From the water, a canoeist can look in three directions and see nothing but woods around the lake, with hills rising up in the background. Mount Blue, at nearly 3,000 feet, dominates the landscape.

Fire swept over Mount Blue the early 1900s, baring rocky ledges that today offer spectacular views of the 313-acre lake, nearby Crane Mountain, and undulating green hills. Although no trail leads to the summit, hikers can reach it by a fairly easy bushwhack from a snowmobile trail that leads to Lixard Pond. The trail can be reached only by water.

From a car-top launch on Garnet Lake's southern shore, paddle southwest about 0.75 mile to a narrow channel in the lake. The trail begins at grassy opening in the woods along the western shore. Start the bushwhack after about 0.75 mile, when the vly east of Lixard Pond comes into view. Turn right off the trail, taking a north-northwest course up the mountain.

At the outset, one passes through a hardwood forest, but as the elevation increases, the deciduous trees give way to red spruce (*Picea rubens*) and balsam fir (*Abies balsamea*). Several kinds of wildflowers adorn the woods, including Canada mayflower (*Maianthemum canadense*), bunchberry (*Cornus canadensis*), foamflower (*Tiarella cordifolia*), star flower (*Trientalis borealis*), and pink lady's slipper (*Cypripedium acaule*). After arriving at the first ledge, just keep going up from one ledge to the next. The higher one goes, the better the view—although the summit itself is enclosed by spruce and fir.

Garnet Lake can be fished for largemouth bass (*Micropterus salmoides*), chain pickerel (*Esox niger*), yellow perch (*Perca flavescens*), and panfish. Ice fishing is permitted. Several primitive campsites can be found along the shores.

Directions: See Crane Mountain, page 169. To reach Garnet Lake, continue down Garnet Lake Road about 5 miles past the turn for Crane Mountain (the road soon turns to dirt) to the turn for the lake, a road also called Garnet Lake Road; turn left and go 0.8 mile to the lake; turn left and go 0.8 mile to a parking area on the left for the Round Pond trailhead. The launch is opposite the trailhead.

Trail: About 2 miles to summit.

Elevation: 1,462 feet to 2,925 feet.

Degree of difficulty: Moderate.

Surface and blaze: Natural forest floor. Yellow snowmobile blazes for first 0.7 mile.

WILCOX LAKE

[Fig. 25] There's nothing quite like waking up to a loon's maniacal laughter emanating from a mist-shrouded lake, echoing off the surrounding hills. Those who camp overnight here may be able to see not only loons (*Gavia immer*) but also great blue herons (*Ardea herodias*) and cedar waxwings (*Bombycilla cedrorum*). The waxwings live on an island near the southeastern shore.

The 115-acre lake can be visited in a day, but it requires more than 10 miles of walking round-trip if taking the scenic route along East Stony Creek. For much of the way, the wooded trail follows the creek, whose banks often are adorned with wildflowers, such as joe-pye weed, cardinal flower (*Lobelia cardinalis*), and Canada lily (*Lilium canadense*).

After crossing the creek on a suspension bridge, the trail climbs over the shoulder of Wilcox Mountain and descends to the lake. There are two lean-tos. Turn left after reaching the lake to reach the newer lean-to. The other is to the right. The state stocks the lake with brook trout (*Salvelinus fontinalis*). No bait fish are allowed.

Directions: From NY 30, turn east onto Old Northville Road, about 4.3 miles north of Northville; go 1.5 miles to Hope Falls Road; turn left and go about 7.4 miles, almost to the end, to a parking area on the left. The trail begins on the left side of the road.

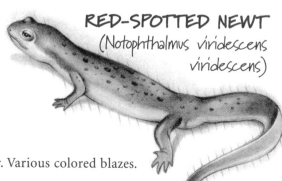

RED-SPOTTED NEWT
(*Notophthalmus viridescens viridescens*)

Trail: 5.2 miles to lake.

Elevation: About 1,060 feet at trailhead to 1,445 feet at lake.

Degree of difficulty: Moderate.

Surface and blaze: Natural forest floor. Various colored blazes.

TENANT CREEK FALLS

[Fig. 25(6)] In its last few miles, Tenant Creek flows over three waterfalls before joining East Stony Creek. An unmaintained trail starting near the confluence of the creeks leads through a mixed wood to all three falls. The boulders, rock ledges and pools at the first, reached in less than 1 mile, make a pleasant picnic spot. The trail becomes fainter beyond these falls, but if hikers keep the creek within sight or earshot they can't go wrong. The second falls is another mile upstream, and third falls is slightly farther. There is a good swimming hole at the base of the third falls, but the water can be chilly.

Directions: See Wilcox Lake, page 171. Take the trail to Wilcox Lake a short distance to the bridge over Tenant Creek. Turn right just before the bridge to go to the falls.

Trail: 0.9 mile to first falls, 2 miles to second falls, 2.1 miles to third falls.

Degree of difficulty: Easy.

Surface: Natural forest floor.

BENNETT, MIDDLE, AND MURPHY LAKES

[Fig. 25] Three trout waters lie along an 8.3-mile trail that goes from Hope Falls to Pumpkin Hollow. The trail follows an old road through a mixed forest. Occasionally, hikers will come across foundations, apple trees, and other signs of settlement.

Heading north from Hope Falls, one reaches Bennett Lake after 1.3 miles (a side trail leads to the shore), Middle Lake after 2.6 miles, and Murphy Lake after 3.8 miles. If skiing or walking the whole route, it's better to spot a car at Hope Falls and head south from Pumpkin Hollow, thus taking advantage of the overall descent (Bennett Lake is about 320 feet lower in elevation than Murphy Lake). If mountain biking to Murphy Lake, start from the south, for the north end of the trail is rockier and wetter.

Hikers can extend the adventure by bushwhacking up the cliffs on the east shore of Murphy Lake. There is a lean-to on the lake's southeastern shore. The state stocks Bennett and Murphy lakes with brook trout (*Salvelinus fontinalis*) and Middle Lake with brown trout (*Salmo trutta*). Anglers are forbidden to use baitfish in any of the lakes. Snowmobilers use the trail in winter.

Directions: Southern trailhead: From the Northville bridge, drive north on NY 30 about 4.3 miles to Old Northville Road; turn right and go 1.4 miles to Hope Falls Road; turn left and go 2.8 miles to Creek Road; turn left and go 0.6 mile to the trailhead on the right. (The other end of Creek Road meets NY 30 south of the hamlet of Wells. If coming from the north, turn left onto Creek Road at this junction and go 2.5 miles to the trailhead.) Northern trailhead: From the Northville bridge, drive north on NY 30 about 11.5 miles to Pumpkin Hollow Road, shortly after crossing Wells town line; turn right and go 1.6 miles to the trailhead.

Trail: 8.3 miles end to end.

Degree of difficulty: Easy to moderate, depending on distance.

Surface and blaze: Old road, natural forest floor. Yellow blazes.

▓ PINE ORCHARD

[Fig. 25(2)] An easy walk along an old tote road leads to a stand of giant white pine (*Pinus strobus*) more than 200 years old that escaped the ax when loggers worked in the region in the 1800s. A grown man cannot stretch his arms halfway around the trunks of the biggest trees. The trail passes through a mixed wood of yellow birch (*Betula alleghaniensis*), American beech (*Fagus americanus*), hemlock (*Tsuga canadensis*), and red spruce (*Picea rubens*), among other species, before reaching the big pines. Hikers will arrive at Pine Orchard soon after fording a stream near a marsh filled with snags and climbing a ridge.

Mountain bikers may want to continue on the trail as far as Jimmy Creek, about 5 miles from the trailhead. Snowmobilers use the trail in winter. It also is suitable for skiing or snowshoeing.

Directions: From NY 8 in the hamlet of Wells, turn north onto Griffin Road, a little north of the State Police barracks, and go 0.8 mile to a righthand turn; then go 1.1 miles to another righthand turn, Flaters Road. Drive 2.1 miles to a parking area at the end of the road near the Flater residence. Do not block the road. You must cross the Flaters' property to get to the trail. The Flaters don't mind, but if they are home, it's courteous to ask permission.

Trail: 1.6 miles to Pine Orchard, though the trail continues for several more miles.

Degree of difficulty: Easy.

Surface: Old tote road, natural forest floor.

Caroga Lake Public Campground

[Fig. 25(8)] The hamlet of Caroga Lake, conspicuous for its carousel and Ferris wheel, lies just 4 miles inside the Adirondack Park's southern boundary. East Caroga and West Caroga lakes, which sit on either side of the hamlet, are popular fishing spots. Although most of the shoreline of both lakes is privately owned and dotted with camps, boats can be launched at the state campground on East Caroga Lake.

The two lakes, each about 1 mile long, are connected by a channel. The state stocks West Caroga with Atlantic salmon (*Salmo salar*) and splake, a hybrid of brook (speckled) and lake trout. Other species found in the lakes include smallmouth bass (*Micropterus dolomieui*), chain pickerel (*Esox niger*), walleye (*Stizostedion vitreum vitreum*), and brown bullhead (*Ictalurus nebulosus*). Ice fishing is permitted on both lakes.

Directions: From Gloversville, drive west on NY 29A about 7 miles to the campground entrance on the left.

Activities: Camping, picnicking, boating, fishing, swimming.

Facilities: 161 campsites, picnic area, sand beach, exercise course, small-boat launch, toilets, hot showers, trailer dump station. Some of the campsites are accessible to the handicapped.

Dates: Open mid-May through Labor Day.

Fees: There is a charge for camping or day use.

Closest town: Caroga Lake hamlet is about 2 miles west.

For more information: Campground office, phone (518) 835-4241. For reservations, phone (800) 456-2267 .

Kane Mountain

[Fig. 25] The hike to the unstaffed fire tower atop Kane Mountain north of Caroga Lake in the Shaker Mountain Wild Forest makes an excellent adventure for young children. The trail is short, the grade is moderate, and the views from the tower are wonderful. There also is a vacant ranger's cabin on the summit.

Hardwood species dominate the boulder-strewn woods on the way up, though red spruce (*Picea rubens*) and hemlock (*Tsuga canadensis*) are scattered about. Kane Mountain lies far enough south that red oak (*Quercus rubra*) grows here along with the more typical Adirondack hardwoods. From the tower, one can see forested mountains and hills in all directions as well as several lakes. On a clear day, it's possible to see the Catskills far to the south.

Directions: From Caroga Lake hamlet, drive north about 3.6 miles on NY 10/29A to Green Lake Road; turn right and go about 0.5 mile to a short road on the left that leads to a parking area. The trail begins on the left.

Trail: 0.9 mile to summit.

Elevation: About 1,600 feet to 2,180 feet.

Degree of difficulty: Moderate.

Surface and blaze: Natural forest floor.

Cathead Mountain

[Fig. 25] This popular summit offers views of Great Sacandaga Lake and the rugged country of the Silver Lake Wilderness and Wilcox Wild Forest. On a clear day, it's possible to see some of the High Peaks.

The trail, rocky and steep in sections, passes through a hardwood forest whose species include northern red oak (*Quercus rubra borealis*), America beech (*Fagus grandifolia*), and sugar maple (*Acer saccharum*). Look for trout lilies (*Erythronium americanum*) along the way and blueberries on the mostly open summit.

An unstaffed fire tower, a radio antenna, and a windmill generator are at the top. The generator can be noisy. Cathead's summit is privately held. The trail is classified as a primitive area rather than as part of the adjacent Silver Lake Wilderness.

Directions: From Northville, drive north 3.4 miles on NY 30 to Benson Road; turn left and go about 2.7 miles to North Road; turn right and continue to a parking area about 1 mile down the road. The trail begins on the left side of the road.

Trail: 1.6 miles to summit.

Elevation: 1,140 feet to 2,423 feet.

Degree of difficulty: Moderate.

Surface and blaze: Natural forest floor. Red blazes.

Silver Lake Wilderness

The Silver Lake Wilderness encompasses more than 105,000 acres of rolling hills and small lakes between NY 30 and NY 10 in Hamilton County. Only four peaks exceed 3,000 feet—none of them reachable by a maintained trail. In fact, the only official trail in the Silver Lake Wilderness is the Northville-Lake Placid Trail, which runs for 22 miles through the heart of the forest. Old-growth trees can be seen on the trail between Benson and Whitehouse.

LABRADOR TEA
(Ledum groenlandicum)
Growing up to three feet tall, this is an evergreen with white blooms.

The West Branch of the Sacandaga River rises near Silver Lake Mountain and takes a meandering course through the wilderness. Much of it is canoeable and easily accessible. The state stocks several ponds in the region with brook trout (*Salvelinus fontinalis*). The use of baitfish is prohibited.

For the best view of the Silver Lake Wilderness, climb Cathead Mountain, located on its southern border (*see* page 174).

For more information: State Department of Environmental Conservation at 701 S. Main Street, Northville, NY 12134. Phone (518) 863-4545. Ask for the leaflet *The Northville-Lake Placid Trail.*

NORTHVILLE-LAKE PLACID TRAIL

[Fig. 25(5)] The first leg of this 133-mile trail, for those walking north, cuts through the middle of the Silver Lake Wilderness. Officially, the trail begins on NY 30 in Northville, following back roads for the first 10 miles before entering the woods at Benson. Thereafter, it stays in the woods for the next 22 miles, exiting on NY 8 near Piseco Lake.

About 2.5 miles north of Benson, the trail enters an old-growth stand where the yellow birch (*Betula alleghaniensis*) stand as tall as 80 feet, with diameters of more than 4 feet. There also are majestic specimens of sugar maple (*Acer saccharum*), hemlock (*Tsuga canadensis*), and red spruce (*Picea rubens*).

Hikers cross the West Branch of the Sacandaga River on a large suspension bridge about 16 miles north of Benson. This spot is known as Whitehouse, once the site of a hunting lodge. Hikes also can begin here, for Whitehouse can be reached by a dirt road that leads from Wells.

For those who wish to do the whole section in two or three days, three lean-tos exist along the way: at Silver Lake 7.4 miles north of Benson, at Mud Lake 13.2 miles north of Benson, and at Hamilton Lake Stream about 2.3 miles north of Whitehouse. The lean-tos also make good destinations for day hikes, but the walk through the lovely forest, not the destination, is the real goal.

If spotting a second car, walk south to take advantage of the slight decrease in elevation. It's 6 miles from NY 8 to Whitehouse and 16.25 miles from Whitehouse to Benson.

The state stocks brook trout in four waters along the trail: Rock Lake, Canary Pond, Mud Lake, and Buckhorn Lake. There also is good fishing in Silver Lake.

Directions: To reach the Benson trailhead, drive north from Northville about 3.4 miles on NY 30 to Benson Road; turn left and go about 5.9 miles to the dirt Washburn Road; turn right and, bearing right at a fork, go 0.6 mile to Godfrey Road near the Trailhead Lodge; turn left and go 0.6 mile to a parking area on the right. To reach the Whitehouse trailhead, turn west on Algonquin Drive from NY 30 near the dam in Wells, drive a short distance to West River Road; turn left and follow this road 8.6 miles to its end. To reach the NY 8 trailhead, drive west on NY 8 about 9.3 miles from the junction of NY 8 and NY 30 in Speculator.

Trail: 22.3 miles from Benson to NY 8.

Elevation: 1,441 to 1,726 feet.

Degree of difficulty: Easy to moderate, depending on length.

Surface and blaze: Natural forest floor. Blue blazes.

BIG EDDY AND WEST SACANDAGA GORGE

[Fig. 25(3)] A few miles west of Whitehouse, the West Branch of the Sacandaga River runs through a gorge whose rock walls rise 200 to 300 feet above the water. After this frenetic show of energy, the river relaxes in a large pool called Big Eddy.

Both Big Eddy and the gorge can be reached by an unmarked trail that branches off the Northville-Lake Placid Trail about 0.7 mile north of Whitehouse. At the fork, the marked trail bears right, while the trail to Big Eddy starts down an old road to the left. After crossing Hamilton Lake Stream, the trail becomes less distinct, but it follows the West Branch the rest of the way to Big Eddy.

Those who push on to the gorge will find the going more arduous after crossing Cold Brook. The river plunges over several waterfalls in the gorge, but reaching them all is a tough assignment. In high water, the gorge may be impassable—in which case it must be appreciated from its eastern end or from the cliffs above. Hikers need to be careful walking through the gorge or atop the cliffs.

Directions: See directions to Northville-Lake Placid Trail's Whitehouse trailhead, page 175–176.

Trail: About 2 miles from Whitehouse to Big Eddy, 2.8 miles to gorge.

Degree of difficulty: Moderate to strenuous, depending on distance.

Surface: Old woods road, natural forest floor.

WEST BRANCH OF SACANDAGA RIVER

[Fig. 25] The West Branch rises near Silver Lake Mountain in the Silver Lake Wilderness and takes its sweet time getting where it's going— flowing first southwest, then west, then north, and finally east. By the time it reaches the main branch, a little south of the hamlet

Northville-Lake Placid Trail

The Adirondack Mountain Club cut the Northville-Lake Placid Trail in 1922 as one of the club's first projects. The trail stretches 133 miles from Northville in the south to Lake Placid in the north, passing through some of the wildest parts of the Adirondacks, including stands of old growth. The club offers a patch to anyone who walks the entire trail, either in one expedition or at different times. One hiker took 50 years to do it all. Most people who make an end-to-end trek take two weeks, give or take a few days. There are numerous lean-tos along the route. The trail emerges from the woods to cross NY 8 near Piseco, NY 30 near Blue Mountain Lake, and NY 28N near Long Lake. Some trekkers mail themselves provisions to the post offices in these hamlets. A state leaflet, *The Northville-Lake Placid Trail*, has a bare-bones description of the trail, but anyone planning to make an end-to-end trip should get a copy of the club's guidebook *The Northville-Lake Placid Trail*. It contains detailed descriptions of the trail and possible side trips. Plus, it comes with an excellent topographical map.

For more information: Adirondack Mountain Club, 814 Goggins Road, Lake George, NY 12845-9523. Phone (518) 668-4447.

of Wells, the West Sacandaga has flowed more than 36 miles, but as the crow flies it is only about 6 miles from its origin.

The river offers some exceptional flat-water canoeing as it meanders north through a broad valley along NY 10. Black ducks (*Anas rubripes*), mergansers, and other waterfowl often visit this quiet stretch, where wild raisin, holly, and elderberry grow along the banks. NY 10 crosses the river twice. The bridges are about 1 mile apart. From the northernmost bridge, canoeists can go upstream past the outlet of Good Luck Lake or downstream past the outlets of Chub Lake and Trout Lake. The lakes can be explored as side trips.

In early spring, whitewater enthusiasts can canoe the last 8 miles of the river, putting in just below the suspension bridge at Whitehouse at the end of West River Road in Wells. Alec Proskine rates the rapids as Class II – III in *Adirondack Canoe Waters: South Flow*. The Northville-Lake Placid Trail crosses the West Sacandaga at the bridge. North of the bridge, a side trail goes west to a scenic gorge (*see* page 176).

The river joins the main branch at Sacandaga Public Campground.

The state stocks the lower river with brown trout (*Salmo trutta*) and brook trout (*Salvelinus fontinalis*).

Directions: From the junction of NY 29A and NY 10 near Pine Lake, drive north on NY 10 about 5 miles to the first bridge or about 6 miles to the second bridge. There is a parking area just past the second bridge. For the lower river, see directions for Northville-Lake Placid Trail's trailhead at Whitehouse, page 175.

Ferris Lake Wild Forest

The Ferris Lake Wild Forest, one of the larger wild forests in the Adirondack Park, contains numerous small ponds and lakes, many of them reachable by trails that follow old logging roads. None of the official trails climbs to summits, but an un-marked path leads to a marvelous view from Good Luck Cliffs. Many trails are used in winter by snowmobilers, skiers, and snowshoers.

The Powley-Piseco Road bisects the region, making it more accessible, but it also contains large tracts of unbroken forest. East Canada Creek, a fine trout stream, can be reached from this road.

The Ferris Lake Wild Forest occupies the southwestern corner of the Adirondack Park. Most of it lies south of NY 8 and west NY 10.

For more information: State Department of Environmental Conservation, 701 S. Main Street, Northville, NY 12134. Phone (518) 863-4545.

CANADA LAKE, WEST LAKE, LILY LAKE

[Fig. 26] At 525 acres, Canada Lake is one of the larger waters in the Ferris Lake Wild Forest. Most of the shoreline is privately owned—much of it lined with camps—but boaters can reach the lake easily from a state launch on West Lake. The state stocks the lake with lake trout (*Salvelinus namaycush*) and brown trout (*Salmo trutta*). Anglers are allowed to take up to three lakers and two browns. Minimum length is 21 inches. Other species include pickerel (*Esox americanus*), smallmouth bass (*Mircopterus dolomieui*), and panfish. Ice fishing is permitted.

Canoeists who put in at the boat launch have several options. For a short trip, they can limit themselves to West Lake, but most will want to enter Canada Lake around Dolgeville Point and head west toward Lily Lake, which is surrounded by state land. From Lily Lake, it's possible to canoe down the outlet a few miles farther to a launch at Stewart Landing. Great blue heron (*Ardea herodias*), osprey (*Pandion haliaetus*), kingfisher (*Megaceryle alcyon*), and several kinds of ducks frequent the marshes along the way.

Directions: From the Ferris wheel in Caroga Lake, drive north on NY 29A-NY 10 about 4.1 miles to West Lake Road; turn left and bear right at the fork; the launch is about 0.5 mile down the road. From the north, the boat launch is on the right about 1.4 miles south of the junction of NY 29A and NY10.

GOOD LUCK CLIFFS AND GOOD LUCK LAKE

[Fig. 26(3)] An unmarked path from a snowmobile trail winds to the top of sheer cliffs for a great view that looks south over lakes and rolling hills to the Mohawk Valley. The path follows a stream along the base of the cliffs, past a jumble of mossy boulders that form miniature caves. Hemlock (*Tsuga canadensis*) and red spruce (*Picea rubens*) grow near the stream, but hardwoods such as American beech (*Fagus grandifolia*) and yellow birch (*Betula alleghaniensis*) predominate elsewhere until reaching the higher elevations. The hike makes a wonderful snowshoe trip. In winter, the ice hangs like melted wax from rock ledges along the stream. In *Climbing in the Adirondacks*, Don Mellor describes 14 rock-climbing routes up the cliffs. Since the path curls around the back end of the cliffs, hikers can save time by bushwhacking along a more direct route back to the snowmobile trail.

About 1.3 miles from the start, before reaching the path to the cliffs, the snowmobile trail passes Good Luck Lake's western shore. To reach the southern shore, where there is a sandy beach, continue on the trail another 0.1mile to a junction. Turn left here on an unmarked path and go 0.4 mile. The lake also can be reached by a 0.3-mile hike down an unmarked path from NY 10. This path begins a couple of yards south of the official trailhead. There are several campsites around the lake.

Directions: From the junction of NY 29A and NY 10 north of Canada Lake, drive 6.4 miles north on NY 10 to a parking area on the right. The trailhead is across the road. Go 0.5 mile up the trail to the trail register at a junction. Take the trail to the left toward Spectacle Lake. About 0.9 mile from the intersection, just past Good Luck Lake, the trail crosses two snowmobile bridges in quick succession. The path to Good Luck Cliffs begins on the right just before the second bridge.

Trail: 2.5 miles from parking lot to summit.

Elevation: About 1,680 feet to about 2,300 feet.

Degree of difficulty: Moderate.

Surface: Snowmobile trail, natural forest floor.

JOCKEYBUSH LAKE

[Fig. 26] This clear pond with its rock ledges makes a nice place for a picnic and a swim. The trail follows the lake's outlet stream for much of the way, passing through a mixed wood where violets, trout lily (*Erythronium americanum*), and painted trillium (*Trillium undulatum*) grow. There is a small waterfall about halfway to the lake. Jockeybush Lake is a narrow pond about 0.75 mile long. Walk along the north shore to find a good swimming spot by the rocks. The state stocks the water with brook trout (*Salvelinus fontinalis*). The use of baitfish is prohibited. Snowmobilers use the trail in winter.

Powley-Piseco Road

Powley-Piseco Road runs nearly 20 miles with only 6.6 miles of it paved. From there, a two-lane dirt road continues northward through a leafy corridor, passing many scenic picnic and camping spots.

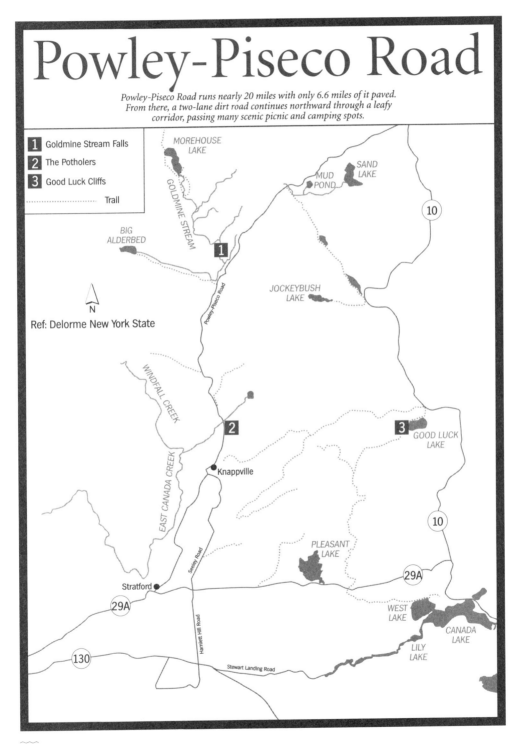

1 Goldmine Stream Falls

2 The Potholers

3 Good Luck Cliffs

·········· Trail

Ref: Delorme New York State

Directions: From the junction of NY 29A and NY 10 just past Pine Lake, drive north on NY 10 for 10.2 miles to a parking area on the left.

Trail: 1.1 miles to the lake.

Degree of difficulty: Easy.

Surface and blaze: Natural forest floor. Orange blazes.

POWLEY-PISECO ROAD

[Fig. 26] For a pleasant introduction to the forests and streams of the Southern Adirondacks, take a drive on the Powley-Piseco Road on a sunny day. The road runs nearly 20 miles from NY 29A in Stratford in Fulton County to its end on NY 10 just south of Piseco Outlet in Hamilton County. The pavement ends after 6.6 miles, just before the road crosses East Canada Creek. From there, a two-lane dirt road continues northward through a leafy corridor, passing many scenic picnic and camping spots.

Near Powley Place, the site of a peaceful meadow, an iron bridge crosses the west branch of the East Canada Creek. It's a quiet stretch of water suitable for canoeing. Numerous roadside trails, most unmarked, beckon hikers to explore, but simply driving along the road is an adventure. Several of the possible hikes are described below. In winter, the unpaved portion of the road, which is unplowed, is a snowmobile corridor. The road reopens to cars usually in May.

Directions: The south end of Powley-Piseco Road (where it is called Piseco Road) begins in Stratford on the north side of NY 29A about 10.1 miles west of the junction of NY 29A and NY 10. The north end (where it is called Powley Road) begins on the west side of NY 10 about 1.3 miles south of the junction of NY 10 and NY 8.

THE POTHOLERS

[Fig. 26(2)] Just north of its confluence with Brayhouse Brook, East Canada Creek cascades over a series of small falls and chutes. In spring, when the creek is full, the foaming water resembles a multi-tiered wedding cake. Later in the season, after the creek quiets down, bathers can laze in the potholes in the bedrock created by swirling waters. The rock ledges and boulders along the creek make the Potholers an excellent picnic spot, especially since it's just a short walk from the road. An unmarked trail follows Brayhouse Brook to East Canada Creek. From there, follow one of the paths upstream to the falls. Look for painted trillium (*Trillium undulatum*) in the woods in spring.

Directions: See Powley-Piseco Road, above. From NY 29A, drive north 8.4 miles, just past the big culvert at Brayhouse Brook. From NY 10, drive south about 11.2 miles. The path begins on the east side of the road.

Trail: A few hundred yards to Potholers.

Degree of difficulty: Easy.

Surface: Natural forest floor.

GOLDMINE STREAM FALLS

[Fig. 26(1)] An unmarked but well-beaten path leads through a mixed forest, including old specimens of red spruce (*Picea rubens*), to a delightful series of water-falls in a small rocky gorge shaded by hemlocks (*Tsuga canadensis*). Although it's not an official trail, someone has cut through the blowdown, built a log bridge over one stream, and placed log rounds in a few mucky spots. Don't let a young child step on the rounds without a helping hand: They can be unstable and extremely slippery.

Spring wildflowers that bloom in the woods include painted trillium (*Trillium undulatum*), goldthread (*Coptis groenlandica*), trout lily (*Erythronium americanum*), wild oats (*Uvularia sessilfloria*), and white baneberry (*Actaea pachypoda*). The ledges beside the lower falls are a good place to sit and have lunch. Take the path to the top of the falls to look at the water rushing over a flat expanse of reddish-gold bedrock—which may account for the stream's name.

Directions: See Powley-Piseco Road, page 181. From NY 29A, drive north about 12.8 miles. About 0.2 mile before the trailhead, the road passes a clearing and side road on the right before descending to a small meadow drained by a culvert. The trail begins on the west side of the road just south of this meadow. From NY 10, drive south about 6.8 miles. Before reaching the meadow, the road passes a campsite on the right and then descends.

Trail: 1.2 miles to falls.

Degree of difficulty: Easy. But wooden stepping-stones can be slippery.

Surface: Natural forest floor.

MUD POND

[Fig. 26] Bogs can be found throughout the Adirondacks, but few are more accessible than the one at the edge of tiny Mud Pond. The pond lies 100 yards or so from the road. There are no official trails: just park the car and cut through the woods. Visitors can walk onto the quaking bog mat, though it is squishy and damp. Typical bog flora such as cranberries, the purple pitcher plant (*Sarracenia purpurea*), and leatherleaf (*Chamaedaphne calyculata*) grow here. A few small spruces have managed to take root. Both painted trillium (*Trillium undulatum*) and red trillium (*Trillium erectum*) grow in the woods between the road and the pond.

Directions: See Powley-Piseco Road, page 181. From NY 29A, drive north about 15.9 miles. From NY 10, drive south about 3.7 miles. Mud Pond lies just east of the road. The snowmobile trail to Meco Lake begins on the opposite side of the road.

Trail: About 0.1 mile.

Degree of difficulty: Easy.

Surface: Natural forest floor, bog mat.

EAST CANADA CREEK

[Fig. 26] The cold current, riffles, and deep pockets make this a popular fly-fishing stream even in summer. The state stocks the creek with brown trout (*Salmo trutta*) and has posted several stretches in Stratford as a public fishing stream. Anglers are allowed to take up to five brook trout (*Salvelinus fontinalis*) and five other trout. The minimum length is 8 inches.

Novice canoeists can paddle a 2-mile stretch of calm water downstream of the iron bridge at Powley Place. In spring, whitewater enthusiasts can put in farther downstream at another bridge on the Powley-Piseco Road. The rapids in the 7.1 miles between the bridge and NY 29A in Stratford can reach Class IV intensity, according to Alec Proskine in *Adirondack Canoe Waters: South Flow*.

Directions: See directions to Powley-Piseco Road, page 181. To reach the bridge at Powley Place, drive north about 11.2 miles from NY 29A or south about 8.4 miles from NY 10.

Lake Pleasant

[Fig. 25] One of the larger lakes in the Southern Adirondacks, Lake Pleasant stretches 3.5 miles between the hamlet of Lake Pleasant and the village of Speculator. Although most of the shore is in private hands, the public can put in boats and canoes at a launch off NY 30 in Speculator. There also is a municipal beach in the village.

The state stocks the lake with rainbow trout (*Oncorhynchus myss*) and brown trout (*Salmo trutta*). Other fish include lake trout (*Salvelinus namaycush*), northern pike (*Esox lucius*), chain pickerel (*Esox niger*), walleye (*Stizostedion vitreum vitreum*), smallmouth bass (*Micropterus dolomieui*), and largemouth bass (*Micropterus salmoides*). Anglers are allowed to catch up to five trout a day of any size. Ice fishing is permitted.

Directions: Both the boat launch and municipal beach can be reached by driving south on NY 30 from the junction of NY 30 and NY 8 in Speculator. The launch is located near the bridge over the lake's outlet, the Sacandaga River. The beach is reached shortly before the launch.

Facilities: Boat launch for up to 10-foot fishing boat, sand beach. Marina with rentals available.

Activities: Canoeing, boating, fishing, swimming.

Fees: There is a charge for rentals at the marina.

Closest town: The launch and beach are within the village of Speculator.

For more information: Adirondack-Speculator Region Chamber of Commerce, Route 30, Speculator, NY 12164. Phone (518) 548-4521.

Col. Loring Peck's Grave

[Fig. 25(1)] Here's a chance to combine history with a pleasant walk through the woods. Col. Loring Peck, who fought in the Revolutionary War, moved to the Lake Pleasant area in 1811. He lies buried with his wife and son in a quaint little cemetery,

Hudson River Recreation Area

*The Hudson River Recreation Area encompasses 1,132 acres, including
16.5 miles of shoreline on the east side of the Hudson and 0.4 mile on the west side.*

NO. 9 BROOK

Warrensburg

1

418

87

North Road

Woods Road

Truesdale Hill

Mouth Road

Hildebrand Rd.

Welle Pond Road

9

HUDSON RIVER

Lanfear Road

Warrensberg

**Black Spruce
Mountain**

2

87

Eddie Road

STEWART
LAKE

Welle Pond Road

Kenyan Mountain

Thomas Road

9N

River Road

Hall Hill Road

LAKE
VANARE

Galley Road

LAKE
FOREST

Buck Bee Road

FOURTH
LAKE

3

1

SECOND
LAKE

Butler Road

1	Warren County Fish Hatchery
2	Hudson River Recreation Area
3	Luzerne Campground
....	Trail

N

Ref: Delorme New York State

LAKE LUCERNE

enclosed by walls of piled stone, in a dark wood that has grown up on land the Pecks once cleared for a farm. A small flag decorates the colonel's simple headstone. In spring, painted trillium (*Trillium undulatum*) blooms near the graves. Nearby, a towering white pine (*Strobus pinus*) stands sentinel. There is something poignant about the scene: One wonders how long the tiny burial ground can ward off the encroaching forest.

Directions: From NY 8 in the hamlet of Lake Pleasant, drive south on South Shore Road about 4.4 miles. The sign for the trail will be on the right. Alternatively, from NY 30 in Speculator, take Downey Avenue to South Shore Road and continue on South Shore Road about 1.7 miles past Gilmantown Road.

Trail: About 0.5 mile.

Degree of difficulty: Easy to moderate.

Surface and blaze: Old woods road, natural forest floor. Tin can blazes, some orange.

For more information: Adirondack-Speculator Region Chamber of Commerce, Route 30, Speculator, NY 12164. Phone (518) 548-4521.

Hudson River Recreation Area

[Fig. 27(2)] The state owns 1,132 acres along the Hudson between Lake Luzerne and Warrensburg, including 16.5 miles of the eastern shoreline. The Department of Environmental Conservation has designated a large tract as a day-use area for picnicking, hiking, canoeing, mountain biking, and horseback riding. Overnight camping is allowed at designated sites.

Motorists can reach the property by River Road, which follows the east bank of the Hudson north of Lake Luzerne. There is a parking area and canoe launch near the entrance, but visitors can continue driving on the rutty dirt road past stands of tall white pine (*Pinus strobus*) to reach the picnic areas, trailheads, and campsites. After a few miles, the road intersects with Gay Pond Road, another dirt road, which goes to Gay Pond and Viele Pond. Near this intersection is a second canoe launch. Several campsites can be found a little farther up River Road.

The Hudson in this stretch is ideal for flat-water canoeists. Paddlers can travel between the two canoe launches, perhaps picnicking on one of the islands along the way, or they can extend their trip by putting in farther upstream near the confluence of the Schroon River or taking out farther downstream before the falls at Lake Luzerne.

The stands of pines along the river are lovely to walk among, since little grows in the understory. The pine needles make a soft bed for laying down a picnic blanket.

Vehicles and horses can take Gay Pond Road as far as Gay Pond, which is stocked with brook trout (*Salvelinus fontinalis*). The rocky road is not recommended for cars with low clearance. Hikers and bikers may take the road all the way to Viele Pond. In winter, snowmobilers are allowed to travel over the River and Gay Pond roads.

Perhaps the best hike follows an old woods road about 0.5 mile to Bear Slide, where Buttermilk Brook rushes over bare bedrock for a few hundred yards. Local legend says a bear once escaped a hunter by sliding down the rock. Upstream of Bear Slide there is a series of small waterfalls and pools. The trail begins at a pull-off on the right about 0.2 mile from the entrance, just past a culvert for the brook.

Directions: From Northway Exit 21, drive west on NY 9N about 8.2 miles to Gailey Hill Road; turn right and go 2.6 miles to Thomas Road; turn left and go 0.8 mile to River Road; turn right and go 1.4 miles to the entrance.

Activities: Camping, hiking, canoeing, picnicking, fishing, mountain biking, horseback riding, cross-country skiing, snowmobiling.

Facilities: Primitive campsites, hiking trails, 2 canoe launches.

Dates: Open year-round.

Fees: None.

Closest town: The village of Lake Luzerne is about 5.5 miles away.

For more information: Contact the local office of the state Department of Environmental Conservation at PO Box 220, Hudson Street Extension, Warrensburg, NY 12885. Phone (518) 623-3671.

Luzerne Public Campground

[Fig. 27(3)] In the 1920s, Earl and Jay Woodward opened the Lazy Jay Ranch in the town of Lake Luzerne and succeeded so well that soon dude ranches opened all over town. Larry Bennett, who owns a riding stable in the town, says of that era: "It was a phenomenal business. They were selling the Old West idea to people in New York City."

Although that heyday has passed, a rodeo and several riding stables and dude ranches still operate in Lake Luzerne and neighboring towns, and the Old West theme lives on in the names of restaurants and motels along NY 9N in Lake Luzerne.

The Luzerne Public Campground, located on Fourth Lake, capitalizes on the tradition: It offers equestrians about 5 miles of horse trails that connect to about 60 miles of private trails. The campground also has two corrals.

No motorboats are allowed on Fourth Lake. Largemouth bass (*Micropterus salmoides*), northern pike (*Esox lucius*), and yellow perch (*Perca flavescens*) are among the fish dwelling in the 0.5-mile-long lake.

Directions: From Northway Exit 21, drive about 7 miles west on NY 9N to the campground on the left.

Activities: Camping, horseback riding, swimming, canoeing, fishing, picnicking.

Facilities: 172 trailer and tent sites, 2 beaches, 2 horse corrals, horse trails, picnic area, small-boat launch, hot showers, trailer dump station. Facilities are accessible to the handicapped.

Dates: Open mid-May through Labor Day.

Fees: There is a charge for camping or day use.

Closest town: The village of Lake Luzerne is approximately 2 miles south on NY 9N.

For more information: Campground office, phone (518) 696-2031. For reservations, phone (800) 456-2267. For information about local dude ranches, phone the Warren County Department of Tourism at (800) 958-4748.

Warren County Fish Hatchery

[Fig. 27(1)] The county raises rainbow trout (*Oncorhynchus mykiss*) and brook trout (*Salvelinus fontinalis*) at a hatchery along the Hudson River a little west of the village of Warrensburg. The fish are stocked in numerous waters around the county. The county also raises native brook trout that are stocked in reclaimed ponds throughout the Adirondacks.

The hatchery publishes a brochure for visitors who want to take a self-guided tour of the 72-acre grounds. Trout can be seen in three concrete ponds and, in summer, in a "Living Stream" in the Visitor Center. The center also shows an educational video. The hatchery has a picnic pavilion and canoe launch.

Directions: From Northway Exit 23 at Warrensburg, drive west briefly to US 9; turn right and drive 1.3 miles on US 9 to County 40; turn left and drive to Fish Hatchery Road on the left. The hatchery is at the end of this road.

Activities: Picnicking, walking.

Facilities: Visitor center, picnic pavilion, playground, restrooms, canoe launch.

Dates: Open year-round.

Fees: No fee.

Closest town: Warrensburg.

For more information: Warren County Division of Parks and Recreation, 261 Main Street, Warrensburg, NY 12885. Phone (518)-623-2877 or (518)-623-5576.

Warren County Nature Trail and Nordic Ski Trails

[Fig. 24(3)] This attractive nature trail winds through woods that have reclaimed old farmland. For part of the way, it follows a stretch of the Hudson River where the buildup of ice floes in spring has created an unusual plant habitat known as an ice meadow. A brochure available at the trailhead explains what to look for at 19 stops along the 0.75-mile route.

Many species of trees grow here, including white pine (*Pinus strobus*), black cherry

(*Prunus serotina*), American beech (*Fagus grandifolia*), American elm (*Ulmus americana*), Amercian basswood (*Tilia americana*), and paper birch (*Betula papyrifea*). Pileated woodpeckers (*Dryocopus pileatus*) are among the birds living in the woods.

The ice floes, by prolonging the spring thaw and scouring the shore, create a chilly microclimate for northern plants not usually found along rivers this far south, such as Clinton's club brush and New England violet. In all, the ice meadows stretch for more than 10 miles. The ice meadow is a globally rare natural community.

In winter, the county maintains several miles of groomed cross-country ski trails, all marked for novice, intermediate, or expert. The trails connect with private trails at Cronin's Golf Resort.

Directions: From Northway Exit 23 at Warrensburg, drive west briefly to US 9; turn right and drive 1.3 miles on US 9 to County 40; turn left and drive 2.7 miles to the parking area on the left (just past Cronin's Golf Course).

Trail: About 0.75 mile.

Degree of difficulty: Easy.

Surface: Old woods road, natural forest floor.

For more information: Warren County Division of Parks and Recreation, 261 Main Street, Warrensburg, NY 12885. Phone (518)-623-2877 or (518)-623-5576.

Pack Demonstration Forest

[Fig. 24(2)] Charles Lathrop Pack, the son of a lumber baron, bought most of this 2,500-acre tract north of Warrensburg in 1927 as an experiment in conservation-friendly forestry. Today, the State University of New York College of Environmental Science and Forestry owns and logs the land, but it has set aside a preserve that includes white pines (*Pinus strobus*) and hemlocks (*Tsuga canadensis*) more than 300 years old. One massive hemlock, nicknamed the Grandmother Tree, stands more than 175 feet tall.

The forestry students have built a gravel path, suitable for wheelchairs, with interpretive stops explained in a brochure available at the trailhead. Besides pines and hemlocks, trees seen along the way include red maple (*Acer rubrum*), striped maple (*Acer pensylvanicum*), black ash (*Fraxinus nigra*), yellow birch (*Betula alleghaniensis*), and Eastern hophornbeam (*Ostrya virginiana*). Wildflowers include common wood sorrel (*Oxalis montana*), goldthread (*Coptis groenlandica*), and partridgeberry (*Mitchella repens*). At least three types of ferns—cinnamon, royal, and interrupted—also grow in the preserve.

Directions: From Warrensburg, take US 9 north about 0.7 mile past the junction with NY 28 to an entrance road on the left. Drive about 0.5 mile to the parking lot.

Trail: 1-mile loop.

Degree of difficulty: Easy.

Surface: Gravel path, old road. Designed to accommodate wheelchairs.

For more information: Pack Demonstration Forest, PO Box 158, Warrensburg, NY 12885. Phone (518) 623-9679.

Camp Dippikill

[Fig. 24(1)] The State University of New York at Albany owns 847 acres of forest north of Warrensburg with about 8 miles of hiking trails (easy to moderate) and a 50-acre pond. The university keeps several cabins on the property that can be rented only by those affiliated with the school. The public, however, is welcome to walk or ski the trails and swim, fish, and canoe at the pond. Day visitors must check in at the camp office and leave by sundown. Trail maps are available at the office. Canoes, paddles, and life jackets are left at the pond during warm weather.

PAPER BIRCH
(Betula papyrifera)
This birch has chalky white bark that peels in strips, adding decorative texture to the winter landscape. It grows by water and on moist hillsides.

The best way to explore Camp Dippikill is to walk the Ridge Trail to the top of Dippikill Mountain and return via Dippikill Pond and the Valley Trail. From a lookout on the mountain, hikers can enjoy vistas in three directions, taking in the High Peaks to the north and the Hudson River to the south. At the pond, anglers can fish for largemouth bass (*Micropterus salmoides*) and yellow perch (*Perca flavescens*).

Directions: From Warrensburg, take US 9 north a few miles to NY 28; turn left and go about 5.6 miles to Glen Creek Road, a left-hand turn reached shortly after crossing the Hudson River; take Glen Creek Road about 2.5 miles to Dippikill Road; turn left and go about 0.7 mile to the office on the left.

Activities: Hiking, swimming, canoeing, fishing, cross-country skiing, snowshoeing, ice skating, volleyball.

Facilities: Bathhouse, 8 cabins, 8 campsites.

Dates: Grounds open year-round. Day visitors must leave by sundown.

Fees: There is a charge for rentals.

Closest town: Warrensburg is about 10 miles south.

For more information: Phone Camp Dippikill at (518) 623-9917.

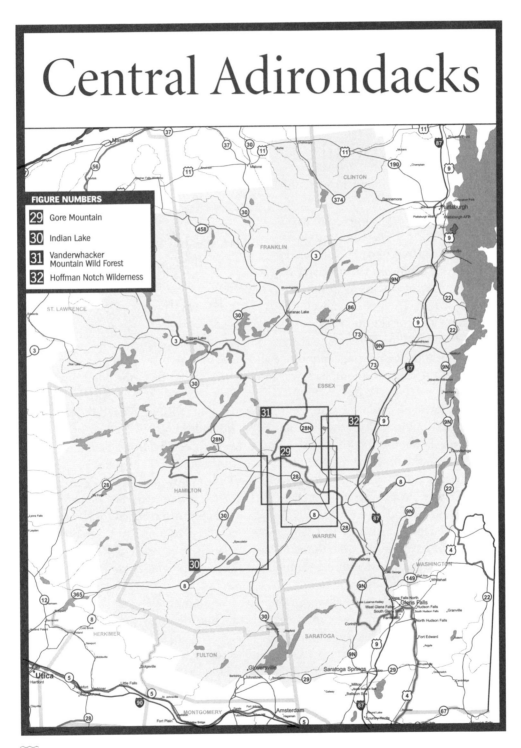

Central Adirondacks

FIGURE NUMBERS

29 Gore Mountain

30 Indian Lake

31 Vanderwhacker Mountain Wild Forest

32 Hoffman Notch Wilderness

Central Adirondacks

Many people see the Central Adirondacks only from a car window as they fly past on their way to the High Peaks. Those who do stop to explore the region discover that it offers something that can be hard to come by in the High Peaks: solitude.

As defined here, the Central Adirondacks is bounded by national and state highways: the Northway to the east, NY 30 to the west, NY 8 to the south, and NY 28N and Blue Ridge Road to the north. The region thus encompasses the Siamese Ponds Wilderness, the Hoffman Notch Wilderness, the Blue Mountain Wild Forest, most of the Vanderwhacker Wild Forest, and small parts of the Jessup River Wild Forest. The Hudson Gorge Primitive Area, although it lies within the region's boundaries, is discussed in a separate chapter on the Hudson River (*see* page 81).

At 113,674 acres, the Siamese Ponds Wilderness accounts for much of the state

[*Above:* Augur Falls is one of the noteworthy geographical features in the Central Adirondacks]

land. The landscape of this wilderness—low mountains creased by rivers and streams, dotted by small lakes and ponds—epitomizes the region as a whole. Not surprisingly, most of the hiking trails in the Central Adirondacks lead not to summits but to interior waters, destinations suitable for a day trip or backpacking excursion.

The region does boast one peak that falls just short of 4,000 feet: Blue Mountain. Located near the Adirondack Museum, each year this mountain attracts thousands of hikers who climb the summit's fire tower for gorgeous views of Blue Mountain Lake and the High Peaks. Great views also can be had from the towers on Vanderwhacker and Goodnow mountains.

Most of the Central Adirondacks' peaks consist of either granitic or syenitic gneiss, a metaplutonic rock somewhat less durable than the anorthosite found in the High Peaks. The largest mass of anorthosite outside the High Peaks, however, can be found in the Siamese Ponds Wilderness. Chimney Mountain, east of Indian Lake, is a geological oddity in the Adirondacks in that much of it consists of metamorphosed sedimentary rock. Erosion of this soft rock has created an unusual rock tower and caves.

One of the region's main attractions is Indian Lake, the eighth-largest lake wholly within the Adirondack Park. Like many lakes in the Adirondacks, Indian Lake lies in a northeast-trending fault zone, hemmed in by hills on both sides. Indian Lake stretches 15 miles and covers 4,365 acres. Thirteenth Lake, the region's second-biggest lake, is about 2 miles long and covers 326 acres. This lake also lies in a fault valley that trends northeast.

Six major rivers besides the Hudson course through the Central Adirondacks: the Boreas, Kunjamuk, Cedar, Rock, Indian, and East Branch of the Sacandaga. All of these rivers have been designated wild, scenic, or recreational, protecting them from development. In the old lumbering days, the rivers were used to float logs to the Hudson.

Although the early settlers cut the primeval forests for timber, tanning bark, or agriculture, few hikers will realize that the dense woods they walk through is recovering from old wounds inflicted by the ax and saw. As in most of the Adirondacks, hardwoods dominate the forest, the most typical species being sugar maple (*Acer saccharum*), American beech (*Fagus grandifolia*), and yellow birch (*Betula alleghaniensis*). Conifers grow in moist lowlands, along rivers and lakes, and at higher elevations.

Black bear, white-tailed deer, beaver, mink, otter, common loon, great blue heron, osprey—virtually the whole Adirondack collection—dwell within the Central Adirondacks. Indian Lake has numerous species of fish, including Atlantic salmon and lake trout. The rivers and ponds often contain brook trout or brown trout.

State-maintained foot trails enable visitors to reach the interior of the forests without difficulty, but large tracts in the Siamese Ponds and Hoffman Notch wildernesses remain trailless—offering bushwhackers a true wilderness experience. Backpackers who stick to the trails will find many primitive campsites and seven lean-tos scattered throughout the region.

The Central Adirondacks has only one state-run campground, the Indian Lake

Islands Public Campground, which has primitive campsites along the shores and islands of the lake. However, several state campgrounds exist just outside the region, such as those at Lake Durant, Lake Lewey, Lake Harris, and Moffitt Beach.

The state also runs a major alpine ski center at Gore Mountain near North Creek (*see* page 201). In summer, Gore opens its trails to mountain bikers and runs the chairlift for those who want to enjoy the view.

For more information: State Department of Environmental Conservation, PO Box 296, Route 86, Ray Brook, NY 12977. Phone (518) 897-1200. Ask for the leaflets *The Siamese Ponds Wilderness* and *Trails in the Blue Mountain Lake Region.*

Siamese Ponds Wilderness

[Fig. 30(14)] The Siamese Ponds Wilderness east of Indian Lake encompasses more than 113,000 acres, making it the third largest wilderness in the Adirondacks. The 33 miles of trails crisscrossing the region are suitable for day trips or multiday excursions. Most trails lead to water, not summits. There are four lean-tos: two at Puffer Pond, one at John Pond, and one on the East Branch of the Sacandaga River.

Only eight peaks in the wilderness top 3,000 feet. The highest, at 3,472 feet, is Puffer Mountain. Other noteworthy geographical features include Thirteenth Lake, a 2-mile lake on the region's northern border; Chimney Mountain, a place of geological oddities; and Augur Falls, a gorge on the Sacandaga River's main branch. For hardy bushwhackers, about 21,000 acres in the west-central sector of the region remain trailless.

Granitic and syenitic gneisses form most of the bedrock, but a large mass of anorthosite—the rock that makes up the High Peaks—exists in the southern sector. The red gemstone garnet has been mined at several places in and around the region. Hikers can reach the old Hooper mine near Garnet Hill Lodge by a short walk (*see* page 199). The more adventuresome can hunt for the remains of a pit mine on Humphrey Mountain south of Kings Flow. The Barton Mines Corporation continues to operate the world's largest garnet mine near North River, just outside the wilderness.

Two rivers originate in the Siamese Ponds Wilderness: the East Branch of the Sacandaga River and the Kunjamuk. The East Sacandaga is easily accessible from NY 8 and a major foot trail (*see* page 194). The upper Kunjamuk is more remote but can reached by foot trail. The lower Kunjamuk—the canoeable section—flows through private timberlands.

Black bear (*Ursus americanus*) and white-tailed deer (*Odocoileus virginianus*) live in the Siamese Ponds Wilderness, along with the smaller Adirondack mammals. Common loon (*Gavia immer*), great blue heron (*Ardea herodias*), and various ducks frequent the ponds and wetlands. Wild trout dwell in some of the waters.

The Siamese Ponds Wilderness constitutes the bulk of the state lands east of Indian Lake, west of Gore Mountain, north of NY 8, and south of NY 28. Trailheads on NY 8 and at Thirteenth Lake and Kings Flow are the region's major gateways. Those trails starting on the eastern shore of Indian Lake, reachable by boat, are discussed in the section on Indian Lake (*see* page 203).

For more information: State Department of Environmental Conservation, PO Box 296, Route 86, Ray Brook, NY 12977. Phone (518) 897-1200. Ask for the leaflet *The Siamese Ponds Wilderness.*

EAST SACANDAGA/SIAMESE PONDS TRAILS

[Fig. 29(4)] The main trail in the Siamese Ponds Wilderness runs from NY 8 north about 9.5 miles to Old Farm Clearing at Thirteenth Lake (*see* page 198). From there, it's another 1.2 miles along an abandoned woods road to a parking area. Hikers and cross-country skiers who spot a car at the other end of the trail can make the 10.7-mile trek in a single day.

For much of the way, the trail follows an old wagon road and parallels the East Branch of the Sacandaga River. This trout stream also is accessible from NY 8, which it follows for several miles south of the trailhead. White-water canoeists can navigate sections of the river in spring.

A short distance from the start, the trail climbs 200 feet over the shoulder of Eleventh Mountain, whose cliffs are visible on the right, and then descends 400 feet to the river. This section can be difficult for skiers. The rest of the way is mostly level, affording a pleasant journey through hardwoods and hemlocks.

For those not making a through trip, a popular destination is Siamese Ponds, reached by a spur trail that begins at a lean-to and suspension bridge 4.0 miles from NY 8. The marked trail ends at the lower pond after 2.3 miles—and a climb of nearly 500 feet. Fishermen's paths lead around the shore to the smaller, upper pond. There are several places to camp and swim on the lower pond. The ponds contain brook trout (*Salvelinus fontinalis*) and lake trout (*Salvelinus namaycush*).

Directions: For southern trailhead: from Bakers Mills, drive south about 4 miles on NY 8 to parking area on the right. For northern trailhead: see directions to eastern parking area on Thirteenth Lake, page 198.

Trail: 6.3 miles to Siamese Ponds; 10.7 miles to Thirteenth Lake, not including detour to Siamese Ponds.

Degree of difficulty: Moderate.

Surface and blaze: Natural forest floor. Blue hiking blazes, yellow skiing blazes.

AUGUR FALLS

[Fig. 30(17)] North of Wells, the Sacandaga River's main branch plunges over a series of cascades in a beautiful rocky gorge that can be reached by a short hike. Hemlocks grow atop the gorge, while lichen, moss, and grasses cling to the mist-drenched walls. The flat rocks on the west side have been worn slippery smooth, with several potholes created by swirling waters.

The trail, starting in a large parking area off NY 30, cuts through a forest of northern hardwoods and hemlock, crossing a small stream and passing several mossy boulders. It's possible to take a herd path along the river back to the parking area.

The gorge is pleasant place to picnic, but adults will need to keep an eye on young children.

Canoeists may want to explore Augur Flats, a large area of still water just upriver from the falls. There is a put-in the parking area. Do not paddle downstream from the put-in.

MAIDENHAIR FERN
(Adiantum pedatum)

Directions: From the junction of NY 30 and NY 8 north of Wells, drive 1.8 miles north on NY 30 to a dirt parking area on the right. Just after making the turn, park on the right near an old dirt road that parallels the highway. Follow the road to the trailhead on the left. If canoeing Augur Flats, drive through the parking area to the riverbank.

Trail: About 0.6 mile to the gorge.

Degree of difficulty: Easy.

Surface and blaze: Natural forest floor. Yellow blazes.

CHIMNEY MOUNTAIN

[Fig. 30(10)] The unusual rock formations and caves on Chimney Mountain have long fascinated geologists and spelunkers. Children, too, will love exploring the area, but they must be warned to watch their step, for there are many precipitous ledges and deep crevices. Parents will need to keep an eye on young children.

The Chimney is a rock tower on the eastern wall of a 600-foot-long rift valley. It rises about 80 feet from its base in the rift and about 35 feet above the rest of the wall. The Chimney cannot be scaled without technical rock-climbing skills. There are smaller towers of rock on the east wall, separated by narrow passageways and tunnels.

Numerous caves have been found in the rift and the vicinity, including one more than 100 feet deep. Many of these should be left to expert spelunkers, but there are places that can be safely explored by amateurs. To enter the rift, return to an unmarked path that branches off the main trail just before the rock towers. Hikers may notice a cold draft as they descend past a large crevice in the eastern wall. Turn left to get to the bottom of the rift, with its jumbled blocks of rock and maze of pathways. Walk about 20 yards to the left to reach an accessible cave where ice persists into summer.

In a 1914 paper, the geologist William J. Miller theorized that the rift formed when the eastern wall, undercut by erosion, broke off from the main rock and toppled to the east, leaving a chasm up to 300 feet wide. Another theory is that the rift formed when rock "slumped" off the mountain's higher slopes. In either case, geologists believe that the rift formed after the glaciers retreated about 10,000 years ago. Later, huge blocks of rock—up to 20 feet wide—tumbled into the chasm, creating the caves and passageways.

The rocks in the rift and on both walls are among the oldest in the Adirondacks. Originally, they were sedimentary rocks that formed in the Grenville Sea about 1.2 billion years ago. They were metamorphosed during the Grenville Orogeny, or mountain-building event, about 1.1 billion years ago. Erosion of these soft rocks has created the sand seen along the trail and around the Chimney. Because the metasedimentary Grenville rock is easily eroded, it rarely is found at this height in the Adirondacks.

The actual summit of Chimney Mountain, located about 0.25 mile east of the Chimney, consists of granitic gneiss and stands about 220 feet higher than the trail at the Chimney. The summit can be reached by a bushwhack, but those who don't go will still be able to enjoy nice views of Kings Flow and Bullhead Mountain from lookouts near the Chimney.

The trail to the Chimney begins on private land but soon enters the Forest Preserve. The trail passes through a forest of mostly hardwoods. It can be muddy. Look for outcrops of quartzite on the upper slope. In places, the weathered bedrock looks as though it were flowing downhill.

Directions: From the junction of NY 30 and NY 28 in Indian Lake, drive south 0.6 mile on NY 30 to Big Brook Road; turn left and go 5.7 miles to the junction of Hutchins and Moulton roads; turn right and go 2.7 miles to the Chimney Mountain Wilderness Lodge. The lodge charges a small parking fee. Walk east from the lot. The trail will be straight ahead.

Trail: 1.4 miles to the Chimney.

Elevation: 1,440 feet to 2,500 feet.

Degree of difficulty: Moderate.

Surface and blaze: Natural forest floor. Blue blazes.

For more information: See William J. Miller, "The Great Rift on Chimney Mountain," *New York State Museum Bulletin*, 177 (Albany: The University of the State of New York, 1914), pp. 143–46. For a copy, phone the state library at (518) 474-5352. Indian Lake Chamber of Commerce, phone (518) 648-5112 or (800) 328-5253.

PUFFER POND LOOP

[Fig. 30(12)] Puffer Pond is an excellent destination for fishermen, backpackers, and day-trippers. The state stocks the 38-acre pond from the air with brook trout (*Salvelinus fontinalis*). The trout often range from 9 to 12 inches, but trophy fish weighing 2 to 3 pounds are sometimes caught. There are two lean-tos on the northern shore. Puffer Mountain rises from the opposite shore. Rock climbers occasionally bushwhack to the other side of the mountain to scale the 70- to 180-foot cliffs.

Hikers can reach Puffer Pond from the north, west, or east. The trails belong to a network that crisscrosses the Siamese Ponds Wilderness, so the pond can be a primary destination or a stop on a multiday trek. For day-trippers, it's best to hike to Puffer from the Chimney Mountain Wilderness Lodge and return by way of Kings Flow—a 5-mile loop.

From the lodge, the trail passes through a mostly deciduous forest. At about 0.6 mile, the trail crosses Carroll Brook, which winds through an open meadow with lots of raspberries. Leaving the brook, the trail climbs to a marked junction. The way left leads to John Pond, see below. Go straight to reach the first lean-to at 1.9 miles. From there, turn left to reach the second lean-to or right to begin the walk to Kings Flow.

The trail to Kings Flow passes the marshy western end of Puffer Pond, a feeding ground for heron, and follows Puffer Pond Brook for much of the way. The 1.9-mile route is mostly downhill. At Kings Flow, which can be seen through the trees, the trail joins an old road that can be taken north to return to the lodge. This part of the route is level.

Several kinds of wildflowers can be seen in the woods during the loop, including Indian pipe (*Monotropa uniflora*), round-leaved pyrola (*Pyrola rotundifolia*), common wood sorrel (*Oxalis montana*), and bunchberry (*Cornus canadensis*). Numerous field flowers adorn sections of the Kings Flow trail.

Directions: Same as for Chimney Mountain (*see* page 195). Walk east from the parking lot. The trail will be on the right.

Trail: About 5 miles.

Degree of difficulty: Moderate.

Surface and blaze: Natural forest floor, old road. Red blazes. West of Puffer Pond, the trail is sparsely marked.

JOHN POND

[Fig. 30(5)] An old road passes through meadows and stands of white pine (*Pinus strobus*) on its way to this trout pond just northwest of Bullhead Mountain. On the southern shore, there is a lean-to that faces the water. Those spending a day at the pond might want to bushwhack up the rocky ridge to the west for a view of the countryside.

The trail follows gentle grades. Many wildflowers grow along the way in summer, especially in the open sections at the beginning, including yarrow (*Achilles millefolium*), common fleabane (*Erigeron philadelphicus*), orange hawkeye (*Hieracium aurantiacum*), yellow goatsbeard (*Tragopogon pratensis*), tall meadow rue (*Thalictrum polygamen*), and swamp candles (*Lysimachia terrestris*).

At 1.7 miles, a trail to the left leads about 0.1 mile to the burial site of two children who died of diphtheria in 1897. The graves are marked by small wooden crosses. The trail to John Pond bears left at the marked junction at 2.7 miles. The right fork leads to the trail from Kings Flow to Puffer Pond (*see* page 196).

The state stocks John Pond with brook trout (*Salvelinus fontinalis*). No baitfish

WHITE-THROATED SPARROW
(Zonotrichia albicollis)

are allowed. It's possible to swim near the lean-to. The bottom of the pond is mucky.

Directions: From the junction of NY 30 and NY 28 in Indian Lake, drive south on NY 30 about 0.6 mile to Big Brook Road; turn left and go 3.6 miles to Starbuck Road; turn left and go 1 mile to a T intersection; and turn right and go 0.2 mile to a parking area. From the lot, walk up a dirt road a short distance to the trail register.

Trail: 3 miles to John Pond.

Degree of difficulty: Easy.

Surface and blaze: Old road, natural forest floor. Blue blazes.

THIRTEENTH LAKE

[Fig. 30(8)] Thirteenth Lake is one of the more heavily used areas of the Siamese Ponds Wilderness. The campsites at the northern end of the lake are easy to reach and can be used for a variety of outdoor activities and excursions. More remote campsites can be found on the eastern and western shores.

The 2-mile-long lake lies in a fault valley and drains by Thirteenth Brook into the Hudson. Canoeists can reach the water by a short carry. Motorboats are not allowed. Day-trippers may want to visit Elizabeth Point on the eastern shore for a picnic and swim. To reach the point, walk 0.5 mile north of the parking lot and then take a right to go to the shore.

Thirteenth Lake has a reputation for fly fishing. Stocked with brown trout (*Salmo trutta*) and rainbow trout (*Oncorhynchus mykiss*), the lake also holds landlocked salmon (*Salmo salar*) and some brook trout (*Salvelinus fontinalis*). Anglers may keep up to three salmon over 15 inches long and up to five trout of any size. The use of baitfish is prohibited.

Thirteenth Lake has parking areas near its northern and eastern shores. Park in the northern lot if putting in a canoe or hiking to Peaked Mountain Pond or Peaked Mountain. Park in the eastern lot if hiking to Elizabeth Point or into the interior of the Siamese Ponds Wilderness.

Directions: For the northern parking area: from the junction of NY 28 and NY 30 in Indian Lake, drive east on NY 28 for 12.4 miles to Thirteenth Lake Road near the hamlet of North River; turn right and go about 3.4 miles to Beach Road; turn right and go 0.8 mile to a parking area at the end. For the eastern parking area: instead of turning onto Beach Road, continue on Thirteenth Lake Road to its end, bearing right at the sign for Garnet Hill Lodge.

Activities: Hiking, camping, fishing, canoeing, picnicking, swimming.

Facilities: Primitive campsites, privies, canoe launch.

Dates: Accessible year-round.

Fees: None.

Closest town: North Creek is about 9 miles away.

PEAKED MOUNTAIN

[Fig. 30(6)] Blink during the hike to Peaked Mountain and you may miss some of the ever-changing scenery. From the parking lot at the northern end of Thirteenth Lake, the trail skirts the western shore of the lake for about 0.5 mile, then begins a gradual ascent through a mixed forest along Peaked Mountain Brook. After crossing the brook, the trail passes several grassy vlies, or wetlands, and beaver ponds before reaching Peaked Mountain Pond.

Baitfish are prohibited in the trout pond. There are a number of informal campsites around the water. The rocky cliffs of Peaked Mountain, visible from the shore, were once home to nesting peregrine falcons (*Falco peregrinus*). The summit is about 0.5 mile farther. The trail continues counterclockwise around the pond until it reaches a cove at the northeast corner, where it turns uphill. From here the trail is quite steep in places. As you approach the top, the trees sometimes give way to patches of open rock. The summit offers a lovely view of the route you have just hiked from Thirteenth Lake; Peaked Mountain Pond and the fold in the landscape followed by Peaked Mountain Brook are directly below. The High Peaks can be seen to the north. Slide Mountain is directly to the east.

Directions: See directions to northern parking area at Thirteenth Lake (*see* page 198).

Trail: 2.5 miles to Peaked Mountain Pond, 3 miles to the top of Peaked Mountain.

Elevation: 1,674 feet to 2,250 feet at the pond. An additional 669 feet to the summit.

Degree of difficulty: Moderate

Surface and blaze: Natural forest floor, bare rock. Red blazes.

HOOPER MINE

[Fig. 29(1)] This abandoned garnet mine was established by Frank Hooper in 1905. The mine closed in the late 1920s, but the remains of blasting shacks and other processing buildings are still visible around the site. The easy hike is ideal for small children, who may enjoy searching for red garnet deposits at the base of the orange cliffs of oxidized rock that mark the boundaries of the mine. For a good overall view of the mine, as well as a glimpse of the active Ruby Mountain Mine to the north, follow the path up the outcrop to the left of the entrance to the amphitheater. The point also offers a nice view of Bullhead and Puffer mountains beyond Thirteenth Lake.

The trail begins on the property of the Garnet Hill Lodge, a center for cross-country skiing and mountain biking. Another hiking trail begins in the same spot. This trail soon forks to give hikers a choice of destinations: the summit of Balm of Gilead Mountain or William Blake Pond. Both are easy hikes of about 0.8 mile. All three hikes can be done in a few hours.

Directions: Follow the directions for the parking area on the eastern shore of

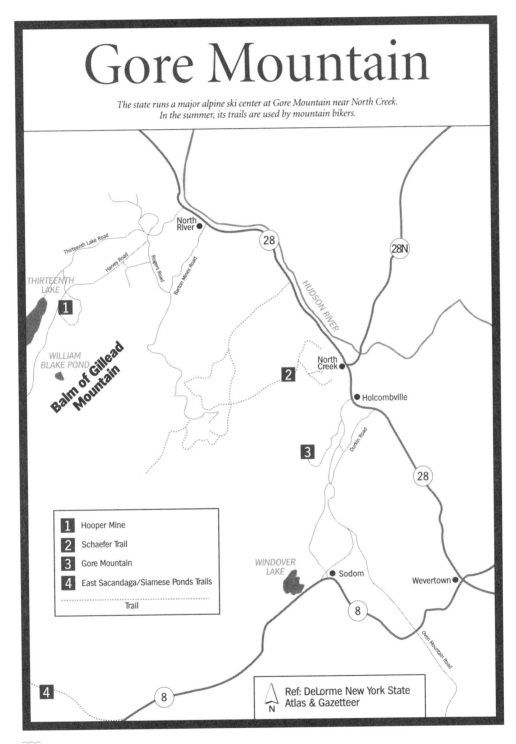

Gore Mountain

The state runs a major alpine ski center at Gore Mountain near North Creek.
In the summer, its trails are used by mountain bikers.

1 Hooper Mine
2 Schaefer Trail
3 Gore Mountain
4 East Sacandaga/Siamese Ponds Trails
.... Trail

Ref: DeLorme New York State
Atlas & Gazetteer

Thirteenth Lake (*see* page 198), but bear left at the sign for Garnet Hill Lodge. Park off the road near the cross-country ski shop, located about 0.2 mile past a junction, and walk a short distance up the dirt road that passes to the left of the lodge's tennis courts. The trailhead is on the right. Note that the parking area and trailhead are on private property. In winter, visitors should purchase a ski ticket.

Trail: 0.4 mile.

Degree of difficulty: Easy.

Surface: Gravel path, natural forest floor.

Gore Mountain

[Fig. 29(3)] The 3,583-foot Gore Mountain boasts one of the two state-owned ski centers in the Adirondacks. The other is at Whiteface Mountain (*see* page 27). For downhill skiers, Gore offers 44 trails—the longest is 3 miles—and eight lifts. It also has more than 6.5 miles of cross-country ski trails, ranging from a 0.5-mile novice loop to a 3-mile wilderness trail.

In summer, Gore maintains a network of mountain bike trails. Bikers take a chairlift up the mountain and ride down. Chairlift rides also are available to those who just want to enjoy the scenery. These patrons can return to the base lodge by chairlift or foot. It's also possible to walk to the top of Gore by the Schaefer Trail, which opened in 1997.

Directions: From NY 28 in North Creek, turn south on Peaceful Valley Road (look for the sign for Gore Mountain) and drive to the ski center's access road.

Activities: Downhill and cross-country skiing, snow-boarding, mountain biking, hiking, chairlift rides.

Facilities: Alpine and Nordic ski trails, mountain bike trails, hiking trail, lodges, restaurant, nursery.

Dates: Open to skiing while snow lasts. Open to mountain biking and chairlift rides from early June to early Sept.

Fees: There is a charge for skiing, biking, and chairlift rides.

Closest town: Gore is located just outside the hamlet of North Creek.

For more information: Gore Mountain, Peaceful Valley Road, North Creek, NY 12853. Phone (518) 251-2411 or (800) 342-1234.

SCHAEFER TRAIL

[Fig. 29(2)] In the 1990s, volunteers blazed a trail up Burnt Ridge and Gore Mountain in honor of Paul, Vincent, and Carl Schaefer. Paul had been a tireless advocate for preservation of the Adirondack wilderness. His two brothers did much to promote skiing in the North Creek region.

The trail, which opened in 1997, begins at the North Creek Ski Bowl, a small ski

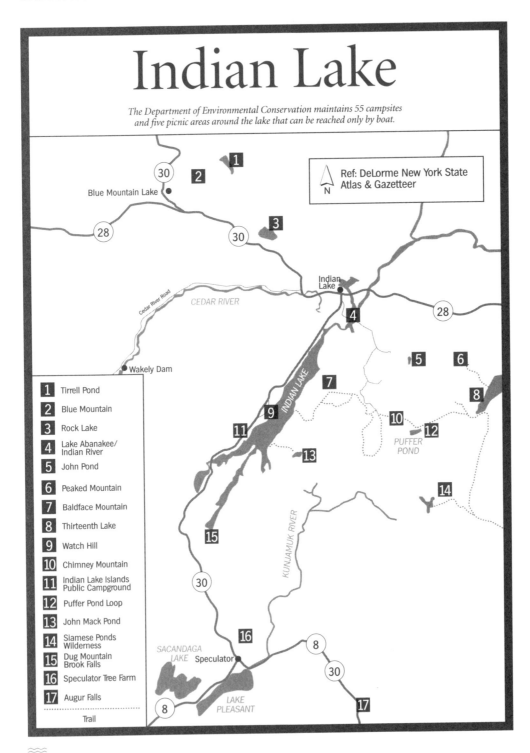

Indian Lake

*The Department of Environmental Conservation maintains 55 campsites
and five picnic areas around the lake that can be reached only by boat.*

Ref: DeLorme New York State
Atlas & Gazetteer

Blue Mountain Lake

CEDAR RIVER

Cedar River Road

Indian
Lake

Wakely Dam

INDIAN LAKE

PUFFER
POND

KUNJAMUK RIVER

SACANDAGA
LAKE   Speculator

LAKE
PLEASANT

1 Tirrell Pond
2 Blue Mountain
3 Rock Lake
4 Lake Abanakee/
  Indian River
5 John Pond
6 Peaked Mountain
7 Baldface Mountain
8 Thirteenth Lake
9 Watch Hill
10 Chimney Mountain
11 Indian Lake Islands
   Public Campground
12 Puffer Pond Loop
13 John Mack Pond
14 Siamese Ponds
   Wilderness
15 Dug Mountain
   Brook Falls
16 Speculator Tree Farm
17 Augur Falls
    Trail

slope owned by the town, and ascends through mostly hardwood forests to Saddle Lodge part way up Gore Mountain, sometimes following ski and mountain bike routes. From Saddle Lodge, hikers can reach the 3,583-foot summit of Gore by following the skiers' Cloud Trail and a work road. Eventually, the Schaefer trail may be extended so hikers can continue to the summit through woods.

For those who don't want to hike all the way to the summit, Burnt Ridge's rock ledge—dubbed Paul's Ledge—is a logical turnaround point. The ledge offers fine views to the south and west of Crane Mountain, the Wilcox Lake Wild Forest, and nearby Bear Mountain. Do not let children get too close to the edge: There is a long drop. One highlight en route to the ledge is a natural amphitheater with steep rock walls and enormous boulders—some jumbled together like abstract sculptures.

In snow season, hikers are not allowed to continue past Paul's Ledge, for beyond it, the trail makes use of alpine ski trails for short stretches. At Saddle Lodge (elevation 2,950 feet), the trail markers end. Those going to the summit can consult a large outdoor map near the lodge for the rest of the route.

Gore offers chairlift rides from early June to early September, so it's possible to ride up the mountain and walk down the Schaefer Trail. At the rock amphitheater, hikers should turn right off the Schaefer Trail to follow the mountain bike trail back to Gore's base lodge.

Directions: From NY 28 in North Creek, turn south on Ski Bowl Road and drive 0.3 mile, bearing right at a junction, to the parking area on the right.

Trail: 2.5 miles to Burnt Ridge ledge, 3.3 miles to Saddle Lodge, 4.5 miles to Gore's summit.

Elevation: 1,050 feet at trailhead to 2,700 feet at Burnt Ridge ledge to 3,583 feet at summit.

Degree of difficulty: Moderate if going to Burnt Ridge ledge, strenuous if going to summit.

Surface and blaze: Roads, ski trails, natural forest floor. Blue blazes to Saddle Lodge.

Indian Lake

[Fig. 30] Indian Lake, the eighth-largest lake wholly within the Adirondack Park, lies in a long fault valley. The lake stretches about 15 miles from the Jessup River to a dam at its northern end. The dam has raised the lake level about 33 feet. The water reaches a maximum depth of 85 feet.

The state owns nearly all of the eastern shore, most of the western shore, and most of the islands. The Department of Environmental Conservation maintains 55 campsites and five picnic areas around the lake that can be reached only by boat. Campers must pay a fee to use the campsites. The picnic areas are open to everyone without charge. Several hiking trails, also reachable only by boat, begin on the eastern shore.

On windy days, the choppy water can be too dangerous for canoes, although the lake has many coves and bays that offer some protection. Those worried about waves can try paddling down the narrow arm of the lake known as Jessup's Bay, which leads to the mouth of the Jessup River.

Swimmers will delight in Indian Lake's clear water. Beware that the water depth can increase quickly off the rock ledges and islands. Parents might want to bring young children to the sandy beach at Normans Cove or one of the other picnic areas.

Many kinds of fish dwell in the lake, including landlocked salmon (*Salmo salar*), lake trout (*Salvelinus namaycush*), brown trout (*Salmo trutta*), northern pike (*Esox lucius*), smallmouth bass (*Micropterus dolomieui*), and various panfish. Fishermen are allowed to keep three salmon greater than 15 inches, two lake trout greater than 21 inches, and five other trout of any size. Ice fishing for salmon and all kinds of trout is permitted.

There is a state-owned boat launch at the Indian Lake Islands Public Campground.

For more information: Indian Lake Chamber of Commerce, PO Box 18, Indian Lake, NY 12842. Phone (518) 648-5112 or (800) 328-5253.

INDIAN LAKE ISLANDS PUBLIC CAMPGROUND

[Fig. 30(11)] Each of the 55 campsites on the shores and islands of Indian Lake has a picnic table, fireplace, and pit privy. Most are located in the southern half of the lake. Canoeists may want to take a campsite in Jessup Bay, a narrow arm of water at the southeastern end of the lake. The bay is more protected than the open part of the lake.

Canoes and rowboats can be rented and launched at Lewey Lake Public Campground, located just 0.2 mile south of the Indian Lake campground. From Lewey Lake, it's a short trip by water to Indian Lake. There also is a boat launch at the Indian Lake campground's headquarters.

Directions: From Speculator, drive 12 miles north on NY 30 to the campground headquarters on the right. From Indian Lake, drive 12 miles south on NY 30. The campground will be on the left.

Activities: Camping, hiking, canoeing, boating, fishing, swimming.

Facilities: 55 campsites, 5 picnic areas, pit toilets, hiking trails, boat launch.

Dates: Open mid-May to Labor Day.

Fees: There is a charge for camping, day use, and boat rentals.

Closest town: Speculator is 12 miles south, Indian Lake 12 miles north.

For more information: Campground office, phone (518) 648-5300. For reservations, phone (800) 456-2267.

BALDFACE MOUNTAIN

[Fig. 30(7)] The short climb up Baldface has a big reward: a magnificent vista of Indian Lake and many of the region's prominent peaks, including Snowy and Blue mountains. The trail ascends at once through a deciduous forest, gradually at first but steepening as it approaches the base of Baldface's cliffs. The trail curls around the cliffs and emerges onto an open rock ledge with a 180-degree view. Red spruce (*Picea rubens*) and red pine (*Pinus resinosa*) grow on the summit. Blueberries also are found. Hawks sometimes can be seen riding the wind currents near the cliffs. After the climb, hikers can take a swim at the beach at the entrance to Normans Cove, where there is also a picnic area.

Directions: The trailhead is reachable only by water. Enter Normans Cove on the eastern shore of Indian Lake, opposite the hamlet of Sabael, and head across the cove to a large rock marked by a white circle. The trail begins just to the left of this rock.

Trail: 1.1 miles to summit.

Elevation: 1,650 feet to 2,230 feet.

Degree of difficulty: Moderate.

Surface and blaze: Natural forest floor. Red blazes.

JOHN MACK POND

[Fig. 30(13)] A little-used trail leads to this 17-acre pond, stocked with brook trout (*Salvelinus fontinalis*), on the western edge of the Siamese Ponds Wilderness. It's a nice excursion for those staying at the Indian Lake Islands Campground. Just before reaching the pond, another trail forks right to go to Long Pond. Rock climbers sometimes scale the 150-foot cliffs rising above the eastern shore of Long Pond. Don Mellor describes several climbing routes in *Climbing in the Adirondacks*. The use of baitfish is not allowed in either pond.

Directions: Go to a sandy cove near campsite 26 on the eastern shore of John Mack Bay. The trail begins at the end of the cove near a trailhead sign.

Trail: 1.6 miles to John Mack Pond, 3.6 miles to Long Pond.

Elevation: 1,650 feet at Indian Lake to 1,760 at John Mack Pond.

Degree of difficulty: Easy.

Surface and blaze: Natural forest floor. Red blazes.

DUG MOUNTAIN BROOK FALLS

[Fig. 30(15)] Dug Mountain Brook creates a charming waterfall as it enters the Jessup River. Hikers will find a larger falls—about 40 feet high—by walking about 0.4 mile up an unmarked path that follows the brook. Canoeists can include this hike as part of an exploration of the lower Jessup.

Directions: Go to the end of Jessup Bay and look for the waterfall at the mouth of Dug Mountain Brook on the bay's eastern shore. The trail follows the north bank of the brook.

Trail: 0.4 mile to falls.

Degree of difficulty: Easy.

Surface and blaze: Natural forest floor.

WATCH HILL

[Fig. 30(9)] This small summit is a great hike for young climbers. The rock ledge at the top can be reached by a trail that begins on the west side of Indian Lake, but most people climb it from NY 30. It offers a great view of Snowy Mountain and nearby peaks. The southern portion of Indian Lake also can be seen.

The usual starting point is the southern end of an old dirt road. The road crosses a creek and rises gradually through a mostly hardwood forest. At 0.7 mile, a sign points right for Watch Hill. The trail is unmarked but easy to follow. Avoid a left-hand turn about 0.2 mile from the junction. As the trail climbs up the hill, it passes through stands of hemlock (*Tsuga canadensis*) and reaches a nice lookout at 1 mile. The summit offers an even better view 0.2 mile farther up the trail. Indian pipe (*Monotropa uniflora*) can be seen along the way. It's also possible to begin the hike from the northern end of the dirt road.

Directions: From the junction of NY 30 and NY 28 in Indian Lake, drive south on NY 30 for about 8.6 miles to the southern end of an old dirt road on the left that angles east from the highway. Park on the shoulder of the highway. Alternatively, park at the Snowy Mountain lot 7.5 miles from Indian Lake. From the lot, walk south on NY 30 along a guardrail. At the eighth guardrail post, turn left. A short trail leads to the northern end of the dirt road.

Trail: 1.2 miles to summit.

Elevation: 1,768 feet to 2,125 feet.

Degree of difficulty: Easy to moderate.

Surface and blaze: Old road, natural forest floor. No blazes.

Lake Abanakee/Indian River

[Fig. 30(4)] The Indian River once flowed from Indian Lake to the Hudson River without interruption, but a dam has created Lake Abanakee just north of the larger lake. Most of Lake Abanakee's shoreline is in private hands, but canoeists can explore the water by putting in near a causeway that splits the lake in two. The lake offers fine views of the surrounding hills, including Snowy Mountain. The lake south of the causeway is less developed. Bass and northern pike can be caught.

North of NY 28, the town of Indian Lake runs a small beach off Chain of Lakes Road just above the Lake Abanakee dam. Below the dam, the Indian River reverts to its natural self, coursing over boulders. There is an access site for whitewater canoeists who wish to ride the river to the Hudson Gorge (*see* page 81). Several informal paths lead from the road to the river, which is stocked with brown trout (*Salmo trutta*).

Directions: To reach the Lake Abanakee causeway, from the junction of NY 30 and NY 28 in Indian Lake, drive 0.6 mile south on NY 30 to Big Brook Road, turn left and go 1.6 miles to the causeway. Cross the causeway and park in an area on the right. To reach the town beach, from the same starting point in Indian Lake, drive 1.4 miles east on NY 28 to Chain of Lakes Road; turn left and go 0.6 mile to the beach on the right.

Activities: Canoeing, fishing, swimming.
Facilities: Canoe launch, beach.
Dates: The beach is open during the summer. Access to the lake is year-round.
Fees: None.
Closest town: Indian Lake.
For more information: Indian Lake Chamber of Commerce, phone (518) 648-5112 or (800) 328-5253.

Speculator Tree Farm

[Fig. 30(16)] International Paper Company owns more than 24,000 acres of timberlands adjacent to the Siamese Ponds Wilderness near the village of Speculator. Most of the land is open to the public for hiking, fishing, hunting, and canoeing, but a permit must be purchased. Camping and campfires are prohibited. Hunting clubs own exclusive rights to two tracts on the tree farm.

A seasonal town road, called East Road or Elm Lake Road, runs through the property to a state parking area at the northern boundary, where the Siamese Ponds Wilderness begins. Visitors may drive over the town road without paying a fee, but the going can be rough. This road and the others are closed during the winter and the spring mud season. From the parking area, hikers can enter the wilderness by an unmarked trail that leads to the Kunjamuk River, Rock Pond, Long Pond, and other destinations.

The numerous woods roads crisscrossing the Speculator Tree Farm, including those branching off East Road, cannot be used for driving, hiking, or mountain biking without a permit. The conditions of these roads vary, but most can be driven by ordinary cars. All-terrain vehicles and motorcycles are not allowed. Logging trucks also use these roads, so drive carefully.

There are no marked trails or road signs on the tree farm, but purchasers of a daily permit receive a leaflet with a map that shows the property's roads, streams, ponds, and major peaks. Possible destinations shown on the map include Elm Lake, Pine Lakes, the Kunjamuk River and several streams. Kunjamuk Cave, thought to be an old mine, also is on the property.

Daily, three-day, and annual permits for the Speculator Tree Farm can be purchased directly from the tree farm headquarters or from several sporting goods stores in the region.

Directions: Turn east at the intersection of NY 30 and NY 8 in the village of Speculator. This is known as East Road or Elm Lake Road. The tree farm is reached in less than 2 miles. The tree farm's headquarters is on Old Route 30 in Speculator.
Activities: Hiking, canoeing, hunting, fishing, cross-country skiing.
Facilities: Woods roads.
Dates: Year-round, but roads are not plowed in winter.

Fees: There is a charge for using the land.

Closest town: The village of Speculator is just east of the tree farm.

For more information: International Paper, PO Box 174, Speculator, NY 12164. Phone (518) 548-7931.

Kunjamuk River

[Fig. 30] The Kunjamuk originates at South Pond in the trailless interior of the Siamese Ponds Wilderness. The river starts off heading northwest, but after bumping into Humphrey Mountain, it turns southwest to flow through the Speculator Tree Farm owned by International Paper Company. The Kunjamuk joins the main branch of the Sacandaga River at Kunjamuk Bay a few miles outside of the village of Speculator.

Most of the Kunjamuk can be canoed, but paddlers may encounter many beaver dams and obstacles above Elm Lake. Paddling up the Kunjamuk from its mouth is fairly easy, as the river rises only 3 feet in the 3 miles to the lake. Canoeists can enter the river from Kunjamuk Bay on the Sacandaga River. Park at a dirt lot on the east side of NY 30 about 2 miles south of the junction of NY 8 and NY 30 in Speculator. For a longer paddle, put in at a parking area on the east side of NY 30 where the road crosses the Sacandaga in Speculator. From there, it's a 1.6-mile paddle to Kunjamuk Bay.

Canoeists with two cars can put in the river or Elm Lake from the Speculator Tree Farm, but this requires a permit from International Paper Company (*see* page 207). For a longer trip, drive through the tree farm to a state parking area and canoe down Cisco Creek a short ways to the pool above a fish barrier dam on the Kunjamuk. If the water is high enough, the river can be canoed below the dam to its mouth, but be prepared to carry around obstacles. No permit is required if the trip starts on state land.

Brook trout (*Salvelinus fontinalis*) live in the river above the dam. Baitfish are not allowed in this stretch of the river. Largemouth and smallmouth bass, northern pike, chain pickerel, and various panfish can be found below the dam. Ice fishing is permitted.

Blue Mountain Wild Forest

The flat-topped summit of Blue Mountain dominates the landscape of the rugged terrain located north of NY 28/30 between the hamlets of Blue Mountain Lake and Indian Lake. This summit is by far the most popular attraction in the region, but there are others: Tirrell Pond, with its sandy beach; Rock Lake, reachable by an easy hike; and the scenic Rock River.

The Blue Mountain Wild Forest encompasses 37,800 acres broken into two discrete parcels. The southern section, bordering NY 28/30, has more trails and sees more use. The northern section's main draw is Tirrell Pond, where there are two lean-tos. The

Northville-Lake Placid Trail passes by Tirrell Pond on its way from Lake Durant to Long Lake, a 14.8-mile route that cuts through both sections of the wild forest.

Most peaks in the region are made of granitic or syenitic gneiss, a relatively durable metamorphic rock born from igneous rock. Marble and other softer rocks, metamorphosed from sedimentary rock, can be found in the Rock River and Cedar River valleys.

Those driving on NY 28/30 between Indian Lake and Blue Mountain Lake may notice a small sign just east of Blue Mountain Lake that marks the divide between the watersheds of the Hudson and Saint Lawrence rivers. The divide is a barely perceptible rise in glacial drift.

For more information: State Department of Environmental Conservation, 701 S. Main Street, Northville, NY 12134. Phone (518) 863-4545.

COMMON WOOD
SORREL
(Oxalis montana)

BLUE MOUNTAIN

[Fig. 30(2)] Blue Mountain, a mass of granitic gneiss, rises nearly 2,000 feet above Blue Mountain Lake. The trail up the mountain, though challenging, is one of the most popular hikes in the Adirondacks. In one year recently, more than 11,000 people climbed to the summit for the gorgeous views from the fire tower.

The hike begins just up the road from the Adirondack Museum (*see* page 13), which helps account for the trail's popularity. A leaflet available at the trailhead points out what to look for at 14 interpretive stops along the way.

At the outset, the trail passes through a hardwood forest, but red spruce (*Picea rubens*) and balsam fir (*Abies balsamea*) appear with greater frequency as elevation increases. American mountain ash (*Sorbus americana*) also crops up near the summit. Common wood sorrel (*Oxalis montana*) often adorns the trailside. Other wildflowers include bunchberry (*Cornus canadensis*), Canada mayflower (*Maianthemum canadense*), and clintonia (*Clintonia borealis*).

The trail can be rocky and muddy. Planks cross the wettest sections. As the way steepens, hikers find themselves traversing bare slabs of bedrock, which can be slippery if wet. Approaching the summit, the trail levels off as it winds through a fragrant balsam wood.

On summer weekends, a volunteer steward may be at the summit to answer questions. If a steward is on duty, the observation deck of the fire tower will be open. Otherwise, hikers will have to be content with enjoying the views from the tower stairs. The magnificent panorama includes the High Peaks to the northeast and the Fulton Chain of Lakes to the southwest, beyond beautiful Blue Mountain Lake.

Verplanck Colvin, the famed Adirondack surveyor, placed a benchmark on the summit in the late 1800s. The bronze disk is located about 10 steps north of the tower.

Directions: From the junction of NY 30 and NY 28 in Blue Mountain Lake, drive north 1.6 miles on NY 30 to the parking lot on the right.

Trail: 2 miles to summit.

Elevation: 2,209 feet to 3,759 feet.

Degree of difficulty: Moderate to difficult.

Surface and blaze: Natural forest floor, bedrock. Red blazes.

TIRRELL POND

[Fig. 30(1)] This scenic 146-acre pond located just east of Blue Mountain has a large sandy beach on the northern shore and lean-tos on the northern and southern shores. There also are primitive campsites. Brook trout (*Salvelinus fontinalis*) can be caught. The pond is a popular destination. Float planes occasionally land on the water. Tirrell Pond can be reached from the south by the Northville-Lake Placid Trail or from the west along a separate trail. If taking the latter route, turn right upon reaching the Northville-Lake Placid Trail shortly before the pond.

Directions: For the southern trailhead, from the junction of NY 30 and NY 28 in Blue Mountain Lake, drive 2.7 miles east on NY 30/NY 28 to a parking area on the left for the Northville-Lake Placid Trail. For the western trailhead, from the Blue Mountain junction, drive 1.6 miles north on NY 30 to a parking area on the right. The Tirrell Pond Trail begins on the left.

Trail: From the south, 3.5 miles to southern lean-to, 4.6 miles to beach and nothern lean-to. From the west, 3.6 miles to beach and northern lean-to.

Elevation: 1,800 feet at southern trailhead, 2,209 feet at western trailhead, 1,918 feet at pond.

Degree of difficulty: Moderate.

Surface and blaze: Natural forest floor. Blue blazes from south. Red blazes from west.

ROCK LAKE

[Fig. 30(3)] This 235-acre lake surrounded by Forest Preserve can be reached by an easy hike from the highway. The trail leads to a primitive campsite on the shore, a good swimming spot. Blue Mountain, with its distinctive flat top, can be seen across the water. There are several other campsites located around the lake.

Anglers fish for smallmouth bass (*Micropterus dolomieui*) and tiger muskies (*Esox masquinongy*). The muskies, migrating from Lake Durant, are best caught in winter.

The trail passes through stands of pine and balsam fir before crossing Johnny Mack Brook on a wooden bridge. Just before the bridge, the trail merges with a snowmobile trail and bears right. A short distance past the bridge, the marked foot trail veers left, away from the snowmobile route. It soon reaches an unmarked path that leads to the shore. The trail to Rock Lake is suitable for mountain bikes.

Directions: From the junction of NY 30 and NY 28 in Blue Mountain Lake, drive east 7.1 miles on NY 30/NY 28 to the parking lot on the left. From the junction of NY 30 and NY 28 in Indian Lake, drive west about 6.3 miles on NY 30/NY 28 to the trailhead.

Trail: About 0.8 mile to the lakeshore.

Degree of difficulty: Easy.

Surface and blaze: Natural forest floor. Red blazes.

CEDAR RIVER

[Fig. 30] The Cedar River flows out of Cedar Lakes in the West Canada Wilderness and reaches the Hudson River after about 37 miles. Near the village of Indian Lake, there is a pretty swimming hole on the river featuring a small beach and clear water. Camping is not allowed. Canoeists can put in here and explore the still water that stretches for about a mile downriver. The state stocks the Cedar with brown trout (*Salmo trutta*).

Directions: From the junction of NY 30 and NY 28 in Indian Lake, drive 0.3 mile west on NY 30/NY 28 to Pelon Road; turn right and then bear left onto Benson Road at the fork after 0.2 mile; go another 1.1 miles to the river.

Activities: Swimming, canoeing, fishing, picnicking.

Facilities: None.

Fees: None.

Closest town: Indian Lake.

For more information: State Department of Environmental Conservation, 701 S. Main Street, Northville, NY 12134. Phone (518) 863-4545.

Goodnow Mountain

[Fig. 31] Goodnow Mountain's fire tower offers a stupendous view of the High Peaks. The New York State College of Environmental Science and Forestry, which maintains the trail, has published a brochure that explains what to look for at stops along the way. There are benches on the trail for the weary. Both the tower and the ranger's cabin at the summit are in excellent shape. In short, this is one of the best hikes in the Adirondacks.

Directions: From the Adirondack Visitor Center in Newcomb, drive about 1.5 miles west on NY 28N to a parking area on the left.

Trail: 1.9 miles to summit.

Elevation: 1,650 feet to 2,690 feet.

Degree of difficulty: Moderate.

Surface and blaze: Natural forest floor. Red blazes.

Vanderwhacker Mountain Wild Forest

The Vanderwhacker Mountain summit offers a superb view of the High Peaks.

RICH LAKE

HARRIS LAKE

BOREAS RIVER

28N

Newcomb

✕ **Goodnow Mountain**

Goodnow Road

HUDSON RIVER

2

2

ZACK POND

28N

CHENEY POND

GOODNOW FLOWAGE

LESTER FLOW

Vanderwhacker ✕**Mountain**

1

MOOSE POND

HEWITT POND

Moose Pond Club

Alden Lair

BALFOUR LAKE

3

STONY POND

BOREAS RIVER

North Woods Club Road

HUNTLEY POND

HUDSON RIVER

2

LAKE FRANCIS

HUDSON RIVER

LAKE ABANAKEE

Minerva

Olmsteadville Road

1	Hewitt Eddy & Boreas River Trail
2	Irishtown Snowmobile Trail
3	Blue Ledge Trail

N

28N

Vanderwhacker Mountain Wild Forest

[Fig. 31] This wild forest's attractions include Vanderwhacker Mountain, an isolated summit with a superb view of the High Peaks, and the Boreas River, a scenic river stocked with brown trout (*Salmo trutta*). Several ponds can be reached by fairly easy hikes. The peaks are considerably shorter than the High Peaks located just to the north. The state highway NY 28N cuts through the heart of the wild forest, facilitating access.

STONY POND

[Fig. 31] Three trails lead to this large pond surrounded by wooded hills. A lean-to on the western shore looks across the water to Green Mountain. The flat rocks on the shore are ideal for basking in the sun after a swim. Stony and four other ponds along the trails are stocked with brook trout (*Salvelinus fontinalis*).

The shortest and easiest route to Stony begins on NY 28N. The trail follows an old woods road that can be muddy in places. At one point, it skirts an old beaver dam. If the trail is flooded here, as can happen in wet weather, hikers may want to tiptoe across the top of the dam.

Those with two cars can return by way of Sherman Pond to the southern trailhead near Irishtown. The return entails a descent of 900 feet from Stony Pond, so expect some climbing if you reverse the direction of this end-to-end trip. The 5.9-mile journey from NY 28N to the Irishtown trailhead can be traveled by advanced mountain bikers able to handle roots and rocks. Intermediate mountain bikers should turn back at Stony Pond. In winter, these two trails are used by snowmobilers.

The third route to Stony Pond begins on Hewitt Lake Club Road. It passes Hewitt Pond, Barnes Pond, and a 0.2-mile spur trail that leads to Center Pond. Since all three ponds are stocked with trout, this route may appeal to fishermen. Beware, however, that the trail is overgrown in places and sometimes hard to follow.

Directions: For the NY 28N trailhead, from the junction of Olmstedville Road and NY 28N north of Olmstedville, drive 6.7 miles north on NY 28N to the trailhead on the right. For the Hewitt Lake Club Road trailhead, continue 2.9 miles north on NY 28N; turn right onto Hewitt Lake Club Road and go 0.6 mile to the trailhead on the right. For the Irishtown trailhead, from the Olmstedville traffic light, drive north 0.3 mile toward Minerva; turn right onto County 24 and go 1.8 miles to Irishtown, where there is a baseball field; turn left onto County 37 and go 0.4 mile to Brannon Road, just past Minerva Stream; turn right and go 0.4 to the trailhead.

Trail: The Stony Pond lean-to is 2.0 miles from NY 28N, 3.9 miles from the Irishtown trailhead, and 4.0 miles from Hewitt Lake Club Road.

Elevation: About 2,015 feet at NY 28N, 1,180 feet at Irishtown, 1,680 feet at Hewitt Lake Club Road, and 2,078 feet at Stony Pond.

Degree of difficulty: Easy to moderate, depending on route.

Surface and blaze: Old road, natural forest floor. Red blazes.

BOREAS RIVER

[Fig. 31] The Boreas River—named after the Greek god of the north wind—originates in the High Peaks and flows about 20 miles to the Hudson River. Roads cross the river in three places, affording easy access for anglers, canoeists, and hikers. There also is a marked trail that follows the river.

Alec Proskine cautions in *Adirondack Canoe Waters: South and West Flow* that the Boreas should be run only by experts, usually in a closed boat. The river has numerous rapids reaching Class IV – V intensity. In one 2.2-mile stretch, Proskine notes, the Boreas drops 254 feet, "making it the steepest canoeable river in the Adirondacks for this distance." Flat-water canoeists, however, can paddle to a stillwater section known as the Lester Flow from Cheney Pond (*see* page 215).

The state stocks the Boreas with brown trout (*Salmo trutta*). Brook trout (*Salvelinus fontinalis*) and rainbow trout (*Oncorhynchus mykiss*) also can be caught. Anglers can get to the river from bridges at NY 28N or North Woods Club Road (*see* page 82).

Hikers can experience the Boreas in all its moods by walking the short hike below.

HEWITT EDDY/BOREAS RIVER TRAIL

[Fig. 31(1)] At Hewitt Eddy, the Boreas River relaxes after a headlong rush over boulders and widens to form a big bend. Ferns and field flowers, such as orange hawkeye (*Hieracium aurantiacum*) and tall meadow rue (*Thalictrum polygamum*), flourish along this peaceful stretch of river.

Hewitt Eddy can be reached by a short walk from NY 28N through a forest dominated by conifers, including a giant white pine (*Strobus pinus*) near the start. The trail parallels Stony Pond Brook for a while before reaching the Boreas.

From Hewitt Eddy, hikers can either turn back or walk north along the river to another trailhead on NY 28N. Since the trailheads are just 0.8 mile apart, hikers can walk along the road to return to their car. Another option is to leave a bike at the second trailhead and pedal back to the car.

Directions: From the junction of Olmstedville Road and NY 28N north of Olmstedville, drive 10.7 miles north on NY 28N to the Hewitt Eddy trailhead on the left. Continue another 0.8 mile to reach the second trailhead just before the Boreas River bridge. There is a pull-off on the right side of the road.

Trail: 0.8 mile to Hewitt Eddy, 2 miles to Boreas River bridge.

Degree of difficulty: Easy.

Surface and blaze: Natural forest floor. Blue blazes.

VANDERWHACKER MOUNTAIN

[Fig. 31] The isolated Vanderwhacker Mountain offers one of the best views of the High Peaks from the south. The course of the Hudson River to the west also can be discerned.

Soon after the start, the trail to the summit passes a marsh and skirts a beaver pond with many gnawed logs and stumps on the shore. After passing another wetland, the trail climbs more steeply to an abandoned ranger's cabin. Up to this point, hardwoods dominate the forest, but as elevation increases, they will yield to red spruce (*Picea rubens*) and balsam fir (*Abies balsamea*). Trout lily (*Erythronium americanum*) and yellow violets bloom on the trail in early spring.

On the summit, a ledge looks north toward the High Peaks. Although trees enclose the rest of the summit, hikers can get a panoramic view by climbing the steps of the fire tower. Mount Marcy, Algonquin Peak, Gothics, and numerous other peaks can be observed.

Vanderwhacker consists of granitic gneiss, but a large boulder of anorthosite has been found about 300 feet east of the summit, proving that a glacier once rode over the mountain. Presumably, the glacier plucked the boulder from the High Peaks.

There are several primitive campsites along the dirt road that leads to the trailhead. The road passes through thick woods and crosses Vanderwhacker Brook. It makes a good mountain bike route. Experienced bikers may be able to ride the hiking trail as far as the ranger's cabin. In winter, the road can be skied, since it is unplowed.

Directions: From the junction of NY 28N and Olmstedville Road, north of Olmstedville, drive 11.7 miles north on NY 28N to Moose Pond Road, a dirt road just past the Boreas River; turn left and go 2.6 miles to the trailhead on the right. The dirt road can be rough. It is not plowed in winter.

Trail: 2.5 miles to summit.

Elevation: 1,735 feet to 3,385 feet.

Degree of difficulty: Moderate to difficult.

Surface and blaze: Natural forest floor. Red blazes.

CHENEY POND AND LESTER FLOW

[Fig. 31] Named for John Cheney, a nineteenth-century Adirondack guide, this good-size pond can be reached by a short walk from Blue Ridge Road. It is possible to drive to the shore down a rutty, rocky access road. It's rough going in an ordinary car, but those with a canoe may want to give it a try.

The access road ends on the western shore, where there is a canoe launch, primitive campsite, and privy. Canoeists may be able to paddle across the pond to Lester Flow on the Boreas River if the water is high enough. There is a sandy beach on the eastern shore of Cheney. The state stocks the pond with brown trout (*Salmo trutta*) and brook trout (*Salvelinus fontinalis*). A fishermen's path from the canoe launch follows the southern shore.

It's also possible to hike or bike to Lester Flow. The 2.6-mile trail follows an old woods road that has evolved into a grassy corridor decorated with meadow flowers such as yarrow (*Achillea millefolium*), daisies (*Chrysanthemum leucanthemum*), bluets (*Houstonia caerulea*), yellow goatsbeard (*Tragopogon pratensis*), and orange hawkeye (*Hieracium aurantiacum*).

Hoffman Notch Wilderness

Although the Hoffman Notch Wilderness is not large, it contains some of the most rugged trailless terrain in the Adirondacks. The region's highest peak, Hoffman Mountain, has no official trail that leads to its summit.

Ref: DeLorme New York State Atlas & Gazetteer

N

Elk Lake Road

Boreas Road

North Hudson

2

2

87

9

1 Hoffman Notch Trail

2 Mt. Severance

Trail

HOFFMAN NOTCH WILDERNESS

× **Hoffman Mountain**

1

BAILEY POND

74

2

Loch Muller

NORTH POND

BIG POND

Lester Flow offers nice views of the High Peaks to the north. It's also a good place to watch waterfowl. The remains of a wooden dam can be seen at the south end of the flow, where the Boreas River resumes its course.

Directions: From Northway Exit 29 in North Hudson, drive 14.1 miles west on Blue Ridge Road to the trailhead on the left. An access road leads 0.3 mile to the Lester Flow trailhead on the right and ends at the shore after 0.6 mile.

Activities: Fishing, canoeing, swimming, camping, hiking.

Facilities: Canoe launch, primitive campsite, picnic table, privy.

Dates: Accessible year-round.

Fees: None.

Closest town: North Hudson is 14.6 miles east.

For more information: State Department of Environmental Conservation, PO Box 296, Route 86, Ray Brook, NY 12977. Phone (518) 897-1200.

IRISHTOWN SNOWMOBILE TRAIL

[Fig. 31(2)] Advanced mountain bikers who don't mind fording streams and riding over rocks and roots can make an 11.5-mile trek along snowmobile trails, starting at Blue Ridge Road and ending north of Olmstedville. Bikers will want to travel from north to south to take advantage of the 600-foot drop in elevation.

Take the trail to Lester Flow (*see* page 215). Cross the Boreas River, if the water is low enough, and pick up the trail again about 150 feet into the woods. The trail goes northeast and then turns southeast, crossing a tributary of Minerva Stream. For the last 5.5 miles or so, the trail parallels Minerva Stream, crossing it three times. Since the trail is remote and receives little maintainence, the journey should be undertaken only by experienced riders.

Directions: Same as Lester Flow for northern trailhead. For southern trailhead, from the village of Schroon Lake drive west on Hoffman Road (County 24) to Byrnes Road; turn right and go 0.6 mile to the parking area.

Trail: 11.5 miles from Blue Ridge Road to southern trailhead.

Elevation: 1,871 feet at Blue Ridge Road to 1,274 feet at southern trailhead.

Degree of difficulty: Strenuous mountain bike ride.

Surface and blaze: Old road, natural forest floor. Orange snowmobile blazes.

Hoffman Notch Wilderness

[Fig. 32] Although the Hoffman Notch Wilderness is not large, it contains some of the most rugged trailless terrain in the Adirondacks, with many large specimens of northern hardwoods and red spruce. Three mountain ridges run north to south through the region: the Washburn Ridge, Texas Ridge, and Blue Ridge Range. The wilderness encompasses about 36,230 acres.

Hoffman Mountain, at 3,693 feet, is the region's highest peak. No official trail leads to the summit—or to any summit in the Hoffman Notch Wilderness. The sole trail that enters deep into the interior passes between mountains. The only two other marked trails lead to a lookout on the eastern flank of Mount Severance and to a trout pond.

Most of the Hoffman Notch Wilderness lies in the towns of North Hudson and Schroon. Roughly, the wilderness encompasses the state lands south of Blue Ridge Road in North Hudson, north of Hoffman Road in Schroon, east of Minerva Stream, and west of the Northway. There is a good view of the region's northern mountains from a buffalo farm on Blue Ridge Road, about 4 miles west of the Northway.

HOFFMAN NOTCH TRAIL

[Fig. 32(1)] Those who make the end-to-end trek on this 7.4-mile trail through a remote mountain pass—the only lengthy trail in the Hoffman Notch Wilderness—will be treated to a variety of scenery: 200-foot cliffs, gigantic glacial erratics, a large marsh pond, clear alpine streams, lush fern meadows, and dark woods. If an end-to-end journey is impossible, a good turnaround destination is Big Marsh, located about halfway between the northern and southern trailheads.

The trail follows an old wagon route between the Washburn Ridge to the west and the Texas Ridge, Blue Ridge Range, and Hornet Cobbles to the east. Hoffman Mountain and several other peaks to the east can be seen at Big Marsh. The notch—the highest point on the trail, at nearly 1,800 feet—is just north of Big Marsh.

If going end to end, hikers may want to walk south to north to take advantage of the grade. The southern trailhead is almost 500 feet higher in elevation than the northern. At the northern end, the trail passes through private land where camping, hunting, and fishing are prohibited.

The route can be skied in winter, but skiers should be strong and experienced, since they may have to break trail. Another trail that starts at the southern trailhead leads 1 mile to Bailey Pond, which is stocked with brook trout (*Salvelinus fontinalis*).

Directions: To southern trailhead: From US 9 in Schroon Lake village, drive east 6.7 miles on Hoffman Road (County 24) to Loch Muller Road; turn right and go 2.7 miles to the parking area. The last 0.4 mile is dirt. The road bears right just before the trailhead to avoid private land. To northern trailhead: From Northway Exit 29 in North Hudson, drive about 5.8 miles east on Blue Ridge Road to the trailhead on the left, immediately past the Branch River.

Trail: 7.4 miles.

Elevation: 1,720 feet at southern trailhead, 1,780 feet at notch, 1,244 feet at northern trailhead.

Degree of difficulty: Moderate.

Surface and blaze: Natural forest floor. Yellow blazes.

White Birch

The cream-colored bark of the white birch (*Betula papyrifela*) makes it not only one of the most beautiful hardwood trees in the Adirondacks, but also the easiest for an amateur naturalist to identify. Unlike yellow birch, this birch craves sunlight, and so it rushes in where fire, logging, or blowdown has opened up the forest canopy. As the white birch matures, it creates a canopy that shades out its own seedlings, and so over time, the birch surrenders its territory to more shade-tolerant species and moves on to the next clearing in the forest. Its abundance in the High Peaks—the species can be found right up to the timberline—is attributable in part to severe forest fires in the early 1900s, but wherever it appears, it is a sign of a disturbance in the not-too-distant past. Also known as paper birch or canoe birch, the white birch lives for up to 80 years and grows up to 70 feet. Native Americans made lightweight canoes by stretching its bark over cedar frames, sewing the pieces together with stringy tamarack roots, and caulking the seams with resin from pine or balsam fir. The thin bark peels off in long, curly strips, revealing an orangish underside. Hikers should avoid the temptation to pull off the strips of a live tree for a souvenir: It leaves a black scar.

MOUNT SEVERANCE

[Fig. 32(2)] This small mountain is popular among families vacationing in the Schroon Lake area. The trail begins just north of the village, passing through tunnels under the Northway to reach the eastern margin of the Hoffman Notch Wilderness.

The official trail does not reach the summit but ends at two rocky lookouts. The first view takes in Schroon Lake to the east and the Pharaoh Mountain Wilderness beyond. The second, about 75 yards up the trail, takes in Paradox Lake and the mountains north of NY 74.

Hikers pass several large specimens of hemlock (*Tsuga canadensis*) and white pine (*Pinus strobus*) on the trail. Northern white cedar (*Thuja occidentalis*) and northern red oak (*Quercus rubra borealis*) also grow on Mount Severance.

No bicycles are allowed on the mountain.

Directions: From Northway Exit 28, drive east about 0.1 mile to US 9; turn right and go south about 0.6 mile to the trailhead on the right. From the village of Schroon Lake, drive north about 1.9 miles to the trailhead on the left.

Trail: 1.2 miles to lookout.

Elevation: 925 feet to 1,638 feet.

Degree of difficulty: Moderate.

Surface and blaze: Natural forest floor. Yellow blazes.

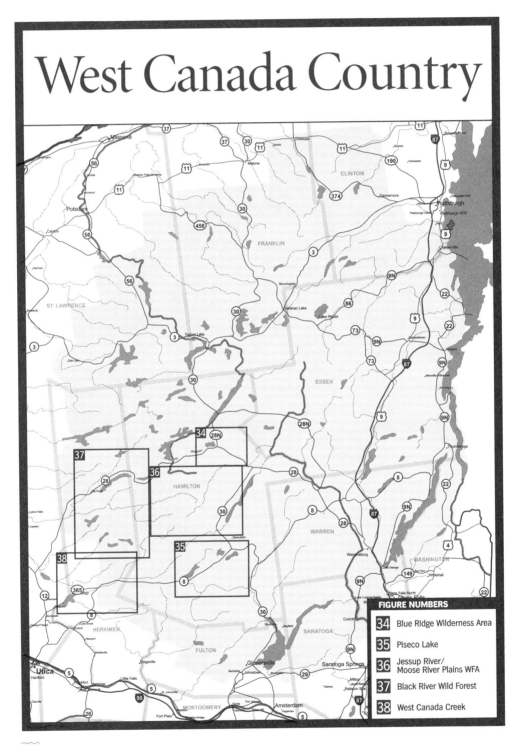

West Canada Country

FIGURE NUMBERS

34 Blue Ridge Wilderness Area

35 Piseco Lake

36 Jessup River/
Moose River Plains WFA

37 Black River Wild Forest

38 West Canada Creek

West Canada Country

Wcst Canada Country contains some of the Adirondack Park's most remote wilderness—once the haunt of French Louie, a legendary hermit—as well as some of its most accessible wild forest.

As defined here, West Canada Country encompasses the region bounded by NY 8 and NY 365 to the south; NY 30 to the east; NY 28 and the Fulton Chain of Lakes to the north; and the Adirondack Park line to the west. It thus includes the West Canada Lakes Wilderness, the Moose River Recreation Area, the Black River Wild Forest, and most of the Jessup River Wild Forest—all told, more than 400,000 acres of state land.

The region has several high mountains in the east. Snowy Mountain, the highest at 3,899 feet, is made of anorthosite, the same durable rock found in the High Peaks. Excellent views can be had from Snowy, Wakely Mountain, and Pillsbury Mountain. As one moves west toward the park boundary, the terrain becomes more gentle. Not

[*Above:* A conifer forest in West Canada Country]

Blue Ridge Wilderness Area

Striking vistas of the Blue Ridge Wilderness may be seen when driving between the hamlets of Indian Lake and Blue Mountain Lake past Lake Durant. There is also a roadside picnic area there.

Ref: DeLorme New York State Atlas & Gazetteer

N

1   Lake Durant Public Campground

     Trail

UPPER POND

BLUE MOUNTAIN LAKE

Blue Mountain Lake

UTOWANA LAKE

30

28N

28

TIRRELL POND

LAKE DURANT

CASCADE POND

STEPHENS POND

BLUE RIDGE WILDERNESS

To Wakely Mountain

28

30

ROCK POND

SPRAGUE POND

Cedar River Road

× Sawyer Mountain

28

To Indian Lake

surprisingly, few trails in the west lead to summits.

Nine rivers designated as wild, scenic, or recreational flow through West Canada Country. Several large lakes and reservoirs can be found in the region. Two large lakes, Piseco and Sacandaga, lie in the southeastern corner of the region. Both are well developed, but the public has access to both at state campgrounds. Three large reservoirs in the Black River Wild Forest—Woodhull, North, and South lakes—offer water-based recreation in a somewhat wilder setting.

Many smaller lakes and ponds surrounded by unbroken forest are sprinkled throughout the region, including the remote and lovely West Canada Lakes and Cedar Lakes. The three West Canada Lakes are the source of West Canada Creek, one of the finest trout streams in the Adirondacks. French Louie—born Louis Seymour—hunted and trapped in the West Lakes region in the late 1800s and early 1900s. He also worked as a lumberjack around Lewey Lake, which is named for him.

West Canada Country had been lumbered heavily in the past. In fact, International Paper Company continues to log a large tract north of Speculator. Nonetheless, old-growth stands survive. In the Moose River Plains, a scrub forest of small trees, shrubs, and grasses replaces the more typical Adirondack woods found elsewhere in the region.

The returning moose (*Alces alces*), once extirpated from the Adirondacks, seems to be drawn to these parts. They have been spotted in the West Canada Lakes Wilderness, Jessup River Wild Forest, and, of course, the Moose River Plains. In the 1990s, the state put up its first moose-crossing signs on NY 30 north of Speculator.

The state operates eight conventional campgrounds in West Canada Country, all easily accessible from major highways. In addition, there are 140 drive-up campsites in the Moose River Recreation Area, available for free on a first-come basis.

For more information: The state Department of Environmental Conservation keeps offices in Northville and Herkimer. The Northville office's address is 701 S. Main Street, Northville, NY 12134. Phone (518) 863-4545. The Herkimer office's address is 225 N. Main Street, Herkimer, NY 13350. Phone (315) 866-6330. Information about the region can be found in the leaflets *Moose River Recreation Area*, *Trails in the Blue Mountain Lake Region*, *The Northville-Lake Placid Trail*, and *Trails in the Old Forge-Brantingham Lake Region*.

Blue Ridge Wilderness

[Fig. 34] People driving between the hamlets of Indian Lake and Blue Mountain Lake enjoy a striking vista of the Blue Ridge Wilderness as they pass Lake Durant: rugged hills rising up behind the marshy waters. There is a roadside picnic area at the spot.

The wilderness takes its name from the 6-mile Blue Ridge. No trails lead to the 3,500-foot ridge, but hikers can reach two other summits without having to bushwhack. Sawyer Mountain is an easy climb ideal for young children. Hikers seeking a

Great Camps

From 1870 to 1930, some of America's richest families—the Vanderbilts, the Whitneys, and the Carnegies, among others—built or purchased the enormous lodges in the Adirondacks that came to be known as the Great Camps. The architects designed the camps to blend in with the woods, using native stone and timber, but no amount of rusticity can disguise the opulence in a lodge that has, say, 40 bedrooms and 20 bathrooms. Today, the public can tour two of the Great Camps for a Fees: Camp Sagamore, once owned by the Vanderbilts, and White Pine Camp, which served as President Coolidge's vacation home in 1926. Or you can visit Camp Santanoni for free. This camp, now owned by the state, can be reached by a 4.5-mile hike or bike ride into the forest north of Newcomb (*see* page 47). Although rundown, Santanoni remains a fine example of Great Camp architecture.

For more information: Great Camp Sagamore, Sagamore Road, Raquette Lake, NY 13436. Phone (315) 354-5311. White Pine Camp, White Pine Road, Paul Smiths, NY 12970. Phone (518) 327-3030.

greater challenge can try Wakely Mountain on the southern edge of the wilderness. Wakely's fire tower offers a superb panorama.

A 6-mile stretch of the Northville-Lake Placid Trail cuts through the Blue Ridge Wilderness as it heads north from Cedar River Road to the Lake Durant Public Campground, passing Stephens Pond along the way. The other marked trails in this wilderness also lead to ponds.

The 45,951-acre Blue Ridge Wilderness is bounded roughly by NY 28 or NY 28/30 to the north and east, Cedar River Road to the south, and Sagamore Road to the west.

For more information: State Department of Environmental Conservation, 701 S. Main Street, Northville, NY 12134. Phone (518) 863-4545.

LAKE DURANT PUBLIC CAMPGROUND

[Fig. 34(1)] Lumbermen created this weedy, shallow lake on the northern edge of the Blue Ridge Wilderness to impound logs that were later floated down the Rock River. Today, the lake can be fished for largemouth bass (*Micropterus salmoides*), northern pike (*Esox lucius*), and tiger muskellunge (*Esox masquinongy*). The muskies are stocked by the state.

The campground lies along the southeastern shore. The Northville-Lake Placid Trail passes through the campground on its way from Cedar River Road to NY 28/30. Hikers can use the trail to reach Stephens Pond and Cascade Pond in the Blue Ridge Wilderness (*see* page 225).

Canoeists also can put in on the western end of the lake at the trailhead for Cascade Pond. From there, it's a short paddle through the channel to Rock Pond, a feeding ground for heron, duck, and kingfishers. Motorboats are not allowed in Rock Pond.

Directions: From the junction of NY 28 and NY 30 in Indian Lake, drive west about 10.3 miles on NY 28/30 to the campground entrance on the left. From the junction of NY 28 and NY 30 in Blue Mountain Lake, drive east about 3.1 miles on NY 28/30. The entrance will be on the right.

Activities: Camping, swimming, hiking, fishing, boating, canoeing.

Facilities: 60 tent and trailer sites, picnic area, sand beach, bathhouse, toilets, showers, trailer dumping station. A fishing pier is accessible to the handicapped.

Dates: Open mid-May through Columbus Day weekend.

Fees: There is a charge for camping or day use.

Closest town: Blue Mountain Lake is 3.1 miles west.

For more information: Campground office, phone (518) 352-7797. For reservations, phone (800) 456-2267.

CASCADE AND STEPHENS PONDS

[Fig. 34] Hikers can visit these trout ponds as part of a loop, end-to-end trip, or round trip. Each pond has a lean-to. The trails to the ponds are used by Nordic skiers in winter.

Stephens Pond lies on the Northville-Lake Placid Trail about 3.3 miles south of Lake Durant Public Campground. Cascade Pond lies along a trail that starts at the opposite end of Lake Durant and meets the Northville-Lake Placid Trail about 2.6 miles south of the campground.

At the outset, the red-blazed trail to Cascade Pond crosses on a long boardwalk the channel connecting Lake Durant with Rock Pond, where hikers may see heron and ducks, and then climbs through a mixed wood to the lean-to, gaining 370 feet in elevation. The lean-to is 2.7 miles from the trailhead.

The Northville-Lake Placid Trail is reached 0.8 mile past the lean-to. Turn right, now following blue blazes, to go to the Stephens Pond lean-to, about 0.6 mile from the junction. If doing an end-to-end trip or loop trip, return on the Northville-Lake Placid Trail all the way to the campground. If you left a second car or bicycle at the campground, drive or pedal west along NY 28/30 to return to the starting point. Otherwise, be prepared to walk 2.6 miles along the highway.

The state includes the trails to Cascade and Stephens ponds in its brochure *Nordic Skiing Trails in New York State*. Skiers can park in the campground. Novices with some experience can try skiing from the campground to Stephens Pond, but the Cascade Pond Trail's steeper grade demands intermediate-level skills. Those making a loop can ski across the frozen lake to return to the campground.

Directions: For the Cascade Pond Trail, from the junction of NY 28 and NY 30 in Blue Mountain Lake, drive east on NY 28/30 about 0.5 mile to Durant Road; turn right and go 0.2 mile to a dirt road on the left. The trail begins at the end of this short road. For the Northville-Lake Placid Trail, follow directions to the Lake Durant Public Campground (*see* page 224).

Trail: 2.7 miles to Cascade Pond Trail lean-to; 4.1 miles to Stephens Pond lean-to; 7.4 miles to visit both lean-tos and campground; 10.3 miles if hiking full loop. From the campground to Stephens Pond lean-to, it's 3.3 miles.

Elevation: 1,769 feet at Lake Durant, 2,139 feet at Cascade Pond, 1,952 feet at Stephens Pond.

Degree of difficulty: Easy to moderate, depending on distance.

Surface and blaze: Natural forest floor. Red and blue blazes.

SAWYER MOUNTAIN

[Fig. 34] This is a good hike for families with young children or anyone who wants an easy mountain to climb. Just past the summit there is a ledge with a scenic lookout.

The trail ascends gradually through a deciduous forest, reaching sloped bedrock shortly before the summit. The trail jogs right to pass above the rock. Look for an opening in the trees at the other end of the exposed rock: There is a lookout to the northeast.

The summit is wooded but rather airy. On a summer day, white admiral butterflies (*Limenitis arthemis*) dance in the sunlight. Continue another 250 feet or so to a rocky ledge, from where Snowy Mountain, Panther Mountain, Blue Mountain, the Blue Ridge, and other peaks can be observed. Garter snakes sometimes hang out about the ledge.

Children may enjoy looking for American toads on the trail. They are numerous in early summer.

Directions: From the junction of NY 28 and NY 30 in Indian Lake, drive west 6.2 miles on NY 28/30 to the trailhead on the left. From the junction of NY 28 and NY 30 in Blue Mountain Lake, drive east 7.2 miles on NY 28/30 to the trailhead on the right.

Trail: 1.1 miles.

Elevation: 1,530 feet to 2,160 feet.

Degree of difficulty: Easy.

Surface and blaze: Natural forest floor. Yellow blazes.

SPRAGUE POND

[Fig. 34] A brief hike through a mixed wood leads to an unspoiled pond where one can listen to loons (*Gavia immer*), fish for brown trout (*Salmo trutta*), or have a picnic and a swim. Paddlers can carry in a canoe to explore the shores and a small island. The island is big enough to accommodate a tent.

The trail is unmarked except for an occasional paint daub, but it is easy to follow. Soon after the trail begins, a short path leads left to a barrier dam on the outlet stream. The dam prevents nonnative fish from reaching the pond and crowding out the trout. Note that anglers are forbidden to use baitfish in Sprague Pond.

The trail soon reaches a grove of hemlock (*Tsuga canadensis*) on the pond's southern shore. White pine (*Pinus strobus*) and other conifers also can be seen along the pond. Turn left to follow a herd path to a spit of land where flat rocks invite visitors to sunbathe or picnic.

Directions: From the junction of NY 28 and NY 30 in Indian Lake, drive 2.2 miles west to Cedar River Road; turn left and go 4.6 miles to a pull-off beside a metal gate on the right side of the road. There is no sign. The trail begins at the gate.

Trail: 0.4 mile to shore.

Degree of difficulty: Easy.

Surface and blaze: Natural forest floor. Sporadic paint daubs.

WAKELY MOUNTAIN

[Fig. 36] From the Wakely fire tower—the tallest in the Adirondacks—hikers can enjoy a panorama that encompasses the Moose River Recreation Area, Cedar River Flow, Blue Ridge Wilderness, Raquette Lake, Blue Mountain, Snowy Mountain, and some of the High Peaks.

The trail follows an old dirt road, passing raspberry patches, before reaching the register after 1.1 miles. After crossing a brook on a wooden bridge, the trail climbs gently through a forest of mostly hardwoods. At 1.9 miles, a sign indicates that the trail takes a sharp right. Before making the turn, hikers may want to visit the meadow that lies straight ahead and look for the remains of the old beaver dam.

After the turn, the real climbing begins. Eventually, the hardwoods give way to balsam fir (*Abies balsamea*) and red spruce (*Picea rubens*). In one attractive section, bedrock winds through an evergreen forest carpeted with ferns, moss, clintonia, bunchberry, and common wood sorrel, each contributing to the miscellany of verdant hues. The summit is wooded, but the Cedar River Flow can be seen to the southeast. The views from the tower are spectacular. There is a privy, picnic table, and abandoned ranger's cabin near the tower. Just before the summit, a short path leads to a wooden helipad.

The trail is marked by red disks for most of the way, but yellow disks appear here and there.

Directions: From the junction of NY 28 and NY 30 in Indian Lake, drive 2.2 miles west to Cedar River Road; turn left and go 12.3 miles to Wakely Road; turn right and go 0.1 mile to a parking area on the right. Wakely Road is about 0.4 mile before the entrance to the Moose River Recreation Area.

Trail: 3 miles to summit.

Elevation: 2,109 feet to 3,744 feet.

Degree of difficulty: Strenuous.

Surface and blaze: Old road, natural forest floor. Red blazes.

ROUND-LEAF SUNDEW (*Drosera rotundifolia*) Insects attracted to a sweet sticky fluid on the tips of the sundew's hairy leaves become stuck among the hairs that bend like tentacles to smother the victim.

Limekiln Lake Public Campground

[Fig. 37(1)] The 406-acre Limekiln Lake is known for its deep, clear water. The state owns most of the land around the lake, but there are private camps on the northwestern shore. Motorboats and canoes share the water. Canoeists will find a peaceful haven at the marshy inlet in the southeastern corner of the lake.

The state stocks the lake with brown trout (*Salmo trutta*) and splake, a cross between brook trout and lake trout.

A 1.2-mile nature trail that circles a pond begins near Campsite 87. Brochures describing the ferns, flowers, and trees found along the way are available at the trailhead. About 0.6 mile from the start, another trail branches right and goes 5 miles to Third Lake. In winter, these trails are part of a cross-country ski network at the campground.

Directions: From NY 28 east of Inlet, turn south on Limekiln Lake Road and go 1.5 miles to a campground sign; turn left and go 0.5 mile to the entrance.

Activities: Camping, hiking, swimming, fishing, canoeing, boating.

Facilities: 271 tent and trailer sites, picnic area, nature trail, sand beach, bathhouse, small-boat launch, toilets, showers, trailer dumping station.

Dates: Open mid-May through Labor Day.

Fees: There is a charge for camping or day use.

Closest town: Inlet is about 4 miles away.

For more information: Campground, phone (315) 357-4401. Reservations, phone (800) 456-2267.

Moose River Recreation Area

Think of a wilderness with roads. Of course, a true wilderness does not have roads, but for those unable to hike in the wild, a drive through the Moose River Recreation Area can approximate the thrill of leaving civilization behind.

The 15-mph speed limit on the 40 miles of dirt roads guarantees that visitors will have plenty of time to drink in the scenery. Often, the hardwood forest forms a canopy over the road, but there are many views of meadows, plains, and streams with mountains rising in the background. Wildflowers add color to sunny patches along the road. Don't be surprised to see a white-tailed deer bound out of the forest.

The roads cross three scenic rivers: Otter Brook, the Red River and the South Branch of the Moose. Most of the Moose River Plains, a flatland characterized by scrub forest and grasses, lies between the South Branch and Sumner Stream to its north. A smaller plain can be found along the Red River.

Visitors enter the area by one of two gates, one on Cedar River Road west of Indian Lake, the other near the Limekiln Public Campground east of Inlet. The Main Road stretches 23.3 miles between the two gates. Branching off it are the 4.6-mile

Rock Dam Road and the 4-mile Cedar Brook Road. The 6.1-mile Indian Lake Road branches off Cedar Brook Road. All three branch roads dead-end at the boundary to wilderness or private land. Maps are available at the gates.

The state maintains 140 drive-up campsites along the roads, available for free on a first-come basis. The roads are open from Memorial Day to the end of deer season.

The Moose River Recreation Area is much more than a drive-through wilderness. Anglers fish for trout in the ponds and rivers. In fall, hunters come in quest of white-tailed deer and black bear. In winter, snowmobilers make use of the roads and designated trails. The area also is a mountain biker's paradise. Not only are the roads themselves good biking, but so are the many old logging roads, now closed to vehicles, that branch off the roads.

The recreation area has not attracted many hikers, perhaps because of its remoteness from main roads, but it has several worthwhile hikes. Rock Dam, where the Red River and South Moose converge, is especially lovely on a sunny afternoon. Many hikes are short, so it's possible to do more than one in a day. The recreation area also can be the starting point for hikes into the adjacent West Canada Lakes Wilderness. The recreation area accounts for the bulk of the Moose River Plains Wild Forest.

Directions: Eastern entrance: From the junction of NY 28 and NY 30 in Indian Lake, drive 2.2 miles west to Cedar River Road; turn left and go 12.7 miles to the register. Western entrance: From NY 28 about 1 mile east of the hamlet of Inlet, turn south onto Campsite Road and drive 1.8 miles; turn left and go 0.2 mile to the register. For the trails below, directions will be given from both entrances.

Activities: Camping, hiking, hunting, fishing, swimming, canoeing, mountain biking, snowmobiling.

Facilities: 140 primitive campsites, 40 miles of roads, hiking trails.

Dates: Roads are open from Memorial Day to the end of deer season. Trailers and RVs are allowed only from Memorial Day through Labor Day. Bicyclists and hikers may enter at any time. Snowmobilers may use the trails as weather permits.

Fees: None.

Closest town: Indian Lake is about 15 miles east of the Cedar River entrance. Inlet is about 3 miles from the Limekiln Lake entrance.

For more information: State Department of Environmental Conservation, 701 S. Main Street, Northville, NY 12134. Phone (518) 863-4545.

ROCK DAM TRAIL

[Fig. 36(4)] At the confluence of the Red River and the Moose River's south branch, boulders and outcrops of bedrock stretch across the water to form a natural dam—one of the prettiest and most serene settings in the Moose River Plains. The flat rocks in the middle of the rivers are ideal for sunbathing. The sandy-bottomed pools behind the rocks make good swimming holes.

Hikers can get to Rock Dam by an easy walk through a forest of hardwoods and red

Return of the Moose

Alvah Dunning, one of the legendary guides of the nineteenth century, boasted that he shot the last moose (*Alces alces*) in the Adirondacks in 1862. Whether he did or not, the moose disappeared from the region about that time, probably as a result of overhunting. Since about 1980, moose have been wandering back into the Adirondacks from New England, where the species has been on the increase for several decades. Al Hicks, who monitors the moose for the state, estimates that 75 to 100 moose live in the Adirondacks, and he expects the population to grow. Moose can turn up in any part of the park and in different habitats, but in summer they often visit wetlands to feed on aquatic plants. They also feed on leaves and twigs of trees and shrubs, such as striped maple, balsam fir, pin cherry, and hobblebush. Their cloven tracks are similar to a deer's but twice as large. Because the animals are reclusive and their numbers still small, count yourself lucky if you see one. But if you do see one, beware that bulls in rut (September to November) and cows with calves can be aggressive. A bull moose weighs up to 1,400 pounds and can run 35 miles an hour.

spruce. The trail ends just below the dam. Turn left to reach a primitive campsite a few yards off the main trail. This is a good place to enter the river to wade to the rocks.

Directions: From the western gate, drive 4.9 miles to a junction with Rock Dam Road; bear right and go 4.2 miles to the trailhead on the left. From the eastern gate, it's 18.4 miles on the Main Road to Rock Dam Road. At 14.3 miles from eastern gate, the Main Road turns right at a T-intersection with Otter Brook Road.

Trail: 1.4 miles.

Degree of difficulty: Easy.

Surface and blaze: Natural forest floor. Yellow blazes.

MITCHELL PONDS TRAIL

[Fig. 36(2)] An old road closed to vehicles leads to two scenic ponds that attract anglers and backpackers. Lower Mitchell Pond is stocked with brown trout (*Salmo trutta*) and red salmon. Upper Mitchell Pond, the first reached, is stocked only with brown trout. At 1.9 miles, the road reaches a junction in a clearing. Continue straight and follow yellow blazes another 0.1 mile to go to Upper Mitchell Pond. Bear right to go to Lower Mitchell Pond, again following yellow blazes. Soon after this junction, a snowmobile trail enters from the right. The hiking trail ends at a natural rock dam. Mitchell Ponds Mountain lies just south of the ponds.

The snowmobile trail offers an alternative way back to the Main Road. It comes out just south of the Red River, about 4 miles from the hiking trailhead. Mountain bikers might want to use this trail to make a loop trip.

Directions: From the western gate, drive 8.6 miles on the Main Road to the trailhead on the right. From the eastern gate, it's 12.7 miles to the trailhead.

Trail: 1.9 miles to Upper Mitchell Pond, 2.8 miles to far side of Lower Mitchell Pond.
Degree of difficulty: Easy.
Surface and blaze: Old road. Yellow blazes.

INDIAN LAKE TRAIL

[Fig. 36(6)] This large lake ringed by wooded hills lies just 0.1 mile from the road in the southwestern corner of the recreation area. The trail ends at a grassy spot on the shore where visitors can take a swim or put in a canoe. There is a campsite on the shore. Those staying at the lake can take day hikes into the adjacent West Canada Lakes Wilderness. At the end of Indian Lake Road, a trail leads into the wilderness to Balsam, Stink, and Horn lakes.

Directions: From the eastern gate, drive 14.3 miles on the Main Road to the junction with Otter Brook Road; turn left and go 3.3 miles on Otter Brook Road to the junction with Indian Lake Road; turn right and go 5.9 miles to the barrier at the end of Indian Lake Road. The official trail begins on the right side of the road about 0.1 mile before the barrier, but it's just as easy to park at the barrier and follow a herd path to the official trail. From the western gate, it's 9 miles on the Main Road to the junction with Otter Brook Road.

Trail: 0.1 mile.
Degree of difficulty: Easy.
Surface and blaze: Natural forest floor. Yellow blazes.

HELLDIVER POND TRAIL

[Fig. 36(3)] A short, pleasant walk through a conifer forest—in summer, it's a prism of green hues—ends at a grassy clearing beside this scenic pond in the Moose River Plains. Loons (*Gavia Immer*) sometimes can be seen diving for fish. Much of the shore is boggy and inaccessible. The water is shallow and the bottom very mucky. There is a picnic table at the trailhead. The level trail makes for an easy canoe carry.

MOOSE

(*Alces alces*)

The largest member of the deer family, the moose can grow up to 10 feet tall and weigh more than 1,000 pounds. Its habitat is the northern forest, often near fresh water, where it feeds on aquatic plants.

Directions: From the eastern gate, drive 13.4 miles along the Main Road to a dirt road on the left; turn and go 0.2 mile to the trailhead. From the western gate, follow the Main Road 9.9 miles to the dirt road. At 9 miles, the Main Road takes a left turn at a T intersection with Otter Brook Road.

Trail: 0.2 mile.

Degree of difficulty: Easy.

Surface and blaze: Natural forest floor. Yellow blazes.

CEDAR RIVER FLOW

[Fig. 36(1)] The Wakely Dam on the Cedar River has created a shallow lake about 3 miles long and 0.5 mile wide. The original wooden dam impounded water so logs could be floated downriver in the spring. The state replaced it with a concrete-and-steel dam in 1966.

The flow, located at the eastern entrance to the Moose River Recreation Area, can be reached by car after a long drive down a dirt road, but since it is surrounded by state-owned forest, it retains a sense of wildness. Loons (*Gavia immer*) and other waterfowl often visit the water. The state stocks the flow with brook trout (*Salvelinus fontinalis*).

The state maintains several primitive campsites near the dam. In summer, it's not unusual to see trailers, screen tents, and barbecue grills in the field near the dam.

Canoeists can find solitude along the flow's marshy shores. About 2 miles from the dam, Buell Brook comes in from the east, offering more opportunities for exploration. Canoeists also can paddle a mile or so up the Cedar River to a lean-to on the western bank. The lean-to is located along the Northville-Lake Placid Trail. The river's entrance is at the southeastern tip of the Flow.

Directions: From the junction of NY 28 and NY 30 in Indian Lake, drive 2.2 miles west on NY 28/30 to Cedar River Road; turn left and go 12.6 miles to a parking area near the entrance to the Moose River Recreation Area. Canoes and small boats can be put in near the dam.

Activities: Camping, canoeing, fishing, swimming.

Facilities: Primitive campsites, privies, small boat launch.

Dates: Year-round.

Fees: None.

Closest town: Indian Lake is about 15 miles east.

For more information: State Department of Environmental Conservation, 701 S. Main Street, Northville, NY 12134. Phone (518) 863-4545.

West Canada Lakes Wilderness

At 170,000 acres, this is the second-largest wilderness in the Adirondacks. The Northville-Lake Placid Trail cuts through the heart of this wild territory, going from the hamlet of Piseco north to the Cedar River Flow in the Moose River Plains and thence to the Blue Ridge Wilderness. Most trails in the West Canada Lakes Wilderness lead to lakes in the northern sector, including the West Canada Lakes themselves—Mud, South, and West lakes.

Hikers tramping through these parts experience the wilderness differently from those who climb the High Peaks. They find beauty not in spectacular panoramas but in more subdued scenes: a beaver meadow adorned with cotton grass, a dark creek snaking through a grassy floodplain, a loon diving beneath the still surface of a sylvan lake. Perhaps more important, they also find solitude. It is possible to walk all day in the West Canada Lakes Wilderness without encountering another soul. Some would argue that this is what wilderness is all about. Snowy Mountain, one of the highest summits outside the High Peaks, sits on the eastern edge of the wilderness. Snowy is made of anorthosite, but most of the other mountains in this region are made of gneiss, a slightly less durable rock.

One of the region's treasures is West Canada Creek, a renowned trout stream that originates in the West Lakes area. Backpacking anglers trek to the upper reaches of the creek to catch brook trout in a wilderness setting. The creek reaches civilization when it passes under NY 8 at Nobleboro. Fly fishermen often can be seen standing in the rapids near the bridge. All told, the state maintains about 80 miles of trails and 11 lean-tos in the West Canada Lakes Wilderness.

For more information: State Department of Environmental Conservation, 701 S. Main Street, Northville, NY 12134. Phone (518) 863-4545. Ask for the leaflet *Moose River Recreation Area* and *The Northville-Lake Placid Trail*.

BROOKTROUT LAKE TRAIL

[Fig. 37(4)] The little-used trail to Brooktrout Lake, though only 5.2 miles, gives hikers a real sense of the remoteness of the West Canada Lakes Wilderness. Just getting to the trailhead is a small adventure, requiring a drive of nearly 14 miles along dirt roads. Acid rain has killed the fish in Brooktrout Lake, but for those who want to swim or picnic, it's a gem. The lake's lean-to faces not the water but a natural rock wall that serves as the back of a fireplace.

The yellow-blazed trail begins with a steady, gradual climb through a mixed forest. Later, it passes through clearings where blueberries and wildflowers grow among slabs of bedrock. In one clearing, the trail makes a right turn that can be hard to spot. Soon afterward, it passes a long serpentine beaver dam in a meadow.

On the approach to Brooktrout Lake the trail descends through an attractive green forest with ferns, common wood sorrel (*Oxalis montana*), and clintonia (*Clintonia borealis*) in the understory—along with numerous glacial boulders.

Hikers will pass two marked junctions on the way. At 1.5 miles, a trail on the right leads 0.45 mile to Falls Pond. At 3.4 miles, a trail on the left leads 1 mile to either Wolf Lake or Deep Lake, depending on which fork is taken. Acid rain has killed the fish in these three lakes.

If hikers continue about 0.3 mile beyond Brooktrout Lake, now following red blazes, they will reach a short unmarked path on the right that leads to a campsite on the western end of West Lake.. Here, the lake is shallow with a sandy bottom. It's another 2 miles to the first West Lake lean-to.

Directions: See directions to the Moose River Recreation Area, page 228. From the western gate, follow the Main Road 9 miles to a T intersection with Otter Brook Road; go straight, along Otter Brook Road, for 3.7 miles to another T intersection; turn right onto Indian Lake Road and drive 1.1 miles to a parking lot on the left. From the eastern gate, the T intersection with Otter Brook Road is 14.3 miles away.

Trail: 5.2 miles to Brooktrout Lake.

Degree of difficulty: Moderate.

Surface and blaze: Old road, natural forest floor. Yellow blazes.

▓ WEST CANADA LAKES LOOP

[Fig. 36(7)] The three West Canada Lakes lie deep in the heart of the wilderness to which they have lent their name. Because of their remoteness, it's best to explore them on a backpacking trip. The 20.7-mile loop described here passes nine lakes and ponds, including the lovely Cedar Lakes, and nine lean-tos. It should leave one with an indelible impression of the West Canada Lakes Wilderness.

The route begins by following the red-blazed French Louie Trail, an old logging road that eventually shrinks to a footpath. At the outset, the trail parallels the Miami River. It reaches a junction at 1.6 miles. Yellow blazes lead straight ahead to the Cedar Lakes dam, but turn left and continue following red blazes another 8.5 miles to the Northville-Lake Placid Trail, passing Pillsbury, Whitney, and Sampson lakes en route.

For the next 6.9 miles the route follows the Northville-Lake Placid Trail's blue blazes. Cross West Canada Creek, a famed trout stream, and go north past the West Canada Lakes—West, South, and Mud. At a junction near West Lake, the trail turns right to head toward Cedar Lakes.

Cedar Lakes is really one lake, about 2 miles long, divided into three segments. The bridge over the Beaver Pond outlet, which flows into First Cedar Lake, offers a marvelous vista of the conifer-ringed lake and surrounding hills. Visitors may hear a loon (*Gavia immer*) while admiring the sights. The deep water and sandy bottom near the bridge make it a good place for a cool dip.

Just past First Cedar Lake, turn right down the yellow-blazed trail. It soon passes a concrete dam that marks the start of the Cedar River, which flows into the Hudson. Follow this trail back to the French Louie Trail and the starting point—4.3 miles in all. Hikers can use this last leg to visit Cedar Lakes on a day trip. The state stocks all of the lakes and ponds on the loop with brook trout (*Salvelinus fontinalis*).

Directions: From the junction of NY 30 and NY 8 in Speculator, drive 8.7 miles north on NY 30 to Perkins Clearing Road on the left, a dirt road just past Mason Lake; go 3.3 miles to a right-hand turn marked by a State Department of Environmental Conservation sign; go 1.8 miles to another right-hand turn marked by a DEC sign; take this road 1.3 miles to its end, where there is a parking area. The last road can be rough in spots.

Trail: 20.7-mile loop.

Degree of difficulty: Moderate if done in two days.

Surface and blaze: Old road, natural forest floor. Red, blue, and yellow blazes.

▓ SNOWY MOUNTAIN

[Fig. 36] At 3,899 feet, Snowy Mountain is the highest mountain outside the High Peaks Region. In fact, it is higher than two of the summits in the Adirondack pantheon—the 46 peaks thought to be over 4,000 feet when Bob and George Marshall climbed them in the 1920s. Snowy's great height can be attributed partly to its durable rock, anorthosite, which is the same rock that underlies most of the High Peaks.

For the first few miles, the trail climbs gently through a mixed forest and crosses several streams, including Beaver Brook twice. In high water, some crossings require wading or difficult rock hopping. Most of the heavy climbing comes in the last mile or so. The trail is especially steep and rocky just before reaching a cliff with a wonderful lookout to the east of Indian Lake and the Siamese Ponds Wilderness. At the cliff, the marked trail turns left and continues another 500 feet or so to the fire tower on the summit. Before making the turn, go straight across the grassy clearing to a herd path that leads 150 feet to a ledge for a good view of Panther and Squaw mountains to the north.

The summit near the tower is enclosed by balsam fir (*Abies balsamea*) and red spruce (*Picea rubens*) and has no view. Since the first two flights of steps have been removed, the tower cannot be climbed. But there is a maze of herd paths that lead to lookouts. Many of the High Peaks can be seen from Snowy.

Directions: From the junction of NY 30 and NY 8 in Speculator, drive north on NY 30 about 17.8 miles to a lot on the right. The trail begins on the opposite side of the road. From Indian Lake, drive south on NY 30 about 6.5 miles.

Trail: 3.8 miles to summit.

Elevation: 1,793 feet to 3,899 feet.

Degree of difficulty: Strenuous.

Surface and blaze: Natural forest floor, rocky in places. Red blazes.

▓ T LAKE

[Fig. 35(2)] This aptly named lake lies west of Piseco Lake. A lean-to near the southern shore makes a good destination for a day trip or overnight excursion.

Piseco Lake

The state operates three small campgrounds on the western shore of this 2,848-acre lake, which is also an attraction for ice fisherman in the winter.

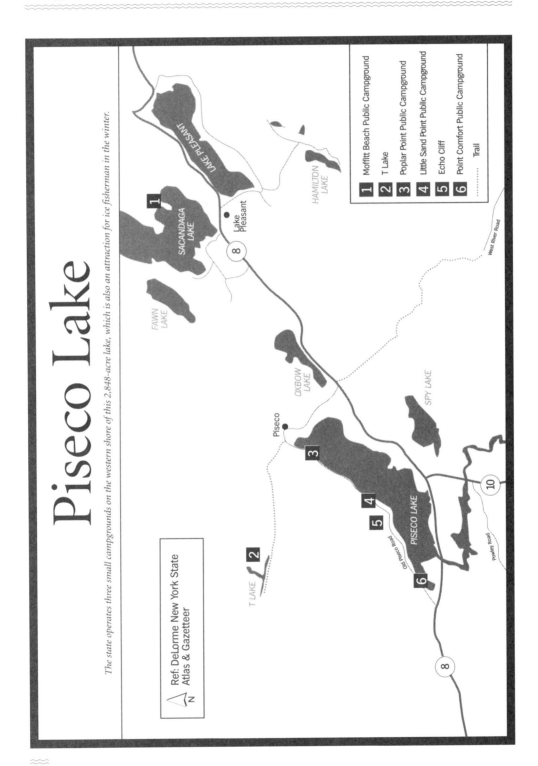

Ref: DeLorme New York State
Atlas & Gazetteer

N

1 Moffitt Beach Public Campground
2 T Lake
3 Poplar Point Public Campground
4 Little Sand Point Public Campground
5 Echo Cliff
6 Point Comfort Public Campground
...... Trail

Farther west, the lake's outlet, a source of the South Branch of West Canada Creek, drops 250 feet at T Lake Falls, one of the largest falls in the Adirondacks. Because hikers have died in accidents there, the state has closed the trail to the falls. It is against the law to go there. The trail to T Lake—which is 800 feet higher than Piseco Lake—has some steep ups and downs.

Directions: From the junction of NY 8 and NY 30 in Speculator, drive west on NY 8 for 16 miles to Old Piseco Road (about 3.1 miles past NY 10); turn right and go 2.3 miles to the trailhead on the left.

Trail: 3.5 miles to lean-to.

Elevation: 1,661 feet at Piseco Lake to 2,467 feet at T Lake.

Degree of difficulty: Moderate.

Surface and blaze: Natural forest floor. Blue blazes.

Echo Cliff

[Fig. 35(5)] This short hike leads to a cliff on Panther Mountain that overlooks Piseco Lake and the mountains to the east and south. The trail cuts through a forest of northern hardwoods and hemlock (*Tsuga canadensis*) and climbs through a rocky gully before making the final, steep ascent. Red spruce (*Picea rubens*), striped maple (*Acer pensylvanicum*), and hemlock grow about the cliff. The trail, worn to smooth slabs in places, passes two curious rocks—one shaped like a giant cube, the other like a chaise longue from *The Flintstones*.

Don Mellor credits Echo Cliff with generating interest in rock climbing in the southern Adirondacks. His rock-climbing guide, *Climbing in the Adirondacks*, describes seven routes up the cliff face that range from 40 to 100 feet. Echo Cliff lies within an isolated piece of the Ferris Lake Wild Forest, most of which lies south of NY 8.

Directions: From the junction of NY 8 and NY 30 in Speculator, drive 16 miles west on NY 8 to Old Piseco Road (about 3.1 miles past NY 10); turn right and go 2.7 miles to the trailhead on the left. Park along the road.

Trail: 0.75 mile to lookout.

Elevation: 1,700 feet to 2,425 feet.

Degree of difficulty: Moderate.

Surface and blaze: Natural forest floor. Blue blazes.

Piseco Lake

[Fig. 35] The state operates three small campgrounds on the western shore of this 2,848-acre lake, giving the public easy access to the 11th-largest lake wholly within the Adirondack Park. Most of the rest of the shoreline is in private hands.

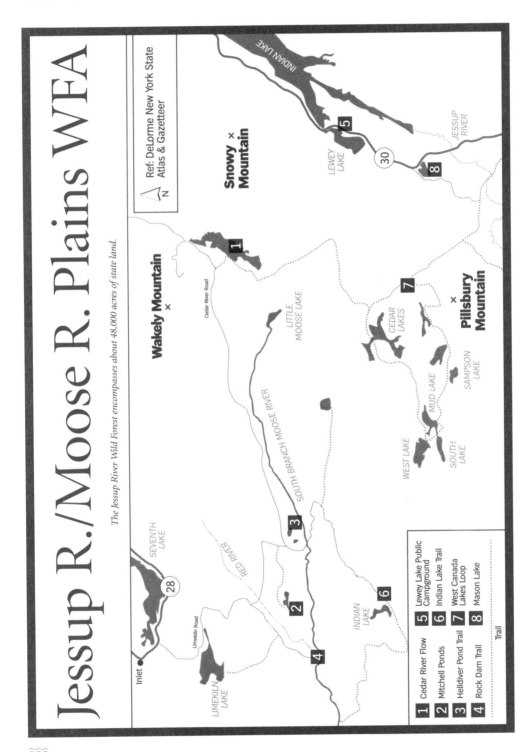

Jessup R./Moose R. Plains WFA

The Jessup River Wild Forest encompasses about 48,000 acres of state land.

Ref: DeLorme New York State Atlas & Gazetteer

N

1 Cedar River Flow
2 Mitchell Ponds
3 Helldiver Pond Trail
4 Rock Dam Trail
5 Lewey Lake Public Campground
6 Indian Lake Trail
7 West Canada Lakes Loop
8 Mason Lake

- - - - - - Trail

INDIAN LAKE

Snowy × Mountain

LEWEY LAKE

JESSUP RIVER

30

Wakely Mountain ×

Cedar River Road

LITTLE MOOSE LAKE

Pillsbury Mountain ×

CEDAR LAKES

MUD LAKE

SAMPSON LAKE

SOUTH BRANCH MOOSE RIVER

WEST LAKE

SOUTH LAKE

SEVENTH LAKE

RED RIVER

28

Inlet

Limekiln Road

INDIAN LAKE

LIMEKILN LAKE

Canoeists looking for a haven away from motorboats can paddle up Fall Stream at the northeastern end of Piseco Lake. If the water is high enough, it's possible to canoe more than 1.5 miles upstream to Vly Lake in the Jessup River Wild Forest. Paddlers may also want to explore Piseco Outlet to the south.

The state stocks Piseco with lake trout (*Salvelinus namaycush*) and Atlantic salmon (*Salmo salar*). Anglers may keep three lake trout and two salmon. The minimum length for both species is 18 inches. Smallmouth bass (*Micropterus dolomieui*) also can be caught. Piseco Lake attracts many ice fishermen in winter.

Those staying at Piseco Lake will find several hiking trails in the vicinity. The Northville-Lake Placid trail leads from the hamlet of Piseco, on the northern end of the lake, into the West Canada Lakes Wilderness (*see* page 232). Shorter trails lead to Echo Cliff and T Lake (*see* pages 237 and 235). In winter, skiers can use 6-mile cross-country loop that starts at the Piseco Airport near the northeastern shore.

▓ POPLAR POINT, LITTLE SAND POINT, AND POINT COMFORT PUBLIC CAMPGROUNDS

[Fig. 35(3), Fig. 35(4), Fig. 35(6)] All three campgrounds can be found along Old Piseco Road on the western shore. Each has a sand beach and boat launch.

Directions: From the junction of NY 8 and NY 30 in Speculator, drive west on NY 8 for 16 miles to Old Piseco Road (about 3.1 miles past NY 10) and turn right. You will reach Point Comfort after 1.2 miles, Little Sand Point after 3.3 miles, and Poplar Point after 4.3 miles.

Activities: Camping, fishing, boating, canoeing, swimming, hiking.

Facilities: 76 campsites at Point Comfort, 78 campsites at Little Sand Point, and 21 campsites at Poplar Point. Each has a sand beach, boat launch, and toilets. Poplar Point and Point Comfort have picnic areas and bathhouses. Little Sand Point has a trailer dumping station.

Dates: Open mid-May to Labor Day. Point Comfort is open until mid-October.

Fees: There is a charge for camping or day use.

Closest town: Speculator is about 17 miles away.

For more information: Poplar Point, phone (518) 548-8031. For reservations, phone (800) 456-2267. Point Comfort, phone (518) 548-7586. Little Sand Point, phone (518) 548-7585.

Jessup River Wild Forest

The Jessup River Wild Forest encompasses about 48,000 acres of state land on both sides of NY 30 between Speculator and Indian Lake. The Jessup River flows through the heart of the wild forest on its way to Indian Lake. The Miami River forms the boundary between the wild forest and West Canada Lakes Wilderness before emptying into Lewey Lake.

Pillsbury Mountain offers a panoramic view from the steps of its fire tower. The summit lies within a 2,240-acre chunk of wild forest isolated by the International Paper lands. Hikers who drive through the International Paper Company timberlands on the way to the trailhead may see logging trucks. The timberlands are open to the public for hunting and hiking, but camping is prohibited.

State campgrounds at Lewey Lake and Sacandaga Lake abut the Jessup River Wild Forest.

For more information: State Department of Environmental Conservation, 701 S. Main Street, Northville, NY 12134. Phone (518) 863-4545.

LEWEY LAKE PUBLIC CAMPGROUND

[Fig. 36(5)] Named for the hermit Louis Seymour—better known as French Louie—the 90-acre Lewey Lake appeals to those who would rather stay at a small lake than at the vastly larger Indian Lake. Since a short channel connects the two, Lewey Lake patrons with a boat or canoe can enjoy the best of both worlds.

Canoeists also can explore the Miami River, which flows into Lewey Lake at its marshy southern end. Hikers can take a 7.2-mile trail from the campground deep into the West Canada Lakes Wilderness. Anglers can fish for Atlantic salmon (*Salmo salar*), lake trout (*Salvelinus namaycush*), and northern pike (*Esox lucius*), among other species.

Directions: From the junction of NY 8 and NY 30 in Speculator, drive 12.7 miles north on NY 30 to the entrance on the left. From the junction of NY 28 and NY 30 in Indian Lake, drive south on NY 30 about 12.6 miles. The entrance will be on the right.

Activities: Camping, swimming, fishing, hiking, canoeing, boating.

Facilities: 209 campsites, picnic area, sand beach, bathhouse, boat launch, toilets, showers, trailer dump station. The picnic area, toilets, showers, and some campsites are accessible to the handicapped.

Dates: Open mid-May through mid-November.

Fees: There is a charge for camping or day use.

Closest town: Speculator is 12 miles south; Indian Lake is 12 miles north.

For more information: Campground office, phone (518) 648-5266. For reservations, phone (800) 456-2267.

MASON LAKE

[Fig. 36(8)] Motorists can see this pretty lake from NY 30 when driving between Speculator and Indian Lake. There are several primitive campsites on the opposite shore, reachable by a dirt road. Canoes and small boats can be launched at the campsites. The lake has many small bays and islands to explore. Anglers can try their luck for brown trout (*Salmo trutta*) and brook trout (*Salvelinus fontinalis*).

Directions: From the junction of NY 30 and NY 8 in Speculator, drive 8.7 miles north on NY 30 to Perkins Clearing Road on the left, about 0.4 mile past the pull-off. The first campsite is on the left about 0.1 mile down this dirt road. Continue down the road to reach other campsites.

Activities: Camping, canoeing, fishing, swimming.

Facilities: Primitive campsites.

Dates: Accessible year-round. The dirt road is unplowed in winter.

Fees: None.

Closest town: Speculator is about 8 miles south on NY 30.

For more information: State Department of Environmental Conservation, 701 S. Main Street, Northville, NY 12134. Phone (518) 863-4545.

PILLSBURY MOUNTAIN

[Fig. 36] Hikers can climb the stairs of an old fire tower for panoramic views of the central and southern Adirondacks.

The trail to the summit begins by descending to the Miami River and then climbing through a deciduous forest past several huge boulders. Hikers may notice some large specimens of paper birch (*Betula papyrifea*), yellow birch (*Betula alleghaniensis*), and red spruce (*Picea rubens*). Higher up, the hardwoods give way to spruce and balsam fir (*Abies balsamea*). The trail often is quite steep, but it levels off before the summit as it passes through a fragrant balsam wood.

Among the wildflowers that bloom along the trail are red trillium (*Trillium erectum*), common wood sorrel (*Oxalis montana*), bunchberry (*Cornus canadensis*), Canada mayflower (*Maianthemum canadense*), and clintonia (*Clintonia borealis*). Orange hawkeye (*Hieracium aurantiacum*) grows on the grassy summit. Don't be surprised if you see a garter snake in the grass. There is a rundown ranger's cabin near the tower.

Directions: From the junction of NY 30 and NY 8 in Speculator, drive 8.7 miles north on NY 30 to Perkins Clearing Road on the left, a dirt road just past Mason Lake; go 3.3 miles to a right-hand turn marked by a State Department of Environmental Conservation sign; go 1.8 miles to another right-hand turn marked by a DEC sign; take this road 1.3 miles to its end, where there is a parking area. The last road can be rough in spots.

Trail: 1.6 miles to summit.

Elevation: 2,260 feet to 3,597 feet.

Degree of difficulty: Moderate.

Surface and blaze: Natural forest floor. Red blazes.

Moffitt Beach Public Campground

[Fig. 35(1)] This state campground gives the public easy access to 1,600-acre Sacandaga Lake. Although it's a big lake with its share of motorboats, canoeists can enjoy a peaceful paddle on Burnt Place Brook, which leads to tiny Mud Pond. The brook can be found at the northernmost tip of the lake, about 1 mile northwest of the campground.

The state stocks Sacandaga Lake with rainbow trout (*Oncorhynchus mykiss*) and

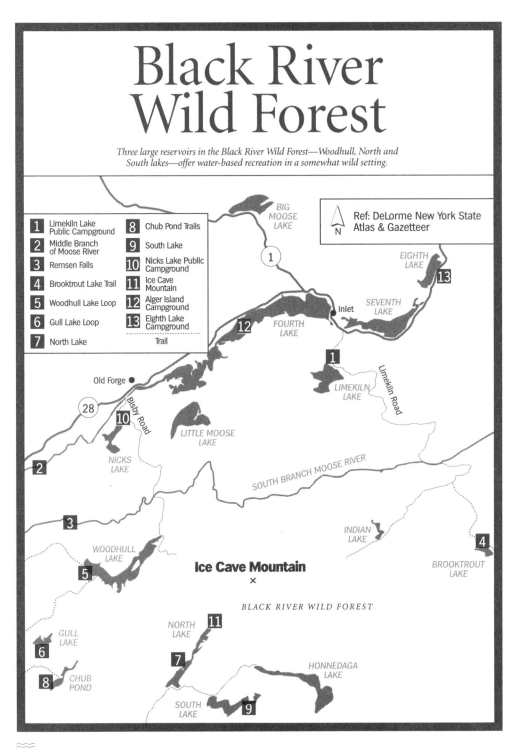

Black River Wild Forest

Three large reservoirs in the Black River Wild Forest—Woodhull, North and South lakes—offer water-based recreation in a somewhat wild setting.

1 Limekiln Lake Public Campground
2 Middle Branch of Moose River
3 Remsen Falls
4 Brooktrout Lake Trail
5 Woodhull Lake Loop
6 Gull Lake Loop
7 North Lake
8 Chub Pond Trails
9 South Lake
10 Nicks Lake Public Campground
11 Ice Cave Mountain
12 Alger Island Campground
13 Eighth Lake Campground
········· Trail

Ref: DeLorme New York State Atlas & Gazetteer

N

BIG MOOSE LAKE

EIGHTH LAKE

SEVENTH LAKE

FOURTH LAKE

Inlet

LIMEKILN LAKE

Limekiln Road

Old Forge

Blisby Road

28

NICKS LAKE

LITTLE MOOSE LAKE

SOUTH BRANCH MOOSE RIVER

INDIAN LAKE

BROOKTROUT LAKE

WOODHULL LAKE

Ice Cave Mountain
×

BLACK RIVER WILD FOREST

GULL LAKE

NORTH LAKE

HONNEDAGA LAKE

CHUB POND

SOUTH LAKE

brown trout (*Salmo trutta*). Several other species can be caught here, including walleye (*Stizostedion vitreum vitreum*) and smallmouth bass (*Micropterus dolomieui*). Fishing is prohibited from March 16 to the opening of walleye season on the first Saturday in May.

Do not confuse Sacandaga Lake with Great Sacandaga Lake, the reservoir that lies several miles to the south.

Directions: From the junction of NY 8 and NY 30 in Speculator, drive west about 2 miles on NY 8 to Page Street; turn right and follow signs for the campground.

Activities: Camping, swimming, fishing, canoeing, boating.

Facilities: 261 campsites, picnic area, sand beach, bathhouse, toilets, showers, 2 small-boat launches, trailer dumping station, general store. Some of the campsites, picnic tables, toilets, and showers are accessible to the handicapped.

Dates: Open mid-May through mid-October.

Fees: There is a charge for camping or day use.

Closest town: Speculator is about 3 miles away.

For more information: Reservations, phone (800) 456-2267.

Black River Wild Forest

[Fig. 37] The Black River Wild Forest contains about 126,000 acres of state land west of the West Canada Lakes Wilderness. This includes the 4,462-acre Pratt-Northam Memorial Park south of South Lake which, though technically not part of the Forest Preserve, is managed as wild forest.

The region lies in the southwestern foothills of the Adirondacks. The highest peak rises to only 2,600 feet, less than half the height of Mount Marcy. The mountains' smaller size can be attributed to two facts: First, these peaks are made of granitic gneiss, which erodes faster than the anorthosite common in the High Peaks, and second, the peaks exist on the fringe of domical uplift that created the Adirondacks.

Three rivers designated scenic or recreational wind through the region: the Black River and the Moose River's south and middle branches. Anglers can get to all three easily. West Canada Creek flows along the region's southeastern and southern boundaries.

The Hudson River-Black River Regulating District manages three large reservoirs that feed into the Black River: Woodhull, North, and South lakes. All three provide excellent opportunities for recreation. Cars can drive to North and South lakes. A jeep trail and hiking trails lead to Woodhull Lake. Many smaller lakes and ponds can be reached by hiking trails. Honnedaga Lake, the region's largest natural lake, is surrounded by private land.

The state runs a campground on Nicks Lake. For backpackers, there are six lean-tos scattered about the region, including one twice the normal size at Woodhull Lake.

For more information: State Department of Environmental Conservation, 225 N. Main Street, Herkimer, NY 13350. Phone (315) 866-6330.

NICKS LAKE PUBLIC CAMPGROUND

[Fig. 37(10)] Located just outside Old Forge, the Nicks Lake Public Campground offers access to the northeastern parts of the Black River Wild Forest. The 154-acre lake—named for Nick Stoner, a famous trapper of Revolutionary days—is home to loons (*Gavia immer*) and other waterfowl.

A 4.4-mile trail starting at the campground beach makes a circuit of the lake. A yellow-blazed trail leaves the circuit trail in two places, making a 17-mile loop that passes Nelson Lake, the Middle Branch of the Moose River, and a lean-to near Remsen Falls (*see* below) on the South Branch of the Moose. Hikers can avoid paying a day-use fee by hiking to the campground trail from another trailhead on Bisby Road.

The state stocks Nicks Lake with brook trout (*Salvelinus fontinalis*) and brown trout (*Salmo trutta*). Rainbow trout (*Oncorhynchus mykiss*) also can be caught. Anglers are forbidden to use baitfish.

Directions: From NY 28 in Old Forge, turn south onto Gilbert Street at sign for the campground and go 0.1 mile to Railroad Avenue; turn right and go 0.1 mile to Joy Tract Road; turn left and go 0.9 mile to Bisby Road; turn left and go about 0.5 mile to the campground's access road on the right. All of the turns should be marked by signs for the campground. The Bisby Road trailhead is 0.2 mile from Joy Tract Road.

Activities: Camping, swimming, hiking, fishing, canoeing, mountain biking.

Facilities: 112 tent and trailer sites, picnic area, sand beach, hiking trails, softball field, playground, bathhouse, showers, flush toilets, trailer dump station.

Dates: Early May to late October.

Fees: There is a charge for camping or day use.

Closest town: Old Forge is about 1 mile north.

For more information: Campground office, phone (315) 369-3314. For reservations, phone (800) 456-2267.

REMSEN FALLS

[Fig. 37(3)] At Remsen Falls, a natural barrier of boulders and flat rocks funnels the South Branch of the Moose River through a narrow flume, creating a small but noisy cataract in a wild setting. Visitors can walk over the rocks to the middle of the river to bask in the sun or admire the scenery. The current near the falls is strong, but the quiet waters above and below the rocks are suitable for a swim.

The falls make an exellent family outing, for they can be reached by walking or biking along a level dirt road that is abandoned but in excellent shape. The hardwood forest often creates a leafy archway, but the road also passes sunny clearings where wildflowers abound, such as steeplebush (*Spiraea tomentosa*), meadowsweet (*Spiraea latifolia*), common Saint-John's-wort (*Hypericum perforatum*), spotted joe-pye weed (*Eupatorium maculatum*), and spotted touch-me-not (*Impatiens capensis*). Raspberries also grow along the way.

Turn left at 2.6 miles at a four-way junction marked by signs. Those going to Remsen Falls turn left and descend on a much rougher road to the river, now less than 0.5 mile away. There are several primitive campsites near the river. An unmarked path continues about 0.2 mile past the falls to Harry's Point, where a memorial tablet sits beneath an old red spruce. Harry's Point lies across the river from the Remsen Falls lean-to, reachable by a foot trail from Nicks Lake Public Campground (*see* page 244).

Directions: From the tourist information center in Old Forge, drive west 11.4 miles on NY 28 to McKeever Road; turn left and go 0.2 mile; turn right onto a dirt road and go 0.6 mile to a parking area; bear left and go another 0.1 mile to a second parking area. Use caution when crossing the railroad tracks.

Trail: 3.1 miles to falls.

Degree of difficulty: Easy.

Surface and blaze: Old road. Red blazes.

WOODHULL LAKE LOOP

[Fig. 37(5)] Woodhull Lake, the largest lake in the Black River Wild Forest, has the largest lean-to in the Adirondack Park: it is twice the normal size and looks out over a scenic, undeveloped part of the lake. The sandy bottom just off the shore invites visitors to take a swim.

Beaver

Hikers forced to tiptoe over beaver dams or wade over flooded trails may find it hard to believe that at the start of the twentieth century the beaver (*Castor canadensis*) had been nearly extirpated from the Adirondacks, the victim of overzealous trappers. The population exploded after the state released about 50 animals near Upper Saranac Lake: Today, more than 50,000 beaver reside in the Adirondacks. Beaver eat the inner bark of the trees they fell to make dams and lodges. In winter, woody plants make up 100 percent of their diet, but in summer the beaver prefer to munch on grasses and aquatic plants. They can grow to up to 110 pounds, but most adults are about 45 pounds. Beavers apparently mate for life, and a typical colony consists of two adults and about four offspring. They work constantly at repairing their dam. Since beavers are nocturnal, hikers rarely get the chance to observe them, but humans can marvel at the animals' feats of engineering. If you do disturb a beaver, you probably will hear the violent slap of its tail—a warning to the colony.

Hikers can walk to this 1,158-acre reservoir along dirt roads and return by a footpath that passes Bear Lake, a loop of 10.1 miles. For an extra mile, they can add Remsen Falls to the itinerary (*see* page 244). For a shorter trip, Bear Lake alone makes a suitable destination.

A jeep trail to Woodhull is open to vehicles, but it is in poor shape, sometimes resembling a muddy motocross track. For hikers, the best route is as follows: Start off down the road for Remsen Falls, marked by red blazes; at 2.6 miles, turn right on a blue-blazed trail that leads 0.2 mile to the jeep trail; turn left and follow the jeep trail

1.9 miles to a vehicle barrier on the right; turn right and follow this trail 0.5 mile to the lean-to. Just before the lean-to, bear left after crossing a creek.

On the return trip, go to Bear Lake via a yellow-blazed trail that starts just before the creek. After 2.2 miles, this trail reaches a junction with a blue trail that skirts the lake. Turn right to go to a grassy campsite on the northeastern shore. The lake bottom is sandy here. Leaving the lake, the blue trail climbs past a talus-filled ravine and eventually reaches the jeep trail. Cross the jeep trail and continue straight until reaching the better road, then turn left to return to the parking lot.

Equestrians can take the same route as hikers to reach Woodhull Lake, but instead of turning at the vehicle barrier, they should continue on the jeep road to reach the lake. Mountain bikers can ride right to the lean-to.

Directions: Same as for Remsen Falls, page 244.

Trail: 10.1-mile loop. Bear Lake is 1.7 miles from the parking lot.

Degree of difficulty: Moderate.

Surface and blaze: Old roads, natural forest floor. Red, blue, and yellow blazes.

GULL LAKE LOOP

[Fig. 37(6)] This 124-acre warm-water lake, where osprey (*Pandion haliaetus*) sometimes nest, can be visited as part of a 7.9-mile loop that also passes Bear Creek, one of the region's best brook trout streams. There is a lean-to on Gull Lake's northern shore.

From the parking lot, take the jeep trail known as Woodhull Road about 0.4 mile to a vehicle barrier on the left. Turn here and follow a yellow-blazed woods road. At 0.8 mile down this road, a grassy lane on the left leads about 0.2 mile to Bear Creek. Blind gentian (*Gentiana clausa*), steeplebush (*Spiraea tomentosa*), and meadowsweet (*Spiraea latifolia*) bloom along the banks. Swimmers can wade into the dark creek from a tiny beach. The water is 3-4 feet deep.

After returning to the main trail, go another 0.8 mile to a junction and bear right on a red-blazed trail. This trail crosses the jeep trail again and reaches the lake at 3 miles. A yellow-blazed trail on the left leads to the lean-to on a point. The fishing in the lake is so-so, but brown bullhead (*Ictalurus nebulosus*) and yellow perch (*Perca flavescens*) can be caught.

On the return trip, follow the red trail for another 2.4 miles around the lake and then south to a junction with the blue Chub Pond Trail. Turn right and follow this dirt road 1.4 miles to the jeep trail. Turn left to return to the parking lot.

Directions: From the blinking light on NY 28 in Woodgate, turn east on Bear Creek Road and drive 3.3 miles to a parking lot on the left.

Trail: 8.1-mile loop, including detour to Bear Creek.

Degree of difficulty: Moderate.

Surface and blaze: Old roads, natural forest floor. Yellow, red, and blue blazes.

CHUB POND TRAIL

[Fig. 37(8)] This 99-acre trout water has a pair of lean-tos. One sits on the northwestern shore, overlooking the conifer-ringed pond. The other's location—about 0.2 mile from the eastern shore—is not nearly as good, but this lean-to is an attraction in itself: Built in 1961 under a special permit, it comes with a propane stove, bunk beds, tables, chairs, and two skylights. The outhouse doubles as a supply shed.

For most of the way, the trail follows old dirt roads through hardwood or mixed forests. One section passes through a stand of large hemlocks (*Tsuga canadensis*). There are scenic views at the crossings of Gull Pond Outlet and Chub Pond Outlet.

From the parking lot, follow the jeep trail about 0.3 mile to the turn for Chub Pond. Turn right and follow the blue-blazed trail for another 3.3 miles to a fork. Bear left on a red-blazed trail to reach the lean-to on the northwestern shore—4.4 miles from the trailhead. Or continue on the blue-blazed trail another 2 miles to the other lean-to—5.3 miles from the trailhead. To get to this lean-to, turn right up a short side trail just after passing a junction with a yellow-blazed trail that leads to Stone Dam Lake. The Chub Pond Trail is suitable for mountain biking.

The elusive pine marten (*Martes americana*) has been known to dwell along Grindstone Creek, which flows into the pond near the lean-to on the northwestern shore. Fishing for brook trout (*Salvelinus fontinalis*) and rainbow trout at Chub Pond (*Oncorhynchus mykiss*) is rated as fair.

Directions: From the blinking light on NY 28 in Woodgate, turn east on Bear Creek Road and drive 3.3 miles to a parking lot on the left.

Trail: 4.4 miles to first lean-to, 5.3 miles to second lean-to.

Degree of difficulty: Moderate.

Surface and blaze: Old road, natural forest floor. Blue and red blazes.

NORTH AND SOUTH LAKES

North Lake [Fig. 37(7)] is a narrow lake about 2.25 miles long that spills into the Black River at a dam about 14 miles northeast of Forestport Station. The state owns most of the shoreline and surrounding territory on the southern end and has purchased conservation easements from timber companies allowing public access on the northern end. There are a few camps along the water, but the lake primarily offers views of wooded shores and rolling hills.

The state maintains several drive-in campsites on the Loop Road that follows the western shore of North Lake. These free campsites—available on a first-come basis—can be found on both the state and the easement lands. In addition, the state maintains several primitive campsites on the eastern shore reachable by boat.

There are three large parking lots on the Loop Road, all of which are located on the easement lands. Camping is permitted only at the third lot. The public is not permitted to drive beyond this lot. The parking lots give hunters and hikers access to 11,490 acres of private timberlands. These lands form a bridge between the Black

River Wild Forest and the West Canada Lakes Wilderness to the east. At times, sections of the timberlands may be closed because of logging.

The 500-acre South Lake [Fig. 37(9)] is located a few miles down the main road from North Lake. Just before South Lake, a dirt road on the right leads to a campsite on the western shore. This is a good picnic spot. From here, a snowmobile trail goes around the southern side of the lake. The state maintains two campsites on the northeastern shore, beyond the narrows, reachable by boat.

Neither lake is stocked, but anglers can catch brook trout (*Salvelinus fontinalis*) and brown bullheads (*Ictalurus nebulosus*), among other species.

Directions: At the Forestport Reservoir on NY 28 in Forestport, turn east at the sign for Forestport Station and drive 1.3 miles to North Lake Road; bear left and go 14.2 miles to North Lake; turn left on the Loop Road to reach trailheads, campsites, and parking lots. The last parking lot is 4.8 miles up the Loop Road. If going to South Lake, do not turn onto the Loop Road.

Activities: Camping, fishing, swimming, boating, canoeing, hiking, mountain biking, snowmobiling.

Facilities: About 16 primitive campsites.

Dates: Accessible year-round, but the Loop Road is not plowed in winter.

Fees: None.

Closest town: Forestport Station is about 14.2 miles west.

For more information: State Department of Environmental Conservation, 225 N. Main Street, Herkimer, NY 13350. Phone (315) 866-6330.

ICE CAVE MOUNTAIN

[Fig. 37(11)] A deep cleft atop the summit ridge of this mountain has been known to keep ice throughout July and August.

The trail to the ice cave begins at a vehicle barrier just past the parking lot. Follow the old road beyond this barrier about 1.2 miles to a small creek that cuts across the road. Turn left to enter the woods just before this creek. The turn and the 0.5-mile herd path up the mountain may be marked by orange ribbons. The path leads north through a hardwood forest and soon reaches mossy cliffs with broken rocks and boulders nearby.

The final climb to the summit ridge is steep. Turn left on the ridge to find the ice cave, which will be on the right of the path. Be careful not to get too close to the edge when peering in. The path leads around the cleft to another narrow fissure and then to a partial lookout through the trees toward North Lake to the southwest and Canachgala Mountain to the northwest.

Ice Cave Mountain lies within an 11,490-acre tract of private timberlands open to the public by virtue of a conservation easement. At times, sections of this tract may be closed because of logging. To check on this, phone the State Department of Environmental Conservation's office in Herkimer at (315) 866-6330.

Directions: Same as for North Lake (*see* above). From North Lake Road, follow the Loop Road 4.8 miles to the last parking lot, which is on the right.

Trail: 1.7 miles to ice cave.

Elevation: About 1,900 feet to 2,400 feet.

Degree of difficulty: Moderate.

Surface and blaze: Old road, natural forest floor. No official blazes.

⬛ MIDDLE BRANCH OF MOOSE RIVER

[Fig. 37(2)] The Middle Branch forms part of the northern boundary of the Black River Wild Forest. Starting at First Lake in Old Forge, the Middle Moose winds about 12 miles before joining forces with the South Branch to form the Moose River's Main Branch. The North Branch of the Moose feeds into the Middle Moose in Thendara, just outside Old Forge.

Novice canoeists can enjoy a 1.3-mile quiet stretch of the Middle Moose from Thendara to an old dam. They can put in near the bridge on Beech Street, which turns east off NY 28 in Thendara. White-water paddlers can continue all the way to McKeever, where NY 28 crosses the Main Branch. The 13-mile trip will require portages around the dam and around Nelson Falls. The rapids reach Class III intensity.

AMERICAN CRANBERRY
(Vaccinium macrocarpon) The cranberry was one of the first crops grown commercially for export from North America.

Canoeists and fishermen also can reach the Middle Branch below Nelson Falls by an easy walk from a state-owned parking lot off NY 28. From a vehicle barrier at the end of the lot, walk straight along an old road for about 0.4 mile. Turn right after crossing the railroad tracks to put in at a quiet stretch of the river. The next rapids are roughly 0.5 mile downriver. Before reaching the rapids, flat-water canoeists can turn left up the Nelson Lake outlet to explore the lake. To get to the parking lot, turn east from NY 28 onto a dirt road, marked by a trailhead sign, about 3 miles north of the McKeever Bridge.

For more information: State Department of Environmental Conservation, 225 N. Main Street, Herkimer, NY 13350. Phone (315) 866-6330.

Hinckley Reservoir State Picnic Area

[Fig. 38(1)] A large dam on West Canada Creek near the hamlet of Hinckley created this 2,784-acre reservoir on the southwestern boundary of the Adirondack Park. The state runs a beach with picnic facilities on the southern shore.

There is no official state launch on the reservoir, but boaters often put in at

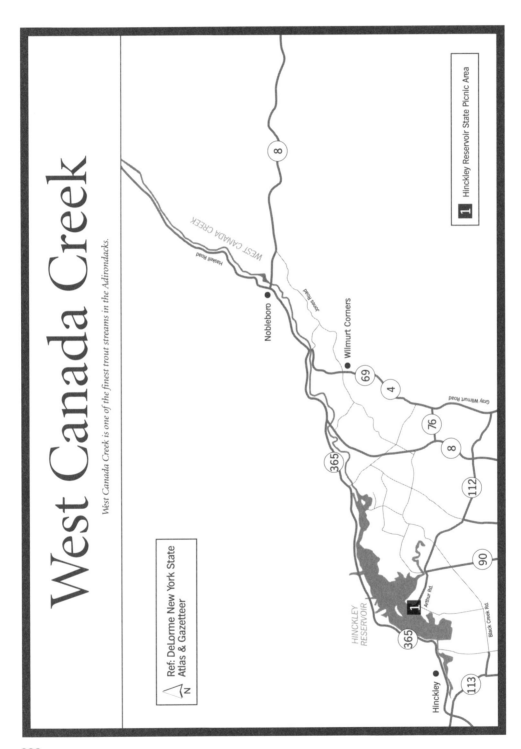

West Canada Creek

West Canada Creek is one of the finest trout streams in the Adirondacks.

Ref: DeLorme New York State
Atlas & Gazetteer

N

Hinckley Reservoir State Picnic Area

WEST CANADA CREEK

Haskell Road

Jones Road

Nobleboro

Wilmurt Corners

Gray Wilmurt Road

69

4

76

8

112

90

365

365

113

Arthur Rd

Black Creek Rd

HINCKLEY
RESERVOIR

Hinckley

8

informal launches along NY 365 on the northern shore. Fishermen catch pickerel, bass, trout, and panfish in the reservoir.

Directions: From NY 12 in Barneveld, take the exit for NY 365 and drive 4.7 miles east to County 151 in Hinckley; turn right and follow the signs for the picnic area.

Activities: Picnicking, swimming, boating, fishing.

Facilities: Sand beach, bathhouse, picnic tables, grills.

Dates: Seasonal.

Fees: There is a charge for the day-use area.

Closest town: Hamlet of Hinckley.

For more information: State Department of Environmental Conservation, 225 N. Main Street, Herkimer, NY 13350. Phone (315) 866-6330.

West Canada Creek

[Fig. 38] The West Canada, one of the best trout streams in the state, begins in the heart of the West Canada Lakes Wilderness and flows southwest to Nobleboro and then west to the Hinckley Reservoir, where it leaves the Adirondack Park. Eventually, after a journey of about 65 miles, it reaches the Mohawk River at Herkimer.

In spring, backpacking anglers fish the wild upper reaches of the West Canada for large brook trout (*Salvelinus fontinalis*). The Northville-Lake Placid Trail crosses the creek as it flows out of Mud Lake. There is a lean-to on the right bank near the bridge. The state stocks Mud Lake and adjacent West and South lakes, all of which feed the creek, with brookies.

The West Canada is easily accessible at Nobleboro from a scenic pull-off at the junction of NY 8 and Haskell Road. Anglers also can get to the creek by driving up Haskell Road about 0.6 mile and turning right down a dirt road. Haskell Road crosses the creek about 4.0 miles from NY 8, but after the first 2.8 miles, the road is very rough and suitable only for high-clearance vehicles.

Below Nobleboro, the creek follows NY 8 and NY 365 for 8.5 miles before reaching the Hinckley Reservoir. The state stocks this part of the river with brook trout and brown trout (*Salmo trutta*) and owns fishing rights in many sections.

Canoeists who put in at Nobleboro will encounter several Class II and Class III rapids on the way to the reservoir—a trip that includes the scenic Ohio Gorge. Before reaching the gorge, there is a carry around a falls above the Wilmurt Bridge. Paddlers can take out at a bridge before the reservoir.

Alec Proskine says in *Adirondack Canoe Waters: South and West Flow* that the West Canada above Nobleboro, starting where Haskell Road crosses the creek, can be canoed by experts in high water, usually from April to early May. Expect Class IV rapids.

For more information: State Department of Environmental Conservation, 225 N. Main Street, Herkimer, NY 13350. Phone (315) 866-6330.

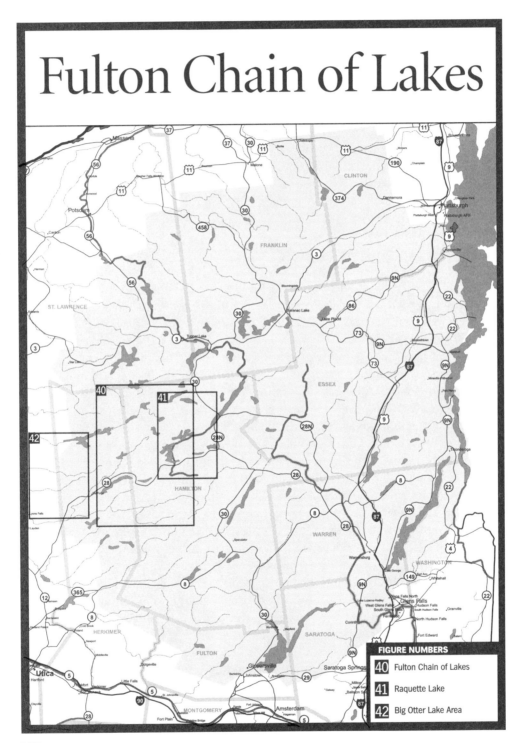

Fulton Chain of Lakes

FIGURE NUMBERS

40	Fulton Chain of Lakes
41	Raquette Lake
42	Big Otter Lake Area

Fulton Chain
of Lakes

Before the arrival of Europeans, the Fulton Chain of Lakes provided Native Americans with a highway to the interior of the Adirondacks. Today, the lakes are a destination in themselves: Summer cottages, hotels, and marinas line much of the shoreline of the Fulton Chain. The highway is now NY 28.

Eight lakes make up the Fulton Chain, and they range in size from tiny Fifth Lake in Inlet, a mere pond, to 2,137-acre Fourth Lake, one of the larger lakes in the Adirondacks. The chain stretches 20 miles, from Old Forge almost to Raquette Lake.

Geologists believe that all eight lakes were once joined, together with Lake Durant and Raquette, Utowana, Eagle, and Blue Mountain lakes, in a large glacial lake that drained into the Hudson River. Today, only Lake Durant lies in the Hudson watershed. The Fulton Chain drains into the Black River via the Middle Branch of the Moose River. The other lakes feed the Raquette River.

[*Above:* The South Branch of the Moose River]

The Fulton Chain lakes sit in a series of depressions at the base of a gneiss scarp. The scarp's cliffs on Bald Mountain and elsewhere offer hikers gorgeous views of the lakes and provide a habitat for ravens (*Corvus corax*). The various types of gneiss that make up the scarp can be seen in road cuts along NY 28.

North of the scarp, the terrain is gentler, characterized by rolling hills, wetlands, streams, and ponds. This territory, too, is part of the Fulton Chain of Lakes Region as defined in this chapter. In addition, the region encompasses some large bodies of water outside the chain, such as the Stillwater Reservoir, Raquette Lake, and Big Moose Lake.

The region is bounded by NY 28 and the Fulton Chain to the south, NY 30 to the east, the Stillwater Reservoir and private lands to the north, and the Adirondack Park border to the west. It thus includes the Ha-de-ron-dah Wilderness, Pigeon Lake Wilderness, Fulton Chain Wild Forest, Sargent Ponds Wild Forest, and Independence River Wild Forest.

The woods do not differ much from those found elsewhere in the Adirondacks, but visitors can find a change of scenery in the sand plains of the Independence River Wild Forest or at Ferd's Bog in the Pigeon Lake Wilderness. The latter is a habitat for a variety of boreal birds relatively uncommon in the Adirondacks.

Several major rivers course through the region, including the Independence, Beaver, and the North Branch of the Moose. The Raquette River begins here but is discussed in the chapter on the Northwest Lakes Region.

The state operates seven campgrounds in the region. In addition, a number of primitive campsites are available for free at Stillwater Reservoir. Two other state campgrounds lie just south of the region.

In winter, the Fulton Chain of Lakes Region, especially the Old Forge area, turns into a mecca for snowmobilers. The region has hundreds of miles of groomed snowmobile trails. They get plenty of use even though Old Forge is one of the coldest spots in the state, with temperatures sometimes sinking to 50 degrees Fahrenheit below zero.

For more information: For questions about Herkimer and Lewis counties, State Department of Environmental Conservation, 225 N. Main Street, Herkimer, NY 13350. Phone (315) 866-6330. For questions about Hamilton County: State Department of Environmental Conservation, 701 S. Main Street, Northville, NY 12134. Phone (518) 863-4545. Several DEC leaflets pertain to the region: *Trails in the Old Forge-Brantingham Lake Region, Otter Creek Horse Trails, Stillwater Reservoir, Adirondack Canoe Routes*, and *Trails in the Blue Mountain Lake Region*.

Ha-de-ron-dah Wilderness

The Ha-de-ron-dah Wilderness encompasses about 26,600 acres west of Old Forge and north of NY 28. The name comes from the same Iroquois word that spawned *Adirondack*—thought to mean "eater of bark," an insult applied to the

Algonquins. *Ha-de-ron-dah* comes closer to the original guttural pronunciation.

Ha-de-ron-dah is a land of rolling hills: The highest mountain reaches only 2,360 feet in elevation. Loggers and fire claimed most of the primeval forest, but a few big white pines (*Pinus strobus*) survive around Big Otter Lake on the region's northern border.

Trails lead to a number of ponds and lakes. Loop hikes of various lengths are possible. The most popular destinations are Big Otter Lake and the lean-tos on Middle Settlement and Middle Branch lakes. Elsewhere, hikers can expect to find solitude, especially on footpaths north of the Big Otter Trail. These trails are lightly maintained and little traveled. The northernmost sector of the wilderness remains trailless.

For more information: State Department of Environmental Conservation, 225 N. Main Street, Herkimer, NY 13350. Phone (315) 866-6330. Ask for the leaflet *Trails in the Old Forge-Brantingham Lake Region.*

🌿 MIDDLE SETTLEMENT LAKE LOOP

[Fig. 42(5)] Day-trippers can experience the Ha-de-ron-dah Wilderness by walking a 7.9-mile loop that passes Middle Settlement Lake. The hike is short enough to allow time for a picnic and swim at the lake's lean-to, beautifully situated on the northwestern shore.

The route passes through hardwood or mixed forests adorned by several types of wildflowers, such as Indian pipe (*Monotropa uniflora*), red trillium (*Trillium erectum*), clintonia (*Clintonia borealis*), and goldthread (*Coptis groenlandica*). Near Middle Settlement Lake, hikers will see immense boulders broken off from a nearby cliff. The state stocks the 39-acre lake with brook trout (*Salvelinus fontinalis*).

Those who camp at the lake might want to spend a day exploring the interior of the Ha-de-ron-dah Wilderness on a 12-mile loop that passes, in this order, Middle Branch Lake, Big Otter Lake, East Pine Pond, Pine Lake, and Lost Lake before returning to Middle Settlement. There also are lean-tos at Middle Branch and Pine lakes.

The Middle Settlement Lake Loop makes use of several trails. From NY 28, take the red-blazed access trail 0.6 mile; turn left and follow the yellow-blazed trail 1.1 miles; turn right and follow the blue-blazed trail 1.2 miles; turn left and follow the yellow-blazed trail 0.5 mile to the lean-to. After returning to the last junction, follow the yellow-blazed trail another 1 mile; turn right and follow the yellow-blazed trail 2.2 miles back to the red-blazed access trail; and turn left to return to NY 28. The junctions are marked by signs.

Directions: From the tourist information center in Old Forge, drive 5 miles south on NY 28 to a rest area on the left. Park in the rest area and cross the highway to reach the trailhead. It is marked by a small sign opposite the eastern end of the rest area. If coming from the south, the rest area will be on the right about 14.2 miles past the blinking light in Woodgate.

Trail: 3.4 miles to lean-to, 7.9 miles for loop.

Degree of difficulty: Moderate.

Surface and blaze: Natural forest floor. Red, yellow, and blue blazes.

Fulton Chain of Lakes

The Fulton Chain, once used by Adirondack guides and Native Americans, remains a popular canoe route.

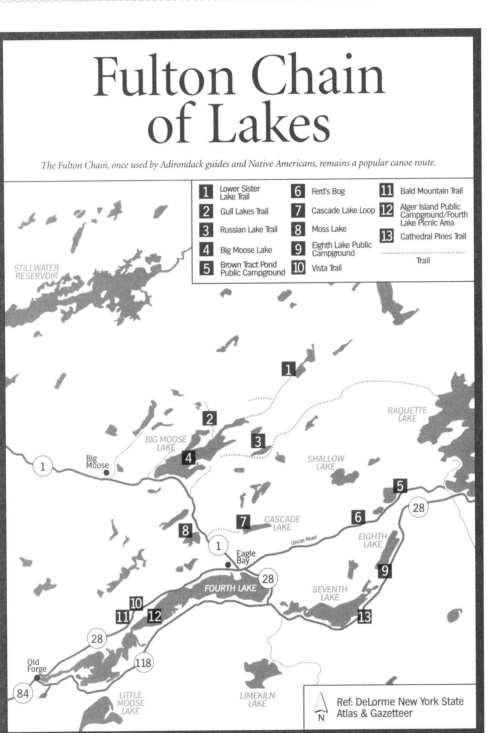

1 Lower Sister Lake Trail	**6** Ferd's Bog	**11** Bald Mountain Trail
2 Gull Lakes Trail	**7** Cascade Lake Loop	**12** Alger Island Public Campground/Fourth Lake Picnic Area
3 Russian Lake Trail	**8** Moss Lake	**13** Cathedral Pines Trail
4 Big Moose Lake	**9** Eighth Lake Public Campground	
5 Brown Tract Pond Public Campground	**10** Vista Trail	·········· Trail

Ref: DeLorme New York State Atlas & Gazetteer

Fulton Chain of Lakes

The steamboat inventor Robert Fulton—after whom the chain is named—dreamed of a canal that would connect all eight lakes. Although the canal was not built, it's still possible to canoe from First Lake in Old Forge to Fifth Lake without a portage. From Fifth Lake, paddlers must carry their canoes 0.5 mile, across NY 28, to Sixth Lake, which is joined to Seventh Lake. At the end of Seventh Lake, there is a 1-mile portage to Eighth Lake.

From Eighth Lake, canoeists can portage to Browns Tract Inlet and then paddle to Raquette Lake (*see* page 263). From Raquette Lake, they can continue east to Blue Mountain Lake via the Marion River or head north to the Raquette River. Once on the Raquette River, long-distance canoeists can extend their trip by several possible routes. Following one historic route, canoeists can go from the Raquette to the Saranac Lakes and end at the village of Saranac Lake.

Canoeists should not expect quiet and solitude on the Fulton Chain. They will share the water with motorboats, jet-skis, and sailboats. On the bigger lakes, winds can whip up whitecaps. Nevertheless, the Fulton Chain remains a popular canoe route—a route used by early Adirondack guides and, even earlier, by Native Americans. The state Department of Environmental Conservation suggests an itinerary in its leaflet *Adirondack Canoe Routes*.

The state runs two campgrounds on the Fulton Chain, one on Alger Island at Fourth Lake and another on the southern end of Eighth Lake. In addition, free campsites and lean-tos exist along the shores and on two islands. DeCamp Island, located between First and Second lakes, has four primitive campsites. Eighth Lake's island has a lean-to. There is a state picnic area on the southern shore of Fourth Lake.

There are state boat launches on Fourth, Seventh, and Eighth lakes. Canoes also can be put in First Lake at Old Forge and Fifth and Sixth lakes at Inlet. Old Forge and Inlet have town beaches.

The Fulton Chain, especially Fourth Lake, is popular among sport fishermen. The state stocks First Lake with tiger muskellunge (*Esox masquinongy*); Third Lake with lake trout (*Salvelinus namaycush*) and rainbow trout (*Oncorhynchus mykiss*); Fourth, Seventh, and Eighth lakes with lake trout, rainbow trout, and Atlantic salmon (*Salmo salar*); and Fifth and Sixth lakes with rainbow trout. Other species can be caught as well.

Big-game hunting is prohibited along the Fulton Chain between NY 28 and South Shore Road from Old Forge to Inlet.

For more information: State Department of Environmental Conservation, 225 N. Main Street, Herkimer, NY 13350. Phone (315) 866-6330. Ask for the leaflet *Adirondack Canoe Routes*. Adirondack Maps Inc. publishes a color map that shows all the canoe carries, boat launches, campsites, and lean-tos along the Fulton Chain and other lakes. Phone (518) 576-9861 or write Adirondack Maps Inc., PO Box 718, Market Street, Keene Valley, NY 12943.

▨ ALGER ISLAND PUBLIC CAMPGROUND/FOURTH LAKE PICNIC AREA

[Fig. 37(12)] The state maintains lean-tos and tent sites on 40-acre Alger Island at the foot of Fourth Lake. A hiking trail follows the perimeter of the island. There is a picnic area on the island's eastern tip. Visitors to the island should register at the Fourth Lake Picnic Area on the adjacent southern shore of the lake. Canoes and car-top boats can be launched from this site.

Directions: From NY 28 in Inlet, drive west on South Shore Road to Petrie Road; turn right and go 1 mile to the Fourth Lake Picnic Area. From NY 28 in Old Forge, turn south onto Gilbert Street; go two blocks to Park Avenue; turn left and go a few blocks to South Shore Road; turn right and drive to Petrie Road; turn left to reach the picnic area.

Activities: Camping, picnicking, boating, hiking, fishing.

Facilities: 15 lean-tos, 2 tent sites, picnic area, hiking trail.

Dates: Open mid-May through Labor Day.

Fees: There is a charge for camping or day use.

Closest town: Old Forge.

For more information: Campground office, phone (315) 369-3224. For reservations, phone (800) 456-2267.

▨ EIGHTH LAKE PUBLIC CAMPGROUND

[Fig. 37(13)] Eighth Lake is the last link in the Fulton Chain of Lakes and the most pristine. The Eighth Lake Public Campround gives access to both Eighth and Seventh lakes. Canoeists paddling the Fulton Chain often stay in lean-tos on the northern shore of both lakes. A hiking trail goes to Eagle's Nest Lake and Bug Lake, two smaller trout waters.

Directions: From Inlet, drive north about 6 miles on NY 28 to the campground entrance on the left. From Raquette Lake, drive about 5 miles south on NY 28 to the entrance on the right.

Activities: Camping, picnicking, swimming, boating, canoeing, fishing, hiking.

Facilities: 126 tent and trailer sites, picnic area, sand beach, bathhouse, showers, toilets, trailer dump station.

Dates: Open mid-Apr. through mid-Nov.

Fees: There is a charge for camping or day use.

Closest town: Raquette Lake is about 5 miles away.

For more information: Campground office, phone (315) 354-4120. For reservations, phone (800) 456-2267.

Fulton Chain Wild Forest

The Fulton Chain Wild Forest covers about 14,775 acres in the vicinity of Old Forge and Eagle Bay. The state land is divided into four chunks divided by narrow strips of private land. The two most popular attractions—Bald Mountain and Moss Lake—both lie within a tract just north of NY 28.

The highest mountains in the region reach about 2,500 feet. Overall, the landscape is characterized by rolling hills, wetlands, and beaver meadows. Trails lead to three summits and a number of ponds.

For more information: State Department of Environmental Conservation, 225 N. Main Street, Herkimer, NY 13350. Phone (315) 866-6330.

NORTHERN PARULA

(Parula americana) Parula means "little titmouse," which refers to the bird's active foraging through foliage for insects.

BALD (RONDAXE) MOUNTAIN TRAIL

[Fig. 40(11)] The trail to the Bald Mountain fire tower crosses over a ridge of open bedrock with gorgeous vistas of Fourth Lake and surrounding mountains. It is one of the most popular hikes in the Adirondacks: About 10,000 people climb the mountain each year.

The trail begins with a steep ascent through a hardwood forest, but once the ridge is reached, the rest of the way is easy walking. Hikers can relax and enjoy the breathtaking views. Red spruce (*Picea rubens*), balsam fir (*Abies balsamea*), white pine (*Pinus strobus*), and mountain ash (*Sorbus* americana) grow on the summit. Ravens (*Corvus corax*) nest on Bald Mountain's cliffs.

The tower steps can be climbed for a 360-degree panorama, though excellent views can be had without climbing the tower. Bald Mountain—also known as Rondaxe Mountain—is an especially popular hike in the fall after the leaves change color.

Directions: From the junction of Big Moose Road and NY 28 in Eagle Bay, drive 4.6 miles west on NY 28 to Rondaxe Road; turn right and go 0.2 mile to the parking lot on the left. The trail begins at the parking lot. If coming from the west, Rondaxe Road is 4.5 miles east of the tourist information center in Old Forge.

Trail: 1 mile.

Elevation: 1,940 feet to 2,350 feet.

Degree of difficulty: Moderate.

Surface and blaze: Natural forest floor, bedrock. Red blazes.

VISTA TRAIL

[Fig. 40(10)] The Vista Trail begins across the road from the Bald Mountain trailhead (*see* above). Like the Bald Mountain Trail, the Vista Trail follows a ridge with views of Fourth Lake and the surrounding countryside, but those who expect continuous vistas will be disappointed. The vistas are few and far between, and most are not as good as those from the Bald Mountain Trail. The Vista Trail, however, passes a greater variety of terrain and offers hikers a greater chance of finding solitude.

The 4.6-mile end-to-end trip has several ups and downs. Shorter hikes utilizing the Vista Trail—to the summit of Cork Mountain, to Mountain Pond, or to Becker's Outlook—are possible.

The blue-blazed trail starts off in a hardwood forest and soon reaches a side trail on the left that leads 0.1 mile to the boggy shore of Fly Pond. About 0.2 mile beyond the junction, the main trail reaches the hemlock-lined shore of Cary Lake. After skirting the pond, the trail comes out on a dirt road that once served as the bed of the Raquette Lake Railroad.

Turn right and walk 200 yards down the road. After passing a wetland, turn left to re-enter the woods. From the road, the trail ascends the shoulder of Cork Mountain, reaching a junction after another 0.5 mile. A red-marked trail on the left leads about 0.1 mile to Cork's summit and a lookout with a view to the northeast.

Beyond the junction, the blue trail descends to Mountain Pond. Those who want to swim can enter the water from an outcrop of bedrock with red spruce growing atop it. Acid rain has killed many fish in the pond. After passing the outcrop, the trail turns right away from the pond and soon reaches another junction. A red-blazed trail leads straight ahead to a trailhead about 0.1 mile away. Turn left to continue on the Vista Trail.

The trail next ascends Onondaga Mountain and follows the ups and downs of a ridge for about 2.5 miles. For most of the way, hikers walk through a hardwood forest, often with ferns in the understory. Far below, Fourth Lake can be glimpsed through the trees, but there are only a few good views of the water. The traffic on NY 28 and the lake can be heard.

Toward the eastern end of the ridge, a sign points left to a short side trail to Becker's Outlook, a rocky ledge with a great lookout to the north. Bubb and Moss lakes lie nestled among wooded hills, while rows of mountains march to the horizon. This is the best view on the trail.

The Vista Trail next descends to a junction with the yellow-blazed Bubb Lake Trail. Turn right to walk 0.2 mile to NY 28. Turn left to walk 0.3 mile to Bubb Lake.

The route described assumes hikers park cars at the western trailhead on Rondaxe Road and the eastern trailhead on NY 28. Shorter hikes are possible using just one car. From the eastern trailhead, it's about 0.7 mile to Becker's Outlook. From the Mountain Pond trailhead, located between the other two trailheads, it's about 0.2 mile to Mountain Pond and 0.6 mile to the lookout on Cork Mountain. From the western trailhead, it's about 1.4 miles to the Cork lookout.

Directions: Western trailhead: From the junction of Big Moose Road and NY 28 in Eagle Bay, drive 4.6 miles west on NY 28 to Rondaxe Road; turn right and go 0.2 mile to the parking lot on the left. The trail begins across Rondaxe Road from the parking lot. If coming from the west, the trailhead is about 4.5 miles east of the tourist information center in Old Forge. Mountain Pond trailhead: From the junction of Big Moose Road and NY 28 in Eagle Bay, drive 3.5 miles west on NY 28; turn right onto an unmarked dirt road, turn left at once, and go about 0.2 mile to the trailhead on the right. If coming from the west, the dirt road is 5.6 miles east of the tourist information center in Old Forge. There is no sign at the trailhead. Look for red trail markers. Eastern trailhead: From the junction of Big Moose Road and NY 28 in Eagle Bay, drive 1.5 miles west on NY 28 to the Bubb Lake trailhead on the right. Park on the shoulder of the road. If coming from the west, this trailhead is 7.6 miles east of the tourist information center in Old Forge.

Trail: 4.6 miles from Rondaxe Road to NY 28.

Elevation: 1,940 feet to 2,340 feet at highest point of Onondaga Mountain. Cork Mountain's summit is 2,280 feet.

Degree of difficulty: Moderate.

Surface and blaze: Natural forest floor. Blue and yellow blazes.

MOSS LAKE

[Fig. 40(8)] A prestigious camp for girls once stood on the grounds around Moss Lake. The state acquired the property in 1973, but a year later a band of Mohawks claiming ancestral land rights moved in and set up the Ganienkeh Indian Territory. The occupation ended in 1978 after the state gave the Mohawks some land in Clinton County. Thereafter, the state demolished all the buildings of the former girls camp.

Since then the state has turned Moss Lake into a year-round attraction. The old bridle trail that circles the 96-acre lake is used for hiking, mountain biking, horseback riding, and Nordic skiing. Canoeists can reach the lake by a short carry from the parking lot to a sand beach. The beach is an excellent swimming spot.

Moss Lake has seven primitive campsites along its shores, each with a privy and fireplace. Three are reachable only by water. The others can be reached by the circuit trail. All are shown on a large color map at the register. The campsites are available for free. No camping is allowed on the lake's island.

Common loons (*Gavia immer*) build nests on the water at Moss Lake. Osprey (*Pandion haliaetus*) have nested on the island. The lake has a self-sustaining population of brook trout (*Salvelinus fontinalis*). Brown bullhead (*Ictalurus nebulosus*) also can be caught.

The yellow-blazed trail makes a 2.5-mile circuit on mostly level terrain. If hikers go clockwise around the lake, they will pass the Bubb Lake Trail on the left after 0.7 mile. From the junction, it's about 0.6 mile to Bubb Lake.

Directions: From NY 28 in Eagle Bay, drive north 2.3 miles on Big Moose Road to the parking lot on the left.

Activities: Camping, swimming, canoeing, fishing, hiking, horseback riding, cross-country skiing.

Facilities: 7 primitive campsites, privies, sand beach, hiking/riding trail.

Dates: Open year-round.

Fees: None.

Closest town: Eagle Bay is 2.3 miles away.

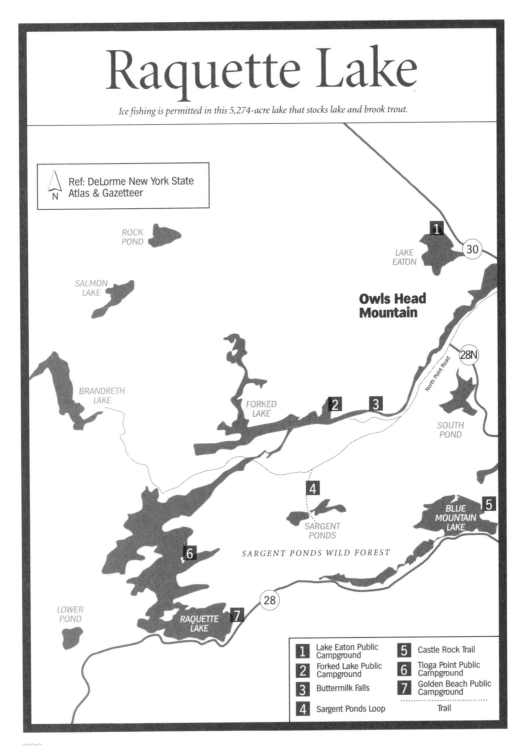

Raquette Lake

Ice fishing is permitted in this 5,274-acre lake that stocks lake and brook trout.

Ref: DeLorme New York State
Atlas & Gazetteer

N

ROCK
POND

SALMON
LAKE

LAKE
EATON

**Owls Head
Mountain**

30

28N

North Point Road

BRANDRETH
LAKE

FORKED
LAKE

SOUTH
POND

SARGENT
PONDS

BLUE
MOUNTAIN
LAKE

SARGENT PONDS WILD FOREST

LOWER
POND

RAQUETTE
LAKE

28

1	Lake Eaton Public Campground	5	Castle Rock Trail
2	Forked Lake Public Campground	6	Tioga Point Public Campground
3	Buttermilk Falls	7	Golden Beach Public Campground
4	Sargent Ponds Loop		Trail

For more information: State Department of Environmental Conservation, 225 N. Main Street, Herkimer, NY. Phone (315) 866-6330.

Cathedral Pines Trail

[Fig. 40(13)] One of the easiest trails in the Adirondacks passes through a small stand of giant white pine (*Pinus strobus*) growing just off the highway between Inlet and Raquette Lake. The largest pines, which are more than 200 years old, soar 100 feet into the air and have diameters of up to 4 feet. The short trail makes a loop through the pines and passes by a memorial for a young airman killed in World War II. A sign marks the trailhead, but the trail itself lacks blazes, except for a few blue paint daubs. Bear right at the start of the trail. It soon reaches a junction, where a short spur goes to the right to an especially large pine. The main trail turns left at this junction.

Directions: The Cathedral Pines are located on the northern side of NY 28 between Inlet and Raquette Lake. If coming from Inlet, they are 1 mile past the state boat launch on Seventh Lake. If coming from Raquette Lake, they are 1 mile past the entrance to the Eighth Lake Public Campground. Park in a pull-off on the south side of the highway, directly across from the trail.

Trail: 0.1-mile loop.

Degree of difficulty: Easy.

Surface and blaze: Natural forest floor. No blazes.

Raquette Lake

[Fig. 41] Several theories about Raquette Lake's name exist, but the most popular one is that it comes from the French word for snowshoe. The story goes that a band of Tories fleeing to Canada during the Revolution left a heap of snowshoes on the shore when they were no longer needed.

At 5,274 acres, Raquette Lake is the sixth largest lake wholly within the Adirondack Park. Two state campgrounds, one reachable by boat, border its shores. In addition, several public lean-tos, available on a first-come basis, can be found on Big Island, Outlet Bay, and Beaver Bay. Primitive campsites exist on Outlet Bay and Sucker Brook Bay.

Because of the lake's size, the surface can become choppy on windy days. To get away from open water, paddlers can explore the marshy waters of South Inlet, located south of NY 28, or the sluggish Marion River, which enters the lake from the east. For a longer trip, portage from the Marion River to Utowana Lake and then canoe all the way to Blue Mountain Lake, a 13.5-mile journey.

The state stocks Raquette Lake with lake trout (*Salvelinus namaycush*) and brook trout (*Salvelinus fontinalis*). Others species that can be caught include smallmouth bass (*Micropterus dolomieui*). Ice fishing is permitted.

Boats can be launched at the village of Raquette Lake or Golden Beach Public Campground. Canoes also can be launched directly into South Inlet from NY 28.

For more information: State Department of Environmental Conservation, 701 S. Main Street, Northville, NY 12134. Phone (518) 863-4545.

GOLDEN BEACH AND TIOGA POINT PUBLIC CAMPGROUNDS

[Fig. 41(7), Fig. 41(6)] Golden Beach Public Campground is a conventional state campground on the southeastern shore of Raquette Lake and is easily accessible from NY 28. Tioga Point Public Campground, on the eastern side of the lake, can be reached only by boat or hiking trail. Canoeists often stay at Tioga Point's 15 lean-tos and 10 primitive campsites. The sites have picnic tables and fireplaces but no other amenities. There is a caretaker at Tioga Point during the camping season.

The information below is for the Golden Beach campground. Those staying at Tioga Point can use the same phone numbers.

Directions: From the junction of NY 28 and NY 30 in Blue Mountain Lake, drive about 9.9 miles south on NY 28 to the campground entrance on the right. From Raquette Lake village, drive 4 miles north on NY 28 to the entrance on the left.

Activities: Camping, picnicking, swimming, boating, canoeing, fishing, hiking.

Facilities: 205 tent and trailer sites, picnic area, sand beach, bathhouse, toilets, showers, trailer dump station. The facilities are accessible to the handicapped.

Dates: Open mid-May through Labor Day.

Fees: There is a charge for camping or day use.

Closest town: Raquette Lake.

For more information: Campground office, phone (315) 354-4230. For reservations, phone (800) 456-2267.

Sargent Ponds Wild Forest

The Sargent Ponds Wild Forest lies east of Raquette Lake and is a land of ponds, conifer swamps, and low mountains. The region can be explored on numerous hiking trails. Although most lead to water, two end at the summits of Castle Rock and Owls Head Mountain. Canoeists pass through the wild forest on the way from Raquette Lake to Long Lake or from Raquette Lake to Blue Mountain Lake.

The state operates campgrounds adjacent to the wild forest at Raquette Lake, Forked Lake, and Lake Eaton.

For more information: State Department of Environmental Conservation, 701 S. Main Street, Northville, NY 12134. Phone (518) 863-4545. Ask for the leaflet *Trails in the Blue Mountain Lake Region*.

FORKED LAKE PUBLIC CAMPGROUND

[Fig. 41(2)] The state's campground on the eastern shore of Forked Lake appeals to those who like to rough it a bit. There are few amenities, and most of the campsites can be reached only by water or by a hiking trail.

Canoeists can put in at the campground or at a public launch on the lake's southern shore. The latter launch is recommended for those who intend to paddle up the marshy Brandreth Lake Outlet at the western end of Forked Lake. The outlet can be canoed for about 2 miles. Paddlers can expect to see common mergansers (*Mergus merganser*) and common loons (*Gavia immer*), among other birds, at Forked Lake.

The state stocks Forked Lake with Atlantic salmon (*Salmo salar*). Other species that can be caught include brook trout (*Salvelinus fontinalis*), smallmouth bass (*Micropterus dolomieui*), and largemouth bass (*Micropterus salmoides*). Ice fishing is permitted.

Directions: From the junction of NY 28 and NY 30 in Blue Mountain Lake, drive north 7.9 miles on NY 30 to North Point Road; turn left and go 3.1 miles to County 3; turn right and go about 2 miles to the campground. If coming from the north, North Point Road is 3.3 miles south of the junction of NY 30 and NY 28N in Long Lake. To reach the launch on the southern shore, continue on North Point Road about 5.5 miles past County 3 to a gravel road; turn right and go 0.3 mile to the launch.

Activities: Camping, fishing, canoeing.

Facilities: 80 primitive campsites, picnic area, pit toilets, boat launch. Canoe and boat rentals.

Dates: Open mid-May through Labor Day.

Fees: There is a charge for camping or day use.

Closest town: Long Lake is about 8.4 miles away.

For more information: Campground office, phone (518) 624-6646. For reservations, phone (800) 456-2267.

CASTLE ROCK TRAIL

[Fig. 41(5)] This is a popular hike for families staying at Blue Mountain Lake. No doubt some children will be excited by the name Castle Rock, which conjures up images of a medieval fortress. Parents

GREAT BLUE HERON
(Ardea herodias)
Often spotted standing or stalking in water, this heron catches fish by using its bill, like scissors. It grows to 4 feet tall and has a wingspan of 6 feet.

ought not to oversell the castle name, however, lest the young ones be disappointed. The real reason for visiting Castle Rock is the wonderful view of Blue Mountain Lake.

The red-blazed trail starts up a private gravel-and-dirt road. At 0.2 mile, the trail leaves the road to follow a stream and soon turns right again to go around Chub Pond. It crosses several streams and muddy sections en route to a marked junction at 1.5 miles. Turn left, following yellow blazes, to go to Castle Rock. The way straight goes to the eastern end of Upper Sargent Pond.

The final scramble up Castle Rock is quite steep. At the summit, several precipitous ledges, separated by rock crevices, offer a variety of views. The ledge with the best view looks out over the lake and east toward Blue Mountain.

Several wildflowers grow along the trail, including Indian pipe (*Monotropa uniflora*), red trillium (*Trillium erectum*), bunchberry (*Cornus canadensis*), wood sorrel (*Oxalis montana*), and spotted touch-me-not (*Impatiens capensis*).

Directions: From the junction of NY 28 and NY 30 in Blue Mountain Lake, drive north on NY 30 for 0.6 mile to Maple Lodge Road; turn left and travel 1.2 miles to the trailhead. There is a pull-off on the left side of the road just before the trailhead.

Trail: 2 miles to summit.

Elevation: 1,840 feet to 2,480 feet.

Degree of difficulty: Moderate.

Surface and blaze: Dirt road, natural forest floor. Red and yellow blazes.

BUTTERMILK FALLS

[Fig. 41(3)] At Buttermilk Falls, the Raquette River spills 40 feet over a series of rock terraces on its way to Long Lake. The scenic falls, just a short walk from the road, is often visited by anglers, picnickers, and sunbathers. The pool beneath the falls is deep enough for swimming, but beware that the current swirls in an eddy and can be strong. Camping is prohibited here.

Directions: From the junction of NY 28 and NY 30 in Blue Mountain Lake, drive north 7.9 miles on NY 30 to North Point Road; turn left and go 2.2 miles to a pull-off on the right. If coming from the north, North Point Road is 3.3 miles south of the junction of NY 30 and NY 28N in Long Lake.

Trail: 0.1 mile.

Degree of difficulty: Easy.

Surface and blaze: Natural forest floor. No blazes.

SARGENT PONDS LOOP

[Fig. 41(4)] Hikers with two cars can visit the scenic Upper and Lower Sargent ponds in a loop with nearly all downhill grades. The ponds make a nice destination for a picnic or a swim. There is a lean-to on Lower Sargent Pond. The loop also makes a good mountain bike route.

Starting at the Upper Sargent Pond trailhead, follow a red-blazed trail through a hardwood forest about 1.2 miles to a marked junction. Just before the junction, there is a rather steep descent. At the junction, go straight about 0.1 mile to a campsite amid tall pines and hemlocks on the northern shore of Upper Sargent Pond.

Return to the junction and turn left, heading west. In many places, the forest is quite airy and ferns cover the ground. Another marked junction is reached at 2.7 miles. You will return to this junction after visiting Lower Sargent Pond. For now, bear left and go 0.1 mile to another junction. Turn left to go to Lower Sargent. The way straight leads to Tioga Point on Raquette Lake (*see* page 263).

Soon after the turn, hikers reach a fork. Bear left to go 0.4 mile to the lean-to on the northern shore of Lower Sargent. Bear right to reach the western shore after just 100 yards. The shallow water and sandy bottom make this spot ideal for wading—especially for young children.

Return to the junction on the Upper Sargent Pond Trail. Turn left and walk about 2 miles to the other trailhead on North Point Road. The trail splits near Grassy Pond, but the two branches soon rejoin.

Directions: From the junction of NY 28 and NY 30 in Blue Mountain Lake, drive north 7.9 miles on NY 30 to North Point Road; turn left and go 6.6 miles to the Upper Sargent Pond trailhead or 8.3 miles to the Lower Sargent Pond trailhead. If coming from the north, North Point Road is 3.3 miles south of the junction of NY 30 and NY 28N in Long Lake.

Trail: 5.2-mile loop with two cars. Add 1.6 miles if walking back along road to first trailhead.

Elevation: 1,900 feet at upper trailhead; 1,824 at Upper Sargent Pond; 1,797 at Lower Sargent Pond; and 1,800 feet at lower trailhead.

Degree of difficulty: Easy.

Surface and blaze: Natural forest floor. Red and yellow blazes.

LAKE EATON PUBLIC CAMPGROUND

[Fig. 41(1)] This state campground on the northern shore of Lake Eaton offers opportunities for fishing, canoeing, boating, and hiking. One of the best hikes in the vicinity leads 3.1 miles to the 2,780-foot summit of Owls Head Mountain, with its scenic views of Raquette Lake, Forked Lake, and Blue Mountain. A short spur trail leads to a secluded shore on Lake Eaton.

The state stocks the 327-acre Lake Eaton with lake trout (*Salvelinus namaycush*), rainbow trout (*Oncorhynchus mykiss*), and Atlantic salmon (*Salmo salar*). Also in the lake are brook trout (*Salvelinus fontinalis*), smallmouth bass (*Micropterus dolomieui*), and brown bullhead (*Ictalurus nebulosus*). Ice fishing is permitted.

Directions: From the junction of NY 28N and NY 30 in Long Lake, drive 2.7 miles west on NY 30 to the campground entrance on the left. For the Owls Head Trail, turn left onto Endion Road from NY 30 about 1.3 miles before the campground entrance and go 2.7 miles to a lot on the right.

Activities: Camping, swimming, fishing, canoeing, hiking.

Facilities: 135 tent and trailer sites, picnic area, sand beach, bathhouse, toilets, showers, trailer dump station. Boat and canoe rentals. The campground is accessible to the handicapped.

Dates: Open mid-May through Labor Day.

Fees: There is a charge for camping or day use.

Closest town: Long Lake is about 1.5 miles east.

For more information: Campground office, phone (518) 624-2641. For reservations, phone (800) 456-2267.

Pigeon Lake Wilderness

The 50,100-acre Pigeon Lake Wilderness, a land of rolling hills and ponds, borders three major lakes: Stillwater Reservoir, Big Moose Lake, and Raquette Lake. The highest summit in the wilderness, West Mountain, rises to 2,902 feet.

The region was heavily logged in the past, but old specimens of white pine (*Pinus strobus*) can be found scattered about. As elsewhere in the Adirondacks, northern hardwood forests and spruce-fir forests—or a mixture of the two—cover most of the landscape. Ferd's Bog, near the southern border of the wilderness, provides a habitat for boreal species of birds, such as the gray jay (*Perisoreus canadensis*), spruce grouse (*Canachites canadensis*), and boreal chickadee (*Parus hudsonicus*).

Acid rain and fish competition have depleted the brook trout population in some lakes, including the remote Pigeon Lake, but brookies can still be caught in Queer, Cascade, and Shallow lakes. A small population of wild trout survives in Windfall Pond.

All told, the wilderness has about 32 miles of trails. Most are found in the southwestern sector. These intersect often, enabling visitors to devise loop hikes that pass a number of small lakes and ponds. The longest trail leads to the summit of West Mountain, which offers a view of Raquette Lake.

Four trails reachable only by water are described in the section on Big Moose Lake (*see* page 271). North of Big Moose Lake, the wilderness remains essentially trailless. There are four lean-tos on the Big Moose Lake trails. The only other lean-to in the region is at Queer Lake. There is one state campground on the wilderness border.

For more information: State Department of Environmental Conservation, 701 S. Main Street, Northville, NY 12134. Phone (518) 863-4545.

▨ BROWN TRACT POND PUBLIC CAMPGROUND

[Fig. 40(5)] This state campground on the eastern shores of Lower Brown Tract Pond on the edge of the Pigeon Lake Wilderness is noted for its quiet and privacy. No motorboats are allowed on the 146-acre pond. Loons (*Gavia immer*) often nest here. The pond's fish include brown bullhead (*Ictalurus nebulosus*), smallmouth bass (*Mi-*

cropterus dolomieui), and an occasional brook trout (*Salvelinus fontinalis*). Hiking trails from the campground lead to Shallow Lake and other places in the Pigeon Lake Wilderness.

Directions: From NY 28 near Raquette Lake, drive north 0.8 mile on County 2 through Raquette Lake village to Browns Tract Road; turn left and go 1.9 miles to the campground.

Activities: Camping, hiking, swimming, fishing, canoeing.

Facilities: 90 tent and trailer sites, picnic area, sand beach, bathhouse, toilets, trailer dump station.

Dates: Open mid-May through Labor Day.

Fees: There is a charge for camping or day use.

Closest town: Raquette Lake is about 1.9 miles east.

For more information: Campground office, phone (315) 354-4412. For reservations, phone (800) 456-2267.

AMERICAN
GOLDFINCH
(Carduelis tristis)
During breeding in late summer,
the male goldfinch is bright
yellow with a black forehead.

🔲 FERD'S BOG

[Fig. 40(6)] Over two summers in the early 1970s, Ferdinand LaFrance identified 69 species of birds in a 170-acre wetland complex now known as Ferd's Bog. Although the trailhead and trail remain unmarked, Ferd's Bog attracts bird watchers from throughout the Northeast.

Most of Ferd's Bog is actually a "poor fen," an acidic wetland dominated by sphagnum moss and sedges. The fen looks like a prairie, but those who walk on it discover that it is a moist mat. Bog plants and coniferous swamps border the fen. Eagle Creek runs through it.

Numerous birds found in boreal or bog habitats can be observed at Ferd's Bog. These species, relatively rare in the Adirondacks, include spruce grouse (*Canachites canadensis*), gray jay (*Perisoreus canadensis*), boreal chickadee (*Parus hudsonicus*), black-backed three-toed woodpecker (*Picoides arcticus*), yellow-bellied flycatcher (*Empidonax flaviventrus*), and rusty blackbird (*Euphagus carolinus*).

The trail, which is easily followed, descends through a hardwood forest to a spruce-fir forest in the moist lowland. At about 0.3 mile, the trail splits. Either way leads to the fen in about 100 yards. After leaving the forest, the paths pass through bog vegetation—such as northern pitcher plant (*Sarracenia purpurea*), Labrador tea (*Ledum groenlandicum*), and rose pogonia (*Pogonia ophioglossoides*)—before reaching the grassy fen. Several herd paths lead into the fen.

The State Department of Environmental Conservation is considering building a boardwalk in the fen to alleviate the trampling of plants.

Directions: From NY 28 in Eagle Bay, turn north on Uncas Road (about 0.3 mile east of Big Moose Road) and drive 3.6 miles to the unmarked trailhead on the left—about 0.5 mile past the trail for Bear Mountain. There is no sign, but there is room for two or three cars to park at the start of the trail. Look for a camp called Hitchy Pants with a red water pump on the lawn. The pull-off is just before the next camp.

Trail: 0.4 mile to edge of fen.

Elevation: About 1,855 feet to 1,780 feet.

Degree of difficulty: Easy.

Surface and blaze: Natural forest floor. No blazes.

CASCADE LAKE LOOP

[Fig. 40(7)] One of the most popular trails in the Pigeon Lake Wilderness follows an old dirt road that makes a circuit of 101-acre Cascade Lake, passing a sand beach as well as the waterfall responsible for the lake's name. The mostly level route is also marked as a Nordic ski trail. Horses are allowed on 1.6 miles of the trail.

From the parking lot, the trail climbs over a small hill to a register, turns left, and soon reaches a junction where the loop begins. Going straight is the quickest way to the cascade near the eastern end of the lake. This part of the trail affords only glimpses of the lake through the trees. Going left is the quickest way to the beach and campsites on the scenic northern shore. This section does offer views of the lake.

Hikers who turn left pass through a large meadow adorned with wildflowers and raspberries and then cross the lake's outlet, where there is a nice view of the hills to the west. At the next junction, marked by signs, turn right to follow the trail along the northern shore.

About halfway up the lake, the beach sits beside a grassy point guarded by large white pines (*Pinus strobus*). The clear water and sandy bottom make this an excellent place to swim. There are four primitive campsites nearby. A little past the beach, hikers may see the remnants of a girls camp.

Toward the eastern end of the lake, the trail gets wetter, but the state has built a detour around the worst of the muck. After crossing a wooden bridge over the lake's inlet, turn left down a side path to see the cascade. The water spills over a rock wall about 25 feet high. On the way back, the road stays far from the southern shore, so there are no views.

Directions: From NY 28 in Eagle Bay, drive north 1.4 miles on Big Moose Road to a parking lot on the right.

Trail: 5.4-mile loop.

Degree of difficulty: Easy.

Surface and blaze: Old road, natural forest floor. Red hiking and yellow ski blazes.

Big Moose Lake

[Fig. 40(4)] Private landowners hold title to most of the shoreline of Big Moose Lake, but the eastern shore falls within the Pigeon Lake Wilderness. Hiking trails lead to four destinations in the wilderness, each with a lean-to.

At 1,286 acres, Big Moose Lake is more suited to powerboats and jet-skis than to canoes, with one major exception: the Inlet, a marshy arm at the northeastern end of the lake. Here, a channel meanders through water lilies, pickerelweed, and rushes, creating a watery trail into a world inhabited by otter, beaver, muskrat, and mink. Ospreys nest nearby and sometimes can be seen gliding overhead.

The Big Moose Property Owners Association asks that no motors be used in the marsh, and most people honor the request. The Inlet makes a great canoe adventure, but there is one drawback: It's a 1.1-mile paddle from the state boat launch off Higby Road and a 3-mile paddle from Dunn's Marina on the western end of the lake. Crossing Big Moose Lake in a canoe when the water is rough can be risky.

Three trails—leading to Gull Lakes, Andy's Creek, and Lower Sister Lake—begin from the Inlet, so it's possible to combine an exploration of the marsh with a hike into the wilderness.

Those with motorboats might want to explore North Bay, a picturesque inlet with bays and islands on the north shore of the lake.

The state stocks Big Moose Lake with brook trout (*Salvelinus fontinalis*) and lake trout (*Salvelinus namaycush*).

Directions: For Higby Road boat launch: From NY 28 in Eagle Bay, drive 4.1 miles north on Big Moose Road to Higby Road; turn right and go 1.6 miles to the access road; turn right and go 0.1 mile to the parking lot. For Dunn's Marina: From NY 28 in Eagle Bay, drive 5.6 miles north on Big Moose Road to the marina on the right.

Activities: Boating, canoeing, hiking, fishing, camping.

Facilities: Boat launch, hiking trails, lean-tos, primitive campsites.

Dates: Seasonal.

Fees: The marina charges for use of its launch and for boat and canoe rentals.

Closest town: The hamlet of Big Moose is on the western end of the lake.

For more information: State Department of Environmental Conservation, 701 S. Main Street, Northville, NY 12134. Phone (518) 863-4545.

GULL LAKES TRAIL

[Fig. 40(2)] The lean-to on Upper Gull Lake undoubtedly would see more visitors if not for the inaccessibility of the trailhead, which is reachable only by water. For those with a canoe or small boat, this lean-to makes a wonderful destination for a day trip or camping trip.

Northern white cedar (*Thuja occidentalis*), hemlock (*Tsuga canadensis*), and red spruce (*Picea rubens*) grow near the landing off the Inlet on Big Moose Lake. The trail climbs gradually to Lower Gull Lake, whose shores were heavily damaged by a windstorm in 1995. After skirting the southern shore, the trail climbs again to Upper Gull. Unlike its counterpart, this lake's shoreline remains beautifully intact.

The lean-to sits amid conifers on the eastern shore of the 26-acre lake. Visitors can swim off a large rock on the water's edge. There may be a canoe with paddles at the lean-to. Neither lake holds fish.

Directions: See directions to Big Moose Lake, page 271. Enter the main channel of the Inlet, the marshy northeastern arm of the lake, and continue another 0.4 mile or so to a small dock and state sign on the left. The trailhead is about 1.5 miles from the Higby Road boat launch and 3.4 miles from Dunn's Marina.

Trail: 1.2 miles to lean-to.

Elevation: 1,825 feet to 1,961 feet.

Degree of difficulty: Easy.

Surface and blaze: Natural forest floor. Blue blazes.

LOWER SISTER LAKE TRAIL

[Fig. 40(1)] Those in search of solitude in a pristine setting likely will find it at Lower Sister Lake. The lean-to on the southeastern shore can be reached only after a long boat trip—usually by canoe, kayak, or rowboat—to the end of the Inlet on Big Moose Lake followed by a 3.3-mile hike.

A windstorm in 1995 downed trees in the area, so forest rangers had to cut a tunnel through the debris to clear the trail. Boreal birds including gray jay (*Perisoreous canadensis*) and boreal chickadee (*Parus hudsonicus*), dwell in these woods.

A channel connects Lower Sister Lake to Upper Sister Lake. Tall white pines (*Pinus strobus*) that survived the blowdown stand along both lakes. Pitcher plants, bog asters, and other bog plants can be found along the shorelines. Lower Sister

COYOTE
(*Canis latrans*)
Easily adapting to the presence of man, the coyote often preys on rodents, small animals, and livestock. It is a member of the dog family and has been known to mate with domestic dogs.

covers about 87 acres and Upper Sister about 77 acres.

Those looking for a shorter hike can visit instead the lean-to on Andy's Creek. At the trail register, turn left and follow the blue-blazed trail 0.3 mile.

Directions: See directions to Big Moose Lake, page 271. Enter the main channel of the Inlet, the marshy northeastern arm of the lake, and follow it 1.5 miles or so to the end, where there is a state sign and small landing. The trailhead is about 2.6 miles from the Higby Road boat launch and 4.5 miles from Dunn's Marina.

Trail: 3.3 miles to lean-to.

Elevation: 1,825 feet to 1,930 feet.

Degree of difficulty: Easy.

Surface and blaze: Natural forest floor. Yellow blazes.

RUSSIAN LAKE TRAIL

[Fig. 40(3)] The short hike to Russian Lake passes a variety of conifers: northern white cedar (*Thuja occidentalis*), hemlock (*Tsuga canadensis*), white pine (*Pinus strobus*), balsam fir (*Abies balsamea*), and red spruce (*Picea rubens*). A lean-to overlooks the 37-acre lake. Visitors can wade into the water on flat rocks in front of the lean-to. There is an island not too far from the shore. Few fish dwell in the acidic water.

Directions: See directions to Big Moose Lake, page 271. The trail begins at a state dock near the end of East Bay, on the northern shore. The dock is about 1.3 miles from the Higby Road boat launch and about 3.4 miles from Dunn's Marina.

Trail: 0.7 mile to lean-to.

Elevation: 1,825 feet to 1,855 feet.

Degree of difficulty: Easy.

Surface and blaze: Natural forest floor. Blue blazes.

Independence River Wild Forest

The Independence River Wild Forest lies in the western foothills of the Adirondacks in Lewis and Herkimer counties. The state acquired most of the 73,560 acres in the 1950s or later.

The wild forest has no big peaks to climb, but those looking for a different Adirondack experience will find it in the region's large sand plains. The sands, deposited by a glacial lake, were exposed after settlers abandoned farms and topsoil blew away. Visitors can spend hours exploring the trails that wend through this unusual landscape of spirea flats, scrub forest, and pine stands.

Small glacial ponds are sprinkled throughout the wild forest. The region's two big water bodies are Big Otter Lake and Francis Lake. Stillwater Reservoir lies on its northern border. The dark Independence River runs through the heart of the forest, carving out a scenic gorge at Gleasman Falls.

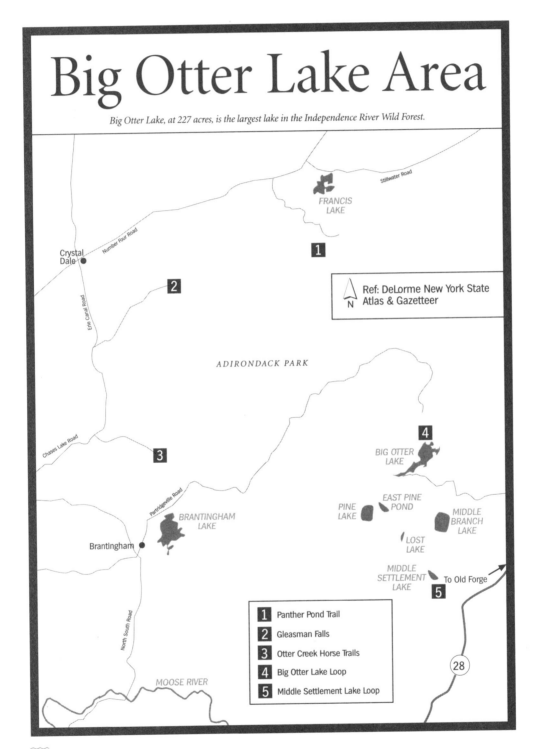

Big Otter Lake Area

Big Otter Lake, at 227 acres, is the largest lake in the Independence River Wild Forest.

Stillwater Road

FRANCIS
LAKE

1

Number Four Road

Crystal
Dale

2

Erie Canal Road

Ref: DeLorme New York State
Atlas & Gazetteer

ADIRONDACK PARK

4

BIG OTTER
LAKE

Chases Lake Road

3

EAST PINE
POND

PINE
LAKE

MIDDLE
BRANCH
LAKE

Partridgeville Road

BRANTINGHAM
LAKE

LOST
LAKE

Brantingham

MIDDLE
SETTLEMENT
LAKE

To Old Forge

5

North South Road

1 Panther Pond Trail

2 Gleasman Falls

3 Otter Creek Horse Trails

4 Big Otter Lake Loop

5 Middle Settlement Lake Loop

28

MOOSE RIVER

The most popular uses of the Independence River Wild Forest are hunting, fishing, and horseback riding. Hikers who do visit the region are likely to find peace and quiet—interrupted, perhaps, by the clatter of a deer in flight.

The region has no state campgrounds and only two lean-tos—at Panther Pond and Pine Lake. Many primitive campsites can be found along the trails, back roads, and shores of ponds.

For more information: State Department of Environmental Conservation, RD3, Box 22A, Route 812, Lowville, NY 13367. Phone (315) 376-3521.

BIG OTTER LAKE LOOP

[Fig. 42(4)] Big Otter Lake, at 227 acres, is the largest lake in the Independence River Wild Forest. The southern shore lies within the Ha-de-ron-dah Wilderness. A campsite on a grassy point on this shore offers a view of the lake and the hills to the east. The state stocks the lake with brook trout (*Salvelinus fontinalis*).

Big Otter can be visited on an 8-mile loop through the Independence Wild Forest that passes by Pine Lake and East Pine Pond on the northern border of the Ha-de-ron-dah Wilderness. It's also possible to reach Big Otter via trails from the Ha-de-ron-dah Wilderness. The 8-mile loop hike will be described here.

From the parking lot, follow an old road through a hardwood forest marked with yellow foot trail markers and orange snowmobile disks. At 0.9 mile, continue straight at a marked junction with the Pico Mountain snowmobile trail coming in from the right. The trail passes through a swampy section where blind gentian (*Gentiana clausa*) and cotton grass grow beside tamarack (*Larix laricina*) and black spruce (*Picea mariana*).

At 2.4 miles, the yellow trail ends at a junction near Pine Lake. Bear left, following red blazes, to go along the northern shore of the 60-acre lake. In another 0.2 mile, a spur trail on the left leads to a lean-to without any view of the lake. If you want to swim, walk a little beyond the spur to a campsite on the right. Here, a path leads to a sandy strand. There is another sandy strand a little farther down the main trail.

The red trail bears left at a junction with a blue-blazed trail at 2.8 miles and soon passes boggy East Pine Pond on the right. At 4.1 miles, it reaches another blue trail on the right. This leads along the southern shore of Big Otter Lake. To reach a campsite on this shore, walk about 0.5 mile on the blue trail to a grassy lane on the left. The turn is not marked.

Those who don't turn on the blue trail will reach the outlet at the western end of Big Otter Lake in about 0.1 mile. Pickerelweed (*Pontederia cordata*) abounds in the marshy waters here. The trail crosses a small rocky island where cardinal flower (*Lobelia cardinalis*), swamp candles (*Lysimachia terrestris*), and meadowsweet (*Spirea latifolia*) bloom.

Soon after crossing the outlet, the trail reaches a T-intersection with a dirt road. Turn left to return to the parking lot, a 3.8-mile hike. The road, marked with orange snowmobile disks, offers an occasional glimpse of Big Otter Creek. Although the road is open to vehicles, it is too rocky, rutted, and flooded even for most high-clearance autos.

Directions: From the light on NY 12 in Port Leyden, drive north 6.3 miles to Burdicks Crossing Road; turn right and go 2.5 miles to a T-intersection; turn left and go 0.8 mile to Brantingham Road; turn right and go 3.8 miles to a four corners; turn left on Partridgeville Road and go 1.7 miles to a fork; bear left and go about 6 miles to a parking lot on the right.

Trail: 8-mile loop.

Degree of difficulty: Moderate.

Surface and blaze: Old road, natural forest floor. Yellow, red, and orange blazes. The south shore trail, branching off the loop, has blue blazes.

OTTER CREEK HORSE TRAILS

[Fig. 42(3)] About 65 miles of horse trails—the largest equestrian network in the Adirondacks—crisscross the sandy plains found on the western edge of the Independence River Wild Forest. The state permits vehicles on many trails, making this unusual landscape very accessible. Hikers also can use the trails.

The state maintains a large equestrian assembly area off Chases Lake Road. The area features 100 roofed stalls, two stud stalls, three mounting platforms for the handicapped, a water system, toilets, picnic tables, and campsites. Most trails follow old sandy roads, often leading to ponds, lakes, or streams. The terrain varies from open meadow to scrub forest to pine stands.

Hikers can enter the network at any one of the many places where trails cross public roads, but perhaps the best entry point is at the Confusion Flats trailhead on Sand Pond Road. As the name suggests, Confusion Flats is something of a maze. The roads pass through open fields, scrub forests, and stands of red pine. One worthwhile destination is the beach on the southern shore of Little Otter Lake.

Several roads in Confusion Flats are open to vehicles, so visitors can drive into the middle of the spirea plains. From the trailhead, start down Confusion Flats Road. Signs indicate which of the side roads are open to autos. Beware that some roads have washed-out sections.

Animals that can be seen in the region include deer, bear, coyote, fox, snowshoe hare, wild turkey, and grouse. Brook trout (*Salvelinus fontinalis*) can be caught in Pitcher Pond, Payne Lake, Independence River, and several creeks. Little Otter Lake holds brown trout (*Salmo trutta*) and brown bullhead (*Ictalurus nebulosus*) as well as brook trout.

Directions: From Lyons Falls, drive north on NY 12 to Grieg Road in the hamlet of Glenfield; turn right and go about 1.9 miles to a T-intersection; turn left onto Pine Grove Road and go 1.2 miles to Chases Lake Road; turn right and go 3.4 miles to the assembly area on the right. To reach the Confusion Flats lot, drive 0.9 mile past the assembly area to Sand Pond Road; turn right and go 1 mile to the lot on the right.

Activities: Horseback riding, hiking, fishing, swimming, picnicking, camping.

Facilities: 100 roofed stalls, 2 stud stalls, 3 mounting platforms for the handi-capped, a water system, toilets, picnic tables, campsites, 65 miles of trails.

Dates: Open year-round.

Closest town: Port Lyons.

For more information: State Department of Conservation, RD 3, PO Box 22A, Lowville, NY 13367. Phone (315) 376-3521. Ask for the leaflet *Otter Creek Horse Trails*.

GLEASMAN FALLS

[Fig. 42(2)] At Gleasman Falls, the Independence River drops 60 feet in a series of falls and rushes beneath 75-foot cliffs. The pink, smooth rocks beside the dark, foaming water are a good spot for sunbathing and picnicking.

The trail to the falls starts downhill through a meadow filled with raspberries and wildflowers, such as blind gentian (*Gentiana clausa*), spotted touch-me-nots (*Impatiens capensis*), and tall meadow rue (*Thalictrum polygamum*), and then crosses Burnt Creek to enter a conifer forest.

Hikers soon come to a muddy stretch of trail that skirts a pond. The route passes through a scrubby forest of young hardwoods and then descends to a bridge over Second Creek, just upstream from its confluence with the Independence River. On the other side of the bridge, the trail climbs slightly through white pine (*Pinus strobus*) to reach the falls. Beyond the falls, the trail continues upriver for 4.2 miles, where it hooks up other trails.

Directions: From Lyons Falls, drive north on NY 12 to Grieg Road in the hamlet of Glenfield; turn right and go about 1.9 miles to a T-intersection; turn left onto Pine Grove Road and go 1.2 miles to Chases Lake Road; turn right and go 6.8 miles to McPhilmy Road; turn right and go 0.3 mile to Beech Mill Road; turn left and go 3 miles to the trailhead at the end.

Trail: 2.9 miles to falls.

Degree of difficulty: Easy.

Surface and blaze: Natural forest floor. Yellow blazes.

PANTHER POND TRAIL

[Fig. 42(1)] Panther Pond has one of the two lean-tos in the Independence River Wild Forest: it sits between two large white pines (*Pinus strobus*) on the northern shore, overlooking the water. The 13-acre pond is scenic, but its water is too acidic for fish. The shores are boggy.

At the outset, the trail crosses Pine Creek and comes to a register, where hikers should bear right. Soon after this, the trail reaches another fork. The two routes will rejoin, but bear left to stay on higher ground and avoid wet sections. Several large pines grow in the vicinity. The trail continues along the along the eastern shore and eventually, 4.8 miles from the start, reaches the Independence River.

Pileated Woodpecker

The pileated woodpecker (*Dryocopus pileated*) usually keeps out of sight, but hikers often come across evidence of its presence in deciduous and mixed woods: large, rectangular cavities dug out of trees. Other woodpeckers tapping away for insects create smaller, more circular holes. The pileated is the biggest woodpecker in the Adirondacks and is about the size of a crow. It is mostly black, with a conspicuous red crest and white stripes on the face and neck. The pileated woodpecker breeds throughout the eastern United States.

Directions: From Lowville, drive east on Number Four Road about 16 miles to Smith Road, located about 0.8 mile before the intersection at Stillwater Road; turn right and go 4 miles to the trailhead. Smith Road can be hard to spot. It's marked by a Department of Environmental Conservation sign.

Trail: 1.3 miles to lean-to.

Degree of difficulty: Easy.

Surface and blaze: Old road, natural forest floor. Yellow blazes.

FRANCIS LAKE

[Fig. 42] At 120 acres, Francis Lake is one of the largest lakes in the Independence River Wild Forest. The lake lies near the Stillwater Road, making it attractive to canoeists who don't like long carries. It's also a nice place for a swim or a picnic. Others may enjoy just strolling through the large pines (*Pinus strobus*) and hemlocks (*Tsuga canadensis*) along the shores.

The state owns most of the shore, but there are private parcels on the northern and eastern shores. From Stillwater Road, three unmarked trails lead to the lake. Hikers should take the westernmost trail. Starting at a vehicle barrier, the trail follows an old road, crosses the lake's outlet, and reaches a campsite on the shore after about 0.2 mile.

Canoeists can reach the lake by an even shorter route that begins about 0.3 mile to the east of the vehicle barrier. From here, a path leads 50 yards to a sandy strand on the shore. About 0.1 mile farther up the Stillwater Road, there is another vehicle barrier. An old road leads from here along the eastern shore. It offers good views of the lake, but the road soon reaches private land.

Directions: From Lowville, drive east on Number Four Road about 17 miles to Stillwater Road; turn right and go 0.6 mile to reach the hiking trail on the right.

Trail: 0.2 mile and 50 yards.

Degree of difficulty: Easy.

Surface and blaze: Old road, footpath. No blazes.

Beaver River Canoe Route

Niagara Mohawk Power Corporation has designated 12 miles of the dammed-up Beaver River as a canoe route that passes through six reservoirs. Motorboats also ply the larger waters. Canoeists who paddle the entire route will have four portages, totaling a little more than 1 mile. If breaking the trip into two days, they may camp on Soft Maple's southwestern shore, in a designated area near a sandy bay.

For more information: Niagara Mohawk Power Corporation, Hydro Generation and Engineering Services, 300 Erie Boulevard West, Syracuse, NY 13202. Phone (800) 642-4272. Ask for the leaflet *Beaver River Canoe Route.*

Stillwater Reservoir

[Fig. 40] The 6,195-acre Stillwater Reservoir—the fifth largest lake wholly within the Adirondack Park—borders the Independence Wild Forest, Pepperbox Wilderness, and Five Ponds Wilderness. The reservoir has become popular with motorboaters who enjoy staying at the primitive campsites along the shores and islands.

The state built the first dam on the Beaver River at Stillwater in 1887, isolating thousands of acres owned by William Seward Webb. After Webb sued, the state bought 47,326 acres of his unharvested timberland, the largest purchase of Forest Preserve. The hamlet of Beaver River, on the southern shore, remains isolated to this day, reachable only by water or foot trail.

The reservoir has been identified as one of the major nesting sites for the common loon (*Gavia immer*) in the Adirondacks. Occasionally, a bald eagle (*Haliaeetus leucocephalus*) has been spotted soaring overhead.

The state stocks the reservoir with splake, a hybrid of lake trout (*Salvelinus namaycush*) and brook trout (*Salvelinus fontinalis*). Other species that can be caught include bass, perch, and bullheads.

Stumps, rocks, and other obstacles limit the number of large motorboats in the reservoir. Thus, canoeists can explore many of the islands and inlets in relative quiet. For more privacy, canoeists can portage to Salmon Lake, Witchhopple Lake, or Clear Lake via a hiking trail that begins on the northern shore. Another trail on the northern shore leads to Raven Lake.

Directions: From NY 28 in Eagle Bay, drive north and west on Big Moose Road about 18.5 miles to a junction; turn right and go 0.5 mile to a parking lot. Big Moose Road takes a sharp left just past Big Moose Lake and a sharp right just past Big Moose Station. It turns to dirt at Big Moose Station.

Activities: Camping, canoeing, boating, fishing, swimming, hiking, snowmobiling, hunting.

Facilities: 46 primitive campsites, boat launch, hiking trails.

Dates: Open year-round.

Closest town: The hamlet of Big Moose Station is about 11 miles away.

For more information: Stillwater forest ranger, phone (315) 376-8030. Ask for the leaflet *Stillwater Reservoir.*

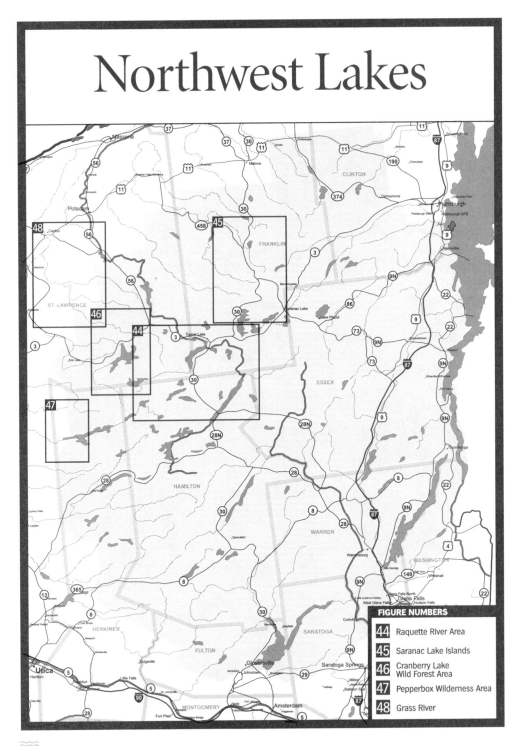

Northwest Lakes

FIGURE NUMBERS

44 Raquette River Area

45 Saranac Lake Islands

46 Cranberry Lake Wild Forest Area

47 Pepperbox Wilderness Area

48 Grass River

Northwest Lakes

Most of the lakes in the Northwest Lakes Region lie in a basin that stretches 35 miles from Tupper Lake to Lower Saint Regis Lake. Within this narrow belt, bordered by mountains on either side, are more than 150 lakes, including 50 or so with a diameter of at least 1 mile.

The geologist Bradford B. Van Diver, noting that the lake belt is aligned in the same direction as many Adirondack faults, surmises that the basin formed when blocks of crust dropped between faults.

The Northwest Lakes Region has numerous lakes outside this basin, including two of the largest in the Adirondacks: Cranberry Lake and Carry Falls Reservoir. The region also lays claim to many large rivers that flow north from the highlands to the Saint Lawrence Valley. Most prominent among these are the Raquette and Oswegatchie rivers.

All this water makes a paddler's paradise. It comes as no surprise that the region

[*Above:* Lampson Falls is one of the most spectacular cascades in the Adirondacks]

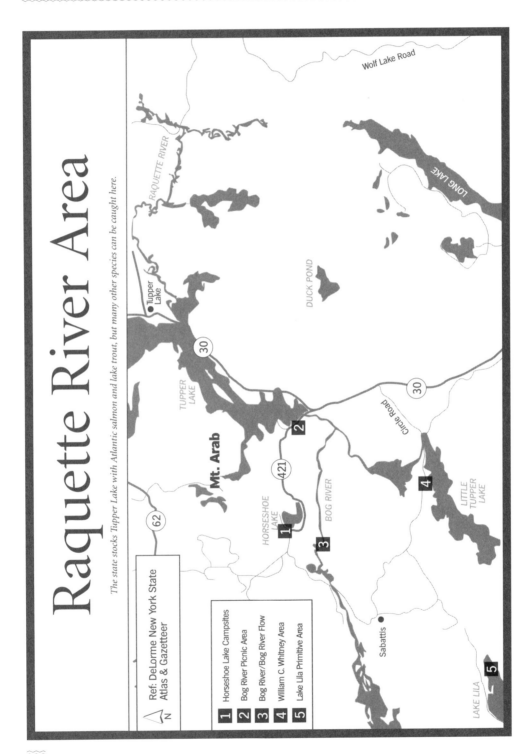

Raquette River Area

The state stocks Tupper Lake with Atlantic salmon and lake trout, but many other species can be caught here.

N

Ref: DeLorme New York State
Atlas & Gazetteer

1 Horseshoe Lake Campsites
2 Bog River Picnic Area
3 Bog River/Bog River Flow
4 William C. Whitney Area
5 Lake Lila Primitve Area

Wolf Lake Road

RAQUETTE RIVER

LONG LAKE

DUCK POND

Tupper Lake

30

TUPPER LAKE

Mt. Arab

30

Circle Road

62

421

HORSESHOE LAKE

BOG RIVER

LITTLE TUPPER LAKE

4

2

1

3

Sabattis

LAKE LILA

5

contains the Adirondack Park's only realm dedicated to the canoe: the Saint Regis Canoe Area, a land of pristine trout ponds where motors are verboten.

Hikers need not feel left out. In the vast Five Ponds Wilderness, one can tramp through one of the largest stands of virgin timber in the Northeast on a trail that ends at a lean-to on a lake 15 miles from the road. If that's not wild enough for you, the Northwest Lakes Region has one wilderness—the Pepperbox—that has no trails at all.

Those who do much hiking may notice that the Northwest Lakes Region has a great number of downed and broken trees. This is the result of a strong windstorm that ripped through the region in July 1995, damaging about 970,000 acres of forest, including 435,000 acres of state land. The Five Ponds Wilderness and the area south of Star Lake took the heaviest hit.

The ice age that ended about 10,000 years ago left its stamp all over the region. Some of the Adirondacks' finest examples of eskers, big ribbons of sandy till deposited by glacial rivers, exist at Star Lake, Massawepie Lake, Five Ponds, and elsewhere. Melting blocks of ice led to the creation of many of the ponds and bogs that dot the landscape.

The region contains a 350,000-acre tract that has been identified as a low-elevation boreal biome, a land of coniferous forests, swamps, and sphagnum bogs that resembles the taiga of Canada. The biome provides a home for a variety of boreal birds, such as the gray jay (*Perisoreus canadensis*), and it's thought that the area could one day become a prime habitat for the returning moose (*Alces alces*). The state, however, owns only about a fifth of the biome, mostly in scattered parcels. Boreal birds can be seen other places in the region, including the William C. Whitney Area acquired in 1998.

As defined in this chapter, the Northwest Lakes Region encompasses all of the Adirondack Park north of Stillwater Reservoir and the Sargent Ponds Wild Forest and west of NY 30. The state-owned lands include the Lake Lila Primitive Area, Horseshoe Lake Wild Forest, Cranberry Lake Wild Forest, Saranac Lakes Wild Forest, Five Ponds Wilderness, Pepperbox Wilderness, and Saint Regis Canoe Area.

The state operates campgrounds at Cranberry Lake, Fish Creek Pond, Rollins Pond, and Saranac Lakes. Primitive campsites available for free are scattered throughout the region.

For more information: State Department of Environmental Conservation, 317 Washington Street, Watertown, NY 13601. Phone (315) 785-2263. The DEC publishes several leaflets on hiking, fishing, and canoeing in the Northwest Lakes Region.

Raquette River

The second longest river in the state, the Raquette flows 146 miles from Raquette Lake to the Saint Lawrence River. Over its 95-mile course within the Adirondack Park, the river exhibits a protean personality, changing from raging whitewater to placid marsh to open lake.

The Raquette's most thrilling whitewater can be found in the 23 miles from

Piercefield to Carry Falls Reservoir. The river courses over several difficult rapids and two dangerous waterfalls. The trip demands expert whitewater skills and arduous carries. Also, the water level fluctuates because of dam releases upriver. Anyone contemplating the journey should consult *Adirondack Canoe Waters: North Flow* by Paul Jamieson and Donald Morris.

For those looking for a day trip, the best bets lie in the tortuous stretch between Raquette Falls and Tupper Lake. The river twists so much that in one spot, known as the Oxbow, canoeists sometimes get turned around and unwittingly head back to their starting point. The marshes and inlets throughout the entire stretch offer wonderful opportunities for seeing waterfowl. The river flows past a large stand of old-growth silver maple (*Acer saccharinum*) between Trombley Landing and the outlet of Follensby Pond.

All told, it's about 22 miles from the falls to Tupper Lake Marsh, where the river flows into the lake, but shorter trips are possible. Canoes can be launched on Tupper Lake, just south of the marsh, or directly into the river at two places east of the lake—off NY 3/30 or at Axton Landing. From Axton Landing, canoeists can paddle upriver about 6 miles and then walk along a carry trail about 1 mile to the falls. The NY 3/30 launch lies about 7.5 miles downriver from Axton Landing and about 9 miles upriver from Tupper Lake.

Because the main channel can be difficult to follow at times, canoeists should consult Jamieson and Morris for details and carry a good map. Several lean-tos and tent sites are located along the shores. Beware that motorboats also travel the Raquette.

Fish that can be caught in the river include brown trout (*Salmo trutta*), northern pike (*Esox lucius*), and walleye (*Stizostedion vitreum vitreum*).

Directions: The Tupper Lake boat launch is located on NY 30 about 2.1 miles south of the village of Tupper Lake, about 0.6 mile past the causeway over Tupper Lake Marsh. The second launch is located off NY 3/30 about 4 miles east of the village. To reach Axton Landing, drive east from the village of Tupper Lake on NY 3/30 about 5 miles to Wawbeek Corners; turn right onto NY 3 and go about 2.5 miles to Coreys Road; turn right and go about 3 miles to the landing on the right.

Activities: Canoeing, boating, fishing, camping, hiking.

Facilities: Boat launches, lean-tos, tent sites, carry trail.

Dates: Seasonal.

Closest town: Tupper Lake.

For more information: The Adirondack Canoe Map shows channels, lean-tos, campsites, hiking trails, and other features. It is published by Adirondack Maps Inc., PO Box 718, Market Street, Keene Valley, NY 12943. Phone (518) 576-9861.

Long Lake

[Fig. 44] Lying in a fault valley excavated by glaciers, Long Lake often resembles a river: It is 14 miles long but only, on average, 0.5 mile wide. Nevertheless, the water can get choppy in a breeze, so canoeists should pick a calm day to explore the lake. A paddle south from the village of Long Lake toward the Raquette River offers gorgeous views of the High Peaks and takes one past several marshes and sandy beaches.

The state owns much of the eastern shore below the village. There are 10 lean-tos and numerous tent sites on this side. Nine of the lean-tos lie along the Northville-Lake Placid Trail. It's a 9.5-mile paddle to the foot of the lake. Canoeists should keep in mind that the northward return trip goes against the current and often against the wind.

From the foot of the lake, canoeists can travel another 6 miles down the meandering Raquette to Raquette Falls, where there is a 1.3-mile portage. A side trip up the Cold River in the High Peaks Wilderness also is possible (*see* page 53). It's sometimes difficult to follow the Raquette's main channel, so canoeists should consult *Adirondack Canoe Waters: North Flow* by Paul Jamieson and Donald Morris for details and bring a good map.

Directions: From NY 30 in the hamlet of Long Lake, turn north near the post office onto Town Dock Road and take this 0.4 mile to a state boat launch.

Activities: Boating, canoeing, fishing, camping, swimming, hiking.

Facilities: Boat launch, town dock, lean-tos, campsites, hiking trails, natural beaches.

Dates: Year-round.

Fees: None.

Closest town: Long Lake village.

For more information: The Adirondack Canoe Map shows channels, lean-tos, campsites, beaches, hiking trails, and other features. It is published by Adirondack Maps Inc., PO Box 718, Market Street, Keene Valley, NY 12943. Phone (518) 576-9861.

William C. Whitney Area

[Fig. 44(4)] In 1998, to the delight of conservationists, the state purchased from the Whitney family a 15,000-acre parcel that includes Little Tupper Lake, one of the largest lakes in the eastern United States that still harbors its original strain of trout.

Little Tupper, stretching nearly 6 miles, is the centerpiece of the Whitney Area, but the property also has 10 ponds. The terrain is relatively flat, with extensive wetlands. The highest point, the 2,297-foot summit of Antediluvian Mountain, stands less than 500 feet higher than Little Tupper's shoreline. Because of past logging, a young forest covers most of the land, but mature trees line the shores of Little Tupper and the ponds and streams.

Many Adirondack animals dwell in the Whitney Area, including black bear (*Ursus*

Raquette River Reservoirs

Niagara Mohawk Power Corporation operates a series of hydroelectric dams that have created a chain of seven reservoirs on the Raquette River in the northwestern Adirondacks. The land around the reservoirs, though privately owned, remains quite wild. Bald eagles have been seen along the water. Niagara Mohawk maintains campsites, picnic areas, boat launches, and portage trails on the reservoirs. Carry Falls Reservoir, at 6,458 acres, is one of the largest water in the Adirondacks. Canoeists probably will want to stick to the smaller reservoirs.

For more information: Niagara Mohawk Power Corporation publishes a leaflet about its public facilities. Phone (800) 642-4272.

americanus), river otter (*Lutra canadensis*), snowshoe hare (*Lepus americanus*), and pine marten (*Martes americana*). Bird watchers will want to keep an eye out for the boreal species found in the region's wetlands, such as the Cape May warbler (*Dendroica tigrina*), yellow-bellied flycatcher (*Empidonax flaviventrus*), three-toed woodpecker (*Picoides tridactylus*), and spruce grouse (*Canachites canadensis*).

The Whitney Area probably will appeal primarily to canoeists, who can explore Little Tupper's islands, marshes, and beaches. It's also possible to reach Rock Pond from the lake via the pond's outlet stream and a carry trail. Canoes may be launched only at the Whitney Area headquarters off Sabattis Road. Motorboats are not allowed.

In 1998, the state established 30 primitive campsites, most reachable only by water, on the shores of Little Tupper, Rock Pond, and Rock Pond Outlet. Camping is allowed only at designated sites. Campers must register at the headquarters.

Hikers can reach most of the Whitney Area ponds by logging roads that now serve as walking trails. The 13.5-mile trail network starts at the Burn Road trailhead west of the headquarters. Because the roads are wide and level, they may appeal to novice cross-country skiers. The state may establish campsites along the trails in the future. Logging trucks have the right to use the roads until April 30, 2000.

In addition to the hiking trails, the state has set aside Stony Pond Road on the south side of Little Tupper as a horse trail. The 4-mile trail begins at Circle Road about 0.4 mile south of Sabattis Road, but equestrians must park their trailers in a lot located just east of the headquarters and ride to the trailhead.

The Little Tupper strain of trout—descendants of trout that arrived soon after the glaciers melted about 10,000 years ago—also can be found in Rock and Bum ponds. The state sometimes stocks other ponds in the Adirondacks with the offspring of Little Tupper trout. Other ponds in the Whitney Area hold trout as well, but not the pure strain.

To protect the heritage trout, the state's interim management plan for the Whitney Area forbids the use of baitfish or worms in all waters and requires anglers to return all brook trout. The plan also forbids the use of snowmobiles and bicycles in the area.

Directions: From the junction of NY 28N and NY 30 in Long Lake, drive west and north on NY 30 for about 7.6 miles to County 10A, also known as Circle Road; turn left and go 3.2 miles to a junction with County 10, also known as the Sabattis Road; turn left and go 1.4 miles to the headquarters on the left. The Burn Road trailhead is on the Sabattis Road about 1.4 miles past the headquarters. After the NY 10 turn, Circle Road curves to rejoin NY 30. If coming from Tupper Lake, turn right from NY 30 onto the northern end of Circle Road about 11.6 miles south of the village; go 3.2 miles to the County 10 junction and bear right. From there, follow the above directions.

Activities: Canoeing, hiking, horseback riding, cross-country skiing.

Facilities: Canoe launch, hiking trails, primitive campsites.

Dates: Open year-round.

Fees: None.

Closest town: Long Lake is about 12 miles away.

For more information: State Department of Environmental Conservation, 701 S. Main Street, Northville, NY 12134. Phone (518) 863-4545. Ask for the leaflet *William C. Whitney Area.*

Lake Lila Primitive Area

[Fig. 44(5)] The 7,125-acre Lake Lila Primitive Area once belonged to W. Seward Webb, a railroad financier who built Nehasne Lodge on the lake's western shore. The area bears signs of its past—dirt roads, a railroad track, the remains of the lodge— but it is still a wild place where visitors might see an osprey (*Pandion haliaetus*) or even a bald eagle (*Haliaaetus leucocephalus*) soaring above the giant white pines (*Pinus strobus*) that grow along the lake's shoreline.

Lake Lila's sandy beaches and seven islands make it ideal for canoe camping. No motors are allowed. The state has designated 22 campsites around the lake, including one each on Snell, Spruce, Buck, and Canada islands. Four campsites for large groups and one lean-to are on the western shore. Up to nine people may stay at a campsite. Camping on beaches is prohibited. Those who plan to stay more than three nights must obtain a permit from DEC.

At 1,446 acres, Lake Lila is the largest lake in the Adirondack Park that is sur-rounded by state land. The surface can get choppy in a breeze. Canoeists can also explore Shingle Shanty Brook, which enters the lake from southeast, and the Beaver River, which drains the lake to the southwest.

The state stocks Lake Lila with Atlantic salmon (*Salmo salar*). Other species that can be caught include lake trout (*Salvelinus namaycush*), brook trout (*Salvelinus fontinalis*), smallmouth bass (*Micropterus dolomieui*), and yellow perch (*Perca flavescens*). The use of baitfish is prohibited.

The lake can be reached by a 0.3-mile portage trail, marked with red blazes, from the parking lot to a large sandy beach on the eastern shore. A 4.4-mile trail, marked with blue blazes, leads from the lot to the western shore and Frederica Mountain. There is a superb view of the lake from the 2,200-foot summit. Canoeists can pick up the trail near the lean-to on the western shore.

Directions: From the junction of NY 28N and NY 30 in Long Lake, drive west and north on NY 30 for about 7.6 miles to County 10A, also known as Circle Road; turn left and go 3.2 miles to a junction with County 10, also known as the Sabattis Road; turn left and go 4.8 miles to a dirt road marked by a sign for Lake Lila; turn left and go 6.1 miles to the parking area. After the NY 10 turn, Circle Road curves to rejoin NY 30. If coming from Tupper Lake, turn right from NY 30 onto the northern end of Circle Road about 11.6 miles south of the village; go 3.2 miles to the County 10 junction and bear right. From there, follow the above directions. Note that it is illegal to park on the road between Sabattis Road and the parking lot.

Activities: Camping, canoeing, hiking, swimming, fishing, hunting.

Facilities: 22 campsites, 1 lean-to, canoe carry trail, hiking road/trail.

Dates: Open year-round, but the access road might not be plowed in winter.

Fees: None.

Closest town: Long Lake is about 19 miles away.

For more information: State Department of Environmental Conservation, 701 S. Main Street, Northville, NY 12134. Phone (518) 863-4545. Ask for the leaflet *Lake Lila Primitive Area.*

Bog River Picnic Area

[Fig. 44(2)] The Bog River spills over a shelving-rock falls just before entering Tupper Lake. The falls and the lake can be viewed from a handsome stone bridge on County 421. Park in the lot next to the bridge to walk to the bedrock slabs beside the falls. Roadside picnic tables can be found on either side of the bridge. Camping in the picnic area is prohibited, but there is a designated campsite with a privy and picnic table on the left side of the road just past the picnic area. The Bog River is stocked with brook trout (*Salvelinus fontinalis*). The river can be canoed upstream for about 2 miles above the falls.

Directions: From the village of Tupper Lake, drive south 8.8 miles on NY 30 to County 421; turn right and go 0.7 mile to the parking lot on the left, just past the bridge, or stop at one of the picnic sites on the way.

Activities: Picnicking, fishing, canoeing.

Facilities: Picnic sites.

Dates: Open year-round.

Fees: None.

Closest town: Tupper Lake is about 9.5 miles away.

Horseshoe Lake Campsites

[Fig. 44(1)] The state maintains 16 designated campsites on Horseshoe Lake, about 3 miles west of Tupper Lake. The campsites, available for free on a first-come basis, can be reached by car off County 421. Most are wooded, but some can be found in a grassy swath on the western shore. Only two of the campsites—numbers 8 and 16—have privies. Except for a few inholdings, the state owns all the land around the lake, which is stocked with tiger muskellunge (*Esox masquinongy*). The Horseshoe Lake Outlet can be canoed to the Bog River (*see* below). There is a launch along the road. Mountain bikers will find miles of dirt roads just west of the lake.

Directions: From the village of Tupper Lake, drive south 8.8 miles on NY 30 to County 421 and turn right. The lake is reached in about 5 miles.

Activities: Camping, picnicking, swimming, fishing, canoeing, hiking, biking.

Facilities: 16 primitive campsites, 2 with privies.

Dates: Open year-round.

Fees: None.

Closest town: Tupper Lake is about 14 miles away.

For more information: State Department of Environmental Conservation, 6739 US Hwy. 11, Canton, NY 13617. Phone (315) 265-3090. Ask for the leaflet *Bog River Flow.*

Bog River/Bog River Flow

[Fig. 44(3)] A wealthy inventor named A. Augustus Low built two dams on the Bog River in the early 1900s to generate power for his Horse Shoe Forestry Co., whose diverse enterprises—ranging from lumbering to jam-making—reflected the eclectic interests of its owner. Low returned to his native Brooklyn after a fire raged over his timberlands in 1908, but he forever left his stamp on the Adirondacks: The two dams, now owned by the state, have created a paddler's paradise.

Canoeists usually put in at the lower dam, canoe upstream to lovely Hitchins Pond, and carry around the upper dam to reach the Bog River Flow, also known as Lows Lake. The Bog River Flow—one of the Adirondacks' premier nesting sites for loons (*Gavia immer*)—stretches about 11 miles to the eastern edge of the Five Ponds Wilderness. Adventurous canoeists can portage 3 miles through the wilderness, via Big Deer Pond, to the Oswegatchie River (*see* page 309).

The state maintains 39 primitive campsites along the canoe route—3 in the 3-mile stretch to Hitchins Pond, 4 on the pond itself, and 32 on the Bog River Flow. Seven of the campsites have privies. Campers staying more than three nights at one site must get a permit from DEC. Groups of more than nine are not allowed.

Paddlers will find numerous islands and inlets, such as Grass Pond and Bog Lake, to explore in the flow. The Boy Scouts, however, have exclusive use of Pole, Goose-

The Saranac Cure

When Dr. Edward Livingston Trudeau arrived in the Adirondacks in 1873, dying of tuberculosis, his old hunting guide exclaimed, "Why, Doc, you ain't no heavier than a dried lambskin!" Miraculously, Trudeau survived, and he attributed his recovery to the clean air of the mountains. He devoted the rest of his life to treating tubercular patients and seeking a cure for the disease. The Adirondack Cottage Sanitarium he founded at Saranac Lake became a model for other sanitariums in the United States. He also opened a laboratory that trained physicians in the treatment of TB. Many celebrities came to Saranac Lake to take the cure, among them the British author Robert Louis Stevenson and the great pitcher Christy Mathewson. The discovery of a TB antibiotic in the 1940s rendered the Saranac cure obsolete. The sanitarium closed in 1954, but the lab lives on as the Trudeau Institute, conducting research on a variety of diseases. The farmhouse where Stevenson stayed from 1887–1888, while writing most of *The Master of Ballantrae*, is now a museum.

For more information: Robert Louis Stevenson Memorial Cottage, 11 Stevenson Lane, Saranac Lake, NY 12983. Phone (518) 891-1462.

neck, and Frying Pan islands in June, July, and August. Canoeists may encounter floating bogs in the flow. If so, avoid walking on the fragile vegetation. Beware that the flow widens in the west, and its waters can be quite choppy.

If you're only making a day trip, paddle the 3.5 miles to Hitchins Pond and the upper dam. There is a picnic table on the southwestern shore of the pond, just below the dam.

From the pond, it's a short walk to an unmarked trail up Lows Ridge, which has a great view of the Bog River region. The short trail begins near the vacant stone lodge near the upper dam. Look for some old stone steps. These cliffs are too dangerous for young children to climb.

Along the Bog River and Bog River Flow visitors will see many kinds of birds besides loons, including osprey (*Pandion haliaetus*), great blue heron (*Ardea herodias*), raven (*Corvus corax*), and spruce grouse (*Canachites canadensis*). Black bears (*Ursus americanus*) are fairly common.

Although most people begin their trip at the lower dam, it's also possible to canoe down the outlet of Horseshoe Lake to the Bog River below Hitchins Pond. There is a launch site along County 421.

Directions: From the village of Tupper Lake, drive south 8.8 miles on NY 30 to County 421 and turn right. To reach the lower dam, drive 6.2 miles on County 421 to a dirt road; turn left and go 0.7 mile to a parking area at the end of the road. To reach the Horseshoe Lake Outlet, drive 6.7 miles on County 421 to the launch on the left.

Activities: Canoeing, camping, picnicking, hiking, fishing.

Facilities: 38 campsites, including 7 with privies; canoe launches.

Dates: Seasonal for canoeing.

Fees: None.

Closest town: Tupper Lake is about 15.7 miles from the lower dam.

For more information: State Department of Environmental Conservation, 6739 US Hwy. 11, Canton, NY 13617. Phone (315) 265-3090. The leaflet *Bog River Flow* contains a map showing all the campsites.

Mount Arab

[Fig. 44] The summit of Mount Arab rewards hikers with a wonderful panorama from its fire tower, offering views of the Raquette River to the northeast, the mountains of the Cranberry Lake Wild Forest and the Five Ponds Wilderness to the west, and Horseshoe Lake to the south.

At the outset, the trail to the summit climbs through a hardwood forest on private timberlands, reaching a junction at 0.25 mile. Turn right to follow the official route. Toward the summit, the trail goes around a rock wall and then emerges into an opening of grasses, wildflowers, shrubs, and stunted trees. Good views can be found without climbing the tower.

Directions: From Tupper Lake, drive 4.8 miles west on NY 3 to County 62, about 2.6 miles past the Saint Lawrence County Line; turn left and go 1.9 miles to Eagle Crag Lake Road; turn left and go 0.9 mile to the parking lot on the right. The trail begins across the road.

Trail: 1 mile to summit.

Elevation: 1,780 feet to 2,545 feet.

Degree of difficulty: Moderate.

Surface and blaze: Natural forest floor. Red blazes.

Tupper Lake

[Fig. 44] At 6,240 acres, Tupper is the fourth largest lake wholly within the Adirondack Park. Although most of the shoreline is in private hands, the state owns considerable stretches on both sides of the lake. Several primitive campsites can be found on the southeastern shore. Campers also can stay at lean-tos on Black Bay and Indian Point on the western shore.

There is a state boat launch off NY 30, about 2.1 miles south of Tupper Lake village or 0.6 mile south of the causeway over the Tupper Lake Marsh.

On most days, the open water gets too rough for canoes. Paddlers, however, can explore the 1,100-acre marsh, where the twisting Raquette River enters the lake (*see* page 283). On especially calm days, canoeists might also explore the southern end of the lake. Two highlights of this trip are Devil's Pulpit, the 100-foot cliffs on Bluff Island, and the 30-foot Bog River Falls, located at the tip of the lake (*see* page 288).

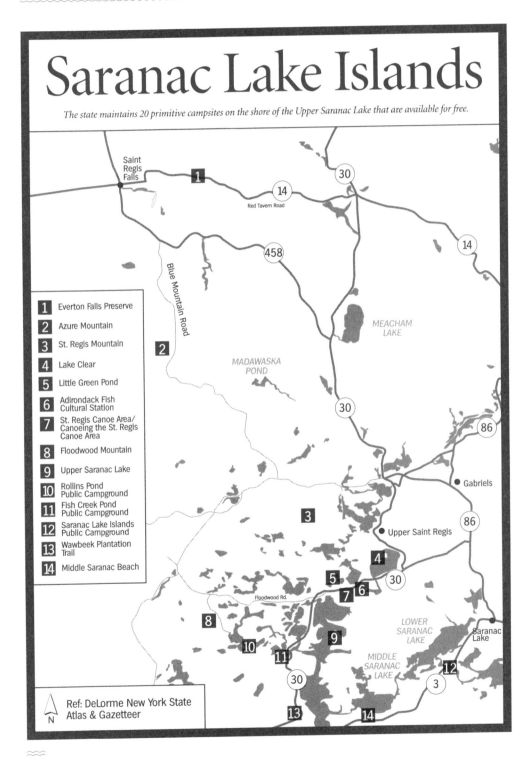

Saranac Lake Islands

The state maintains 20 primitive campsites on the shore of the Upper Saranac Lake that are available for free.

1 Everton Falls Preserve

2 Azure Mountain

3 St. Regis Mountain

4 Lake Clear

5 Little Green Pond

6 Adirondack Fish Cultural Station

7 St. Regis Canoe Area/ Canoeing the St. Regis Canoe Area

8 Floodwood Mountain

9 Upper Saranac Lake

10 Rollins Pond Public Campground

11 Fish Creek Pond Public Campground

12 Saranac Lake Islands Public Campground

13 Wawbeek Plantation Trail

14 Middle Saranac Beach

Ref: DeLorme New York State Atlas & Gazetteer

Saint Regis Falls

Red Tavern Road

Blue Mountain Road

MEACHAM LAKE

MADAWASKA POND

Gabriels

Upper Saint Regis

Floodwood Rd.

LOWER SARANAC LAKE

Saranac Lake

MIDDLE SARANAC LAKE

The state stocks Tupper Lake with Atlantic salmon (*Salmo salar*) and lake trout (*Salvelinus namaycush*), but many other species, such as northern pike and bass, can be caught here. Ice fishing is permitted.

For more information: State Department of Environmental Conservation, Route 86, PO Box 296, Ray Brook, NY 12977. Phone (518) 897-1200. Ask for the leaflet *Adirondack Canoe Routes.*

Saranac Lake Islands Public Campground

[Fig. 45(12)] The state maintains 87 primitive campsites, most reachable only by boat, on the shores and islands of Lower and Middle Saranac lakes. Most sites have a picnic table, fireplace, and privy. Five of the sites have lean-tos.

Although both lakes have seen some development, state-owned lands in the Saranac Lakes Wild Forest border most of the shores. The lakes remain wild enough to attract ring-necked duck (*Aythya collaris*), common loon (*Gavia immer*), great blue heron (*Ardea herodias*), and other waterfowl. Fishermen come here for the northern pike and bass.

Lower Saranac covers 2,285 acres and Middle Saranac 1,376 acres. They are two of the region's larger lakes, but their combined acreage still falls short of Upper Saranac Lake (*see* page 294). A short stretch of the Saranac River connects the lower and middle lakes.

Canoeists may prefer to stay at Middle Saranac, since it is less accessible to powerboats than Lower Saranac. The campsites on Weller Pond, at the northern end of the lake, are especially prized for their remote setting. The easiest way to reach Middle Saranac is to put in at a car-top boat launch on South Creek on NY 3. Paddlers also can carry 0.5 mile from NY 3 to Middle Saranac Beach (*see* page 294).

The state has a boat launch on Lower Saranac at the campground office on NY 3. Boaters also can put in Lake Flower from a launch on NY 86 in the village of Saranac Lake and reach Lower Saranac via Oseetah Lake and the Saranac River. Canoeists can put in at a car-top launch off Ampersand Avenue in the village.

To travel between Lower and Middle Saranac lakes, boats must pass through a pair of manual locks. If no lock operator is on duty, boaters can operate the locks themselves by following the instructions on a sign. Canoeists have the option of carrying around the locks.

Directions: From the junction of NY 3 and NY 86 in Saranac Lake, drive 4.3 miles west on NY 3 to the campground office on the left. The launch for Middle Saranac Lake is 6 miles west of the office.

Activities: Camping, boating, canoeing, fishing, swimming.

Facilities: 87 campsites, privies, boat launch. 5 campsites have lean-tos.

Dates: Open May through Labor Day.

Fees: There is a charge for camping or day use.

Closest town: Saranac Lake is about 4 miles east.

For more information: Campground office, phone (518) 891-4590. For reservations, phone (800) 456-2267.

Middle Saranac Beach

[Fig. 45(14)] This lovely sand beach on the south shore of Middle Saranac Lake can be reached by a flat 0.5-mile hike through the forest from NY 3—a hike just long enough to keep out crowds. The beach is an ideal swimming spot for families with young children, because the bottom is sandy and the water deepens gradually. Nearby are an outhouse and a few campsites. The campsites are part of the Saranac Lake Islands Public Campground (*see* page 293). The trail to the beach begins across the road from the Ampersand Mountain Trail, so hikers can combine a climb and a swim.

Directions: From the junction of NY 3 and NY 86 in Saranac Lake, drive 8.7 miles west on NY 3 to a parking lot on the right. The trail begins at the lot.

Activities: Swimming, camping, canoeing, fishing, hiking.

Facilities: Sand beach, privy, campsites.

Dates: Seasonal.

Fees: There is no fee for day use. There is a fee for camping.

Closest town: Saranac Lake is about 8 miles east.

Upper Saranac Lake

[Fig. 45(9)] Upper Saranac is one of the largest lakes in the Adirondacks, covering 5,056 acres, and one of the deepest, reaching more than 80 feet in places. Most of the shoreline is in private hands, although the state owns a lot of land around the northern half of the lake.

Because of its size and development, Upper Saranac appeals more to motorboaters than to canoeists. Paddlers, however, cross the southern end of the lake when traveling the historic canoe route from Old Forge to the village of Saranac Lake. The 0.4-mile Bartlett Carry Trail links Upper Saranac to Middle Saranac Lake.

The state maintains 20 primitive campsites on the shores of Upper Saranac, available for free. Five of the sites, including one with a lean-to, are along Saginaw Bay, a narrow inlet on the eastern shore. There is a canoe carry trail from the southeastern end of Saginaw Bay to Weller Pond, an arm of Middle Saranac Lake. Seven campsites can be found on islands—five on Buck Island, just north of Saginaw Bay, and two on Green Island, in the northwestern part of the lake. Campers need a permit if they plan to stay more than four days or if the party exceeds 10 people.

The state stocks Upper Saranac Lake with lake trout (*Salvelinus namaycush*), rainbow trout (*Oncorhynchus mykiss*), and brown trout (*Salmo trutta*). Among the other species that can be caught are northern pike (*Esox lucius*) and bass. Ice fishing is permitted, but tip-ups are prohibited.

Motorboats can be put in at state launch sites at Saranac Inn, a hamlet off NY 30 on the northern end of the lake, or at the Fish Creek Pond Public Campground (*see* page 296). Canoes can be launched on the southern end of the lake at the Indian Carry Trail off NY 3.

Directions: To get to Saranac Inn from the junction of NY 3 and NY 86 in Saranac Lake, drive north on NY 86 for 5.6 miles to NY 186; turn left and go 4.1 miles to NY 30; bear left, go 5.2 miles, and look for a sign for Saranac Inn on the left. If coming from the village of Tupper Lake, follow NY 30 about 14.6 miles east. To get to the Indian Carry Trail from the junction of NY 3 and NY 86 in Saranac Lake, drive 13.2 miles west on NY 3 and look for a sign for the trail on the right. If coming from Tupper Lake, follow NY 3 about 8 miles east.

Activities: Boating, canoeing, camping, swimming, fishing.

Facilities: Boat launches, primitive campsites, 1 lean-to, canoe carry trails.

Dates: Open year-round.

Fees: There is a charge for using the state campground.

Closest town: Tupper Lake is about 8 miles west from the Indian Carry Trail. Saranac Lake is about 14 miles east of Saranac Inn.

For more information: State Department of Environmental Conservation, PO Box 96, Ray Brook, NY 12977. Phone (518) 897-1277. Ask for the leaflet *Camping Upper Saranac Lake.*

Wawbeek Plantation Trail

[Fig. 45(13)] In the early 1900s, one of America's pioneer foresters, Bernard E. Fernow, cleared about 68 acres of hardwoods and planted in their stead white pine (*Pinus strobus*) and the exotic Norway spruce (*Picea abies*). Fernow wanted to prove that softwoods—the more valuable trees, from the loggers' point of view—could be grown on hardwood sites. Today, students of Paul Smiths College maintain an interpretive trail with 15 stops that wanders among these tall trees. A leaflet is available at the trailhead.

Directions: From Tupper Lake, drive about 5.8 miles east and north on NY 30 to the parking lot on the left. From the junction of NY 3 and NY 86 in Saranac Lake, drive about 16.1 miles west to NY 30; turn right and go about 0.8 mile to the lot on the left.

Trail: 1-mile loop.

Degree of difficulty: Easy.

Surface and blaze: Natural forest floor. Red blazes.

Fish Creek Pond and Rollins Pond Public Campgrounds

[Fig. 45(11), Fig. 45(10)] These two state campgrounds, which share an entrance off NY 30, give access to a network of ponds in the Saranac Lakes Wild Forest. The ponds, connected by channels or portage trails, are a canoeist's delight. Many are stocked with trout or salmon. Hikers and mountain bikers can reach the ponds via trails shown on the campground leaflet.

The Fish Creek Pond Public Campground fronts Fish Creek Pond and Square Pond. Campers with large boats should stay here, since Fish Creek Pond gives access to the 7.5-mile-long Upper Saranac Lake (*see* page 294). The Rollins Pond Public Campground, on Rollins and Whey ponds, is a little more private. It prohibits motorboats with more than 25 horsepower engines.

Those who can do without the amenities of a public campground can stay for free at primitive campsites along Floodwood Road (*see* below), which also gives access to the ponds. Free campsites also exist on the shores of many of the ponds.

Directions: From Tupper Lake, drive about 10.8 miles east on NY 30 to the campground entrance on the left. If starting in Saranac Lake, drive east on NY 3/30 about 14 miles to NY 30; turn right and go 5.8 miles to the campground entrance on the left.

Activities: Camping, canoeing, boating, fishing, swimming, hiking, picnicking.

Facilities: Fish Creek Pond has 355 tent and RV sites, boat launch, hiking trails, beach, playground, picnic area, showers, trailer dumping station. Rollins Pond has 287 tent and RV sites, boat launch, hiking trails, showers, trailer dumping station. Boats and canoes can be rented at both.

Dates: Fish Pond is open from mid-April to mid-November. Rollins Pond is open from mid-May through Labor Day.

Fees: There is a charge for camping or day use.

Closest town: Tupper Lake is about 10.8 miles west.

For more information: Fish Pond office, phone (518) 891-4560. Rollins Pond office, phone (518) 891-3239. For reservations, phone (800) 456-2267.

Floodwood Road

[Fig. 45] This dirt road can be the starting point for canoe trips into either the Saranac Lakes Wild Forest to the south or the Saint Regis Canoe Area to the north. It also provides opportunities for roadside camping, mountain biking, hiking, fishing, and cross-country skiing.

The state maintains 19 campsites along the 7-mile road, available on a first-come basis. The prettiest sites are on the shores of ponds. Camping is allowed only at designated sites.

Paddlers can put in canoes at four ponds in the Saranac Lakes Wild Forest—Polliwog, Middle, Floodwood, and East Pine—from launch sites on the south side of the road. From any of these ponds, canoeists can reach numerous other ponds connected by either waterways or portage trails. The ponds also can be reached by trails from the road. Primitive campsites can be found at most of the waters.

Those who want to explore the Saint Regis Canoe Area can portage north from the road to Long Pond. For more on the Saint Regis Canoe Area, see page 298.

Novice mountain bikers will enjoy riding on Floodwood Road. More adventurous bikers will be tempted to turn off the road onto the trails. Note that bicycles are prohibited in the Saint Regis Canoe Area.

Hikers and fishermen also can use the trails to visit the ponds—most of which are stocked with trout or salmon. Those in search of a more strenuous hike can climb Floodwood Mountain (*see* page 298).

Spruce Grouse

Wildlife biologists believe spruce grouse (*Canachites canadensis*) were more common in the Adirondacks before loggers in the nineteenth century starting cutting down the conifers that constitute their habitat. Spruce grouse eat the buds and needles of evergreens. They survive in the lowland swamps of the northwestern Adirondacks, but the state lists the species as threatened. The ruffed grouse (*Bonasa umbellus*) exists in large numbers in the Adirondacks. Hikers often unwittingly startle the birds and set them into noisy flight. The males of both species court females in spring by beating their wings to make a drumming sound. Both birds resemble chickens. The spruce grouse can be distinguished from the ruffed by its red eyebrows and chestnut-tipped tail.

Directions: From the junction of NY 3 and NY 86 in Saranac Lake, drive north on NY 86 for 5.6 miles to NY 186; turn left and go 4.1 miles to NY 30; bear left and go 6.2 miles to Floodwood Road on the right.

Activities: Camping, canoeing, hiking, fishing, mountain biking, cross-country skiing, hunting.

Facilities: 19 drive-up campsites, canoe launches, carry trails. There also is a state boat launch at Follensby Clear Pond off NY 30, about 1.9 miles north of the Fish Creek Pond Public Campground.

Dates: Open year-round.

Fees: None.

Closest town: Saranac Lake is about 15 miles away.

For more information: Saint Regis Canoe Outfitters, located on Floodwood Road, can offer tips for exploring either the Saranac Lakes Wild Forest or the Saint Regis Canoe Area from Floodwood Road. Phone (518) 891-1838.

Floodwood Mountain

[Fig. 45(8)] This modest summit rewards hikers with nice views of several peaks, including Saint Regis Mountain, as well as several ponds in the nearby canoe country. The state bought Floodwood Mountain from the Boy Scouts in 1990, but the road from which the trail to the summit starts remains in private hands and the public parking lot is about 0.5 mile from the trailhead.

Hikers walk about 1 mile from the parking lot before they start to climb. Once the ascent begins, the trail makes use of switchbacks and rock stairs in the steepest sections. After reaching the summit, be sure to continue 0.1 mile to the south summit, where the views are even better.

Directions: From the junction of NY 3 and NY 86 in Saranac Lake, drive north on NY 86 for 5.6 miles to NY 186; turn left and go 4.1 miles to NY 30; bear left and go 6.2 miles to Floodwood Road on the right. Take Floodwood Road 6.7 miles to a left-hand turn for the Floodwood Boy Scout reservation; make the turn and go another 0.2 mile to a public parking lot on the left. The trail begins about 0.5 mile farther down the road on the right.

Trail: 1 mile from road to summit, 1.5 miles from parking lot to summit.

Elevation: 1,640 feet at parking lot to 2,315 feet at summit.

Degree of difficulty: Moderate.

Surface and blaze: Natural forest floor. Red blazes.

Saint Regis Canoe Area

The Saint Regis Canoe Area is blessed with water: There are 58 ponds scattered over its 18,231 acres. Geologically, the canoe area is similar to the land of small ponds just to the south in the Saranac Lake Wild Forest. The canoe area, however, is managed like a wilderness. No motorboats, snowmobiles, or bicycles are allowed. Anglers may not use baitfish. In general, it is more remote and more pristine than the Saranac Lake Wild Forest.

The Wisconsin glacier, which retreated about 10,000 years ago, shaped the landscape and created the region's spring-fed ponds. Some of the portage trails follow eskers—narrow ridges of sand and gravel deposited by rivers that once flowed through or atop the ice. Most of the ponds are cold and deep enough to support brook trout (*Salvelinus fontinalis*).

The terrain gives way to hills and mountains in the northern sector of the canoe area. Two peaks—Saint Regis Mountain and Long Pond Mountain—can be climbed for spectacular views of the waters. The trail to the latter can be reached only by water.

Fire raged over the region in 1903, but many trees escaped destruction, especially those growing near water or in swampy places. Large specimens of white pine (*Pinus* strobus), hemlock (*Tsuga canadensis*), and red spruce (*Picea rubens*) are common along the canoe routes.

You don't have to have a canoe to enjoy the region. Hikers and cross-country skiers can enter the region via the Fish Pond Truck Trail, a 5.1-mile dirt road closed to vehicles. Campers can stay for free at drive-up campsites on Little Green Pond on the southern fringe of the area.

Visitors who spent some time in the canoe area have a good chance of seeing loons (*Gavia immer*), mergansers (*Mergus merganser*), great blue heron (*Ardea herodias*), and other waterfowl at the ponds. With luck, they may also see black bear (*Ursus americanus*), white-tailed deer (*Odocoileus virginianus*), beaver (*Castor canadensis*), and river otter (*Lutra canadensis*).

For more information: State Department of Environmental Conservation, Route 86, PO Box 296, Ray Brook, NY 12977. Phone (518) 897-1200. Ask for the leaflet *Adirondack Canoe Routes.*

CANOEING THE SAINT REGIS CANOE AREA

[Fig. 45(7)] Since portage trails connect many of the ponds, paddlers can spend days hopping from one water to the next. Numerous primitive campsites exist along the shores. There are two lean-tos at Fish Pond and one at Saint Regis Pond. Trips also can be extended to waters outside the area.

When planning a trip, consult the Adirondack Canoe Map published by Adirondack Maps Inc. of Keene Valley. This large color map shows contours, trails, campsites, lean-tos, and launch sites not only in the Saint Regis Canoe Area but also in the neighboring regions. Saint Regis Canoe Outfitters, located on Floodwood Road at the start of a canoe carry to Long Pond, also can help plan a trip. The outfitter rents canoes and kayaks and provides a shuttle service.

Canoeists can put in without a carry at Little Clear Pond or Little Green Pond or they can portage from Floodwood Road to Long Pond. The Saint Regis Canoe Area also can be reached via two adjacent waters, Hoel Pond and Upper Saint Regis Lake. Both have public launch sites near roads. Hoel Pond also can be reached by a portage trail from Floodwood Road.

A canoe isn't necessary to enjoy the region. Campers can stay for free at drive-up campsites on Little Green Pond on the southern edge of the area. Hikers and cross-country skiers can enter the region via the Fish Pond Truck Trail, a 5.2-mile dirt road, closed to vehicles, that starts near Campsite 12 at Little Green.

A popular day trip begins at Long Pond, passes through Slang and Turtle ponds, and ends at Hoel Pond. The 6-mile route requires three carries totaling about 0.6 mile. If canoeists have time, they can climb climb Long Pond Mountain. The trail to the summit begins on the northwestern shore of a large inlet on Long Pond.

Two longer trips, the Seven Carries Route and Nine Carries Route, begin at Little Clear Pond. Both are described in detail in *Adirondack Canoe Waters: North Flow* by

Paul Jamieson and Donald Morris, but the basics are as follows:

Seven Carries. This can be done as a long day trip or more leisurely overnight trip. The traditional route begins at Little Green Pond, but many people put in at Little Clear, reducing the number of carries to six. From Little Clear, the route passes through Saint Regis, Green, Little Long, Bear, and Bog ponds before reaching Upper Saint Regis Lake. The trip is 9 to 12 miles, depending on whether canoeists take out at Upper Saint Regis Lake or Lower Saint Regis Lake. The six carries add up to about 1.3 miles.

Nine Carries. This arduous circuit of the region's ponds is best done over several days. From Little Clear, the route passes through nine other ponds: Saint Regis, Ochre, Mud, Fish, Little Fish, Little Long, Kit Fox, Nellie, and Long. (Little Long differs from the pond of the same name on the Seven Carries Route.) A variant route passes through Clamshell Pond and ends at Hoel Pond. Several short side trips are possible. The nine carries add up to about 4.8 miles.

Directions: The two main carry trails to Long Pond begin on the north side of Floodwood Road (*see* page 296). The first, located across from Saint Regis Canoe Outfitters, about 4.2 miles from NY 30, is 0.7 mile long. The second, located about 5.3 miles from NY 30, is about 0.3 mile long. To reach Hoel Pond, turn right from Floodwood Road at the fork about 0.4 mile from NY 30 and follow this road a short distance to the access site. For directions to Little Green and Little Clear ponds, see below. Canoeists can put in Lower Saint Regis Lake at Paul Smiths College, which is located in Paul Smiths near the junction of NY 30 and NY 86. For the Upper Saint Regis put-in, drive 4 miles south from Paul Smiths to a gravel road on the right and follow this 0.4 mile to a public dock. From Lake Clear Junction, the gravel road will be on the left after about 2.9 miles.

For more information: Adirondack Maps Inc., PO Box 718, Market Street, Keene Valley, NY 12943. Phone (518) 576-9861. Saint Regis Canoe Outfitters, Floodwood Road, PO Box 318, Lake Clear, NY 12945. Phone (518) 891-1838.

LITTLE GREEN POND CAMPSITES

[Fig. 45(5)] The state maintains 12 drive-up campsites on the shore of Little Green Pond, available for free. Campers should register at the nearby Adirondack Fish Cultural Station (*see* page 301). Because the hatchery raises trout and salmon in Little Green and neighboring Little Clear Pond, fishing in both ponds is prohibited. Little Green's sandy bottom tempts swimmers, but beware that leeches live in the water. A short carry trail leads from the northern shore to tiny Bone Pond.

Directions: From the junction of NY 3 and NY 86 in Saranac Lake, drive north on NY 86 for 5.6 miles to NY 186; turn left and go 4.1 miles to NY 30; bear left and go about 3 miles to Fish Hatchery Road; turn right and go about 0.3 mile to a dirt road; turn right and cross the railroad tracks. At a junction just past the tracks, turn left to go to Campsites 7–12 or go straight for Campsites 1–6 and for Little Clear Pond.

Activities: Camping, canoeing, swimming, hiking.

Facilities: 15 primitive campsites.

Dates: Open year-round.

Fees: None.

Closest town: Saranac Lake is about 11 miles east.

For more information: Adirondack Fish Cultural Station, PO Box 1, Saranac Lake, 12983. Phone (518) 891-3358.

SAINT REGIS MOUNTAIN

[Fig. 45(3)] The bare summit of Saint Regis Mountain provides spectacular vistas in all sirections: Debar Mountain to the northeast, Upper Saint Regis Lake to the east, the High Peaks to the southeast, Upper Saranac Lake to the south, and the shimmering waters of the Saint Regis Canoe Area to the south and southwest.

The trail starts just before the imposing gate to Topridge, the Great Camp formerly owned by Marjorie Merriweather Post, the cereal heiress. At 0.9 mile, just after the trail crosses a wooden bridge, a short spur to the left leads to a grassy clearing with a picnic table. Shortly before the summit, the trail skirts a rock-walled valley filled with paper birch (*Betula papyrifea*). The tops of many of the birch were snapped off during an ice storm in 1998. The fire tower is inaccessible.

Directions: From the junction of NY 30 and NY 86 in Paul Smiths, drive about 0.1 mile north on NY 30 to Keese Mill Road; turn left and go 2.7 miles to a dirt road on the left; go 0.5 mile down this road to the trailhead on the right.

Trail: 2.5 miles to summit.

Elevation: 1,650 feet to 2,875 feet.

Degree of difficulty: Moderate.

Surface and blaze: Natural forest floor. Red blazes.

Adirondack Fish Cultural Station

[Fig. 45(6)] The state fish hatchery near Saranac Lake specializes in raising Atlantic salmon (*Salmo salar*) from both hatchery and wild stock. Each year, it stocks about 500,000 salmon and trout in 120 waters in five Adirondack counties. Visitors can see the fish in various stages of life as well as the large salmon and trout used for breeding.

Directions: From the junction of NY 3 and NY 86 in Saranac Lake, drive north on NY 86 for 5.6 miles to NY 186; turn left and go 4.1 miles to NY 30; bear left and go 5.2 miles to Fish Hatchery Road on the right.

Facilities: Visitor center.

Dates: Open year-round.

Fees: None.

Closest town: Saranac Lake is about 14 miles east.

For more information: Adirondack Fish Cultural Station, PO Box 1, Saranac Lake, 12983. Phone (518) 891-3358. Ask for their leaflet.

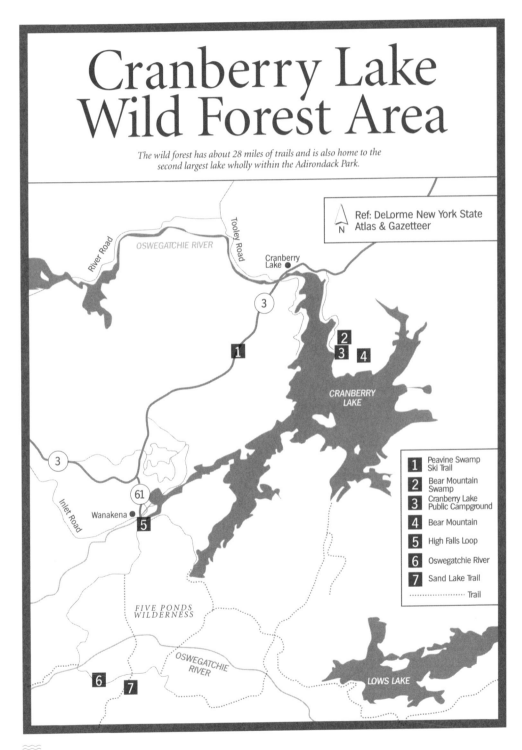

Cranberry Lake Wild Forest Area

The wild forest has about 28 miles of trails and is also home to the second largest lake wholly within the Adirondack Park.

Ref: DeLorme New York State Atlas & Gazetteer

N

OSWEGATCHIE RIVER

River Road

Tooley Road

Cranberry Lake

CRANBERRY LAKE

Inlet Road

Wanakena

FIVE PONDS WILDERNESS

OSWEGATCHIE RIVER

LOWS LAKE

1 Peavine Swamp Ski Trail

2 Bear Mountain Swamp

3 Cranberry Lake Public Campground

4 Bear Mountain

5 High Falls Loop

6 Oswegatchie River

7 Sand Lake Trail

.... Trail

Lake Clear

[Fig. 45(4)] The state owns a large sandy beach just off NY 30 on the eastern shore of this large lake. The swimming is excellent, but there is no lifeguard. No camping is allowed. Canoes can be launched at the beach, but paddlers should beware that the large lake can get choppy in a breeze. The state stocks the water with brown trout (*Salmo trutta*) and Atlantic salmon (*Salmo salar*). Ice fishing is permitted.

Directions: From the junction of NY 3 and NY 86 in Saranac Lake, drive north on NY 86 for 5.6 miles to NY 186; turn left and go 4.1 miles to NY 30; turn right and go 1.3 miles to an entrance road on the left. The entrance is hard to spot.

Activities: Swimming, canoeing, fishing.

Facilities: Sand beach, outhouse.

Dates: Year-round.

Fees: None.

Closest town: Saranac Lake is about 11 miles away.

For more information: State Department of Environmental Conservation, RD3, PO Box 22A, Lowville, NY 13367. Phone (315) 376-3521.

Cranberry Lake Wild Forest

[Fig. 46] The Cranberry Lake Wild Forest encompasses more than 24,000 acres on both sides of Cranberry Lake. Although the woods throughout the region were lumbered in the past, old-growth trees can be seen along the Peavine Swamp Ski Trail west of the lake.

The wild forest contains some small mountains, but overall the elevation is fairly low, making the region excellent habitat for white-tailed deer (*Odocoileus virginianus*). Hunters in quest of deer and black bear (*Ursus americanus*) enjoy success here. Trout fishermen frequent the ponds east of Cranberry Lake.

Cranberry Lake is one of the Adirondacks' prime breeding grounds for the common loon (*Gavia immer*). Other birds dwelling in the region include wood duck (*Aix sponsa*), black duck (*Anas platyrhynchus*), cedar waxwing (*Bombycilla cedrorum*), and ruffed grouse (*Bonasa umbellus*).

The state runs the Cranberry Lake Public Campground on the lake's eastern shore. The wild forest's most popular trail leads from the campground to the 2,520-foot summit of Bear Mountain. Other trails east of the lake lead to Bear Mountain Swamp and the trout ponds. All told, the wild forest has about 28 miles of trails. It has two lean-tos, one on the Bear Mountain Trail and one on the Peavine Swamp Trail.

For more information: State Department of Environmental Conservation, 6739 US Hwy. 11, Canton, NY 13617. Phone (315) 265-3090. Ask for the leaflet *Trails in the Cranberry Lake Region*.

CRANBERRY LAKE

[Fig. 46] Cranberry Lake, encompassing 6,976 acres, is the second largest lake wholly within the Adirondack Park, after Lake George. More than three-fourths of its shoreline is owned by the state. Although the state runs a conventional campground on the eastern shore, hikers, boaters, and canoeists can stay for free at 46 primitive campsites scattered around the lake and on its islands.

A dam built in 1867 doubled the size of the lake, creating several long inlets. The lake's unusual shape has been compared to both a starfish and a Rorschach ink blot. The Oswegatchie River is the lake's main feeder and its outlet (*see* page 309).

Cranberry Lake sees motorboat traffic but not as much as Lake George and some of the other big Adirondack waters. The open water can get rough, so most canoeists prefer to explore the inlets. In these more peaceful, more remote waters, visitors will observe a variety of wildlife, such as river otter (*Lutra canadensis*), common merganser (*Mergus merganser*), wood duck, great blue heron (*Ardea herodias*), and osprey (*Pandion haliaetus*). One possible way to visit is to paddle down Brandy Brook Flow, on the eastern side of the lake, and then head north to Bear Mountain Swamp.

Several hiking trails lead into the Five Ponds Wilderness from the lake's southern shore. Two good day-hike destinations are High Falls on the Oswegatchie River and the Cat Mountain summit. Both can be reached from Janacks Landing on the southwestern end of Dead Creek Flow, the longest arm of the lake.

The state stocks Cranberry Lake with brook trout (*Salvelinus fontinalis*). Other species that can be caught include smallmouth bass (*Micropterus dolomieui*) and northern pike (*Esox lucius*).

There is a state boat launch in the village of Cranberry Lake. Canoeists also can put in at the state Rangers School in Wanakena. By putting in at the Rangers School, canoeists heading to the southern part of the lake, including Dead Creek Flow, can avoid much open water. For a fee, canoeists also can launch at the state campground (*see* page 305).

Directions: To reach the state boat launch from NY 3 in Cranberry Lake, turn south onto Columbian Road, just west of the bridge over the Oswegatchie River, and drive 0.2 mile to the launch. To reach the Rangers School, continue west on NY 3 about 7 miles past the boat launch to County 61; turn left and go about 0.9 mile to Ranger School Road; turn left and go about 0.4 mile to the launch on the right.

Activities: Camping, canoeing, boating, fishing, hiking.

Facilities: Boat launch and 46 campsites, including two lean-tos. Some sites have privies.

Dates: Seasonal.

Fees: None.

Closest town: The village of Cranberry Lake is on the northern shore.

For more information: State Department of Environmental Conservation, 6739 US Hwy. 11, Canton, NY 13676. Phone (315) 265-3090. The leaflet *Trails in the Cranberry Lake Region* shows the campsites and trails.

CRANBERRY LAKE PUBLIC CAMPGROUND

[Fig. 46(3)] The state operates a 173-site campground on the northern arm of Cranberry Lake. A trail leads from the campground to the summit of Bear Mountain. Another trail branches off this one to go to Bear Mountain Swamp. It later hooks up with a trail network that penetrates deeper into the Cranberry Lake Wild Forest.

Directions: From NY 3 just east of the hamlet of Cranberry Lake, turn south on Lone Pine Road and drive to 1.3 miles to the campground entrance on the left.

Activities: Camping, hiking, swimming, fishing, boating, canoeing, picnicking.

Facilities: 173 campsites, picnic area, sand beach, bathhouse, flush toilets, hot showers, trailer dump station. Some campsites, a fishing pier, and toilets and showers are accessible to the handicapped.

Dates: Open May through October.

Fees: There is a charge for camping or day use.

Closest town: Cranberry Lake is a short distance to the west.

For more information. Campground office, phone (315) 848-2315. For reservations, phone (800) 456-2267.

BEAR MOUNTAIN

[Fig. 46(4)] A rocky overlook on Bear Mountain offers a good view of Cranberry Lake and the mountains of the Five Ponds Wilderness beyond. Since the trail to the overlook begins at the Cranberry Lake Public Campground, it gets a lot of use.

From a parking lot near Campsite 27, the trail climbs the mountain's northwestern slope. Bear right at the marked junction 0.15 mile from the start. The trail crosses a few creeks and ascends through a hardwood forest with large specimens of yellow birch (*Betula alleghaniensis*) and sugar maple (*Acer saccharum*) before passing a lean-to at 0.8 mile.

The trail levels off when it reaches the summit. There are no views here. Continue walking, past numerous glacial boulders, until reaching the lookout on the right after a short descent. From the lookout, hikers can continue 1 mile down the trail, which ends near Campsite 133. Since this requires a long walk along campground roads to return to the original trailhead, most people simply turn around at the lookout.

Directions: The trail begins just past Campsite 27 and ends near Campsite 133. If not doing the loop, start and finish at Campsite 27. To avoid a day-use fee, park in a small lot near the pay phone at the campground entrance and walk about 0.4 mile to the trailhead.

Trail: 1.7 mile to overlook.

Elevation: About 1,500 feet to 2,520 feet at summit.

Degree of difficulty: Moderate.

Surface and blaze: Natural forest floor. Red blazes.

BEAR MOUNTAIN SWAMP

[Fig. 46(2)] The trails to Bear Mountain Swamp and

TROUT LILY
(*Erythronium americanum*)

the Bear Mountain lookout begin at the same trailhead in the Cranberry Lake Public Campground. Although the swamp trail lacks the popularity of the summit trail, it is just as interesting. A leaflet explaining interpretive stops can be obtained at the campground office.

Two long boardwalks cross the wetland. The first passes through a hummocky swamp dominated by balsam fir (*Abies balsamea*), red spruce (*Picea rubens*), and northern white cedar (*Thuja occidentalis*). Bunchberry (*Cornus canadensis*) and clintonia (*Clintonia borealis*) contribute to the green ground cover. The second boardwalk passes through a section of the swamp where water flows more freely. Turtleheads (*Chelone glabra*) and spotted touch-me-nots (*Impatiens capensis*) bloom amid grasses and shrubs. Tamaracks (*Larix laricina*) also can be seen.

After the second boardwalk, the trail continues to a snowmobile trail that begins on NY 3 and leads to several ponds deep in the Cranberry Lake Wild Forest.

Directions: The trail begins just past Campsite 27. To avoid a day-use fee, park in a small lot near the pay phone at the campground entrance and walk about 0.4 mile to the trailhead.

Trail: About 1.4 miles to swamp, 2.4 miles to snowmobile trail.

Degree of difficulty: Easy.

Surface and blaze: Natural forest floor, boardwalk. Red and yellow blazes.

PEAVINE SWAMP SKI TRAIL

[Fig. 46(1)] Designated a cross-country ski route, this trail passes by the Peavine Swamp, a large acidic bog, on its way to a lean-to on the Inlet Flow near the point where it meets the main body of Cranberry Lake. Old-growth hemlock (*Tsuga canadensis*) and red spruce (*Picea rubens*) are common along the southern part of the trail. This tract, acquired by the state in 1881, has never been extensively logged. About 0.3 mile from the start, the trail reaches a junction with another trail to the left. This trail loops back to rejoin the main trail at 1 mile.

Directions: From the hamlet of Cranberry Lake, drive west about 2 miles on NY 3 to the trailhead on the left.

Trail: 4.2 miles to lean-to.

Degree of difficulty: Easy.

Surface and blaze: Natural forest floor. Red blazes.

Five Ponds Wilderness

Let's start with what the Five Ponds Wilderness doesn't have: mountains and crowds. The only alpine trail leads to the summit of the rather puny Cat Mountain south of Cranberry Lake. In one recent year, the wilderness accounted for less than 1 percent of the trailhead sign-ins in the Adirondack Park, even though it contains

107,208 acres, about 4 percent of the park's state-owned land.

Here's what the Five Ponds Wilderness does have to offer: the Oswegatchie River, famed among canoeists as a watery road through the wild, and one of the biggest tracts of virgin forest in the Northeast. It also contains the Five Ponds Esker, recognized by the Adirondack Park Agency as a natural feature of special interest. This long, narrow ridge of glacial till separates the five small ponds that give the wilderness its name.

Also, solitude. A hiker can walk on the trails for hours without seeing anyone. Bushwhackers who venture into the trailless tracts in the south can count on being alone.

A windstorm ripped through the Five Ponds Wilderness in 1995, toppling thousands of trees and and clogging trails. Although the trails have been reopened—or rerouted—visitors will see evidence of the storm's devastation. Fortunately, most of the old-growth trees escaped unscathed.

A more insidious form of destruction, acid rain, has left most pond in the southern sector of the wilderness without fish. Anglers can still catch brook trout in many ponds in the northern sector. Several ponds are stocked.

In a region as vast as the Five Ponds Wilderness, just about every kind of Adirondack animal, from the tiniest vole to the black bear, can find a home. Moose have been spotted in the region since they began returning to the Adirondacks in the 1980s. The conifer lowlands provide habitat for boreal species, such as the gray jay and Canada warbler. Other relatively uncommon birds that dwell in the Five Ponds Wilderness include osprey, red-shouldered hawk, and Eastern bluebird.

The Five Ponds Wilderness has about 50 miles of trails and 14 lean-tos. Numerous primitive campsites exist along the canoe route on the Oswegatchie.

For more information: State Department of Environmental Conservation, 317 Washington Street, Watertown, NY 13601. Phone (315) 785-2263. Ask for the leaflet *Trails in the Cranberry Lake Region.*

HIGH FALLS LOOP

[Fig. 46(5)] One of the best ways to see the Five Ponds Wilderness is to hike a 15.5-mile loop that includes a visit to High Falls on the Oswegatchie River, a destination popular among canoeists.

Both ends of the loop begin in the hamlet of Wanakena. The eastern section of the loop, starting on the Dead Creek Flow Trail, offers the easiest and quickest route to the falls. Hikers should take this trail if they want to visit the falls without doing the whole loop. It also is used to reach trails leading to Janacks Landing and Cat Mountain. Janacks Landing, on the Dead Creek Flow, is a short detour and well worth a visit.

The western section of the loop follows an old truck trail that eventually shrinks to a footpath. It passes large coniferous wetlands with views of nearby hills. The trail can be hard to follow in places. At times, hikers will find themselves tiptoeing across old beaver dams or wading through flooded stretches. Some of the best scenery comes at bends in the Oswegatchie River.

After about 7 miles, the truck trail reaches a junction with a blue-blazed trail that leads south to Sand Lake (*see* below). Continue straight. The trail soon reaches the western edge of the Oswegatchie Plains, a sandy-soil heath where early settlers once grazed sheep. Trees are starting to overtake the plains. After skirting the plains, hikers reach a spur trail on the right that leads about 0.25 mile to High Falls.

The falls, though only about 15 feet high, are quite powerful: The water gushes through bedrock channels, throwing off a fine mist. The rock slabs are ideal for sunbathing. Fishermen sometimes cast for brook trout (*Salvelinus fontinalis*) at the base of falls. There are two lean-tos at the falls, one on either side of the river.

The trail back to Wanakena has a few ups and downs. It is easier to follow than the western section. It crosses creeks, circumnavigates beaver ponds, and passes several small cascades tumbling down rocky cliffs. Throughout the loop, hikers will see abundant evidence of the windstorm that swept across the region in 1995.

Directions: From Cranberry Lake village, drive west on NY 3 about 7 miles and turn left onto County 61; continue straight at two intersections, reached at 0.8 mile and 1.1 miles, to go to a gravel road on the right at 1.5 miles, just after crossing the Oswegatchie River. The gravel road is the western trailhead. To reach the eastern trailhead, continue about 0.5 mile to a parking lot on the right.

Trail: 15.5-mile loop, including spur trail to High Falls. From the eastern trailhead, it's 6.6 miles to High Falls.

Degree of difficulty: Strenuous, because of length.

Surface and blaze: Old road, natural forest floor. Red blazes.

SAND LAKE TRAIL

[Fig. 46(7)] Hikers who want to visit the remoter parts of the Five Ponds Wilderness can take this trail south from the High Falls Loop (*see* page 307) for 7.2 miles—a walk of at least 14 miles from the trailhead in Wanakena.

The Sand Lake Trail passes through the 40,000-acre tract of virgin forest purchased by the state in 1896. Large specimens of red spruce (*Picea rubens*), yellow birch (*Betula alleghaniensis*), and white pine (*Pinus strobus*) can be seen. The tract begins as the trail enters Herkimer County, a little south of the Oswegatchie River.

After crossing the outlet to Big Shallow Pond, the trail skirts the Five Ponds Esker, one of the largest eskers in the Adirondacks. Hikers may want to leave the trail to walk along the knifelike ridge, among big pines and hemlocks, until they see Big Shallow Pond on the left. At Big Shallow, the trail turns away from the esker en route to Washbowl and Little Shallow ponds.

The trail ends near the lean-to on Sand Lake. Lean-tos also exist at Big Shallow and Little Shallow ponds. A smaller esker separates Sand Lake from Rock Lake. About 2.5 miles before Sand Lake, a yellow-blazed trail on the right leads 0.5 mile to a lean-to at Wolf Pond.

Directions: Same as for High Falls Loop (*see* page 307).

Trail: 7.3 miles from High Falls Loop.

Degree of difficulty: Moderate.

Surface and blaze: Natural forest floor. Blue blazes.

OSWEGATCHIE RIVER

[Fig. 46(6)] No river provides a better passage into the Adirondack wilds than the Oswegatchie. Canoeists who travel the 20 miles upriver through the Five Ponds Wilderness enjoy a meandering journey past marsh and virgin forest and waterfall, a journey that always holds out the promise of a surprise around the next bend—perhaps a deer, an otter, or a cedar waxwing.

The state maintains 44 campsites on the river, including two lean-tos at High Falls, a small but powerful cascade 13 miles from the launch site at Inlet. Many people turn around at the falls. Above the falls, the river narrows and canoeists encounter numerous beaver dams, but it is possible to continue another 7 miles or so. A few miles below the falls, a footbridge crosses the river where a trail leads south to the Five Ponds Wilderness and beyond. Camping canoeists might want to reserve time to explore this country of old-growth timber on the Sand Lake Trail (*see* page 308).

For the ultimate Oswegatchie trip, canoeists can paddle up the Bog River Flow to the eastern edge of the Five Ponds Wilderness, portage 0.9 mile along a trail to Big Deer Pond, paddle across the pond, and then carry another 2.1 miles to the upper river (*see* Bog River/Bog River Flow, page 289).

Most trips, however, will begin at a still water known as Inlet where there is a large grass parking lot, a register, and a privy. Upriver from Inlet, canoeists can look forward to smooth water and an occasional Class I rapid. Downriver from Inlet, the Oswegatchie rushes through a boulder garden that is seldom canoed. Hikers and anglers, however, can walk a 2-mile hiking trail marked by yellow blazes between Inlet and the hamlet of Wanakena. This stretch is stocked with brook trout (*Salvelinus fontinalis*) and brown trout (*Salmo trutta*). Trout also can be caught upriver from Inlet.

At Wanakena, the Oswegatchie widens to become Inlet Flow, an arm of Cranberry Lake. The river flows northwest from the lake and joins forces with the west and middle branches before reaching the Saint Lawrence River in Ogdensburg. Other canoeing ideas for all three branches can be found in *Adirondack Canoe Waters: North Flow* by Paul Jamieson and Donald Morris.

Directions: From the village of Cranberry Lake, drive about 10 miles west on NY 3 to Sunny Lake Road; turn left and immediately take another left onto Inlet Road; take this road 3.4 miles to the parking lot at the end. The trail to Wanakena begins on the left about 0.1 mile before the lot.

Activities: Canoeing, camping, fishing, hiking.

Facilities: Canoe launch, 44 campsites, including 4 lean-tos, hiking trails. Some campsites have privies. There are 2 other campsites on the canoe carry from Bog River Flow.

Dates: The river is canoeable in spring, summer, and fall.

Pepperbox Wilderness Area

The second smallest wilderness in the Adirondack Park is home to about two dozen ponds, ranging in size from 1 acre to 64 acres.

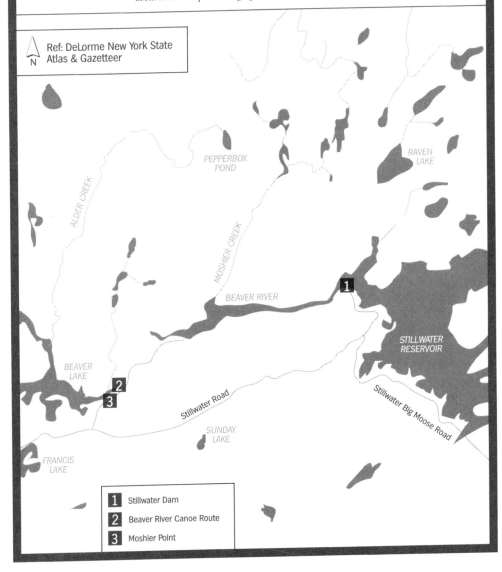

Ref: DeLorme New York State Atlas & Gazetteer

N

PEPPERBOX POND

RAVEN LAKE

ALDER CREEK

MOSHIER CREEK

BEAVER RIVER

1

STILLWATER RESERVOIR

BEAVER LAKE

2
3

Stillwater Road

Stillwater Big Moose Road

SUNDAY LAKE

FRANCIS LAKE

1 Stillwater Dam

2 Beaver River Canoe Route

3 Moshier Point

Fees: None.

Closest town: Star Lake is about 1.7 miles west of Sunny Lake Road.

For more information: State Department of Environmental Conservation, 6739 US Hwy. 11, Canton, NY 13617. Phone (315) 265-3090. The leaflet *Trails in the Cranberry Lake Region* shows the campsites and trails. Another leaflet, *Fishing/Canoeing the Oswegatchie River*, covers the river from Cranberry Lake to the Saint Lawrence.

Pepperbox Wilderness

[Fig. 47] This 14,600-acre trailless tract, the second smallest wilderness in the Adirondack Park, lies just west of Stillwater Reservoir and the Five Ponds Wilderness. The region has about two dozen ponds, ranging in size from 1 acre to 64 acres, but acid rain has killed off the fish. The terrain varies from beaver meadows and wetland flats to small mountains reaching 2,160 feet in height. Deciduous forests cover most of the region.

Because of its remoteness and lack of trails, the Pepperbox Wilderness sees few visitors besides hunters. The very characteristics that discourage others may appeal to bushwhackers in search of solitude and a true wilderness experience. The Pepperbox is small enough—roughly 5 square miles—to be traversed in a day.

The region has two entry points. A short trail on land owned by Niagara Mohawk Power Corporation crosses the Beaver River near the Moshier hydroelectric plant to give access to the southwestern portion. Near the Stillwater dam, a dirt road closed to vehicles gives access to the southeastern portion. The road forms part of the wilderness boundary.

Directions: Stillwater dam: From NY 28 in Eagle Bay, drive north and west on Big Moose Road about 18.5 miles to Stillwater Road; turn right and go 0.4 mile to a gravel road on the left, near a restaurant; go about 1.1 miles on the gravel road to a vehicle barrier. Moshier plant: From Eagle Bay, take Big Moose Road north and west 18.5 miles to Stillwater Road; turn left and go 5.5 miles to Moshier Road; turn right and go 0.7 mile to a lot on the right. Starting on the other side of the road, a blue-blazed trail leads 0.4 mile to the edge of the wilderness. The trail will end soon after crossing the Beaver River. If starting in Lowville, take the Number Four Road about 17 miles; turn right onto Stillwater Road and go about 3.5 miles to Moshier Road on the left.

Activities: Bushwhacking, primitive camping, hunting, snowshoeing, cross-country skiing.

Facilities: None.

Dates: Year-round.

Fees: None.

Closest town: Eagle Bay is about 19 miles away.

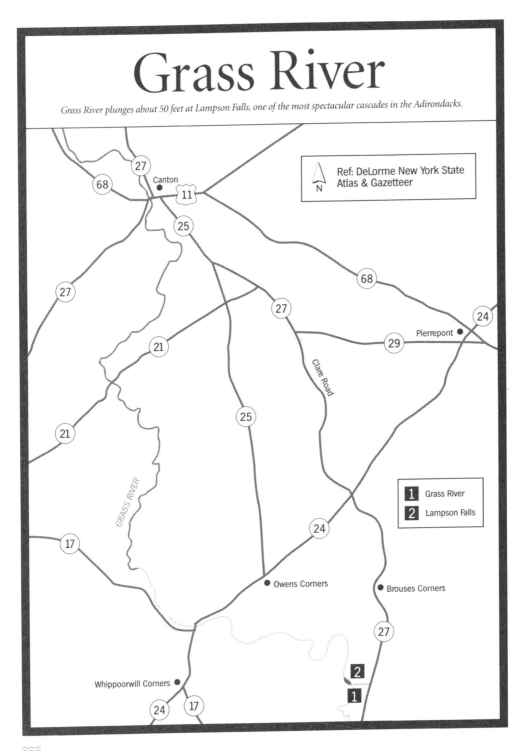

Grass River

Grass River plunges about 50 feet at Lampson Falls, one of the most spectacular cascades in the Adirondacks.

Ref: DeLorme New York State Atlas & Gazetteer

N

27

68

Canton

11

25

27

21

27

68

29   Pierrepont

24

Clare Road

25

21

17

GRASS RIVER

24

Owens Corners

Brouses Corners

27

1 Grass River
2 Lampson Falls

2

1

Whippoorwill Corners

24   17

Grass River

[Fig. 48(1)] Before reaching Lampson Falls, the Grass River meanders sluggishly through flats for about 5 miles, a scenic stretch that can be easily canoed. The most convenient launch is located off Clare Road on the Middle Branch of the Grass. The Middle Branch meets the main river about 0.75 mile downstream from the put-in. From the confluence, the main branch can be canoed in either direction. Lampson Falls is about 3 miles downriver. It's possible to take out on either side of the river when the roar of the falls is heard. If making a one-way trip, take out on the right, where there is an obvious path to Lampson Falls Road (*see* below). The state stocks the Grass River with brown trout (*Salmo trutta*).

For other canoeing possibilities on all the branches of the Grass, see *Adirondack Canoe Waters: North Flow* by Paul Jamieson and Donald Morris.

Directions: From the junction of County 17 and County 27 in Degrasse, drive about 2 miles north on County 27, or Clare Road, to a short carry trail on the left. The trail begins on the left about 0.25 miles past Dean Road.

For more information: State Department of Environmental Conservation, 6739 US Hwy. 11, Canton, NY 13617. Phone (315) 265-3090. Ask for the leaflet *Fishing and Canoeing the Grass River.*

Lampson Falls

[Fig. 48(2)] At Lampson Falls, the Grass River plunges about 50 feet in a thunderous roar, one of the most spectacular cascades in the Adirondacks. This wide, powerful falls can be reached by an old dirt road—Lampson Falls Road—that is now closed to vehicles. Below the falls, a foot trail follows the river past smaller cascades and flumes. Old-growth white pine (*Pinus strobus*) and hemlock (*Tsuga canadensis*) can be seen on much of the hike.

Hikers may begin to hear the falls as they pass through a stand of pine about 0.25 mile from the trailhead. As the trail nears the falls, several herd paths lead left to the top of the cascade. At 0.5 mile, the main trail reaches a sandy campsite beside the large, foamy pool below the falls.

From the campsite, the trail climbs a pine knoll, where there is a privy. Most hikers, however, will want to turn left before the knoll to view the falls from bedrock outcrops that form a small peninsula. Those who want to continue the hike down the river should turn right near the tip of the peninsula to rejoin the marked trail. Since the trail follows the river, it's easy to find.

At 1.5 miles, the trail reaches a boisterous flume where the river is squeezed into a narrow rock channel. A bridge that once enabled hikers to cross the river here has been washed out, but the state may rebuild it. The old road on the right leads back to Lampson

Falls Road. At 1.7 miles, the trail reaches another flume and, just beyond it, a tiny gorge.

Lampson Falls and the foot trail belong to the 1,275-acre Grass Lake Wild Forest. The forest also boasts Harper Falls, a smaller cascade on the North Branch of the Grass River.

Directions: From the junction of County 17 and County 27 in Degrasse, drive 4.4 miles north on County 27, or Clare Road, to the trailhead on the left. Park along the road.

Trail: 0.5 mile to campsite below falls, 1.7 miles to second flume and gorge.

Degree of difficulty: Easy.

Surface and blaze: Old road, natural forest floor. Red blazes.

Azure Mountain

[Fig. 45(2)] Even though its fire tower is inaccessible, Azure Mountain offers superb views in several directions: Debar Mountain to the northeast, Saint Regis Mountain to the southeast, and the Saint Lawrence valley to the north. On a clear day, the High Peaks can be discerned. The Saint Regis River winds through a boreal forest directly below the mountain.

The trail to the summit is fairly level until reaching the remains of a ranger's cabin at 0.3 mile. It then begins climbing steeply through the hardwood forest, making use of switchbacks. An ice storm in 1998 snapped the tops off many of the trees, especially those closer to the summit. During the ascent, be sure to look back occasionally for nice views of the mountains to the south.

PITCHER PLANT
(Sarracenia sp.)
This insect-eating plant grows in boggy soil and uses its leafstalks or "pitchers" to hold pools of water. Insects are attracted by the odor of decay inside, then are forced downward by a hairy lining to the water where a narcotic kills them.

Blueberries, chokecherries, and various wildflowers, including meadowsweet (*Spiraea latifolia*), fireweed (*Epilobium augustifolium*), and yarrow (*Achillea millefolium*), grow on the rocky summit.

Directions: From the junction of NY 458 and County 5 in the hamlet of Saint Regis Falls, drive 4 miles south on NY 458 to Blue Mountain Road; turn right and go 7.7 miles to the trailhead parking lot on the right. There is a spring on the right about 0.4 mile before the parking lot.

Trail: 1 mile to summit.

Elevation: 1,575 feet to 2,518 feet.

Degree of difficulty: Moderate.

Surface and blaze: Old road, natural forest floor. Red blazes.

Everton Falls Preserve

[Fig. 45(1)] The Adirondack Nature Conservancy owns a 530-acre preserve along the East Branch of the Saint Regis that gives canoeists access to 9 miles of still water above Everton Falls. The small falls is located just off the road, where the conservancy has a register. Visitors can park along the road to walk to the flat rocks above the cascade. Paddlers will find a short carry trail about 0.2 mile upriver.

The East Branch above the falls is canoeable all summer. It winds through a wide marsh that harbors a variety of waterfowl. The Nature Conservancy forbids fishing in the preserve above the falls. The preserve ends about 1 mile above the falls. Thereafter, the land is posted, though the river can be canoed.

The conservancy has laid out two short nature trails in the preserve. If coming from the village of Saint Regis Falls, the Balsam Trail begins about 0.5 mile before Everton Falls, on the right side of the road. The Hardwood Trail begins about 0.3 mile past the falls, on the left side of the road. Each trail, marked by a wooden post, is roughly 0.25 mile long.

Directions: From the junction of NY 458 and County 5 in the hamlet of Saint Regis Falls, drive north on County 5 for 0.2 mile to Duane Street, or County 14; turn right and go 7.5 miles to the falls on the right. County 14, also known as Red Tavern Road, continues 8.7 miles past the falls and ends at NY 30.

Activities: Canoeing, fishing, hiking.

Facilities: Canoe launch, hiking trails.

Dates: Open year-round.

Fees: None.

Closest town: Saint Regis Falls is about 7.5 miles away.

For more information: Adirondack Nature Conservancy and Adirondack Land Trust, PO Box 65, Keene Valley, NY 12943. Phone (518) 576-2082.

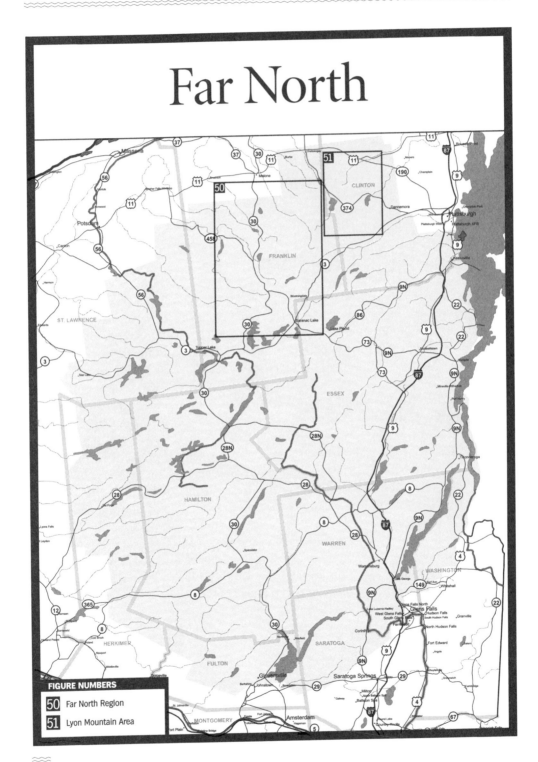

Far North

FIGURE NUMBERS

| 50 | Far North Region |
| 51 | Lyon Mountain Area |

Far North

North of the High Peaks Region, the proportion of state land in the Adirondacks drops off significantly. Substantial chunks of contiguous public land exist in the Debar Mountain Wild Forest and Taylor Pond Wild Forest but nothing to rival those found in the wilderness areas to the south.

For those who enjoy alpine vistas, two of the best hikes end at the summits of Debar and Lyon mountains. These isolated peaks offer wonderful views of the northern Adirondacks and the Saint Lawrence valley. Hikers looking for a change of scenery can visit the Bloomingdale Bog, Silver Lake Bog, or Clintonville Pine Barrens.

The Far North includes three lakes over 1,000 acres: Upper Chateaugay Lake, Union Falls Pond, and Meacham Lake. The Saranac River flows through the region.

The state operates three campgrounds in the Far North, at Buck Pond, Taylor Pond, and Meacham Lake.

[*Above:* Canoeists on the Saranac River]

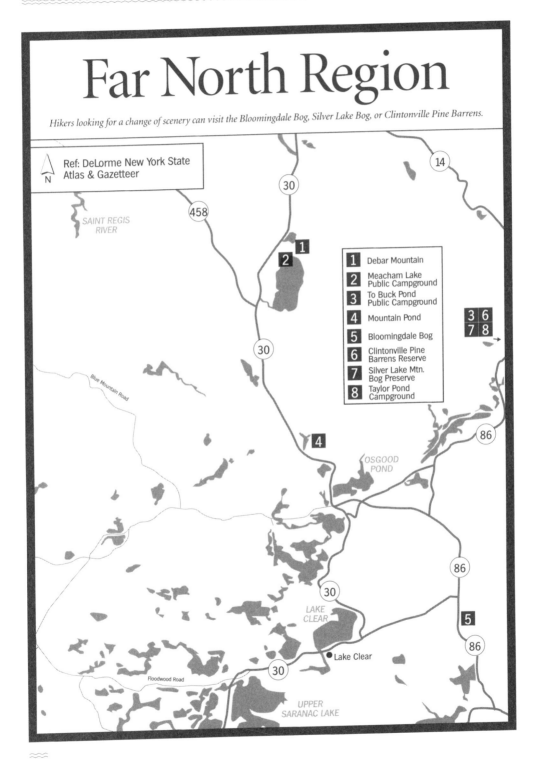

Far North Region

Hikers looking for a change of scenery can visit the Bloomingdale Bog, Silver Lake Bog, or Clintonville Pine Barrens.

Ref: DeLorme New York State
Atlas & Gazetteer

N

14

30

458

SAINT REGIS
RIVER

2 **1**

1 Debar Mountain

2 Meacham Lake
Public Campground

3 To Buck Pond
Public Campground

4 Mountain Pond

5 Bloomingdale Bog

6 Clintonville Pine
Barrens Reserve

7 Silver Lake Mtn.
Bog Preserve

8 Taylor Pond
Campground

30

Blue Mountain Road

3 **6**
7 **8** →

4

OSGOOD
POND

86

86

30

LAKE
CLEAR

5

86

• Lake Clear

30

Floodwood Road

UPPER
SARANAC LAKE

As defined in this chapter, the Far North encompasses the Adirondack Park east of NY 30, west of the Northway, and north of the McKenzie Mountain Wilderness, Whiteface Mountain, and Ausable River.

For more information: State Department of Environmental Conservation, Route 86, PO Box 296, Ray Brook, NY 12977. Phone (518) 897-1200.

Sites in the Far North Region

BLOOMINGDALE BOG

[Fig. 50(5)] This 1,100-acre bog, one of the largest in the Adirondacks, provides a habitat for boreal birds and several rare plants. Hikers can walk through the bog along an abandoned railroad bed now designated as a snowmobile route. Since the ties have been removed, the trail also makes an excellent mountain bike route.

The trail begins just off NY 86 northwest of Saranac Lake. It's possible to walk 4 miles all the way to County 55 west of Bloomingdale. Most visitors probably will not walk that far, unless they have cars at each end, but they will need to walk at least 1 mile to experience the bog. At the outset, trees line both sides of trail, but as one progresses, they become more scarce, opening up for vistas across the bog to the surrounding mountains.

The bog actually contains several ecological communities: boreal acid bog, black spruce-tamarack swamp, deep emergent marsh, shallow marsh, sedge meadow, and shrub swamp. Among the birds that breed here are the spruce grouse (*Canachites canadensis*), gray jay (*Perisoreus canadensis*), boreal chickadee (*Parus hudsonicus*), and black-backed three-toed woodpecker (*Picoides arcticus*).

Blind gentian (*Gentiana clausa*), meadowsweet (*Spiraea latifolia*), yarrow (*Achillea millefolium*), and other wildflowers bloom along the trail. Rhodora (*Rhododendron canadense*), a rare rhododendron, grows in the bog. Other rare plants found here include dwarf birch (*Betula minor*), mountain rice (*Oryzopis canadensis*), and ground-fir (*Lycopodium sabinaefolium*).

Directions: From the junction of NY 3 and NY 86 in Saranac Lake drive north on NY 86 for 3.4 miles to a dirt road on the right; turn down this road and park in a lot on the left. The trail begins next to the lot.

Trail: 1 to 4 miles.

Degree of difficulty: Easy.

Surface and blaze: Old railroad bed. No blazes.

BUCK POND PUBLIC CAMPGROUND

[Fig. 50(3)] Canoeists who stay at this state campground north of Gabriels will find plenty of paddling opportunities. Canoes can be launched from the campground into Buck Pond or Lake Kushaqua.

Buck Pond is rather small and surrounded by state land. Motorboats are not allowed on it. Lake Kushaqua does see motorboat traffic, but canoeists can seek out quiet places. One possibility is to paddle south from the launch to the narrows connecting Lake Kushaqua and Rainbow Lake and then go up the North Branch of the Saranac River to explore its mashes.

For a longer trip, keep going south until reaching a break in the Rainbow Lake Esker, a 4-mile ridge of glacial till that bisects the lake. Rainbow Lake can get busy, but on the other side of the esker lie three quiet waters: the Inlet, the Flow, and Clear Pond.

The state stocks Lake Kushaqua with red salmon and lake trout. Other species found in the lake as well as in Buck Pond include northern pike, brown bullhead, and yellow perch. Brook trout can be caught in the Saranac's north branch.

Directions: From the junction of NY 30 and NY 86 in Paul Smiths, drive east on NY 86 about 4 miles to Gabriels; turn left on the Gabriels-Onchiota Road and go about 6 miles, following the signs for the campground.

Activities: Camping, fishing, canoeing, boating.

Facilities: 116 campsites, sand beach, bathhouse, hot showers, boat launches, trailer dump station.

Dates: May through Labor Day.

Fees: There is a charge for camping or day use.

For more information: Campground office, phone (518) 891-3449. For reservations, phone (800) 456-2267.

▩ MOUNTAIN POND

[Fig. 50(4)] The state maintains several drive-up campsites, available for free, on the edge of this small lake, located just off NY 30 north of Paul Smiths. On the southern end of the lake, rock cliffs rise straight out of the water. Just beyond the northern end is the start of the Hayes Brook Truck Trail, a hiking and equestrian trail that leads about 3.5 miles to a horse barn and two lean-tos in a former sheep meadow. The state stocks the lake with brook trout (*Salvelinus fontinalis*), but a catch-and-release rule is in effect. Anglers may use only artificial lures.

Directions: From the junction of NY 30 and NY 86 in Paul Smiths, drive 3.1 miles north on NY 30 to Mountain Pond Road on the right. The campsites lie along this road.

Activities: Camping, canoeing, fishing, hiking, horseback riding.

Facilities: Primitive campsites, hitching posts, horseback trail. Lean-tos and horse barn on trail.

Dates: Open year-round.

Fees: None.

For more information: State Department of Environmental Conservation, Route 86, PO Box 296, Ray Brook, NY 12977. Phone (518) 897-1200.

MEACHAM LAKE PUBLIC CAMPGROUND

[Fig. 50(2)] At 1,203 acres, Meacham Lake is the second largest lake in the Adirondack Park wholly surrounded by state land. The campground on the northern shore can be used as a base for canoeing, hiking, or fishing.

From the southern end of Meacham Lake, canoeists can enter the marshy inlet of the Osgood River and paddle upriver for about 4 miles. It's about 2 miles from the campground to the river.

For hikers, several trails lead from the campground into the adjacent DeBar Mountain Wild Forest, including one to the summit of DeBar Mountain (*see below*).

The state stocks the lake with Atlantic salmon (*Salmo salar*), brown trout (*Salmo trutta*), and splake, a cross between lake trout and brook trout. Other species that can be caught include northern pike (*Esox lucius*) and yellow perch (*Perca flavenscens*).

From the end of June to Labor Day, the campground conducts nature hikes, crafts, games, and other recreation.

Directions: From the junction of NY 30 and NY 86 in Paul Smiths, drive about 9.5 miles north on NY 30 to the entrance road on the right; turn and go 0.6 mile to the campground.

Activities: Camping, picnicking, hiking, swimming, canoeing, boating.

Facilities: 224 campsites, picnic area, playground, sand beach, bathhouse, showers, boat launch.

Dates: Open mid-May through Columbus Day.

Fees: There is a charge for camping or day use.

For more information: Campground office, phone (518) 483-5116. For reservations, phone (800) 456-2267.

DEBAR MOUNTAIN

[Fig. 50(1)] The 3,300-foot summit of this isolated peak affords good views of the northern Adirondacks, including Saint Regis Mountain and Meacham Lake. The trail begins on the Debar Game Management Trail in the Meacham Lake Public Campground. After about 1 mile, the summit trail bears left at a junction. Hikers may want to take a breather in a lean-to about 0.75 mile from the top: the final ascent is steep.

Directions: See directions for Meacham Lake Public Campground. Turn down a dirt road near Campsite 48 to reach trailhead.

Trail: 3.7 miles to summit.

Elevation: 1,575 feet to 3,300 feet.

Degree of difficulty: Moderate.

Surface and blaze: Dirt road, natural forest floor. Red blazes.

SARANAC RIVER

[Fig. 50] From Upper Saranac Lake, the Saranac River flows about 80 miles to Lake Champlain at Plattsburgh. When Atlantic salmon (*Salmo salar*) head up the river to feed or spawn, anglers often hook them right in the city.

The Saranac flows through a series of lakes before reaching the village of Saranac Lake. From the village to the Blue Line, the river alternates between rapids and slack water. There also are several impoundments. Theoretically, the whole stretch can be canoed when water levels are high, but it entails numerous portages. Anyone contemplating a long trip should consult *Adirondack Canoe Waters: North Flow* by Paul Jamieson and Donald Morris.

Flat-water enthusiasts will enjoy Franklin Falls Pond and Union Falls Pond, two reservoirs several miles outside Saranac Lake. Nearly all the land around these waters is either owned by the state or protected by conservation easements. Bald eagles (*Haliaeetus leucocephalus*) have been known to nest in the vicinity.

The two reservoirs are separated by County 48 at the Franklin Falls Pond dam. Canoes can be launched from the road. Union Falls Pond, at 1,376 acres is easily the larger of the two. Both lakes offer a great view of Whiteface Mountain to the southeast.

Walleye (*Stizostedion vitreum vitreum*) and northern pike (*Esox lucius*) are among the fish that can be caught in the reservoirs. Below the reservoirs, several stretches of the Saranac enjoy a reputation as good places for catching rainbow and brown trout.

Directions: From the village of Bloomingdale, located north of Saranac Lake, drive east on County 18, or River Road, which becomes County 48. The Franklin Falls Pond dam is reached in about 8 miles, but canoe and fishing access sites will be passed en route.

Activities: Boating, canoeing, fishing.

Facilities: Canoe launches on Franklin Falls Pond. Informal launches on Union Falls Pond.

Dates: Seasonal.

Fees: None.

Closest town: Bloomingdale is about 8 miles west.

For more information: State Department of Environmental Conservation, Route 86, PO Box 296, Ray Brook, NY 12977. Phone (518) 897-1200.

CLINTONVILLE PINE BARRENS PRESERVE

[Fig. 50(6)] Some 10,000 years ago, glacial meltwater deposited the sands that underlie these pitch pine–heath barrens owned by the Adirondack Nature Conservancy. Pitch pine (*Pinus rigida*)—recognizable by its scaly bark and prickly, pineapple-shaped cones—thrives in the infertile soil. Pitch pine communities depend on fire for survival: The flames destroy competing trees while the heat opens pine cones to release seeds. The conservancy periodically sets small fires, managed by burn crews, in the preserve.

Blueberries grow in abundance here. Prairie redroot (*Ceanothus herbacea*), a small shrub rare in New York State, also can be found. Other understory plants include sheep laurel (*Kalmia angustifolia*), pipsissiwa (*Chimaphilia umbrellata*), and sweet fern (*Comptonia peregrina*). A rare moth, the pine pinion moth (*Lithophane lepida lepida*), makes its home in the barrens, although it only comes out at night.

The Nature Conservancy has marked a trail that follows old logging roads, but blazes and signs are sometimes scarce. Since several roads crisscross the 900-acre preserve, visitors need to be careful to make the proper turn at junctions. The terrain is flat, so novice cross-country skiers may want to visit the preserve in winter. Leaflets are available at the trail register.

Directions: From the blinking light in Ausable Forks, drive northeast on North Main Street about 0.2 mile to the stop sign; go straight about 2 miles on Golf Course Road to Dry Bridge Road; turn right and go 0.3 mile to Buck Hill Road; turn left and go 0.5 mile to the trailhead on the left.

Trail: 1-mile loop.

Degree of difficulty: Easy.

Surface and blaze: Old roads. Red blazes.

TAYLOR POND PUBLIC CAMPGROUND

[Fig. 50(8)] For those who can do without the usual amenities, the Taylor Pond Public Campground offers primitive camping in a remote and peaceful setting. Each of the 30 campsites comes with an outhouse, picnic table, and fire grate. Some sites can be reached only by boat. There also are three lean-tos on the lake.

Surrounded by state forest, with Catamount Mountain rising nearby, Taylor Pond attracts anglers and canoeists who appreciate its unspoiled beauty. Hikers will find solitude on a 10.5-mile trail that circles the 813-acre lake—although a 1998 ice storm clogged the way with fallen trees and limbs.

The state stocks the water with Atlantic salmon (*Salmo salar*), rainbow trout (*Oncorhynchus mykiss*), and lake trout (*Salvelinus namaycush*).

Directions: From the blinking light in Ausable Forks, drive northeast on North Main Street about 0.2 mile to a stop sign; turn left onto County 1—also known as Turnpike Road or Silver Lake Road—and go about 9.5 miles to the campground entrance road on the left. Note: Silver Lake Road forks left about 3 miles north of the stop sign.

Activities: Camping, picnicking, canoeing, boating, fishing, hiking.

Facilities: 30 campsites, 3 lean-tos, showers, boat launch, hiking trail.

Dates: Open mid-May to mid-Sept.

Fees: There is a fee for camping or day use.

For more information: Campground office, phone (518) 647-5250. For reservations, phone (800) 456-2267.

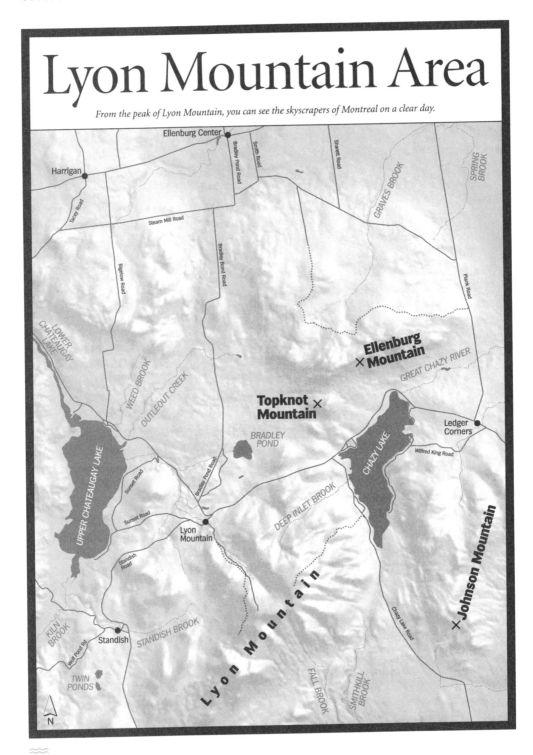

Lyon Mountain Area

From the peak of Lyon Mountain, you can see the skyscrapers of Montreal on a clear day.

LYON MOUNTAIN

[Fig. 51] This giant of the Far North misses High Peak status by less than 200 feet. From its bare summit, one can see almost 180 degrees. The views from the fire tower are even better, but beware that some steps are missing. Bring your binoculars: on a clear day, you can see the skyscrapers of Montreal.

The trail to the summit follows an old jeep trail whose loose rock makes a tough climb even tougher. At the start, the trail ascends through a young hardwood forest. At about 0.75 mile, hikers pass a stand of white birch (*Betula papyrifea*) bent over like ballerinas: they have been frozen in that pose since an ice storm in 1998. Toward the summit, the hardwoods give way to balsam fir (*Abies balsamea*) and red spruce (*Picea rubens*), which become more stunted as elevation increases.

Several kinds of flowers bloom along the trail: spotted touch-me-nots (*Impatiens capensis*), clintonia (*Clintonia borealis*), and Indian pipe (*Monotropa uniflora*).

Directions: From the village of Dannemora, drive 9.3 miles northwest on NY 374 to Chazy Lake Road; turn left and go 1.9 miles to a gravel road on the right; go 0.9 mile up this road to the trailhead.

Trail: 2.5 miles to summit.

Elevation: About 1,900 feet to 3,830 feet.

Degree of difficulty: Strenuous.

Surface and blaze: Old jeep trail, natural forest floor. No blazes.

SILVER LAKE MOUNTAIN

[Fig. 50] The short climb to the summit of this mountain rewards the hiker with interesting views of Silver Lake, Taylor Pond, and, toward the horizon, Whiteface Mountain. The mountain supports not only the typical Adirondack trees, but also red pine (*Pinus resinosa*), northern white cedar (*Thuja occidentalis*), and northern red oak (*Quercus rubra borealis*).

Many trees were damaged in an ice storm in 1998. Look for bent and broken white birch (*Betula papyrifea*) in a ravine about two-thirds of the way to the summit. The trail passes several bedrock outcrops with good lookouts en route to the rock ledges at the top. Wildflowers along the way include clintonia (*Clintonia borealis*) and bunchberry (*Cornus canadensis*). The trail follows an old road for a short distance at the outset and then veers to the left. The climb begins soon after the turn.

Directions: From the blinking light in Ausable Forks, drive northeast on North Main Street about 0.2 mile to a stop sign; turn left onto County 1—also known as Turnpike Road or Silver Lake Road—and go about 11.5 miles to a parking area on the right. The trail begins from the lot. Note: Silver Lake Road forks left about 3 miles north of the stop sign.

Trail: 1 mile to summit.

Elevation: 1,475 feet to 2,375 feet.

Degree of difficulty: Moderate.

Surface and blaze: Natural forest floor. Red blazes.

SILVER LAKE BOG PRESERVE

[Fig. 50(7)] The Adirondack Nature Conservancy has built an excellent boardwalk, with benches and interpretive stops, across a bog and swamp, affording visitors a close-up look at wetlands that are usually inaccessible. Beyond the boardwalk, the trail climbs through a hardwood forest to a piney bluff overlooking Silver Lake.

The boardwalk passes through a green world of sphagnum moss, ferns, pitcher plants, mountain holly, and trees adapted to the wet environment: black spruce (*Picea mariana*), tamarack (*Larix laricina*), northern white cedar (*Thuja occidentalis*), and balsam fir (*Abies balsamea*).

Leaving the bog, the trail passes through a forest of typical Adirondack hardwoods—yellow birch (*Betula alleghaniensis*), sugar maple (*Acer saccharum*), and American beech (*Fagus grandifolia*)—and hemlock (*Tsuga canadensis*). An ice storm in 1998 snapped off the tops of many trees, creating an open canopy in places. The trail gains 200 feet in elevation before reaching the bluff dominated by tall red pines (*Pinus resinosa*).

Informative leaflets are available at the trail register.

Directions: From the blinking light in Ausable Forks, drive northeast on North Main Street about 0.2 mile to a stop sign; turn left onto County 1—also known as Turnpike Road or Silver Lake Road—and go about 12.5 miles to Union Falls Road, just past Silver Lake; turn left and go 1.1 mile to a dirt road on the left; go 0.3 mile down this road to the trailhead on the right. Note: Silver Lake Road forks left about 3 miles north of the stop sign.

Trail: 0.5 mile to end of boardwalk, 1.25 miles to Silver Lake lookout.

Degree of difficulty: Easy.

Surface and blaze: Boardwalk, natural forest floor. Green blazes.

CHATEAUGAY LAKES

[Fig. 51] Although private lands surround Upper and Lower Chateaugay lakes, boaters and canoeists have access to the water at a boat launch on the narrows that separates the two lakes. There is a good view from the water of Lyon Mountain to the southeast. Canoeists should be prepared for powerboat traffic. Together, the lakes and the narrows stretch for 10.5 miles. Upper Chateaugay, at 2,605 acres, is by far the larger of the lakes.

Directions: From the hamlet of Merrill, on the eastern shore of Upper Chateaugay, drive about 0.5 mile north on County 374 to the launch.

Activities: Boating, canoeing, fishing.

Facilities: Hard-surface boat launch.

Dates: Seasonal.

Fees: None.

Closest town: The hamlet of Merrill is 0.5 mile south of the launch.

For more information: State Department of Environmental Conservation, Route 86, PO Box 296, Ray Brook, NY 12977. Phone (518) 897-1200.

Appendixes

A. Books and References

Adirondack Canoe Waters: North Flow by Paul Jamieson and Donald Morris, Adirondack Mountain Club, Lake George, NY 1987.

Adirondack Canoe Waters: South and West Flow by Alec Proskine, Adirondack Mountain Club, Lake George, NY 1994.

Adirondack Cross-Country Skiing: A Guide to Seventy Trails by Dennis Conroy with Shirley Matzke, Backcountry Publications, Woodstock, VT 1992.

Adirondack Mammals by D. Andrew Saunders, State University of New York College of Environmental Science and Forestry, Syracuse, NY 1988.

Adirondack Park 1994 Mountain Bike Preliminary Trail and Route Listing, Adirondack Mountain Club, Lake George, NY, and Adirondack North Country Association, Saranac Lake, NY 1994.

Adirondack Wildguide: A Natural History of the Adirondack Park by Michael G. DiNunzio, Adirondack Mountain Club, Lake George, NY, and Adirondack Conservancy.

An Adirondack Sampler: Day Hikes for All Seasons by Bruce Wadsworth, Adirondack Mountain Club, Lake George, NY 1996.

An Adirondack Sampler II: Backpacking Trips for All Seasons by Bruce Wadsworth, Adirondack Mountain Club, Lake George, NY 1996.

Birds of the Adirondacks by Alan Bessette and William K. Chapman, North Country Books, Utica, NY 1993.

Classic Adirondack Ski Tours by Tony Goodwin, Adirondack Mountain Club, Lake George, NY 1993.

Climbing in the Adirondacks: A Guide to Rock and Ice Routes in the Adirondack Park by Don Mellor, Adirondack Mountain Club, Lake George, NY 1995.

Discover the Adirondacks, 11 volumes, by Barbara McMartin, originally published by Backcountry Publications, Woodstock, VT. Now being distributed by North Country Books, Utica, NY.

85 Acres: A Field Guide to the Adirondack Alpine Summits by Nancy G. Slack and Allison W. Bell, Adirondack Mountain Club, Lake George, NY 1993.

50 Hikes in the Adirondacks by Barbara McMartin, Backcountry Publications, Woodstock, VT 1993.

Fishing the Adirondacks by Francis Betters, Adirondack Sports Publications, Wilmington, NY 1987.

Forest and Trees of the Adirondack High Peaks Region by E.H. Ketchledge, Adirondack Mountain Club, Lake George, NY 1996.

Fun on Flatwater: An Introduction to Adirondack Canoeing by Barbara McMartin, North Country Books, Utica, NY 1995.

Geology of the High Peaks Region: A Hiker's Guide by Howard W. and Elizabeth B. Jaffe, Adirondack Mountain Club, Lake George, NY 1986.

The Geology of New York: A Simplified Account by Yngvar W. Isachsen and others, New York State Geological Survey, Albany 1991.

Good Fishing in the Adirondacks edited by Dennis Aprill, Backcountry Publications, Woodstock, VT 1994.

Guides to Adirondack and Catskill Trails, 8 volumes, edited by Neal S. Burdick, Adirondack Mountain Club, Lake George, NY.

Mammals of the Adirondacks by William K. Chapman, North Country Books, Utica, NY 1991.

North Woods: An Inside Look at the Nature of Forests in the Northeast by Peter J. Marchand, Appalachian Mountain Club, Boston, MA 1987.

Paths Less Traveled: The Adirondack Experience for Walkers, Hikers and Climbers of All Ages by Dennis Aprill, Pinto Press, Mount Kisco, NY 1998.

Quiet Water Canoe Guide: New York by John Hayes and Alex Wilson, Appalachian Mountain Club, Boston, MA 1996.

Roadside Geology of New York by Bradford B. Van Diver, Mountain Press Publishing Company, Missoula, MT 1985.

Trailside Notes: A Naturalist's Companion to Adirondack Plants by Ruth Schottman and Clem Habetler, Adirondack Mountain Club, Lake George, NY 1998.

25 Bicycle Tours in the Adirondacks by Bill McKibben and others, Backcountry Publications, Woodstock, VT 1995.

Wildflowers of the Adirondacks by Anne McGrath and Joanne Treffs, North Country Books, Utica, NY 1981.

Winterwise: A Backpacker's Guide by John M. Dunn, Adirondack Mountain Club, Lake George, NY 1996.

B. Conservation Organizations

Adirondack Council, PO Box D-2, Church Street, Elizabethtown, NY 12932-0640. Phone (518) 873-2240. Satellite office at 342 Hamilton Street, Albany, NY 12210. Phone (518) 432-1770. Lobbies for conservation, monitors land use, and publishes special reports.

Adirondack Mountain Club, 814 Goggins Road, Lake George, NY 12845-4117. Phone (518) 668-4447. Lobbies for conservation, publishes *Adirondac* magazine as well as books and maps, sponsors outdoors workshops and lectures, helps maintain trails and preserve alpine summits, operates two lodges and a campground in High Peaks Region. Uses the abbreviation ADK.

Adirondack Nature Conservancy and Adirondack Land Trust, PO Box 65, Keene Valley, NY 12943. Phone (518) 576-2082. Dedicated to preserving plant and wildlife habitat through conservation easements and outright purchases, often working as a middleman between private landowners and the state. Maintains several nature preserves in the Adirondacks.

Association for the Protection of the Adirondacks, PO Box 951, 30 Roland Place, Schenectady, NY 12304. Phone (518) 377-1452. Oldest organization devoted to protection of the Adirondacks. Maintains the Adirondack and Catskill Research Library, sponsors lectures, publishes *Forest Preserve* magazine as well as newsletters and special reports.

Eastern New York Chapter of The Nature Conservancy, 200 Broadway, 3rd Floor, Troy, NY 12180. Phone (518) 272-0195. Dedicated to preserving plant and wildlife habitat in 16 counties in eastern New York. Owns Dome Island in Lake George.

Lake George Association, PO Box 408, Route 9N, South Luzerne Road, Lake George, NY 12845. Phone (518) 668-3558. The oldest lake association in the nation. Dedicated to preserving and conserving Lake George through education, advocacy and broad-based community involvement. LGA offers Water Quality Programs, Lake-Saving Projects, and the Floating Classroom.

Lake George Basin Land Conservancy, PO Box 1250, Lake Shore Drive, Bolton Landing, NY. Phone (518) 644-9673. Dedicated to preserving land in Lake George's 150,000-acre watershed through outright purchases and conservation easements. Co-owner of Cook Mountain Preserve.

National Audubon Society of New York State, 200 Trillium Lane, Albany, NY 12203. Phone (518) 869-9731. Seeks to preserve land in the Adirondacks through conservation easements and purchases. Chairs the New York Caucus, a group of environmental organizations concerned with conserving the forests of the Adirondacks and Tug Hill to the west. The High Peaks and Southern Adirondacks chapters of Audubon focus on the Adirondacks.

Residents Committee to Protect the Adirondacks, PO Box 27, Main Street, North Creek, NY 12853. Phone (518) 251-4257. Grass-roots organization devoted to protecting the park.

Sierra Club, Atlantic Chapter, 353 Hamilton Street, Albany, NY 12210. Phone (518) 426-9144. Dedicated to preserving wild land through easements, purchases, and land-use regulations.

C. Outfitters

Adirondac Rafting Company, 7 Patch Lane, Lake Placid, NY 12946. Phone (518) 523-1635. Rafting trips on the Hudson and Moose rivers.

Adirondack Alpine Adventures, Route 73, PO Box 179, Keene NY 12942. Phone (518) 576-9881. Rock climbing, ice climbing, mountaineering, backcountry skiing, guide service and instruction.

Adirondack Canoes and Kayaks, 96 Old Piercefield Road & Route 3, Tupper Lake, NY 12986. Phone (518) 359-2174 or (800) 499-2174. Canoe and kayak sales and rentals, shuttle service, guide service.

Adirondack Lakes & Trails Outfitters, 168 Lake Flower Avenue, Saranac Lake, NY 12983. Phone (518) 891-7450 or (800) 491-0414. Canoe and kayak sales and rentals, shuttle service, guide service.

Adirondack River Outfitters (ARO Adventures), PO Box 649, Old Forge, NY 13420. Phone (315) 369-3536 or (800) 525-RAFT. Rafting trips on Sacandaga, Hudson, and Moose rivers.

Adirondack Rock and River, PO Box 219, Keene, NY 12942. Phone (518) 576-2041. Rock and ice climbing, guide service and instruction.

Adventure Sports Rafting Company, Main Street, PO Box 775, Indian Lake, NY 12842. Phone (518) 648-5812 or (800) 441-RAFT. Rafting trips on the Hudson and Moose rivers.

Bear Cub Adventure Tours, 30 Bear Cub Road, Lake Placid, NY 12946. Phone (518) 523-4339. Canoe and kayak rentals, mountaineering, mountain biking, fishing, guide service.

Beaver Brook Outfitters, PO Box 96, Wevertown, NY 12886. Phone (888) 454-8433. Canoe trips and rentals. Rafting trips on the Hudson River.

Blue Mountain Outfitters, Route 28, PO Box 144, Blue Mountain Lake, NY 12812. Phone (518) 352-7306. Canoe and kayak sales and rentals, shuttle service, guide service.

Eastern Mountain Sports, 51 Main Street, Lake Placid, NY 12946. Phone (518) 523-2505. Sales and rental of outdoor gear.

High Peaks Adventure Center, 331 Main Street, Lake Placid, NY 12946. Phone (518) 523-3764 or (800) 550-1455. Rock-climbing gym, equipment, and instruction, canoe and kayak rental, mountain bike rental, shuttle service, guide service.

Hudson River Rafting Company, Cunningham's Ski Barn, North Creek, NY 12853. Phone (518) 696-2964 for Sacandaga River or (518) 251-3215 for Hudson River. Also (800) 888-RAFT. Rafting trips on the Sacandaga, Hudson, and Moose rivers.

Hudson Whitewater World, Main Street, North Creek, NY 12853. Phone (800) 944-8392. Rafting trips on the Hudson and Moose rivers.

Jones Outfitters Ltd., 37 Main Street, Lake Placid, NY 12946. Phone (518) 523-3468. Canoe and kayak sales and rentals, fly-fishing instruction, guide service.

Lake George Kayak, Green Island, PO Box 1575, Bolton Landing, NY 12814. Phone (518) 644-5295. Sales and rentals of kayaks, kayak instruction, guide service.

McDonnell's Adirondack Challenges, Route 30, RR 1, PO Box 262, Lake Clear, NY 12945. Phone (518) 891-1176. Canoe rentals, guided canoe trips, guide service.

Middle Earth Expeditions, Route 73, HCR01 Box 37, Lake Placid, NY 12946-9702. Phone (518) 523-9572. Wilderness canoe and fishing trips, whitewater rafting and canoeing on the Hudson River.

Moose River Company, Box 670, Main Street, Old Forge, NY 13420. Phone (315) 369-3682. Fishing and hunting trips, outdoor skills instruction.

Mountainman Outdoor Supply Company, Route 28, PO Box 659, Inlet, NY 13360. Phone (315) 357-6672. Canoe and kayak rentals, shuttle service, hiking and backpacking supplies.

Placid Bay Ventures, 70 Saranac Avenue, Lake Placid, NY 12946. Phone (518) 523-1744. Fishing and hunting guide service.

Raquette River Outfitters, 131 Moody Road, Route 30, PO Box 653, Tupper Lake, NY 12986. Phone (518) 359-3228. Canoe and kayak rentals, shuttle service.

Stillwaters Guide Service, HC1, Lake Placid, NY 12946-9703. Phone (518) 523-2280. Wilderness fishing trips in High Peaks Region.

Saint Regis Canoe Outfitters, Floodwood Road, PO Box 318, Lake Clear, NY 12945. Phone (518) 891-1838. Canoe and kayak rentals, shuttle service, guide service.

Syd & Dusty's Outfitters, Corner of Routes 9 and 149, Lake George, NY 12845. Phone (518) 745-5130 or (800) 424-0260. Rafting trips on the Hudson River.

Tahawus, Ltd., PO Box 424, Lake Placid, NY 12946. Phone (518) 891-4334. Fishing guides, canoe and guideboat trips.

Whitewater Challengers Inc., Route 28, Okara Lakes, PO Box 657, Old Forge, NY 13420. Phone (315) 369-6699 or (800) 443-7238. Canoe and kayak rental, mountain bike rental, shuttle service. Rafting trips on Hudson and Moose rivers.

W.I.L.D./W.A.T.E.R.S. Outdoor Center, Route 28, HCR01, Box 197A, Warrensburg, NY 12885. Phone (800) 867-2335. Rafting trips on Sacandaga, Hudson, and Moose rivers.

D. Tourism Information

Adirondack Regional Tourism Council, PO Box 51, West Chazy, NY 12992. Phone (518) 846-8016.

Adirondacks Speculator Region Chamber of Commerce, PO Box 184, Speculator, NY 12164. Phone (518) 548-4521.

Bolton Landing Chamber of Commerce, Box 368, Bolton Landing, NY 12814. Phone (518) 644-3831.

Central Adirondack Association, Route 28, PO Box 68, Old Forge, NY 13420. Phone (315) 369-6983.

Franklin County Tourism, 63 West Main Street, Malone, NY 12953. Phone (518) 2900 or (800) 709-4895.

Fulton County Regional Chamber of Commerce & Industry, 2 North Main Street, Gloversville, NY 12078. Phone (518) 725-0641 or (800) 676-3858.

Hamilton County Tourism, White Birch Lane, PO Box 771, Indian Lake, NY 12842. Phone (518) 648-5239.

Indian Lake Chamber of Commerce, PO Box 18, Indian Lake, NY 12842. Phone (518) 648-5112 or (800) 328-5253.

Inlet Chamber of Commerce, PO Box 266-G, Inlet, NY 13360. Phone (315) 357-5501.

Lake Placid/Essex County Visitors Bureau, Olympic Center, Lake Placid, NY 12946. Phone (518) 523-2445 or (800) 275-2243.

Lewis County Chamber of Commerce, 7550 South State Street, Lowville, NY 13367. Phone (315) 376-2213 or (800) 724-0242.

Long Lake Parks, Recreation and Tourism Department, Town Office Building, Route 28N/30, PO Box 496BD, Long Lake, NY 12847-0496. Phone (518) 624-3077.

Plattsburgh/North Country Chamber of Commerce, PO Box 310, Plattsburgh, NY 12901. Phone (518) 563-1000.

Saranac Lake Chamber of Commerce, 30 Main Street, Saranac Lake, NY 12983. Phone (518) 891-1990 or (800) 347-1992.

Saratoga County Chamber of Commerce, 28 Clinton Street, Saratoga Springs, NY 12866. Phone (518) 584-3255.

Schroon Lake Chamber of Commerce, PO Box 726, Schroon Lake, NY 12870. Phone (518) 532-7675 or (800) 923-5687.

Saint Lawrence County Chamber of Commerce, Drawer A, Canton, NY 13617. Phone (315) 386-4000.

Ticonderoga & Crown Point Chamber of Commerce, PO Box 70, Ticonderoga, NY 12883. Phone (518) 585-6619.

Tupper Lake Chamber of Commerce, 60 Park Street, Tupper Lake, NY 12986. Phone (518) 359-3328 or (800) 882-6785.

Warren County Tourism, 1340 Route 9, 908 Municipal Center, Lake George, NY 12845-9803. Phone (518) 761-6366 or (800) 365-1050.

Washington County Tourism Association, County Municipal Center, 383 Broadway, Fort Edward, NY 12828. Phone (518) 746-2294.

Westport Chamber of Commece, Pleasant Street, PO Box 394, Westport, NY 12993. Phone (518) 962-8383.

Whitehall Chamber of Commerce, 259 Broadway, Whitehall, NY 12887. Phone (518) 499-2292.

E. Map Sources

Adirondack Maps Inc., PO Box 718, Market Street, Keene Valley, NY 12943. Phone (518) 576-9861. E-mail: AdackMaps@aol.com. Publishes five large topographical maps of the Adirondacks showing trails and lean-tos. Taken as a group, they cover most of the Adirondack Park. It also sells a detailed canoe map of major canoe areas and routes.

Adirondack Mountain Club, 814 Goggins Road, Lake George, NY 12845-4117. Phone (518) 668-4447. E-mail: adkinfo@adk.org. Each of its seven Adirondack trail guides comes with a topographical map that shows trails, lean-tos, and state lands. The maps can be purchased separately. Each map encompasses only a part of the region covered by the guidebook.

DeLorme, PO Box 298, Freeport, ME 04032. Phone (207) 865-4171. Publishes *New York State Atlas & Gazetteer.*

JIMAPCO, Inc. PO Box 1137, Clifton Park, NY 12065. Phone (518) 899-5091. Publishes Lake George and Lake Champlain boaters maps, Adirondack Park road map, and county road maps.

Map Distribution, United States Geological Survey Map Sales, Box 25286, Federal Center, Building 810, Denver, CO 80225. Phone (800) 872-6277. Sells a variety of topographical and other maps.

Map Information Unit, New York State Department of Transportation, State Campus, Building 4, Room 105, Albany, NY 12232-01415. Phone (518) 457-3555. Sells a variety of topographical and other maps.

Marshall Penn-York Company, 538 Erie Boulevard West, Syracuse, NY 13204-2498. Phone (315) 422-2162. Publishes "Adirondacks Visual Encyclopedia," a detailed road map of the Adirondack Park.

New York State Geological Survey, State Museum, Room 3136, Cultural Education Center, Albany, NY 12230. Phone (518) 474-5816. Publishes "New York State Geological Highway Map," a large color-coded map of the state's bedrock, with commentary. Also includes a composite satellite photograph of the state.

F. Special Events, Fairs, and Festivals

JANUARY
Malone Winter Carnival—A parade, ball, casino night, and snowmobile poker run are among the festivities scheduled here during the last week of January and the first week of February. Phone (518) 483-3760.

FEBRUARY
Febfest—A month-long celebration of winter activities in the village of Speculator, including a dogsled, ice fishing contests, and indoor games and storytelling. Phone (518) 548-4521.

MARCH
Icebreaker Canoe Race—Paddle downriver 3 miles before turning around and heading 2 miles upriver to the finish line in Saranac Lake. Held the third weekend in March. Phone (800) 347-1992.

MAY
Annual White Water Derby—Celebrate the end of winter splashing in the chilly waters of the Hudson River. Visit the street fair if the kayak and canoe races aren't your style. Phone (800) 896-5428.

Bloom-n-Blossom Canoe Race—Meander over a looped course all around the new blooms of spring. Begins and ends at the Tupper Lake Rod & Gun Club the third weekend of May. Phone (888) 887-5253.

JUNE
Flatwater Weekend—Paddle in an 11-mile canoe race on the Raquette River or, for those hardier folks, a 44-mile race starting in Long Lake and ending in Tupper Lake. Both take place the first weekend in June. Phone (888) 887-5253.

Great Adirondack Outdoor Rendezvous—Displays and demonstrations, all touting the outdoors, highlight this family-oriented three-day event in Lake Placid. Phone (518) 523-3961.

June Bug Run/Walk—This annual footrace the first weekend in June begins at North Country Community College in Saranac Lake. Children and adults are welcome. Phone (518) 891-4141, extension 348.

No-Octane Regatta Weekend—Celebrate the history of boats and boating with festivities sponsored by the Adirondack Museum in Blue Mountain Lake. There are also boating-related workshops and demonstrations. Phone (518) 352-7311.

JULY
Black Fly Festival—A weekend of festivities in wry celebration of that bane of the Adirondack vacationer, the blackfly. The town of Bleecker crowns a queen and hosts craft exhibitors in mock honor of the pesky insect. Phone (518) 725-6897.

Mayor's Cup Sailing Race and Landlubber Festival—The sailboat races are just part of the fun in downtown Plattsburgh. There also are musicians, acrobats, and street performers. Held in the middle of the month. Phone (518) 563-1000.

Summer Park Concert Series—A variety of music can be heard at free concerts held every Friday evening in July and August at Riverside Park on Lake Flower in Saranac Lake. Phone (518) 347-1992.

Woodsmen's Days—A weekend full of logging competitions and the North Country's largest horse pull in Tupper Lake in early July. Phone (518) 359-9444.

AUGUST
Adirondack Wildlife Festival—An Adirondack celebration at the Visitor Interpretive Center in Paul Smiths. Phone (518) 327-3000.

Native American Festival—This festival at Whiteface Mountain Ski Center in Wilmington offers storytelling, native dancing, and crafts presentations. Phone (518) 946-2223.

SEPTEMBER
Adirondack Canoe Classic—Travel the original "Highway of the Adirondacks" from Old Forge to Saranac Lake. The 90-mile paddle is held on the second weekend in September. Phone (800) 347-1992.

Fall Foliage Canoe Race—An excellent opportunity to view the spectacular fall foliage in peak color in Tupper Lake. Phone (888) 887-5253.

Lumberjack Festival—Watch lumberjacks throw axes, climb greased poles, and log roll during a weekend of events in Croghan. A parade and a teen pageant round out the festivities. Phone (315) 346-1083.

OCTOBER
Boo Bash and Dash Mountain Bike Race—Bike one day at Dewey Mountain and one day at Big Tupper in the Tupper Lake area. Phone (800) 347-1992.

Octoberfest—Big Tupper's homage to German food, music, and crafts is held at the Ski Center in Tupper Lake. Phone (518) 359-7902 or (518) 359-2904

DECEMBER
Old-Fashioned Christmas Weekend—A Christmas Craft Fair, caroling, and the tree-lighting ceremony highlight this weekend celebration in Northville. Phone (518) 863-4026.

G. Glossary

Anticline—Arching rock fold that is closed at the top and open at bottom. Oldest formation occurs in the center of an anticline.

Basement—Complex of igneous and metamorphic rock that underlies the sedimentary rocks of a region.

Biotic—Pertaining to plants and animals.

Boreal—Relating to the northern biotic area characterized by the dominance of coniferous forests.

Carbonate rock—Collective term including limestone and dolomite.

Coniferous—Describing the cone-bearing trees of the pine family; usually evergreen.

Continental drift—Theory that the continental land masses drift across the Earth as the Earth's plates move and interact in a process called Plate Tectonics.

Deciduous—Plants that shed their leaves seasonally and are leafless for part of the year.

Endemic—Having originated in and being restricted to one particular environment.

Escarpment—Cliff or steep rock face formed by faulting that separates two comparatively level land surfaces.

Extinct—No longer existing.

Extirpated—Extinct in a particular area.

Feldspar—Complex of silicates that make up bulk of the Earth's crust.

Fold—Warped rock including synclines and anticlines.

Gneiss—Metamorphic granitelike rock showing layers.

Granite—Igneous rock composed predominantly of visible grains of feldspar and quartz. Used in building.

Igneous—Rock formed by cooled and hardened magma within the crust or lava on the surface.

Karst—Area of land lying over limestone and characterized by sinkholes, caves, and sinking streams.

Lava—Magma that reaches the surface of the earth.

Magma—Molten rock within the earth's crust.

Metamorphic—Rock that has been changed into present state after being subjected to heat and pressure from the crust, or chemical alteration.

Monadnock—Land that contains more erosion-resistant rock than surrounding area and therefore is higher.

Orogeny—A geologic process which results in the formation of mountain belts.

Outcrop—Exposed bedrock.

Overthrust belt—An area where older rock has been thrust over younger rock.

Rapids—Fast-moving water that flows around rocks and boulders in rivers; classified from I to VI according to degree of difficulty navigating.

Schist—Flaky, metamorphic rock containing parallel layers of minerals such as mica.

Sedimentary—Rocks formed by the accumulation of sediments (sandstone, shale) or the remains of products of animals or plants (limestone, coal).

Shale—Sedimentary rock composed of clay, mud, and silt grains that easily splits into layers.

Syncline—A rock fold shaped like a U that is closed at the bottom and open at the top. The youngest rock is at the center of a syncline.

Talus—Rock debris and boulders that accumulate at the base of a cliff.

Watershed—The area drained by a river and all its tributaries.

Index